D0500654

Homework Helper

Grade 8 Volume 1

PEARSON

Boston, Massachusetts • Chandler, Arizona • Glenview, Illinois • Upper Saddle River, New Jersey

Acknowledgments for Illustrations:
Rory Hensley, David Jackson, Jim Mariano, Rich McMahon, Lorie Park, and Ted Smykal

ISBN-13: 978-0-13-327633-6
ISBN-10: 0-13-327633-3
4 5 6 7 8 9 10 V011 17 16 15 14

Contents

Francis (Skip) Fennell
digits Author

Approaches to mathematics content and curriculum, educational policy, and support for intervention

Dr. Francis (Skip) Fennell is Professor of Education at McDaniel College, and a senior author with Pearson. He is a past president of the National Council of Teachers of Mathematics (NCTM) and a member of the writing team for the Curriculum Focal Points from the NCTM, which influenced the work of the Common Core Standards Initiative. Skip was also one of the writers of the Principles and Standards for School Mathematics.

Art Johnson
digits Author

Approaches to mathematical content and support for English Language Learners

Art Johnson is a Professor of Mathematics at Boston University who taught in public school for over 30 years. He is part of the author team for Pearson's high school mathematics series. Art is the author of numerous books, including Teaching Mathematics to Culturally and Linguistically Diverse Students published by Allyn & Bacon, Teaching Today's Mathematics in the Middle Grades published by Allyn & Bacon, and Guiding Children's Learning of Mathematics, K–6 published by Wadsworth.

Helene Sherman
digits Author

Teacher education and support for struggling students

Helene Sherman is Associate Dean for Undergraduate Education and Professor of Education in the College of Education at the University of Missouri in St. Louis, MO. Helene is the author of Teaching Learners Who Struggle with Mathematics, published by Merrill.

Stuart J. Murphy
digits Author

Visual learning and student engagement

Stuart J. Murphy is a visual learning specialist and the author of the MathStart series. He contributed to the development of the Visual Learning Bridge in enVisionMATH™ as well as many visual elements of the Prentice Hall Algebra 1, Geometry, and Algebra 2 high school program.

Janie Schielack
digits Author

Approaches to mathematical content, building problem solvers,and support for intervention

Janie Schielack is Professor of Mathematics and Associate Dean for Assessment and PreK–12 Education at Texas A&M University. She chaired the writing committee for the NCTM Curriculum Focal Points and was part of the nine-member NCTM feedback and advisory team that responded to and met with CCSSCO and NGA representatives during the development of various drafts of the Common Core State Standards.

Eric Milou
digits Author

Approaches to mathematical content and the use of technology in middle grades classrooms

Eric Milou is Professor in the Department of Mathematics at Rowan University in Glassboro, NJ. Eric teaches pre-service teachers and works with in-service teachers, and is primarily interested in balancing concept development with skill proficiency. He was part of the nine-member NCTM feedback/advisory team that responded to and met with Council of Chief State School Officers (CCSSCO) and National Governors Association (NGA) representatives during the development of various drafts of the Common Core State Standards. Eric is the author of Teaching Mathematics to Middle School Students, published by Allyn & Bacon.

William F. Tate
digits Author

Approaches to intervention, and use of efficacy and research

William Tate is the Edward Mallinckrodt Distinguished University Professor in Arts & Sciences at Washington University in St. Louis, MO. He is a past president of the American Educational Research Association. His research focuses on the social and psychological determinants of mathematics achievement and attainment as well as the political economy of schooling.

Randall I. Charles
digits Advisor

Dr. Randall I. Charles is Professor Emeritus in the Department of Mathematics at San Jose State University in San Jose, CA, and a senior author with Pearson. Randall served on the writing team for the Curriculum Focal Points from NCTM. The NCTM Curriculum Focal Points served as a key inspiration to the writers of the Common Core Standards in bringing focus, depth, and coherence to the curriculum.

> *Pearson tapped leaders in mathematics education to develop* **digits***. This esteemed author team—from diverse areas of expertise including mathematical content, Understanding by Design, and Technology Engagement—came together to construct a highly interactive and personalized learning experience.*

Jim Cummins
digits Advisor

Supporting English Language Learners

Dr. Jim Cummins is Professor and Canada Research Chair in the Centre for Educational Research on Languages and Literacies at the University of Toronto. His research focuses on literacy development in multilingual school contexts as well as on the potential roles of technology in promoting language and literacy development.

Grant Wiggins
digits Consulting Author

Understanding by Design

Grant Wiggins is a cross-curricular Pearson consulting author specializing in curricular change. He is the author of Understanding by Design published by ASCD, and the President of Authentic Education in Hopewell, NJ. Over the past 20 years, he has worked on some of the most influential reform initiatives in the country, including Vermont's portfolio system and Ted Sizer's Coalition of Essential Schools.

Jacquie Moen
digits Advisor

Digital Technology

Jacquie Moen is a consultant specializing in how consumers interact with and use digital technologies. Jacquie worked for AOL for 10 years, and most recently was VP & General Manager for AOL's kids and teen online services, reaching over seven million kids every month. Jacquie has worked with a wide range of organizations to develop interactive content and strategies to reach families and children, including National Geographic, PBS, Pearson Education, National Wildlife Foundation, and the National Children's Museum.

Welcome to digits™

Using the Homework Helper

digits is designed to help you master mathematics skills and concepts in a way that's relevant to you. As the title **digits** suggests, this program takes a digital approach. **digits** is digital, but sometimes you may not be able to access digital resources. When that happens, you can use the Homework Helper because you can refer back to the daily lesson and see all your homework questions right in the book.

Your Homework Helper supports your work on **digits** in so many ways!

The lesson pages capture important elements of the digital lesson that you need to know in order to do your homework.

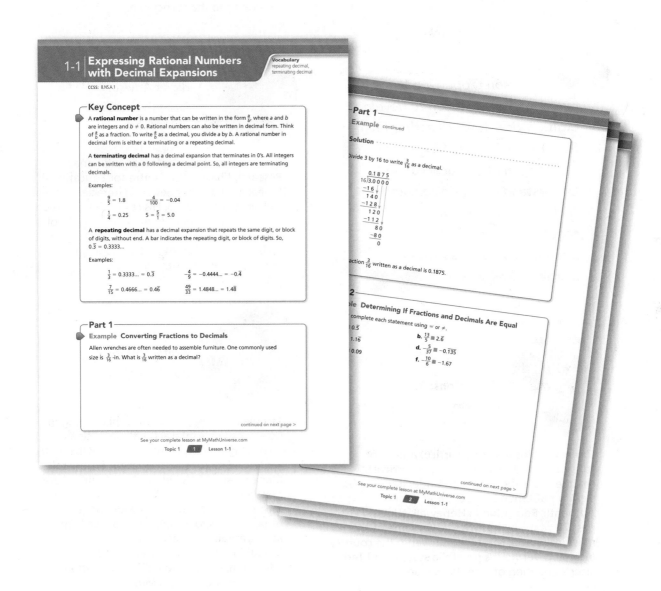

Every lesson in your Homework Helper also includes two pages of homework. The combination of homework exercises includes problems that focus on reasoning, multiple representations, mental math, writing, and error analysis. They vary in difficulty level from thinking about a plan to challenging. The problems come in different formats, like multiple choice, short answer, and open response, to help you prepare for tests.

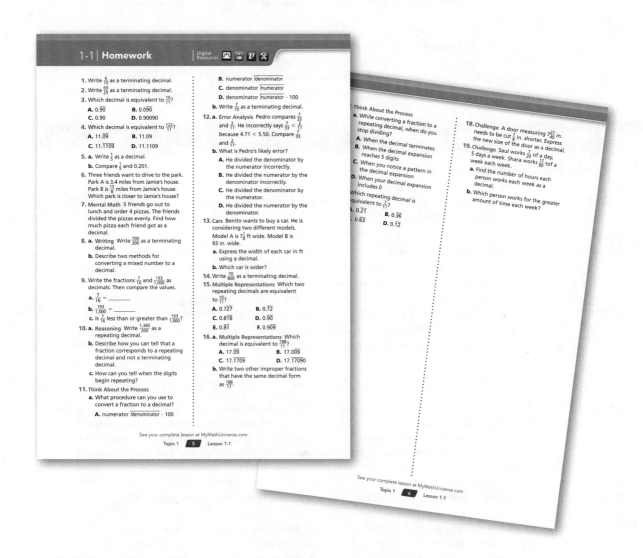

1-1 | Homework

Digital Resources

1. Write $\frac{6}{10}$ as a terminating decimal.
2. Write $\frac{69}{25}$ as a terminating decimal.
3. Which decimal is equivalent to $\frac{10}{11}$?

   A. $0.\overline{90}$ B. 0.090
   C. 0.90 D. 0.90090

4. Which decimal is equivalent to $\frac{122}{11}$?

   A. 11.09 B. 11.09
   C. $11.\overline{1109}$ D. 11.1109

5. a. Write $\frac{1}{5}$ as a decimal.
   b. Compare $\frac{1}{5}$ and 0.201.

6. Three friends want to drive to the park. Park A is 3.4 miles from Jamie's house. Park B is $\frac{15}{8}$ miles from Jamie's house. Which park is closer to Jamie's house?

7. Mental Math 5 friends go out to lunch and order 4 pizzas. The friends divided the pizzas evenly. Find how much pizza each friend got as a decimal.

8. a. Writing Write $\frac{700}{200}$ as a terminating decimal.
   b. Describe two methods for converting a mixed number to a decimal.

9. Write the fractions $\frac{7}{16}$ and $\frac{193}{1,000}$ as decimals. Then compare the values.

   a. $\frac{7}{16} = $ _____
   b. $\frac{193}{1,000} = $ _____
   c. Is $\frac{7}{16}$ less than or greater than $\frac{193}{1,000}$?

10. a. Reasoning Write $\frac{1,360}{200}$ as a repeating decimal.
    b. Describe how you can tell that a fraction corresponds to a repeating decimal and not a terminating decimal.
    c. How can you tell when the digits begin repeating?

11. Think About the Process
    a. What procedure can you use to convert a fraction to a decimal?

    A. numerator $\overline{)\text{denominator}}$ · 100

    B. numerator $\overline{)\text{denominator}}$
    C. denominator $\overline{)\text{numerator}}$
    D. denominator $\overline{)\text{numerator}}$ · 100
    b. Write $\frac{7}{10}$ as a terminating decimal.

12. a. Error Analysis Pedro compares $\frac{7}{33}$ and $\frac{2}{11}$. He incorrectly says $\frac{7}{33} < \frac{2}{11}$ because $4.71 < 5.50$. Compare $\frac{7}{33}$ and $\frac{2}{11}$.
    b. What is Pedro's likely error?

    A. He divided the denominator by the numerator incorrectly.
    B. He divided the numerator by the denominator incorrectly.
    C. He divided the denominator by the numerator.
    D. He divided the numerator by the denominator.

13. Cars Benito wants to buy a car. He is considering two different models. Model A is $7\frac{1}{8}$ ft wide. Model B is 93 in. wide.
    a. Express the width of each car in ft using a decimal.
    b. Which car is wider?

14. Write $\frac{70}{800}$ as a terminating decimal.

15. Multiple Representations Which two repeating decimals are equivalent to $\frac{10}{11}$?

    A. $0.7\overline{27}$ B. $0.\overline{72}$
    C. $0.8\overline{18}$ D. $0.\overline{90}$
    E. $0.\overline{81}$ F. $0.\overline{909}$

16. a. Multiple Representations Which decimal is equivalent to $\frac{188}{11}$?

    A. $17.\overline{09}$ B. $17.0\overline{09}$
    C. $17.\overline{1709}$ D. $17.\overline{17090}$
    b. Write two other improper fractions that have the same decimal form as $\frac{188}{11}$.

See your complete lesson at MyMathUniverse.com

Topic 1   5   Lesson 1-1

17. Think About the Process
    a. While converting a fraction to a repeating decimal, when do you stop dividing?

    A. When the decimal terminates
    B. When the decimal expansion reaches 5 digits
    C. When you notice a pattern in the decimal expansion
    D. When your decimal expansion includes 0

    Which repeating decimal is equivalent to $\frac{7}{11}$?

    A. $0.\overline{21}$ B. $0.\overline{36}$
    C. $0.\overline{63}$ D. $0.\overline{12}$

18. Challenge A door measuring $7\frac{27}{40}$ in. needs to be cut $\frac{7}{8}$ in. shorter. Express the new size of the door as a decimal.

19. Challenge Saul works $\frac{7}{20}$ of a day, 5 days a week. Shara works $\frac{17}{80}$ tof a week each week.
    a. Find the number of hours each person works each week as a decimal.
    b. Which person works for the greater amount of time each week?

See your complete lesson at MyMathUniverse.com

Topic 1   6   Lesson 1-1

Number	Standard for Mathematical Content

8.NS The Number System

Know that there are numbers that are not rational, and approximate them by rational numbers.

8.NS.A.1	Know that numbers that are not rational are called irrational. Understand informally that every number has a decimal expansion; for rational numbers show that the decimal expansion repeats eventually, and convert a decimal expansion which repeats eventually into a rational number.
8.NS.A.2	Use rational approximations of irrational numbers to compare the size of irrational numbers, locate them approximately on a number line diagram, and estimate the value of expressions (e.g., π^2). For example, by truncating the decimal expansion of $\sqrt{2}$, show that $\sqrt{2}$ is between 1 and 2, then between 1.4 and 1.5, and explain how to continue on to get better approximations.

8.EE Expressions and Equations

Work with radicals and integer exponents.

8.EE.A.1	Know and apply the properties of integer exponents to generate equivalent numerical expressions. For example, $3^2 \times 3^{(-5)} = 3^{(-3)} = \frac{1}{(3^3)} = \frac{1}{27}$.
8.EE.A.2	Use square root and cube root symbols to represent solutions to equations of the form $x^2 = p$ and $x^3 = p$, where p is a positive rational number. Evaluate square roots of small perfect squares and cube roots of small perfect cubes. Know that $\sqrt{2}$ is irrational.
8.EE.A.3	Use numbers expressed in the form of a single digit times an integer power of 10 to estimate very large or very small quantities, and to express how many times as much one is than the other. For example, estimate the population of the United States as 3×10^8 and the population of the world as 7×10^9, and determine that the world population is more than 20 times larger.
8.EE.A.4	Perform operations with numbers expressed in scientific notation, including problems where both decimal and scientific notation are used. Use scientific notation and choose units of appropriate size for measurements of very large or very small quantities (e.g., use millimeters per year for seafloor spreading). Interpret scientific notation that has been generated by technology.

Understand the connections between proportional relationships, lines, and linear equations.

8.EE.B.5	Graph proportional relationships, interpreting the unit rate as the slope of the graph. Compare two different proportional relationships represented in different ways. For example, compare a distance-time graph to a distance-time equation to determine which of two moving objects has greater speed.
8.EE.B.6	Use similar triangles to explain why the slope m is the same between any two distinct points on a non-vertical line in the coordinate plane; derive the equation $y = mx$ for a line through the origin and the equation $y = mx + b$ for a line intercepting the vertical axis at b.

Number	Standard for Mathematical Content

8.EE Expressions and Equations (continued)

Analyze and solve linear equations and pairs of simultaneous linear equations.

8.EE.C.7	Solve linear equations in one variable.
8.EE.C.7a	Give examples of linear equations in one variable with one solution, infinitely many solutions, or no solutions. Show which of these possibilities is the case by successively transforming the given equation into simpler forms, until an equivalent equation of the form $x = a$, $a = a$, or $a = b$ results (where a and b are different numbers).
8.EE.C.7b	Solve linear equations with rational number coefficients, including equations whose solutions require expanding expressions using the distributive property and collecting like terms.
8.EE.C.8	Analyze and solve pairs of simultaneous linear equations.
8.EE.C.8a	Understand that solutions to a system of two linear equations in two variables correspond to points of intersection of their graphs, because points of intersection satisfy both equations simultaneously.
8.EE.C.8b	Solve systems of two linear equations in two variables algebraically, and estimate solutions by graphing the equations. Solve simple cases by inspection. For example, $3x + 2y = 5$ and $3x + 2y = 6$ have no solution because $3x + 2y$ cannot simultaneously be 5 and 6.
8.EE.C.8c	Solve real-world and mathematical problems leading to two linear equations in two variables. For example, given coordinates for two pairs of points, determine whether the line through the first pair of points intersects the line through the second pair.

8.F Functions

Define, evaluate, and compare functions.

8.F.A.1	Understand that a function is a rule that assigns to each input exactly one output. The graph of a function is the set of ordered pairs consisting of an input and the corresponding output.
8.F.A.2	Compare properties of two functions each represented in a different way (algebraically, graphically, numerically in tables, or by verbal descriptions). For example, given a linear function represented by a table of values and a linear function represented by an algebraic expression, determine which function has the greater rate of change.
8.F.A.3	Interpret the equation $y = mx + b$ as defining a linear function, whose graph is a straight line; give examples of functions that are not linear. For example, the function $A = s^2$ giving the area of a square as a function of its side length is not linear because its graph contains the points (1,1), (2,4) and (3,9), which are not on a straight line.

Use functions to model relationships between quantities.

8.F.B.4	Construct a function to model a linear relationship between two quantities. Determine the rate of change and initial value of the function from a description of a relationship or from two (x, y) values, including reading these from a table or from a graph. Interpret the rate of change and initial value of a linear function in terms of the situation it models, and in terms of its graph or a table of values.
8.F.B.5	Describe qualitatively the functional relationship between two quantities by analyzing a graph (e.g., where the function is increasing or decreasing, linear or nonlinear). Sketch a graph that exhibits the qualitative features of a function that has been described verbally.

Grade 8 Common Core State Standards *continued*

Number	Standard for Mathematical Content

8.G   Geometry

Understand congruence and similarity using physical models, transparencies, or geometry software.

8.G.A.1	Verify experimentally the properties of rotations, reflections, and translations:
8.G.A.1a	Verify experimentally the properties of rotations, reflections, and translations: Lines are taken to lines, and line segments to line segments of the same length.
8.G.A.1b	Verify experimentally the properties of rotations, reflections, and translations: Angles are taken to angles of the same measure.
8.G.A.1c	Verify experimentally the properties of rotations, reflections, and translations: Parallel lines are taken to parallel lines.
8.G.A.2	Understand that a two-dimensional figure is congruent to another if the second can be obtained from the first by a sequence of rotations, reflections, and translations; given two congruent figures, describe a sequence that exhibits the congruence between them.
8.G.A.3	Describe the effect of dilations, translations, rotations, and reflections on two-dimensional figures using coordinates.
8.G.A.4	Understand that a two-dimensional figure is similar to another if the second can be obtained from the first by a sequence of rotations, reflections, translations, and dilations; given two similar two- dimensional figures, describe a sequence that exhibits the similarity between them.
8.G.A.5	Use informal arguments to establish facts about the angle sum and exterior angle of triangles, about the angles created when parallel lines are cut by a transversal, and the angle-angle criterion for similarity of triangles.

Understand and apply the Pythagorean Theorem.

8.G.B.6	Explain a proof of the Pythagorean Theorem and its converse.
8.G.B.7	Apply the Pythagorean Theorem to determine unknown side lengths in right triangles in real-world and mathematical problems in two and three dimensions.
8.G.B.8	Apply the Pythagorean Theorem to find the distance between two points in a coordinate system.

Solve real-world and mathematical problems involving volume of cylinders, cones, and spheres.

8.G.C.9	Know the formulas for the volumes of cones, cylinders, and spheres and use them to solve real-world and mathematical problems.

Number	Standard for Mathematical Content

8.SP   Statistics and Probability

Investigate patterns of association in bivariate data.

Number	Standard for Mathematical Content
8.SP.A.1	Construct and interpret scatter plots for bivariate measurement data to investigate patterns of association between two quantities. Describe patterns such as clustering, outliers, positive or negative association, linear association, and nonlinear association.
8.SP.A.2	Know that straight lines are widely used to model relationships between two quantitative variables. For scatter plots that suggest a linear association, informally fit a straight line, and informally assess the model fit by judging the closeness of the data points to the line.
8.SP.A.3	Use the equation of a linear model to solve problems in the context of bivariate measurement data, interpreting the slope and intercept.
8.SP.A.4	Understand that patterns of association can also be seen in bivariate categorical data by displaying frequencies and relative frequencies in a two-way table. Construct and interpret a two-way table summarizing data on two categorical variables collected from the same subjects. Use relative frequencies calculated for rows or columns to describe possible association between the two variables.

Number	Standard for Mathematical Practice
MP1	Make sense of problems and persevere in solving them.
MP2	Reason abstractly and quantitatively.
MP3	Construct viable arguments and critique the reasoning of others.
MP4	Model with mathematics.
MP5	Use appropriate tools strategically.
MP6	Attend to precision.
MP7	Look for and make use of structure.
MP8	Look for and express regularity in repeated reasoning.

CCSS: 8.NS.A.1

Key Concept

A **rational number** is a number that can be written in the form $\frac{a}{b}$, where a and b are integers and $b \neq 0$. Rational numbers can also be written in decimal form. Think of $\frac{a}{b}$ as a fraction. To write $\frac{a}{b}$ as a decimal, you divide a by b. A rational number in decimal form is either a terminating or a repeating decimal.

A **terminating decimal** has a decimal expansion that terminates in 0's. All integers can be written with a 0 following a decimal point. So, all integers are terminating decimals.

Examples:

$$\frac{9}{5} = 1.8 \qquad -\frac{4}{100} = -0.04$$

$$\frac{1}{4} = 0.25 \qquad 5 = \frac{5}{1} = 5.0$$

A **repeating decimal** has a decimal expansion that repeats the same digit, or block of digits, without end. A bar indicates the repeating digit, or block of digits. So, $0.\overline{3} = 0.3333...$

Examples:

$$\frac{1}{3} = 0.3333... = 0.\overline{3} \qquad\qquad -\frac{4}{9} = -0.4444... = -0.\overline{4}$$

$$\frac{7}{15} = 0.4666... = 0.4\overline{6} \qquad\qquad \frac{49}{33} = 1.4848... = 1.\overline{48}$$

Part 1

Example Converting Fractions to Decimals

Allen wrenches are often needed to assemble furniture. One commonly used size is $\frac{3}{16}$-in. What is $\frac{3}{16}$ written as a decimal?

continued on next page >

Part 1

Example continued

Solution ·

Divide 3 by 16 to write $\frac{3}{16}$ as a decimal.

```
        0.1 8 7 5
  16)3.0 0 0 0
     −1 6
        1 4 0
       −1 2 8
          1 2 0
         −1 1 2
              8 0
             −8 0
                0
```

The fraction $\frac{3}{16}$ written as a decimal is 0.1875.

Part 2

Example Determining If Fractions and Decimals Are Equal

Correctly complete each statement using = or ≠.

a. $\frac{5}{9}$ ■ $0.\overline{5}$

b. $\frac{13}{5}$ ■ $2.\overline{6}$

c. $\frac{7}{6}$ ■ $1.1\overline{6}$

d. $-\frac{5}{37}$ ■ $-0.\overline{135}$

e. $\frac{1}{11}$ ■ 0.09

f. $-\frac{10}{6}$ ■ -1.67

continued on next page >

Part 2

Example continued

Solution ·

a. Divide 5 by 9 to write $\frac{5}{9}$ as a decimal.

$$
\begin{array}{r}
0.5\,5\,5 \\
9\overline{)5.0\,0\,0} \\
-4\,5 \\
\hline
5\,0 \\
-4\,5 \\
\hline
5\,0 \\
-4\,5 \\
\hline
0
\end{array}
$$

This is a repeating decimal.

$\frac{5}{9} = 0.555...$
  $= 0.\overline{5}$

b. Divide 13 by 5 to write $\frac{13}{5}$ as a decimal.

$$
\begin{array}{r}
2.6\,0 \\
5\overline{)1\,3.0\,0} \\
-1\,0 \\
\hline
3\,0 \\
-3\,0 \\
\hline
0\,0 \\
-0 \\
\hline
0
\end{array}
$$

This is a terminating decimal.

$\frac{13}{5} = 2.6$
  $\neq 2.\overline{6}$

c. Divide 7 by 6 to write $\frac{7}{6}$ as a decimal.

$$
\begin{array}{r}
1.1\,6\,6 \\
6\overline{)7.0\,0\,0} \\
-6 \\
\hline
1\,0 \\
-6 \\
\hline
4\,0 \\
-3\,6 \\
\hline
4\,0 \\
-3\,6 \\
\hline
4
\end{array}
$$

$\frac{7}{6} = 1.166...$
  $= 1.1\overline{6}$

d. Divide 5 by 37 to write $-\frac{5}{37}$ as a decimal.

$$
\begin{array}{r}
0.1\,3\,5\,1\,3\,5 \\
37\overline{)5.0\,0\,0\,0\,0\,0} \\
-\,3\,7 \\
\hline
1\,3\,0 \\
-\,1\,1\,1 \\
\hline
1\,9\,0 \\
-\,1\,8\,5 \\
\hline
5\,0 \\
-\,3\,7 \\
\hline
1\,3\,0 \\
-\,1\,1\,1 \\
\hline
1\,9\,0 \\
-\,1\,8\,5 \\
\hline
5
\end{array}
$$

$-\frac{5}{37} = -0.135135...$
  $= -0.\overline{135}$

continued on next page >

Part 2

Solution continued

e. Divide 1 by 11 to write $\frac{1}{11}$ as a decimal. **f.** Divide 10 by 6 to write $-\frac{10}{6}$ as a decimal.

```
        0.0 9 0 9
  11)1.0 0 0 0
     − 9 9
         1 0
       −   0
         1 0 0
         −  9 9
              1
```

```
        1.6 6 6
   6)1 0.0 0 0
     − 6
        4 0
      − 3 6
         4 0
       − 3 6
          4 0
        − 3 6
            4
```

$$\frac{1}{11} = 0.0909...$$
$$= 0.\overline{09}$$
$$\neq 0.09$$

$$-\frac{10}{6} = -1.666...$$
$$= -1.\overline{6}$$

Part 3

Example Comparing Fractions and Decimals

The main span of the Brooklyn Bridge is about 0.3 mi long. The main span of the Williamsburg Bridge is about $\frac{10}{33}$ mi long. The main span of which bridge is longer?

Solution

To compare 0.3 mi and $\frac{10}{33}$ mi, write both as decimals.

```
         0.3 0 3 0
  33)1 0.0 0 0 0
     − 9 9
         1 0
       −   0
         1 0 0
         −  9 9
              1 0
            −   0
              1 0
```

$$\frac{10}{30} = 0.3030..., \text{ or } 0.\overline{30}$$

Since $0.\overline{30} > 0.3$, the main span of the Williamsburg Bridge is longer than the main span of the Brooklyn Bridge.

1. Write $\frac{6}{10}$ as a terminating decimal.

2. Write $\frac{69}{25}$ as a terminating decimal.

3. Which decimal is equivalent to $\frac{10}{11}$?

   A. $0.\overline{90}$ **B.** $0.0\overline{90}$

   C. 0.90 **D.** 0.90090

4. Which decimal is equivalent to $\frac{122}{11}$?

   A. $11.\overline{09}$ **B.** 11.09

   C. $11.\overline{1109}$ **D.** 11.1109

5. **a.** Write $\frac{1}{5}$ as a decimal.

   b. Compare $\frac{1}{5}$ and 0.201.

6. Three friends want to drive to the park. Park A is 3.4 miles from Jamie's house. Park B is $\frac{15}{8}$ miles from Jamie's house. Which park is closer to Jamie's house?

7. **Mental Math** 5 friends go out to lunch and order 4 pizzas. The friends divided the pizzas evenly. Find how much pizza each friend got as a decimal.

8. **a. Writing** Write $\frac{700}{200}$ as a terminating decimal.

   b. Describe two methods for converting a mixed number to a decimal.

9. Write the fractions $\frac{7}{16}$ and $\frac{193}{1,000}$ as decimals. Then compare the values.

   a. $\frac{7}{16} =$ _____

   b. $\frac{193}{1,000} =$ _____

   c. Is $\frac{7}{16}$ less than or greater than $\frac{193}{1,000}$?

10. **a. Reasoning** Write $\frac{1,360}{220}$ as a repeating decimal.

   b. Describe how you can tell that a fraction corresponds to a repeating decimal and not a terminating decimal.

   c. How can you tell when the digits begin repeating?

11. **Think About the Process**

   a. What procedure can you use to convert a fraction to a decimal?

      A. numerator $\overline{)\text{denominator}}$ $\cdot$ 100

      B. numerator $\overline{)\text{denominator}}$

      C. denominator $\overline{)\text{numerator}}$

      D. denominator $\overline{)\text{numerator}}$ $\cdot$ 100

   b. Write $\frac{7}{10}$ as a terminating decimal.

12. **a. Error Analysis** Pedro compares $\frac{7}{33}$ and $\frac{2}{11}$. He incorrectly says $\frac{7}{33} < \frac{2}{11}$ because $4.71 < 5.50$. Compare $\frac{7}{33}$ and $\frac{2}{11}$.

   b. What is Pedro's likely error?

      A. He divided the denominator by the numerator incorrectly.

      B. He divided the numerator by the denominator incorrectly.

      C. He divided the denominator by the numerator.

      D. He divided the numerator by the denominator.

13. **Cars** Benito wants to buy a car. He is considering two different models. Model A is $7\frac{1}{8}$ ft wide. Model B is 93 in. wide.

   a. Express the width of each car in ft using a decimal.

   b. Which car is wider?

14. Write $\frac{70}{800}$ as a terminating decimal.

15. **Multiple Representations** Which two repeating decimals are equivalent to $\frac{10}{11}$?

   A. $0.7\overline{27}$ **B.** $0.\overline{72}$

   C. $0.8\overline{18}$ **D.** $0.\overline{90}$

   E. $0.\overline{81}$ **F.** $0.9\overline{09}$

16. **a. Multiple Representations** Which decimal is equivalent to $\frac{188}{11}$?

      A. $17.\overline{09}$ **B.** $17.0\overline{09}$

      C. $17.\overline{1709}$ **D.** $17.\overline{17090}$

   b. Write two other improper fractions that have the same decimal form as $\frac{188}{11}$.

17. Think About the Process

    a. While converting a fraction to a repeating decimal, when do you stop dividing?

      A. When the decimal terminates

      B. When the decimal expansion reaches 5 digits

      C. When you notice a pattern in the decimal expansion

      D. When your decimal expansion includes 0

    b. Which repeating decimal is equivalent to $\frac{7}{11}$?

      A. $0.\overline{21}$ **B.** $0.\overline{36}$

      C. $0.\overline{63}$ **D.** $0.\overline{12}$

18. Challenge A door measuring $7\frac{27}{40}$ in. needs to be cut $\frac{7}{8}$ in. shorter. Express the new size of the door as a decimal.

19. Challenge Saul works $\frac{7}{20}$ of a day, 5 days a week. Shara works $\frac{17}{80}$ tof a week each week.

    a. Find the number of hours each person works each week as a decimal.

    b. Which person works for the greater amount of time each week?

Exploring Irrational Numbers

Vocabulary
irrational numbers,
perfect square, real
numbers, square root

CCSS: 8.NS.A.1

Part 1

Intro

A number that is the square of an integer is a **perfect square**. The **square root** of a number is another number that when multiplied by itself is equal to the original number. Some square roots are rational numbers and some are irrational numbers. **Irrational numbers** are numbers that cannot be written in the form $\frac{a}{b}$ where a and b are integers and $b \neq 0$.

Square Roots The symbol $\sqrt{}$ means the square root of a number. In this program, $\sqrt{}$ means the positive square root of a number, unless stated otherwise. So, $\sqrt{9}$ means the positive square root of 9, or 3, and $-\sqrt{9}$ means the opposite of the positive square root of 9, or -3.

$$\sqrt{25} = \sqrt{5^2}$$
$$= 5$$

$$-\sqrt{25} = -\sqrt{5^2}$$
$$= -5$$

Rational Square Roots A number a is a square root of a number b if $a^2 = b$. For any whole number b that is a perfect square, $\sqrt{b}$ is rational.

$81 = 9^2$, so 81 is a perfect square:

$$\sqrt{81} = \sqrt{9^2}$$
$$= 9$$

9 is a rational number, so $\sqrt{81}$ is rational.

Irrational Square Roots A number a is a square root of a number b if $a^2 = b$. For any whole number b that is *not* a perfect square, $\sqrt{b}$ is irrational.

90 cannot be written as the square of a whole number, so 90 is not a perfect square.

Since 90 is not a perfect square, $\sqrt{90}$ is irrational.

Part 1

Example Determining Whether a Square Root is Irrational

Determine if each square root is *rational* or *irrational*.

$$\sqrt{9} \qquad \sqrt{6} \qquad \sqrt{5} \qquad \sqrt{8}$$
$$\sqrt{3} \qquad \sqrt{4} \qquad \sqrt{7} \qquad \sqrt{2}$$

Solution

$$4 = 2^2 \quad \longleftarrow \boxed{\text{4 and 9 are perfect squares.}} \longrightarrow \quad 9 = 3^2$$

$\sqrt{4}$ and $\sqrt{9}$ are rational.

2, 3, 5, 6, 7, and 8 are not perfect squares so $\sqrt{2}$, $\sqrt{3}$, $\sqrt{5}$, $\sqrt{6}$, $\sqrt{7}$, and $\sqrt{8}$ are irrational.

Part 2

Intro

Rational numbers have decimal expansions that terminate in 0's or eventually repeat. Irrational numbers cannot be represented as terminating or repeating decimals.

For example, $\sqrt{10} = 3.16227766...$ is irrational.

Irrational numbers also include nonrepeating decimals that have a pattern in their digits.

For example, 1.1010010001... is irrational.

Since π is an irrational number, the decimal digits do not terminate or repeat.

3.14159265358979323846264338327950288...

Part 2

Determining Whether a Decimal Number
is Rational

Determine if each number is *irrational* or *rational*. Assume each pattern
continues.

    a. 2.125
    b. 2.1111...
    c. 2.01011011101111...
    d. 2.12341234...
    e. 1.80333...

Solution

a. 2.125	is a terminating decimal, so it is **rational**.
b. 2.1111...	is a repeating decimal, with a repeating pattern of 1, so it is **rational**.
c. 2.01011011101111...	shows a pattern, but it does not have a repeating pattern or terminating decimal, so it is **irrational**.
d. 2.12341234...	is a repeating decimal, with a repeating pattern of 1234, so it is **rational**.
e. 1.80333...	is a repeating decimal, with a repeating pattern of 3, so it is **rational**.

Key Concept

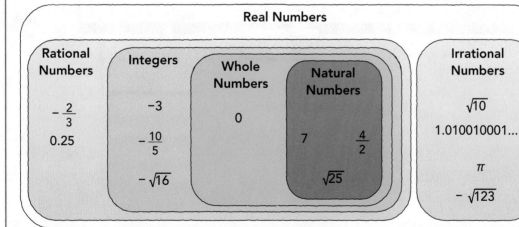

Rational and irrational numbers form the set of **real numbers**.

Part 3

Example Classifying Numbers

Indicate all of the possible names for each number.

	15	−1.232	$\sqrt{45}$	$\frac{121}{35}$	$-\sqrt{16}$	$\frac{21}{3}$
Natural Number	▪	▪	▪	▪	▪	▪
Whole Number	▪	▪	▪	▪	▪	▪
Integer	▪	▪	▪	▪	▪	▪
Rational Number	▪	▪	▪	▪	▪	▪
Irrational Number	▪	▪	▪	▪	▪	▪
Real Number	▪	▪	▪	▪	▪	▪

Solution

	15	−1.232	$\sqrt{45}$	$\frac{121}{35}$	$-\sqrt{16}$	$\frac{21}{3}$
Natural Number	✓					✓
Whole Number	✓					✓
Integer	✓				✓	✓
Rational Number	✓	✓		✓	✓	✓
Irrational Number			✓			
Real Number	✓	✓	✓	✓	✓	✓

$$\frac{21}{3} = 7$$

$$\sqrt{45} \approx 6.71$$

$$-\sqrt{16} = -\sqrt{4^2}$$
$$= {}^-4$$

1. Find the square root $\sqrt{9}$.

2. Which numbers are irrational? Select all that apply.

   A. $\sqrt{45}$ **B.** $\sqrt{100}$
   C. $\sqrt{64}$ **D.** $\sqrt{21}$

3. A square rug has an area 100 ft². Write the side length as a square root. Then decide if the side length is a rational number.

4. **Think About the Process**

   a. How do you decide if a decimal is a rational number?

   A. Check whether the decimal terminates in 0s or repeats.

   B. All decimals are irrational numbers.

   C. All decimals are rational numbers.

   D. Check whether the decimal never terminates nor repeats.

   b. Is 4.87787778... a rational number?

5. Which numbers are rational? The dots, ..., indicate that the pattern continues.

   I. 1.1111111...

   II. 1.567

   III. 1.10110111...

   A. II and III   **B.** III only
   C. II only   **D.** I and II
   E. I only
   F. None of the above.

6. Is 5.78778777... a rational or irrational number?

7. Find the sets of numbers to which $-\frac{8}{9}$ belongs. Select all that apply.

   A. integers
   B. whole numbers
   C. irrational numbers
   D. real numbers
   E. rational numbers
   F. natural numbers

8. Which numbers are rational? Select all that apply.

   A. $\frac{8}{5}$ **B.** π
   C. 0   **D.** $4.\overline{46}$
   E. 10   **F.** $\frac{19}{3}$
   G. -6
   H. There are no rational numbers

9. **Reasoning** The numbers 2.888... and 2.999... are both rational numbers. Which of the following is an irrational number that is between the two rational numbers? Select all that apply.

   A. 2.889   **B.** 3.889888...
   C. 2.998999... **D.** 2.889888...

10. **a. Multiple Representations** Is the decimal form of $\frac{13}{3}$ a rational number?

    b Explain how you can give the answer to this question without identifying the decimal form for the fraction.

11. **a. Writing** Is 8.33333333... a rational or irrational number?

    b Describe how you would explain the difference between rational and irrational numbers to someone who has never heard these terms.

12. **Error Analysis** Deena says that 9.56556555... is a rational number. Elijah disagrees and says the number is irrational. Who is correct? What might likely cause one of them to make the error?

    A. Elijah is correct. Deena may see 9.56556555... as showing a repeating pattern.

    B. Both Deena and Elijah are correct. Numbers like this one are both rational and irrational.

    C. Deena is correct. Elijah may see 9.56556555... as not showing a repeating pattern.

    D. Neither is correct. The numbers cannot be classified as rational or irrational.

See your complete lesson at MyMathUniverse.com

13. Estimated Value of π The circumference of a circle is found using the formula $C = \pi d$. In the formula, d is the diameter of the circle and $\frac{62{,}832}{20{,}000}$ is a number that represents π. Find the sets of numbers to which $\frac{62{,}832}{20{,}000}$ belongs. Select all that apply.

  A. irrational numbers

  B. rational numbers

  C. integers

  D. whole numbers

  E. natural numbers

  F. real numbers

14. You are given the list of numbers $\{-5, 0, 6, -\frac{8}{3}, \sqrt{47}, 3.73773777...\}$.

  a. Which numbers are rational? Select all that apply.

  A. $\sqrt{47}$ **B.** $-\frac{8}{3}$

  C. 0   **D.** -5

  E. 6   **F.** 3.73773777...

  b. Which numbers are irrational? Select all that apply.

  A. 0   **B.** $\sqrt{47}$

  C. 3.73773777...   **D.** 6

  E. $-\frac{8}{3}$ **F.** -5

15. You are given the list of numbers, $\{5.73773777..., -6, \sqrt{45}, -\frac{3}{2}, 0, 9\}$.

  a. Which numbers are rational? Select all that apply.

  A. $\sqrt{45}$ **B.** 0

  C. $-\frac{3}{2}$ **D.** 9

  E. -6 **F.** 5.73773777...

  b. Which numbers are irrational? Select all that apply.

  A. $-\frac{3}{2}$ **B.** 9

  C. $\sqrt{45}$ **D.** -6

  E. 5.73773777...   **F.** 0

16. Evaluate $\sqrt{49} + \sqrt{169}$.

17. a. Simplify $\sqrt{324 + 576}$.

  b. Find the sets of numbers to which the number belongs. Select all that apply.

  A. irrational numbers

  B. real numbers

  C. integers

  D. whole numbers

  E. natural numbers

  F. rational numbers

18. Think About the Process

  a. How do you know if a whole number is a perfect square?

  A. A whole number is a perfect square if it is divisible by 2.

  B. A whole number is a perfect square if its square root is a whole number.

  C. A whole number is a perfect square if its square root is an irrational number.

  D. A whole number is a perfect square if it is divisible by 4.

  b. Is 25 a perfect square?

  A. The whole number 25 is not a perfect square because 25 is not divisible by 4.

  B. The whole number 25 is not a perfect square because the square root of 25 is not an irrational number.

  C. The whole number 25 is a perfect square because the square root of 25 is a whole number.

  D. The whole number 25 is not a perfect square because 25 is not divisible by 2.

19. Challenge You are given the numbers $\sqrt{1{,}815}$ and $\sqrt{3{,}025}$.

  a. Are the numbers rational?

  A. Only $\sqrt{1{,}815}$ is rational.

  B. Only $\sqrt{3{,}025}$ is rational.

  C. Both numbers are rational.

  D. Both numbers are irrational.

  b. How many perfect squares, n, are there that are greater than 1,815 and less than 3,025?

20. Challenge You are given the numbers $\{32 + n, \frac{n}{8}, \sqrt{n} + 225\}$. Find the smallest value of n so that all of the numbers in the set are natural numbers.

See your complete lesson at MyMathUniverse.com

Topic 1   **12**   Lesson 1-2

CCSS: 8.NS.A.2

Key Concept

Show $\sqrt{2}$ as a decimal.

First, label the square roots you know on a number line. $\sqrt{2}$ is between 1 and 2, but it's a little closer to 1 than 2.

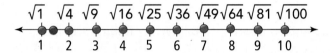

$\sqrt{2}$ must be between 1.4 and 1.5.

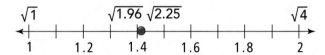

$\sqrt{2}$ is somewhere between 1.41 and 1.42.

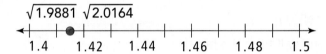

There is no exact decimal expansion for $\sqrt{2}$, but you can find one that is a pretty good approximation.

$$\sqrt{2} = 1.41421356\ldots$$

Part 1

Example Using Square Roots to Solve Real-World Problems

You are designing a booth for a comic convention. The booth is 7 ft wide and 6 ft deep. You plan to place a square rug in the booth, parallel to the walls. Each side of the rug is $\sqrt{33}$ ft long. Will the rug fit?

Solution ·

For the rug to fit, the side length of the rug must be less than or equal to 6 ft.

Estimate the value of $\sqrt{33}$ and compare it to 6. Start by finding the two perfect squares closest to 33.

The perfect squares closest to 33 are 25 and 36.

$$\sqrt{25} < \sqrt{33} < \sqrt{36}$$
$$5 < \sqrt{33} < 6$$

$\sqrt{33}$ is less than 6, so the rug will fit in the booth.

Part 2

Example Using Decimal Approximations of Irrational Square Roots to Solve a Real-World Problem

Your friend points out there will be a gap between the rug and the walls of the booth. To calculate the size of this gap, you need a better approximation for the length of the rug.

  a. Use a number line to estimate $\sqrt{33}$ to the nearest tenth.
  b. Use a number line to estimate $\sqrt{33}$ to the nearest hundredth.

continued on next page >

Solution ·

a. Since $\sqrt{33}$ is between 5 and 6 but closer to 6, look at the squares of numbers between 5.5 and 6 to find a more accurate estimate.

x	5.5	5.6	5.7	5.8	5.9	6.0
x^2	30.25	31.36	32.49	33.64	34.81	36

33

33 is between 32.49 and 33.64.

$$32.49 < 33 < 33.64$$
$$5.7^2 < 33 < 5.8^2$$
$$5.7 < \sqrt{33} < 5.8$$

Draw a number line to visualize the number.

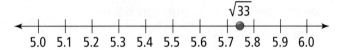

To see if $\sqrt{33}$ is closer to 5.7 or 5.8, compare 33 with 5.75^2.

- If $33 < 5.75^2$, then $5.7 < \sqrt{33} < 5.75$; round down to 5.7.
- If $33 > 5.75^2$, then $5.75 < \sqrt{33} < 5.8$; round up to 5.8.

$5.75^2 = 33.0625$ so $33 < 5.75^2$ and $\sqrt{33}$ rounded to the nearest tenth is 5.7. The rug is about 5.7 ft long.

b. You know from part a that $\sqrt{33}$ is close to 5.7. Now, look at the squares of numbers between 5.72 and 5.76 to estimate its value to the nearest hundredth.

x	5.72	5.73	5.74	5.75	5.76
x^2	32.7184	32.8329	32.9476	33.0625	33.1776

33

33 is between 32.9476 and 33.0625.

$$32.9476 < 33 < 33.0625$$
$$5.74^2 < 33 < 5.75^2$$
$$5.74 < \sqrt{33} < 5.75$$

Draw a number line to visualize the number.

continued on next page >

Part 2

Solution continued

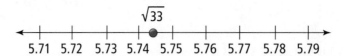

$$\sqrt{33}$$

To see if $\sqrt{33}$ is closer to 5.74 or 5.75, compare 33 with 5.745^2.

- If $33 < 5.745^2$, then $5.74 < \sqrt{33} < 5.745$; round down to 5.74.
- If $33 > 5.745^2$, then $5.745 < \sqrt{33} < 5.75$; round up to 5.75.

$5.745^2 = 33.005025$ so $33 < 5.745^2$ and $\sqrt{33}$ rounded to the nearest hundredth is 5.74. The rug is about 5.74 ft long.

Check

Use your calculator to find $\sqrt{33}$.

$$\sqrt{33} = 5.74456264\ldots$$

5.74456264... rounded to the nearest tenth is 5.7.
5.74456264... rounded to the nearest hundredth is 5.74.
Both answers are correct.

Part 3

Intro

The Know-Need-Plan graphic organizer is a tool that can help you in making sense of problems.

Consider the following problem: A square has an area of 20 ft². A circle has a diameter equal to the side length of the square. What is the approximate diameter of the circle?

Know	Need	Plan
• Area of the square: 20 ft² • Side length of square = diameter of circle	Diameter of the circle	Find the side length of the square, **s**. Since the area of a square is equal to the side length squared, $s = \sqrt{A}$.

Part 3

Example Using Decimal Approximations of Irrational Square Roots to Solve a Real-World Problem

In your booth there is a square-shaped table. The table has an area of 26 ft². You want to hang a table skirt along the edge of the table. Approximately how long must the skirt be to wrap around the perimeter of the table?

Solution

Know	Need	Plan
Area of square: 26 ft²	The perimeter of the table	• Find the side length s of the table. • Use the equation $P = 4s$ to find the perimeter of the table.

Step 1 Find the side length of the table.

The area of the table is 26 ft², so the side length of the table is $\sqrt{26}$ ft.

Step 2 Find the perimeter of the table.

Use the formula for the perimeter of a square.	$P = 4s$
Substitute $\sqrt{26}$ for s.	$= 4(\sqrt{26})$
$\sqrt{26} \approx 5.1$	$\approx 4(5.1)$
Multiply.	$= 20.4$

The perimeter of the table is about 20.4 ft. So you will need about 20.4 ft of the skirt to wrap around the perimeter of the table.

Check

Use a calculator to check your answer.

$4(\sqrt{26}) = 20.39607805...$

20.4 is close to $4\sqrt{26}$, so the answer checks.

1. **Think About the Process**

   a. What is the first step in finding the two consecutive whole numbers between which $\sqrt{845}$ is located?

      A. Find the two perfect squares closest to 845.

      B. Evaluate $\frac{\sqrt{844} + \sqrt{846}}{2}$.

      C. Evaluate $\sqrt{845^2}$.

      D. Evaluate $\sqrt{845}$.

   b. On a number line, between which two whole numbers would $\sqrt{845}$ be located?

      A. 31 and 32

      B. 29 and 30

      C. 28 and 29

      D. 30 and 31

2. On a number line, between which two consecutive whole numbers would $\sqrt{61}$ be located?

   A. 7 and 8   **B.** 9 and 10

   C. 6 and 7   **D.** 8 and 9

3. The height of a painting is $\sqrt{90}$ ft. Between which two consecutive whole numbers is $\sqrt{90}$?

   A. 11 and 12   **B.** 8 and 9

   C. 10 and 11   **D.** 9 and 10

4. Estimate $\sqrt{15}$ to the nearest tenth. Then locate $\sqrt{15}$ on a number line.

5. Estimate $\sqrt{136}$ to the nearest tenth.

6. Estimate $\sqrt{37}$ to the nearest hundredth. Then locate $\sqrt{37}$ on a number line.

7. **Think About the Process**

   a. What is the second step in finding the two consecutive whole numbers between which $\sqrt{185}$ is located?

      A. Evaluate $\frac{\sqrt{184} + \sqrt{186}}{2}$.

      B. Find the square roots of the two perfect squares closest to 185.

      C. Evaluate $\sqrt{185}$.

      D. Evaluate $\sqrt{185^2}$.

   b. Estimate $\sqrt{185}$ to the nearest hundredth.

8. The area of a square poster is 31 in.². Find the length of one side of the poster to the nearest tenth of an inch.

9. A tree is 16 feet tall. A wire runs from the top of the tree to a point 8 feet from its base. The wire is $\sqrt{320}$ feet long. Estimate the length of the wire to the nearest hundredth of a foot.

10. a. **Writing** On a number line, between which two consecutive whole numbers would $\sqrt{381}$ be located?

      A. 19 and 20

      B. 20 and 21

      C. 18 and 19

      D. 21 and 22

    b. Explain why it might be useful to approximate the value rather than use the exact value.

11. **Mental Math** The volume of displacement in an engine is $\sqrt{84}$ L. Between which two consecutive whole numbers is $\sqrt{84}$?

    A. 8 and 9   **B.** 11 and 12

    C. 10 and 11   **D.** 9 and 10

12. **Error Analysis** Diego incorrectly said that $\sqrt{82} = 41$.

    a. Estimate $\sqrt{82}$ to the nearest tenth.

    b. What was his likely error?

      A. He evaluated $\frac{82}{2}$ instead of evaluating $\sqrt{82}$.

      B. He rounded incorrectly.

      C. He did not round.

      D. He evaluated the square root incorrectly.

13. a. **Reasoning** Estimate $\sqrt{35}$ to the nearest hundredth.

    b. Is the estimated value rational or irrational? Explain.

14. The formula $d = \sqrt{2s^2}$ gives the length, d, of a diagonal of a square with side length s. Each side of a square piece of wood is 33 cm long. You paint a stripe along the diagonal of the piece of wood. Estimate the length of the stripe to the nearest hundredth.

15. The length of a car is $\sqrt{162}$ ft. Will this car fit in a garage that measures 11 ft long? If not, what is the minimum length of a garage long enough for this car?

16. Estimate $\sqrt{150}$ to the nearest hundredth.

17. Mrs. Drew wants to build a square sandbox for her children. The area of the sandbox will be 119 ft². To the nearest tenth, what is the total length of wood Mrs. Drew needs to make the sides of the sandbox?

18. **Challenge** A square pool has a volume of 4,528 cubic feet and a depth of 8 feet. A couple builds a fence 3.5 feet high around the pool. How many square feet of fencing surround the pool? Round to the nearest tenth as needed.

19. **Challenge** The formula $D = \sqrt{TR}$ gives the voltage D (in volts) across an electrical circuit that uses power T (in watts) and has resistance R (in ohms).

Electrical Circuits

Circuit	Power (watts)	Resistance (ohms)
A	51	5
B	50	9
C	57	6

a. Estimate the voltage across each of these circuits to the nearest hundredth of a volt.

b. List the circuits in order of the voltages from least to greatest.

CCSS: 8.NS.A.2

Key Concept

All real numbers can be located on a number line. This means that all irrational numbers can be located on a number line. You can use a number line to graph and order real numbers.

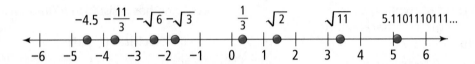

Part 1

Example Comparing Rational and Irrational Numbers

Complete each statement using >, <, or =.

a. $\sqrt{3}$ ■ 1   **b.** 1.5 ■ $\sqrt{2}$ **c.** 3 ■ $\sqrt{12}$

d. $\frac{20}{9}$ ■ $\sqrt{6}$ **e.** $-\sqrt{7}$ ■ -2.6 **f.** 9.5 ■ π^2

Solution

For each pair of values, draw a number line and approximate the placement of the irrational numbers.

a.

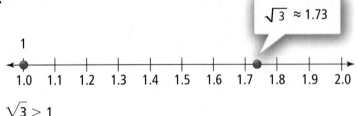

$\sqrt{3} > 1$

b.

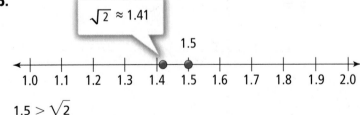

$1.5 > \sqrt{2}$

continued on next page >

Solution continued

c.

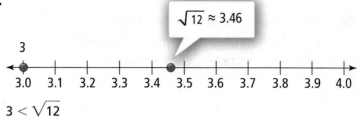

$$3 < \sqrt{12}$$

d.

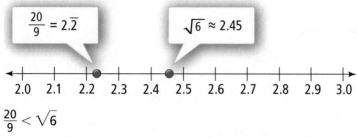

$$\frac{20}{9} < \sqrt{6}$$

e.

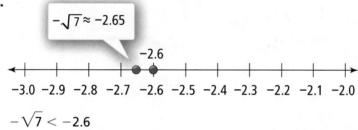

$$-\sqrt{7} < -2.6$$

f.

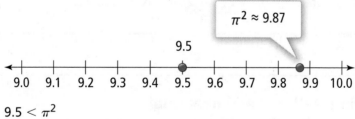

$$9.5 < \pi^2$$

Part 2

Example Ordering Rational and Irrational Numbers to Solve Real-World Problems

You are planning an art exhibit. One of the artists is a former math teacher. Each artist sent you the heights of their paintings. You want to display the paintings from shortest to tallest. List the heights in order.

2 ft $\sqrt{5}$ ft   1.6 ft $\sqrt{7}$ ft $\sqrt{2}$ ft   2.8 ft

Solution ·

Estimate each irrational number.

$$\sqrt{5} \approx 2.24$$
$$\sqrt{2} \approx 1.41$$
$$\sqrt{7} \approx 2.65$$

Draw a number line and plot all of the painting heights.

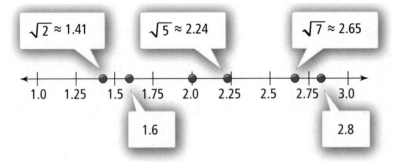

The heights from least to greatest are $\sqrt{2}$, 1.6, 2, $\sqrt{5}$, $\sqrt{7}$, and 2.8.

Part 3

Example Ordering Rational and Irrational Numbers with Negatives

Order the values from greatest to least.

-1.7 $-\sqrt{17}$ $\sqrt{9}$ $\frac{5}{3}$ $-\frac{17}{4}$ $\sqrt{3}$

continued on next page >

Part 3

Example continued

Solution ·

Draw a number line and plot all of the values.

$-\dfrac{17}{4} = -4.25$ $-\sqrt{17} \approx -4.12$ -1.7 $\dfrac{5}{3} = 1.\overline{6}$ $\sqrt{3} \approx 1.73$ $\sqrt{9} = 3$

The numbers from greatest to least are $\sqrt{9}$, $\sqrt{3}$, $\dfrac{5}{3}$, -1.7, $-\sqrt{17}$, and $-\dfrac{17}{4}$.

1. Locate $1\frac{4}{7}$ to the nearest tenth. Draw a point on a number line.

2. Compare $\sqrt{7}$ and 2.1.

3. Which list is in order from least to greatest?
   A. $\sqrt{27}$, 4.6, 5.8, $\sqrt{23}$
   B. $\sqrt{23}$, 5.8, 4.6, $\sqrt{27}$
   C. 4.6, $\sqrt{23}$, $\sqrt{27}$, 5.8
   D. 5.8, $\sqrt{27}$, $\sqrt{23}$, 4.6

4. You have 6 clay pots that you want to display in order form shortest to tallest. Which list has the heights of the pots in order from least to greatest?
   A. 1.8 in., $\sqrt{5}$ in., $2\frac{1}{3}$ in., 2.4 in., 2.5 in., $\sqrt{8}$ in.
   B. $\sqrt{8}$ in., $\sqrt{5}$ in., 2.4 in., 2.5 in., 1.8 in., $2\frac{1}{3}$ in.
   C. $\sqrt{8}$ in., 2.5 in., 2.4 in., $2\frac{1}{3}$ in., $\sqrt{5}$ in., 1.8 in.
   D. 1.8 in., 2.5 in., $\sqrt{5}$ in., 2.4 in., $2\frac{1}{3}$ in., $\sqrt{8}$ in.

5. Which list has the numbers in order from greatest to least?
   A. -0.7, $-\sqrt{5}$, -2.9, $-\frac{2}{9}$, $-\frac{37}{10}$, $-\sqrt{23}$
   B. $-\sqrt{5}$, $-\sqrt{23}$, -2.9, -0.7, $-\frac{37}{10}$, $-\frac{2}{9}$
   C. $-\frac{2}{9}$, -0.7, $-\sqrt{5}$, -2.9, $-\frac{37}{10}$, $-\sqrt{23}$
   D. $-\sqrt{23}$, $-\frac{37}{10}$, -2.9, $-\sqrt{5}$, -0.7, $-\frac{2}{9}$

6. Which list has the numbers in order from least to greatest?
   A. -4, $-\frac{9}{4}$, $\frac{1}{2}$, 3.7, $\sqrt{5}$
   B. -4, $-\frac{9}{4}$, $\frac{1}{2}$, $\sqrt{5}$, 3.7
   C. $\frac{1}{2}$, $-\frac{9}{4}$, 3.7, $\sqrt{5}$, -4
   D. $-\frac{9}{4}$, -4, $\frac{1}{2}$, 3.7, $\sqrt{5}$

7. Four fruit trees are being moved into an orchard. The trees are going to be planted in order from tallest to shortest. Write the heights of the trees in order from greatest to least.

   $2\sqrt{19}$ ft, $\frac{76}{9}$ ft, 9.35 ft, 9.58 ft

   A. $\frac{76}{9}$ ft, $2\sqrt{19}$ ft, 9.58 ft, 9.35 ft
   B. 9.58 ft, 9.35 ft, $2\sqrt{19}$ ft, $\frac{76}{9}$ ft
   C. 9.58 ft, $2\sqrt{19}$ ft, $\frac{76}{9}$ ft, 9.35 ft
   D. $\frac{76}{9}$ ft, $2\sqrt{19}$ ft, 9.35 ft, 9.58 ft

8. a. **Writing** Locate $-\sqrt{23}$ to the nearest tenth. Draw a point on a number line.
   b. Explain why it might be better to use a decimal estimate instead of an exact value to plot this number on a number line.

9. **Error Analysis** Your math class is comparing $\sqrt{7}$ and 3.4. Your friend says that $\sqrt{7} > 3.4$ because $\sqrt{7} = 3.5$.
   a. What is the correct comparison?
   b. What mistake did your friend likely make?
      A. Your friend made an error when rounding the decimal value of $\sqrt{7}$ to the nearest tenth.
      B. Your friend found $7 \div 2$, not $\sqrt{7}$.
      C. Your friend found $-\sqrt{7}$, not $\sqrt{7}$.

10. a. **Open-Ended** Which list shows the numbers in order from least to greatest?
    A. $\sqrt{32}$, 5.2, $4\frac{2}{3}$, $\sqrt{17}$
    B. $\sqrt{17}$, $4\frac{2}{3}$, 5.2, $\sqrt{32}$
    C. $4\frac{2}{3}$, $\sqrt{32}$, $\sqrt{17}$, 5.2
    D. 5.2, $\sqrt{17}$, $\sqrt{32}$, $4\frac{2}{3}$
    b. Find two more irrational numbers that would fall in the middle of the list.

See your complete lesson at MyMathUniverse.com

11. a. Estimation Use decimal estimates of $\sqrt{168}$ and $\sqrt{189}$ to locate the two irrational numbers on a number line.

b. Which list shows the numbers in order from greatest to least?

A. 12.33, $\sqrt{168}$, 13.13, $\sqrt{189}$, 13.77

B. $\sqrt{189}$, $\sqrt{168}$, 12.33, 13.77, 13.13

C. 12.33, $\sqrt{168}$, 13.77, $\sqrt{189}$, 13.13

D. 13.77, $\sqrt{189}$, 13.13, $\sqrt{168}$, 12.33

12. a. Reasoning Does $\frac{1}{6}$, -3, $\sqrt{7}$, $-\frac{6}{5}$, or 4.5 come first when the numbers are listed from least to greatest?

A. -3 because it is the negative number with the greatest absolute value.

B. 4.5 because it is the greatest positive number.

C. $\sqrt{7}$ because it is the greatest positive number.

D. $-\frac{6}{5}$ because it is the negative number with the greatest absolute value.

E. $\frac{1}{6}$ because it is the only number less than 1.

b. Write the numbers in order from least to greatest.

13. Locate $3 + \sqrt{6}$ to the nearest tenth on a number line. Draw a point on a tick mark that is closest to the value of $3 + \sqrt{6}$.

14. Write the numbers in order from greatest to least.

$$-\sqrt{29}, -\sqrt{17}, -5\frac{4}{5}, -4\frac{2}{5}, -4.8, -5.6$$

15. Think About the Process

a. What do you need to do to write $-|-\sqrt{59}|$ as a decimal?

A. Rewrite $-|-\sqrt{59}|$ as an improper fraction.

B. Rewrite $-|-\sqrt{59}|$ as a mixed number.

C. Rewrite $-|-\sqrt{59}|$ as $-\sqrt{59}$.

D. Rewrite $-|-\sqrt{59}|$ as $\sqrt{59}$.

b. Order the numbers from least to greatest.

$$-|-\sqrt{59}|, -\sqrt{40}, -5.6, -8.9, -5\frac{1}{9}, -\frac{95}{10}$$

16. Think About the Process

a. What is the first step to compare $-\pi$ and -4.4?

A. Rewrite $-\pi$ and -4.4 as mixed numbers.

B. Rewrite $-\pi$ as a decimal.

C. Find the absolute value of $-\pi$ and -4.4.

D. Add $-\pi + -4.4$.

b. Is $-\pi$ less than or greater than -4.4?

17. Challenge A pizza store offers 3 pizza specials. Special #1 is a square pizza with side length 13.7 in. that costs $20. Special #2 is a round pizza with diameter 13 in. that costs $22. Special #3 is a rectangular pizza with length $\sqrt{128}$ in. and width $\sqrt{157}$ in. that costs $25.

a. Which special is the best deal?

b. Which special is the worst deal?

18. a. Challenge Which list shows the numbers in order from least to greatest?

A. $-4\sqrt{5}, -\frac{3\pi}{2}, -2.7, \sqrt{10}, \frac{3\pi}{2}, 8\frac{1}{3}$

B. $-2.7, -4\sqrt{5}, 8\frac{1}{3}, \frac{3\pi}{2}, -\frac{3\pi}{2}, \sqrt{10}$

C. $8\frac{1}{3}, \frac{3\pi}{2}, \sqrt{10}, -2.7, -\frac{3\pi}{2}, -4\sqrt{5}$

D. $-4\sqrt{5}, \sqrt{10}, 8\frac{1}{3}, -2.7, -\frac{3\pi}{2}, \frac{3\pi}{2}$

b. Explain how you can split this task into two subtasks. Does this split simplify your work? Explain.

CCSS: 8.NS.A.1, 8.NS.A.2

Part 1

Example Finding Examples of Rational and Irrational Numbers

Find values for x and y to make each statement true, if possible. Assume that x and y are natural numbers less than 11 and $x \neq y$.

a. $\sqrt{x^2 + y^2}$ is rational.

b. $\sqrt{x^2 + y^2}$ is irrational.

c. $\sqrt{(x + y)^2}$ is rational.

d. $\sqrt{(x + y)^2}$ is irrational.

Solution

Answers may vary. Sample answers:

a. Let $x = 3$ and $y = 4$.

> First evaluate exponents, then add the terms.

$$\sqrt{x^2 + y^2} = \sqrt{3^2 + 4^2}$$
$$= \sqrt{9 + 16}$$
$$= \sqrt{25}$$
$$= 5$$

5 is a rational number.

b. Let $x = 1$ and $y = 2$.

$$\sqrt{x^2 + y^2} = \sqrt{1^2 + 2^2}$$
$$= \sqrt{1 + 4}$$
$$= \sqrt{5}$$

$\sqrt{5}$ is a rational number.

c. Let $x = 1$ and $y = 2$.

> First evaluate the expression inside parentheses.

$$\sqrt{(x + y)^2} = \sqrt{(1 + 2)^2}$$
$$= \sqrt{3^2}$$
$$= \sqrt{9}$$
$$= 3$$

3 is a rational number.

d. Not possible. No matter what the values of x and y, the square of the sum will always be a perfect square. So the square root of that perfect square will always be rational.

Part 2

Example Using Irrational Numbers to Solve Real-World Problems

You want to wrap a ribbon around the gift so that the ends meet on the top, without a bow. You have $\frac{1}{3}$ of a 110 in. roll of ribbon. The gift box has a square base and its volume is 875 in³. Do you have enough ribbon to wrap around the box once?

5 in.

Solution

Step 1 Find out how much ribbon you need.

First, use the formula $V = Bh$ to find the area of the base. You know that the volume V is 875 in.³ and the height h is 5 in.

Use the formula for volume	$V = Bh$
Substitute 875 for V and 5 for h.	$875 = B(5)$
Simplify.	$175 = B$

The area of the base is 175 in.², so the side length of the square is $\sqrt{175}$ in.

The ribbon needs to be long enough to run along the top of the box, down the side, along the bottom, and up the other side.

> Down one side, up the other

> Across the top and bottom

$\sqrt{175} \approx 13.2$	$2(5) + 2(\sqrt{175}) \approx 2(5) + 2(13.2)$
Multiply.	$\approx 10 + 26.4$
Add.	≈ 36.4

You need about 36.4 in. of ribbon.

Step 2 Find out how much ribbon you have.

A roll of ribbon is 110 in. and you have $\frac{1}{3}$ of a roll.

$$\frac{1}{3}(110) = \frac{110}{3}$$
$$= 36.\bar{6}$$

You have $36.\bar{6}$ in. of ribbon.

continued on next page >

Part 2

Solution continued

    Step 3 Compare the amount of ribbon you need to the amount of ribbon you have.

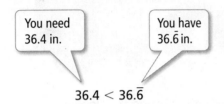

You need 36.4 in.

You have 36.$\overline{6}$ in.

$$36.4 < 36.\overline{6}$$

You have more ribbon than you need, so you have enough ribbon to wrap around the box once.

Part 3

▶ Intro

Recall that all repeating decimals are rational numbers. You can use algebra to write a repeating decimal as a fraction.

Write $0.\overline{72}$ as a fraction in simplest form.

First, write the following equation.

$$n = 0.\overline{72}$$

Since the length of the repetition is 2 decimal places, multiply both sides of the equation by 100. Show the decimal expansions.

$$100n = 72.7272\ldots$$

Then, subtract the original expression.

$$
\begin{array}{r}
100n = 72.72 \\
- n = 0.72 \\
\hline
99n = 72
\end{array}
$$

Now solve for n.

$$n = \frac{8}{11}$$

The repeating decimal $0.\overline{72}$ equals $\frac{8}{11}$.

▶ Example Converting Repeating Decimals into Fractions

Write each decimal as a fraction in simplest form.

    a. $0.\overline{4}$ **b.** $0.\overline{45}$

continued on next page >

Part 3

Example continued

Solution

a. Let $x = 0.\overline{4}$.

> There is 1 repeating digit, so multiply by 10.

$$10x = 4.\overline{4}$$
$$-\quad x = 0.\overline{4}$$
$$\overline{9x = 4.0}$$

Now solve for x.

$$\frac{9x}{9} = \frac{4}{9}$$
$$x = \frac{4}{9}$$

The repeating decimal $0.\overline{4}$ equals $\frac{4}{9}$.

Check

To check your answer, write the fraction as a decimal. Divide 4 by 9.

$$
\begin{array}{r}
0.444 \\
9\overline{)4.000} \\
-\ 3\ 6 \\
\hline
4\ 0 \\
-\ 3\ 6 \\
\hline
4\ 0 \\
-\ 3\ 6 \\
\hline
4
\end{array}
$$

> The quotient is the repeating decimal $0.\overline{4}$, so the answer checks.

> There are 2 repeating digits, so multiply by 100.

b. Let $x = 0.\overline{45}$.

$$100x = 45.\overline{45}$$
$$-\quad x = 0.\overline{45}$$
$$\overline{99x = 45.00}$$

Now solve for x.

$$\frac{99x}{99} = \frac{45}{99}$$
$$x = \frac{45}{99}$$
$$x = \frac{5}{11}$$

The repeating decimal $0.\overline{45}$ equals $\frac{5}{11}$.

continued on next page >

continued on next page >

Solution continued

Check ·

To check your answer, write the fraction as a decimal. Divide 5 by 11.

$$
\begin{array}{r}
0.4545 \\
11{\overline{\smash{\big)}\,5.0000}} \\
\underline{-4\,4} \\
60 \\
\underline{-55} \\
50 \\
\underline{-44} \\
60 \\
\underline{-55} \\
5
\end{array}
$$

> The quotient is the repeating decimal $0.\overline{45}$, so the answer checks.

1. If $x = 36$ and $y = 25$, is $\sqrt{x + y}$ rational or irrational? Simplify your answer.

2. After an accident, police can use the formula $v = 2\sqrt{5L}$ to estimate the speed, v, in miles per hour, that a car was traveling by measuring the length of the skid marks, L, in feet.

   a. Estimate the speed of a car that left skid marks 65 ft long. Round to the nearest tenth as needed.

   b. If the posted speed limit is 40 mi/h, was the car speeding?

3. Write $0.\overline{87}$ as a fraction in simplest form.

4. Find the integer value of x, $1 \le x \le 5$, that makes $\sqrt{x^3 + 41}$ rational.

5. Is $\sqrt{x^2 + y^2}$ rational or irrational when $x = 14$ and $y = 8$? If you pick a whole number value for x, can you always find a whole number value for y to make the expression a rational number? Explain.

6. A couple wants to enclose a square garden with area 141 ft². The wife says that they need about 47.6 ft of fence. The husband disagrees. He says they need about 11.9 ft of fence.

   a. Who is correct?

   b. What error did the person who found the incorrect length make?

   A. The person divided the area of the garden by 4 to find the side length.

   B. The person added 4 to the side length instead of multiplying by 4 to find the perimeter.

   C. The person squared the area instead of finding the square root to find the side length.

   D. The person found the side length of the garden, not the perimeter.

   c. Explain how you found the correct length of fence that the couple needs.

7. **Think About the Process** The length of a rectangle is twice the width. The area of the rectangle is 90 square units. Notice that you can divide the rectangle into two squares with equal area.

   a. How can you estimate the side length of each square?

   A. Estimate $\sqrt{\frac{90}{4}}$.

   B. Estimate $\sqrt{90}$.

   C. Estimate $\sqrt{45}$.

   D. Estimate $\sqrt{\frac{45}{4}}$.

   b. Estimate the length and width of the rectangle.

8. A woman wants to send a framed photograph of her family to her parents. The frame is 10 in. long and 6 in. wide. Will the frame lay flat in a box that has a square base, height 6 in., and volume 564 in.³? Round to the nearest tenth as needed.

9. a. Is $\sqrt{y + x + z}$ rational or irrational for $x = 15$, $y = 22$, and $z = 14$? Simplify your answer.

   b. Is $\sqrt{y + x + z}$ rational or irrational for $x = 14$, $y = 25$, and $z = 10$? Simplify your answer.

   c. Find three different values that make the expression rational.

   d. Find three different values that make the expression irrational.

   e. Describe how you found these sets of numbers.

10. Write $1.\overline{48}$ as a mixed number in simplest form.

11. If $x = 4$ and $y = 5$, is $\sqrt{x^2 + y^2 + 57}$ rational or irrational? Simplify your answer.

12. **Think About the Process**

    a. Evaluate the expression $\sqrt{x^3 + y^2 + 5}$ for $x = 3$ and $y = 2$. Leave your answer in square root form.

    b. How can you decide if the result is rational or irrational?

      A. See if the value under the square root symbol is a perfect square or not.

      B. See if the value under the square root symbol is positive or negative.

      C. See if the value under the square root symbol is a whole number.

      D. See if the value under the square root symbol is a rational or an irrational number.

    c. Is the result rational or irrational?

13. **a.** **Challenge** If $x = 5$, $y = 6$, and $z = 2$, is $\sqrt{x^2 + y^2 + z^2 + 56}$ rational or irrational? Simplify your answer.

    b. If the result is an irrational number, find values for x, y, and z that give a rational number.

    c. Once you've found three values that give a rational number, find three other values for x, y, and z that give a rational number.

14. **Challenge** A toy has various shaped objects that a child is supposed to push through matching holes. The area of the square hole is 5 cm^2. The area of the circular face of the round peg is 5 cm^2. Will the round peg fit through the square hole? Use $\pi = 3.14$. Round to the nearest hundredth as needed.

CCSS: 8.EE.C.7, 8.EE.C.7b

Key Concept

You can think of solving an equation as transforming the equation into a series of simpler equivalent equations. Use the properties of equality to isolate the variable on one side of the equation.

A two-step equation involves two operations. To solve a two-step equation, it is usually easier to perform the order of operations in reverse. So undo addition or subtraction, and then undo multiplication of division.

Solve $\frac{x}{4} + 12 = 32$.

Subtract 12 from each side.	$\frac{x}{4} + 12 - 12 = 32 - 12$
Simplify.	$\frac{x}{4} = 20$
Multiply each side by 4.	$4\left(\frac{x}{4}\right) = 4(20)$
Simplify.	$x = 80$

Check

$$\frac{x}{4} + 12 = 32$$

Substitute 80 for x.	$\frac{80}{4} + 12 \stackrel{?}{=} 32$
Simplify.	$32 = 32 ✔$

$32 = 32$ is a true statement, so when $\frac{x}{4} + 12 = 32$, x equals 80.

Part 1

Intro

Sometimes you have to use the Commutative Property to reorder terms. The step using the Commutative Property is shown in the example below. In future examples in this topic, this step is done mentally.

Solve $3 + 3t = 17$.

Subtract 3 from each side.	$3 + 3t - 3 = 17 - 3$
Use the Commutative Property to reorder items.	$3 - 3 + 3t = 17 - 3$
Simplify.	$3t = 14$
Divide each side by 3.	$\frac{3t}{3} = \frac{14}{3}$
Simplify.	$t = \frac{14}{3}$

Example Finding Solutions of Two-Step Equations

Solve each equation.

a. $\frac{x}{2} + 5 = -10$ **b.** $3x + 7 = -2$

c. $35 = 3 + 5x$ **d.** $10.7 - x - 43$

Solution ·

a. $\frac{x}{2} + 5 = -10$

Subtract 5 from each side.	$\frac{x}{2} + 5 - 5 = -10 - 5$
Simplify.	$\frac{x}{2} = -15$
Multiply each side by 2.	$\frac{x}{2} \cdot 2 = -15 \cdot 2$
Simplify.	$x = -30$

b. $3x + 7 = -2$

Subtract 7 from each side.	$3x + 7 - 7 = -2 - 7$
Simplify.	$3x = -9$
Divide each side by 3.	$\frac{3x}{3} = \frac{-9}{3}$
Simplify.	$x = -3$

continued on next page >

Solution continued

c. $35 = 3 + 5x$

Subtract 3 from each side.	$35 - 3 = 3 + 5x - 3$
Use the Commutative Property.	$35 - 3 = 3 - 3 + 5x$
Simplify.	$32 = 5x$
Divide each side by 5.	$\dfrac{32}{5} = \dfrac{5x}{5}$
Simplify.	$\dfrac{32}{5} = x$

d. $10.7 - x - 43$

Add 43 to each side.	$10.7 + 43 = -x - 43 + 43$
Simplify.	$53.7 = -x$
Divide each side by -1.	$\dfrac{53.7}{-1} = \dfrac{-x}{-1}$
Simplify.	$-53.7 = x$

> You're not finished yet! If 53.7 is the opposite of x; what *is* x?

Check

a. $\dfrac{x}{2} + 5 = -10$

$\dfrac{-30}{2} + 5 \stackrel{?}{=} -10$

$-15 + 5 \stackrel{?}{=} -10$

$-10 = -10$ ✔

b. $3x + 7 = -2$

$3(-3) + 7 \stackrel{?}{=} -2$

$-9 + 7 \stackrel{?}{=} -2$

$-2 = -2$ ✔

c. $35 = 3 + 5x$

$35 \stackrel{?}{=} 3 + 5\left(\dfrac{32}{5}\right)$

$35 \stackrel{?}{=} 3 + 32$

$35 \stackrel{?}{=} 35$ ✔

d. $10.7 = -x - 43$

$10.7 \stackrel{?}{=} -(-53.7) - 43$

$10.7 \stackrel{?}{=} 53.7 - 43$

$10.7 = 10.7$ ✔

Part 2

Intro

You can solve equations with decimals in multiple ways. In one method, you begin by removing all decimals from the equation. To do this, first find the greatest number of digits to the right of any decimal point. Then multiply each term in the equation by that power of 10.

One digit to the right of the decimal point	Two digits to the right of the decimal point

$$4 + 6.8g = 24.14$$

To remove all decimals from this equation, multiply each term by 10^2, or 100.

$$100(4) + 100(6.8g) = 100(24.14)$$

$$400 + 680g = 2{,}414$$

Example Writing and Solving Two-Step Equations

A 22.8-pound cat needs to lose weight. If the owner follows the vet's weight-loss plan, the cat will lose 0.4 pound per month. After how many months will the cat weigh 14 pounds?

Solution

Words	initial weight	minus	weight loss per month	times	number of months	equals	new weight

to

Let m = the number of months the cat is on the plan.

Equation	22.8	–	0.4	×	m	=	14

continued on next page >

Part 2

Solution continued

Method 1 Multiply by a power of 10 to remove the decimals.

> There is at most 1 digit to the right of a decimal.

$$22.8 - 0.4m = 14$$

Multiply each term by 10.	$10(22.8) - 10(0.4m) = 10(14)$
Multiply.	$228 - 4m = 140$
Subtract 228 from each side.	$228 - 228 - 4m = 140 - 228$
Simplify.	$4m = -88$
Divide each side by -4.	$\dfrac{-4m}{-4} = \dfrac{-88}{-4}$
Simplify.	$m = 22$

Method 2 Solve the original equation with decimals.

$$22.8 - 0.4m = 14$$

Subtract 22.8 from each side.	$22.8 - 22.8 - 0.4m = 14 - 22.8$
Simplify.	$-0.4m = -8.8$
Divide each side by -0.4.	$\dfrac{-0.4m}{-0.4} = \dfrac{-8.8}{-0.4}$
Simplify.	$m = 22$

If the plan is followed, the cat will weigh 14 pounds after 22 months.

Check ·

$$22.8 - 0.4m = 14$$
$$22.8 - 0.4(22) \stackrel{?}{=} 14$$
$$22.8 - 8.8 \stackrel{?}{=} 14$$
$$14 = 14 \checkmark$$

Part 3

Intro

Some equations have more than one variable term on the same side of the equal sign. To solve these equations, use the Distributive Property to combine like terms and simplify the equation.

$$13.6n + 12n = 128$$

Use the Distributive Property.	$(13.6 + 12)n = 128$
Add.	$25.6n = 128$
Divide each side by 25.6.	$\dfrac{25.6n}{25.6} = \dfrac{128}{25.6}$
Simplify.	$n = 5$

So when $n = 5$, the expression $13.6n + 12n$ equals 128.

Example Using Two-Step Equations to Solve Problems

You rake leaves for 2 hours on Saturday and 5 hours on Sunday. Your neighbor pays you $63 in total. How much do you earn per hour?

Solution

Words   2 hours times pay per hour plus 5 hours times pay per hour equals total cost

  to

Let r = your pay per hour, in dollars.

Equation   2 • r + 5 • r = 63

$$2r + 5r = 63$$

Combine like terms.	$7r = 63$
Divide each side by 7.	$\dfrac{7r}{7} = \dfrac{63}{7}$
Simplify.	$r = 9$

You earn $9 per hour.

Check

$$2r + 5r = 63$$
$$2(9) + 5(9) \stackrel{?}{=} 63$$
$$18 + 45 \stackrel{?}{=} 63$$
$$63 = 63 \checkmark$$

1. Solve $\dfrac{y}{6} + 6 = -8$.

2. Solve $\dfrac{x}{8} - 4 = \dfrac{15}{16}$.

3. A rental company rents a luxury car at a daily rate of $38.34 plus $.50 per mile. Paul is allotted $100 for car rental each day.

   a. Which equation represents the cost, C, of renting a car and driving x miles?

      A. $C = 38.34x + 0.50$

      B. $38.34 = C + 0.50x$

      C. $38.34 = Cx + 0.50$

      D. $C = 38.34 + 0.50x$

   b. How many miles can Paul travel on the $100?

4. The same number of guests are seated at each of 11 large tables. There are 2 guests seated at one small table.

   a. Which equation represents the total number of guests, T, and the number of people, x, at each large table?

      A. $11 = Tx + 2$

      B. $T = 11x + 2$

      C. $T = 11 + 2x$

      D. $11 = T + 2x$

   b. If there are 90 guests, how many are seated at each large table?

5. Jacek went to a sporting event with some friends. They bought 2 snacks of equal price and a drink that cost $4.09.

   a. Which equation represents the total cost T and the cost s of each snack bought?

      A. $T = 2 + 4.09s$

      B. $2 = Ts + 4.09$

      C. $2 = T + 4.09s$

      D. $T = 2s + 4.09$

   b. How much did each snack cost if they spent $14.85 total?

6. Solve $7x + 11x = 144$. Simplify your answer.

7. A 132-inch board is cut into two pieces. One piece is three times the length of the other. Find the length of the shorter piece.

8. A contractor bought 8.2 ft² of sheet metal. She used 2.1 ft² so far and has $183 worth of sheet metal remaining. The equation $8.2x - 2.1x = 183$ represents how much sheet metal is remaining and the cost of the remaining amount. How much does sheet metal cost per square foot?

9. a. **Writing** Solve $\dfrac{y}{5} - 2 = 1$.

   b. Think of a situation in your own life that could be represented by a two-step equation. Write and solve the two-step equation.

10. **Reasoning** A worker on the production line is paid a base salary of $220.00 per week plus $0.92 for each unit produced.

    a. Which equation represents the weekly salary of $428.84 when she produces x units?

       A. $428.84 = 220x + 0.92$

       B. $220 = 428.84x + 0.92$

       C. $220 = 428.84 + 0.92x$

       D. $428.84 = 220 + 0.92x$

    b. How many units did she produce?

11. **Running** An athlete runs an equal distance 4 days a week. The other 3 days of the week, she runs a total of 11 miles.

    a. Which equation represents the total number of miles run in a week, R, and the number of miles, x, run each of the 4 days?

       A. $4 = R + 11x$

       B. $R = 4 + 11x$

       C. $4 = Rx + 11$

       D. $R = 4x + 11$

    b. If the athlete ran 43 miles last week, how far did she run each of the first 4 days?

12. a. Error Analysis Your friend incorrectly says the solution to this equation is $\frac{8}{9}$. Solve the equation $11y - 7y = 16$ correctly.

  b. What error did your friend likely make?

    A. She added like terms instead of subtracting.

    B. She incorrectly subtracted like terms.

    C. She divided incorrectly.

    D. She solved for $\frac{1}{y}$ instead of for y.

13. Solve $\frac{z}{5} - 4 = 2\frac{1}{4}$. Simplify your answer.

14. Ursula went clothes shopping at the mall. She bought 5 pairs of shorts at the same price and a shirt that cost $18.25.

  a. Which equation represents the total cost, T, and the cost, s, of each pair of shorts bought?

    A. $T = 5s + 18.25$

    B. $5 = T + 18.25s$

    C. $T = 5 + 18.25s$

    D. $5 = Ts + 18.25$

  b. How much did each pair of shorts cost if she spent $143.60 total?

  c. What was the total if she bought 2 more shirts?

15. Solve $6y - 4y - 10 = 31.58$. Simplify your answer.

16. Think About the Process You are given the following equation.

$$\frac{1}{4}y - 3 = -18$$

  a. What is the first operation you would use to solve the equation?

    A. Multiplication

    B. Division

    C. Addition

    D. Subtraction

  b. Solve the equation to find the value of y.

17. Think About the Process A limousine driver earns a daily rate of $123.81 plus $0.82 per mile driven.

  a. Which equation represents the amount T she earns for driving M miles each day?

    A. $T = 123.81M + 0.28$

    B. $T = 123.81 + 0.82M$

    C. $123.81 = TM + 0.82$

    D. $123.81 = M + 0.82T$

  b. What is the first step in solving the equation?

    A. Multiply by a power of 10 to remove the decimals.

    B. Combine all like terms.

    C. Divide by a power of 10 to remove the decimals.

    D. Divide by the coefficient of M.

  c. She earns $■ when she drives 160 miles in a day.

18. Challenge Solve $\frac{2h}{3} - 156 = 3\frac{13}{24}$. Simplify your answer.

19. Challenge An architect plans to buy 8 stone spheres and 4 stone cylinders. For the same amount, she can buy 3 stone spheres and 7 stone cylinders. If one stone cylinder costs $38.83, how much does each stone sphere cost? Round to the nearest cent as needed.

Solving Equations with Variables on Both Sides

CCSS: 8.EE.C.7, 8.EE.C.7b

Key Concept

When you write an equation, you set two expressions equal to each other.

When you solve an equation, you find the value of the variable that makes the two expressions equal.

$$2x + 6 = -3x + 1$$

Variable term on each side of the equation

Sometimes, both expressions contain a variable term.

$$2x - 2x + 6 = -3x - 2x + 1$$
$$6 = -5x + 1$$

To solve this kind of equation, bring all of the variable terms to the same side of the equation.

$$2x + 3x + 6 = -3x + 3x + 1$$
$$5x + 6 = 1$$

Part 1

Intro

You can use algebra tiles to model equations with integer coefficients and variables on both sides of the equation.

Example Using Models to Solve Equations with Variables on Both Sides

What is the value of x when the expression $6x - 9$ equals the expression $4x + 3$?

Solution

Use algebra tiles to solve the equation $6x - 9 = 4x + 3$. Begin by representing the two expressions.

continued on next page >

Part 1

Solution continued

Subtract 4*x* from each side.

Add 9 to each side.

Remove the zero pairs.

Divide the tiles into two equal groups.

Then remove one group from each side.

The solution is $x = 6$.

continued on next page >

Part 1

Solution continued

Check ···

$$6x - 9 = 4x + 3$$
$$6(6) - 9 \stackrel{?}{=} 4(6) + 3$$
$$36 - 9 \stackrel{?}{=} 24 + 3$$
$$27 = 27 \checkmark$$

When $6x - 9$ equals $4x + 3$, the value of x is 6.

Part 2

Intro

Suppose the temperature in your town is 21°F and rising 1.5°F every hour. Your friend lives far away, and the temperature in his town is 28°F and falling 2°F every hour. In how many hours will the temperatures be equal?

Step 1 Write an expression showing the temperature in your town at hour h.

The temperature in your town at hour h is $(21 + 1.5h)$°F.

Words   starting temperature   plus   1.5°F per hour   times   number of hours

⬇ **to**   Let h = the number of hours.

Expression   21   +   1.5   • h

Step 2 Write an expression showing the temperature in your friend's town at hour h.

The temperature in your friend's town at hour h is $(28 - 2h)$°F.

Words   starting temperature   minus   2°F per hour   times   number of hours

⬇ **to**   Let h = the number of hours.

Expression   28   –   2   • h

continued on next page >

Part 2

Intro continued

Step 3 Set the two expressions equal to each other and solve the resulting equation.

$$21 + 1.5h = 28 - 2h$$

Add 2h to each side.	$21 + 1.5h + 2h = 28 - 2h + 2h$
Combine like terms.	$21 + 3.5h = 28$
Subtract 21 from each side.	$21 - 21 + 3.5h = 28 - 21$
Simplify.	$3.5h = 7$
Divide each side by 3.5.	$\dfrac{3.5h}{3.5} = \dfrac{7}{3.5}$
Simplify.	$h = 2$

Step 4 Check the solution: $h = 2$

Check

$$21 + 1.5h = 28 - 2h$$

Substitute 2 for h.	$21 + 1.5(2) \stackrel{?}{=} 28 - 2(2)$
Simplify.	$24 = 24 \checkmark$

When $h = 2$, the expressions are equal. So in 2 hours, the temperatures in the two towns will be equal.

Example Writing and Solving Equations with Variables on Both Sides

A town's population is 14,000, and it is increasing by 160 people every year. A nearby town has a population of 24,000, and it is decreasing by 200 people every year. In about how many years will the populations of the towns be equal?

Solution

Step 1 Write the expression showing the population of the first town in year y.

Words	starting population	plus	160 people per year	times	number of years

to Let y = the number of years.

Expression	14,000	+	160	•	y

An expression showing the population of the first town in year y is $14{,}000 + 160y$.

continued on next page >

See your complete lesson at MyMathUniverse.com

Topic 2   44   Lesson 2-2

Part 2

Solution continued

Step 2 Write the expression showing the population of the second town in year *y*.

Words
| starting population | minus | 200 people per year | times | number of years |

 to Let y = the number of years.

Expression | 24,000 | − | 200 | • | *y* |

An expression that shows the population of the second town in year *y* is 24,000 − 200*y*.

Step 3 Set the two expressions equal to each other and solve the resulting equation.

$$14{,}000 + 160y = 24{,}000 - 200y$$

The population of the first town is increasing.

The population of the second town is decreasing.

Add 200*y* to each side.	$14{,}000 + 160y + 200y = 24{,}000 - 200y + 200y$
Combine like terms.	$14{,}000 + 360y = 24{,}000$
Subtract 14,000 from each side.	$14{,}000 - 14{,}000 + 360y = 24{,}000 - 14{,}000$
Simplify.	$360y = 10{,}000$
Divide each side by 360.	$\dfrac{360y}{360} = \dfrac{10{,}000}{360}$
Simplify.	$y \approx 27.78$

In about 28 years, the populations of the two towns will by equal.

Check ·

$$14{,}000 + 160y = 24{,}000 - 200y$$
$$14{,}000 + 160(27.78) \stackrel{?}{=} 24{,}000 - 200(27.78)$$
$$14{,}000 + 4{,}444.8 \stackrel{?}{=} 24{,}000 - 5{,}556$$
$$18{,}444.8 \approx 18{,}444 \checkmark$$

Since the answer is rounded, the check results in two numbers that are approximately equal.

Part 3

Example Solving Equations with Variables on Both Sides

Find the solution to each equation to find the value of each variable.

$$a = \blacksquare \qquad b = \blacksquare \qquad c = \blacksquare \qquad d = \blacksquare$$

a. $6a + 14 = -7 - a$ **b.** $b + b + 18 = 4b$

c. $-\frac{1}{2}c - 5 = \frac{1}{2}c$ **d.** $2d + 9.7 = -d - 17$

Solution ·

a. $6a + 14 = -7 - a$

Add a to each side.	$6a + a + 14 = -7 - a + a$
Combine like terms.	$7a + 14 = -7$
Subtract 14 from each side.	$7a + 14 - 14 = -7 - 14$
Simplify.	$7a = -21$
Divide each side by 7.	$\frac{7a}{7} = \frac{-21}{7}$
Simplify.	$a = -3$

b. $b + b + 18 = 4b$

Combine like terms.	$2b + 18 = 4b$
Subtract 2b from each side.	$2b - 2b + 18 = 4b - 2b$
Combine like terms.	$18 = 2b$
Divide each side by 2.	$\frac{18}{2} = \frac{2b}{2}$
Simplify.	$9 = b$

c. $-\frac{1}{2}c - 5 = \frac{1}{2}c$

Add $\frac{1}{2}c$ to each side.	$-\frac{1}{2}c + \frac{1}{2}c - 5 = \frac{1}{2}c + \frac{1}{2}c$
Combine like terms.	$-5 = 1c$
Use the Identity Property.	$-5 = c$

d. $2d + 9.7 = -d - 17$

Add d to each side.	$2d + d + 9.7 = -d + d - 17$
Combine like terms.	$3d + 9.7 = -17$
Subtract 9.7 from each side.	$3d + 9.7 - 9.7 = -17 - 9.7$
Simplify.	$3d = -26.7$
Divide each side by 3.	$\frac{3d}{3} = \frac{-26.7}{3}$
Simplify.	$d = -8.9$

continued on next page >

Part 3

Solution continued

Check ·

a. $6a + 14 = -7 - a$

$6(-3) + 14 \stackrel{?}{=} -7 - (-3)$

$-18 + 14 \stackrel{?}{=} -7 + 3$

$-4 = -4$ ✔

b. $b + b + 18 = 4b$

$9 + 9 + 18 \stackrel{?}{=} 4(9)$

$36 = 36$ ✔

c. $-\frac{1}{2}c - 5 = \frac{1}{2}c$

$-\frac{1}{2}(-5) - 5 \stackrel{?}{=} \frac{1}{2}(-5)$

$\frac{5}{2} - 5 \stackrel{?}{=} \frac{-5}{2}$

$\frac{5}{2} - \frac{10}{2} \stackrel{?}{=} \frac{-5}{2}$

$\frac{-5}{2} = \frac{-5}{2}$ ✔

d. $2d + 9.7 = -d - 17$

$2(-8.9) + 9.7 \stackrel{?}{=} -(-8.9) - 17$

$-17.8 + 9.7 \stackrel{?}{=} 8.9 - 17$

$-8.1 = -8.1$ ✔

See your complete lesson at MyMathUniverse.com

1. Use the algebra tiles to find the value of x when the expression $6x + 2$ equals $4x + 10$. Simplify your answer.

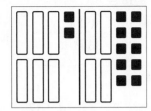

2. Which is the value of n when $6n - 10 = 4n + 6$?

3. A town has accumulated 5 inches of snow, and the snow depth is increasing by 6 inches every hour. A nearby town has accumulated 6 inches, and the depth is increasing by 2 inches every hour. In about how many hours will the snowfall of the towns be equal? Round your answer to the nearest tenth.

4. **Think About the Process** You are given the equation, $34 - 7x = 15 + 12x$.
   a. What would you do first to find x?
   b. What value of x makes the equation true?

5. Find the value of x when $6 - 4x = 6x - 8x + 2$.

6. Solve the equation to find the value of x. $6 - 6x = 5x - 9x - 2$

7. A town's population is 43,425. About 125 people move out of the town each month. Each month, 200 people on average move into town. A nearby town has a population of 45,000. It has no one moving in and an average of 150 people moving away every month.
   a. Write an equation which models the situation.
   b. In about how many months will the population of the towns be equal?

8. a. **Writing** Find the value of g when $5g + 9$ equals $2g + 15$.
   b. Explain how you can check that the value you found for g is correct. If your check does not work, does that mean that your result is incorrect? Explain.

9. **Health Club Fees** You are choosing between two health clubs. Club A offers membership for a fee of $28 plus a monthly fee of $24. Club B offers membership for a fee of $35 plus a monthly fee of $17. After how many months will the total cost of each health club be the same?

10. **Reasoning** To solve an equation in x, you simplify the equation so that it becomes easy to tell which value(s) of x make the equation true.
    a. Simplify $-6x + 13 + 7x = 6 + x + 7$ until you have the equation in the form $x = \blacksquare$. Tell what value(s) of x make the equation true.
    b. What can you conclude about the original equation?

11. **Error Analysis** You and a friend are doing math homework together. You have to solve the equation $5x + 4x - 68 = 34 - 8x$. Your friend arrives at the incorrect answer $x = -2$.
    a. Find the correct value of x.
    b. What possible error could your friend have made to get $x = -2$?
       A. Your friend should have added $8x$ to each side of the equation, but instead subtracted $8x$ from the left side.
       B. Your friend should have added $5x$ and $4x$ to get a sum of $9x$, but instead got a sum of $10x$.
       C. Your friend should have added 68 to each side of the equation, but instead subtracted 68 from the right side.

12. Multiple Representations You can use algebra tiles to model and solve the equation $8x + 4 = 4x + 12$.

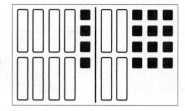

a. What are two other ways to write the equation?

A. $8x + 8 = -4x$ and $4x - 4 = 12$

B. $-8x = 8 - 4x$ and $8x + 8 = -4x$

C. $8x + 8 = 4x$ and $4x + 12 = 4$

D. $8x - 8 = 4x$ and $4x + 4 = 12$

b. Solve the equation to find the value of x.

13. a. Multiple Representations Use the algebra tiles to solve $6x + 12 = 3x + 9$.

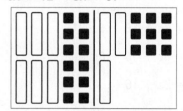

b. Tell what you could do with the x-tiles on each side of the given model for the equation. Draw what the model would look like then.

c. Tell what you could do with the ones-tiles on each side of the given model for the equation. Draw what the model would look like then.

14. Think About the Process

a. How would you set up a model for the equation $7x + 4 = 3x + 8$ using algebra tiles?

A. Place 4 x-tiles and 7 ones-tiles for the left side of the equation. Place 8 x-tiles and 3 ones-tiles for the right side of the equation.

B. Place 7 x-tiles and 4 ones-tiles for the left side of the equation. Place 3 x-tiles and 8 ones-tiles for the right side of the equation.

C. Place 7 x-tiles and 8 ones-tiles for the left side of the equation. Place 3 x-tiles and 4 ones-tiles for the right side of the equation.

D. None of these models the equation.

b. Draw your model.

c. Find the value of x that makes the equation true.

15. Solve $\frac{5}{3}x + \frac{1}{3}x = 13\frac{1}{3} + \frac{8}{3}x$.

16. Challenge The price of stock A at 9 A.M. was $12.73. Since then, the price has been increasing at the rate of $0.06 each hour. At noon the price of Stock B was $13.48. It begins to decrease at the rate of $0.14 each hour. If the two rates continue, in how many hours will the prices of the two stocks be the same? Round to the nearest tenth as needed.

17. Challenge Schools A and B are competing in an academic contest. Correct answers earn 12 points. Incorrect answers lose 5 points. In the final round, School A gives the same number of correct and incorrect answers. School B gives no incorrect answers and the same number of correct answers as School A. School A started the final round with 165 points. School B started with 65. The game ends with the two schools tied. Let x represent the number of correct answers given by School A in the final round.

a. Which equation models the scoring in the final round and the outcome of the contest?

b. How many answers did each school get correct in the final round?

Solving Equations Using the Distributive Property

CCSS: 8.EE.C.7b

Part 1

▶ Intro

You can use the Distributive Property to simplify the expressions $a(b + c)$ and $a(b - c)$, where a, b, and c are numbers.

$$a(b + c) = a \cdot b + a \cdot c \qquad a(b - c) = a \cdot b - a \cdot c$$

Some equations are easier to solve if you use the Distributive Property to simplify them.

▶ Example Using the Distributive Property to Solve Equations

Use the Distributive Property to solve $4(8 - c) = 8c + 16 - 6c$.

Solution

Use the Distributive Property.	$4(8) - 4(c) = 8c + 16 - 6c$
Multiply.	$32 - 4c = 8c + 16 - 6c$
Combine like terms.	$32 - 4c = 2c + 16$
Add 4c to each side.	$32 - 4c + 4c = 2c + 4c + 16$
Combine like terms.	$32 = 6c + 16$
Subtract 16 from each side.	$32 - 16 = 6c + 16 - 16$
Simplify.	$16 = 6c$
Divide each side by 6.	$\dfrac{16}{6} = \dfrac{6c}{6}$
Simplify.	$\dfrac{8}{3} = c$

When $4(8 - c) = 8c + 16 - 6c$, $c = \dfrac{8}{3}$.

Check

$$4(8 - c) = 8c + 16 - 6c$$

$$4\left(8 - \frac{8}{3}\right) \overset{?}{=} 8\left(\frac{8}{3}\right) + 16 - 6\left(\frac{8}{3}\right)$$

$$4\left(\frac{16}{3}\right) \overset{?}{=} \frac{64}{3} + 16 - \frac{48}{3}$$

$$64 \overset{?}{=} 64 + 48 - 48$$

$$64 = 64 \ ✔$$

Part 2

Intro

You can solve an equation with a fraction in multiple ways. One way is to begin by eliminating the fraction from the equation. This is similar to eliminating decimals from an equation by multiplying each term by a power of 10.

To do this, multiply each side of the equation by the denominator of the fraction. You might then have to use the Distributive Property.

To solve equations containing more than one fraction, you can eliminate all fractions by multiplying each side by the least common multiple of the denominators.

Solve the equation $\qquad$ $12 = \frac{3}{4}n + 5$

Multiply each side by 4.	$4(12) = 4\left(\frac{3}{4}n + 5\right)$
Use the Distributive Property.	$4(12) = 4\left(\frac{3}{4}n\right) + 4(5)$
Multiply.	$48 = 3n + 20$
Subtract 20 from each side.	$48 - 20 = 3n + 20 - 20$
Simplify.	$28 = 3n$
Divide each side by 3.	$\frac{28}{3} = \frac{3n}{3}$
Simplify.	$\frac{28}{3} = n$

Example Using the Distributive Property to Eliminate Fractions

Students A and B use different methods to solve the equation $-20 = \frac{x}{2} + 7$. One of the students makes a mistake. Find, describe, and correct the error.

$$-20 = \frac{x}{2} + 7$$
$$-20 - 7 = \frac{x}{2} + 7 - 7$$
$$-27 = \frac{x}{2}$$
$$2(-27) = \left(\frac{x}{2}\right)2$$
$$-54 = x$$

$$-20 = \frac{x}{2} + 7$$
$$2(-20) = \left(\frac{x}{2} + 7\right)2$$
$$-40 = x + 7$$
$$-40 - 7 = x + 7 - 7$$
$$-47 = x$$

continued on next page >

Part 2

Example continued

Solution ·

Student A is correct and Student B is incorrect.

Student B multiplied by the denominator 2 to eliminate the fraction $\frac{x}{2}$ from the equation, but then did not distribute the 2 to each term inside the parentheses.

Student B (corrected work):

$$-20 = \frac{x}{2} + 7$$

$$2(-20) = 2\left(\frac{x}{2} + 7\right)$$

$$2(-20) = 2\left(\frac{x}{2}\right) + 2(7)$$

> Student B did not multiply 2 by 7.

$$-40 = x + 14$$

$$-40 - 14 = x + 14 - 14$$

$$-54 = x$$

Part 3

Example **Writing and Solving Equations with Grouping Symbols**

An apprentice pastry chef has been left alone to make 8 cakes. He cannot remember how much sugar to put in the filling.

He knows the following:

- Each cake (not counting the filling) requires $1\frac{1}{4}$ cups of sugar.
- The head chef told him he would need a total of 12 cups of sugar for all 8 cakes and fillings.

Write an equation to represent the situation. Then find the amount of sugar needed for the filling of one cake.

continued on next page >

Part 3

Example continued

Solution

| Words | total sugar | = | 8 cakes | • | (amount of sugar for one cake | + | amount of sugar for one filling) |

to

Let f = the number of cups of sugar needed for one filling.

| Equation | 12 | = | 8 | • | ($1\frac{1}{4}$ | + | f) |

| Write the mixed number as an improper fraction. | $12 = 8\left(\frac{5}{4} + f\right)$ |

| Use the Distributive Property. Then multiply. | $12 = 10 + 8f$ |

| Subtract 10 from each side. | $12 - 10 = 10 - 10 + 8f$ |

| Simplify. | $2 = 8f$ |

| Divide each side by 8. | $\frac{2}{8} = \frac{8f}{8}$ |

| Simplify. | $\frac{1}{4} = f$ |

Each filling requires $\frac{1}{4}$ cup of sugar.

Check

$$12 = 8\left(1\frac{1}{4} + f\right)$$

| Substitute $\frac{1}{4}$ for f. | $12 \stackrel{?}{=} 8\left(1\frac{1}{4} + \frac{1}{4}\right)$ |

| Simplify. | $12 = 12$ ✔ |

1. **Think About the Process**
   a. Apply the Distributive Property to rewrite $3(6 - x) = 3$.
      A. $6(3) + 6x = 3$
      B. $3(6) - 3x = 3$
      C. $3(6) + 3x = 3$
      D. $6(3) - 6x = 3$
   b. The solution of the equation is ■.

2. Use the Distributive Property to solve the equation $3(x + 4) = 27$.

3. Use the Distributive Property to solve the equation $3(x - 6) + 6 = 5x - 6$.

4. **Think About the Process** You are given the following equation.
   $$\frac{3}{4}k - 10 = 1$$
   a. You want to use the Distributive Property to solve the equation. By what number would you multiply each side of the equation?
   b. What is the solution of the equation?
   c. Describe another way to find the solution.

5. **Estimation**
   a. Approximate the solution of the equation below by rounding all values to the nearest integer.
   $$\frac{4}{5}m + 4 = 12$$
   b. After estimating, use the Distributive Property to solve the equation.

6. Use the Distributive Property to solve the equation $8 + \frac{1}{7}x = 9$.

7. Use the Distributive Property to solve the equation $\frac{z}{2} + 4 = 5 - \frac{z}{2}$.

8. Use the Distributive Property to solve the equation.
   $$4x - 2(x - 2) = -9 + 5x - 8$$

9. Donavon and some friends go to a fair. Donavon spends $\frac{1}{2}$ of his money on rides. He then spends $3 on food. At the end of the day, Donavon has $2 remaining. Let d represent the amount of money Donavon brought to the fair.
   a. Which equation represents the situation?
      A. $\frac{1}{2}d - 3 = 2$
      B. $2d - \frac{1}{2} = 3$
      C. $\frac{1}{2}d + 3 = 2$
      D. $\frac{1}{2} - 3d = 2$
   b. How much money did Donavon bring to the fair?

10. Peter has to use the following information to find the original number. If you double a number and then add 40, you get $\frac{2}{11}$ of the original number. Let x represent the original number.
    a. Which equation represents the situation?
       A. $\frac{2}{11} + 2x = 11$
       B. $2x + \frac{2}{11} = 40$
       C. $2x + 40 = \frac{2}{11}x$
       D. $40x - 2 = \frac{2}{11}x$
    b. What is the original number?

11. a. **Writing** Use the Distributive Property to solve the equation $2(m + 2) = 22$.
    b. Describe what it means to distribute the 2 to each term inside the parentheses.

12. a. **Reasoning** Use the Distributive Property to solve the equation $28 - (3c + 4) = 2(c + 6) + c$.
    b. Explain why the Distributive Property makes it possible to solve this equation.

13. **Error Analysis** A teacher gives her students the equation $\frac{1}{2}t + 3 = 1$. She tells the students to multiply each side of the equation by 2 to eliminate the fraction. Jenna claims the answer is -1.

   a. Use the Distributive Property to solve the equation $\frac{1}{2}t + 3 = 1$.

   b. What error did Jenna likely make?

     A. Jenna did not distribute 2 to 1.

     B. Jenna did not distribute 2 to 3.

     C. Jenna did not add 3 to 1.

     D. Jenna did not subtract 2 from 3.

14. **Mental Math** If you take $\frac{3}{10}$ of a number and add 1, you get 10. Let x represent the original number.

   a. Which equation represents the situation?

     A. $\frac{3}{10}x + 1 = 10$

     B. $\frac{3}{10}x + 10 = 1$

     C. $\frac{3}{10} + x = 10$

     D. $\frac{3}{10} + 10x = 1$

   b. What is the original number?

15. **Manufacturing** Three robots make the same item. Each day, Robot B can make $2\frac{1}{2}$ times as many items as Robot A. Robot C makes 20 items each day. In one day, the three robots combined can make 48 items. Let s be the number of items that Robot A can make each day.

   a. Which equation represents the situation?

     A. $s + 2\frac{1}{2}s + 20s = 48$

     B. $2\frac{1}{2}s + 20s = 48$

     C. $s(48 + 20) = 2\frac{1}{2}$

     D. $s + 2\frac{1}{2}s + 20 = 48$

   b. How many items can Robot A make each day?

16. Use the Distributive Property to solve the equation $\frac{4x}{5} - x = \frac{x}{10} - \frac{9}{2}$.

17. **a. Estimation** Approximate the solution of the equation $2\frac{2}{3} + 3n = \frac{4}{5}n + 12$ by rounding all values to the nearest integer.

   b. After estimating, use the Distributive Property to solve the equation.

18. **Challenge** A recipe calls for $\frac{1}{2}$ cup of bananas and c cups of blueberries for each batch. If you are making 2 batches, you need a total $1\frac{2}{5}$ cups of fruit.

   a. Which equation represents the situation?

     A. $2\left(\frac{1}{2} + c\right) = 1\frac{2}{5}$

     B. $2\left(\frac{1}{2} - c\right) = 1\frac{2}{5}$

     C. $1\frac{2}{5}\left(\frac{1}{2} + c\right) = 2$

     D. $\frac{1}{2} + 2c = 1\frac{2}{5}$

   b. How many cups of blueberries do you need for 1 batch?

   c. How many cups of blueberries do you need for 7 batches?

   d. How many cups of blueberries do you need for n batches?

19. **Challenge** The length of a postage stamp is $4\frac{1}{4}$ mm longer than its width. The perimeter of the stamp is $124\frac{1}{2}$ mm.

   a. Which equation represents the perimeter in terms of the width w?

     A. $2w - 2\left(w + 4\frac{1}{4}\right) = 124\frac{1}{2}$

     B. $w\left(w + 4\frac{1}{4}\right) = 124\frac{1}{2}$

     C. $2w + \left(2w + 124\frac{1}{2}\right) = 4\frac{1}{4}$

     D. $2w + 2\left(w + 4\frac{1}{4}\right) = 124\frac{1}{2}$

   b. What is the width of the postage stamp?

   c. What is the length of the postage stamp?

Solutions – One, None, or Infinitely Many

Vocabulary
infinitely many solutions, no solution

CCSS: 8.EE.C.7, 8.EE.C.7a

Key Concept

One Solution A linear equation in one variable has one solution if only one value of the variable makes the equation true.

In this situation, you transform the original equation into simpler equivalent equations until the variable is alone on one side of the equal sign, and a number is alone on the other. For example:

$$57.9 - 98.2y = 303.4$$

$$57.9 - 57.9 - 98.2y = 303.4 - 57.9$$

$$-98.2y = 245.5$$

$$\frac{-98.2y}{-98.2} = \frac{245.5}{-98.2}$$

$$y = -2.5 \quad \text{The equation has one solution.}$$

No Solution A linear equation in one variable has *no solution* if no value of the variable makes the two sides of the equation equal.

You know that an equation has no solution when, as you solve for the variable, you get a false statement. For example:

$$3(2g + 4) = 6g + 9$$

$$6g + 12 = 6g + 9$$

$$6g - 6g + 12 = 6g - 6g + 9$$

$$12 = 9 \text{ ✗} \quad \text{False statement}$$

The equation has no solution.

Infinitely Many Solutions A linear equation in one variable has *infinitely many solutions* if any value of the variable makes the two sides of the equation equal.

You know that an equation has *infinitely many solutions* when, as you solve for the variable, you get a true statement. For example:

$$9 + 4p - 2 = p + 3p + 7$$

$$9 - 2 + 4p = p + 3p + 7$$

$$7 + 4p = 4p + 7$$

$$7 + 4p - 4p = 4p - 4p + 7$$

$$7 = 7 \text{ ✓} \quad \text{True statement}$$

The equation has infinitely many solutions.

See your complete lesson at MyMathUniverse.com

Part 1

Example Identifying Numbers of Solutions of Equations

You simplify several equations and get each of the following:

a. $4 = 9$ **b.** $\frac{2}{10} = 0.02$ **c.** $3h = 12$

d. $x = \frac{2}{5}$ **e.** $\frac{1}{2} = \frac{5}{10}$ **f.** $2j + 7 = 2j + 7$

Decide if each indicates *no solution, one solution,* or *infinitely many solutions.*

Solution

a. The statement $4 = 9$ is false, so the equation has no solution.

b. $\frac{2}{10}$ equals 0.2, so the statement $\frac{2}{10} = 0.02$ is false. The equation has no solution.

c. $3h = 12$ simplifies to $h = 4$, so the equation has one solution.

d. $x = \frac{2}{5}$ is the only solution of the equation, so the equation has one solution.

e. Since $\frac{1}{2}$ and $\frac{5}{10}$ are equivalent fractions, the statement $\frac{1}{2} = \frac{5}{10}$ is true. So the equation has infinitely many solutions.

f. $2j + 7 = 2j + 7$ simplifies to $7 = 7$, which is a true statement. So the equation has infinitely many solutions.

Part 2

Example Solving Equations with No Solutions

Solve $4 + w + 5w = 3(2w + 1.6)$.

Solution

Use the Distributive Property.	$4 + w + 5w = 6w + 4.8$
Combine like terms.	$4 + 6w = 6w + 4.8$
Subtract 6w from each side.	$4 + 6w - 6w = 6w - 6w + 4.8$
Combine like terms.	$4 \neq 4.8$ ✗

Since $4 \neq 4.8$, the equation $4 + w + 5w = 3(2w + 1.6)$ has no solution.

Part 3

Solve $0.25(4x - 2) = x - \frac{1}{2}$.

Solution ·

$$0.25(4x) = 1x = x$$

Use the Distributive Property.	$0.25(4x) - 0.25(2) = x - \frac{1}{2}$
Multiply.	$x - 0.5 = x - \frac{1}{2}$
Subtract x from each side.	$x - x - 0.5 = x - x - \frac{1}{2}$
Combine like terms.	$-0.5 = -\frac{1}{2}$

-0.5 is equivalent to $-\frac{1}{2}$, so the equation has infinitely many solutions.

1. Classify the equation $7x + 3 = 7x - 4$ as having one solution, no solution, or infinitely many solutions.

2. Classify the equation $4x + 2 = 4x + 2$ as having one solution, no solution, or infinitely many solutions.

3. Classify the equation $5(10x + 6) = 50x - 4$ as having one solution, no solution, or infinitely many solutions.

4. **Think About the Process**

   a. Which operations can be used to find the solution to $17x + 163x - 12 = 18(10x + 17)$?

      A. Addition and multiplication

      B. Addition, multiplication, and division

      C. Subtraction and multiplication

      D. Addition, subtraction, multiplication, and division

      E. Subtraction, multiplication, and division

   b. Solve $17x + 163x - 12 = 18(10x + 17)$.

      A. $x = \blacksquare$

      B. The equation has infinitely many solutions.

      C. The equation has no solution.

5. Which answer shows the correct solution for $6x + 19x - 4 = 5(5x + 4)$?

   A. $x = \blacksquare$

   B. The equation has infinitely many solutions.

   C. The equation has no solution.

6. Which answer shows the correct solution for $10x + 22x - 5 = 8(4x + 7)$?

   A. $x = \blacksquare$

   B. The equation has infinitely many solutions.

   C. The equation has no solution.

7. Which answer shows the correct solution for $4(2x + 4) = 10x + 15 - 2x + 1$?

   A. $x = \blacksquare$

   B. The equation has infinitely many solutions.

   C. The equation has no solutions.

8. Solve $4(2x + 3) = 16x + 3 - 8x + 9$.

   A. $x = \blacksquare$

   B. The equation has infinitely many solutions.

   C. The equation has no solution.

9. Which answer shows the correct solution for $3x + x + 2 = 8x - 4x + 2$?

   A. $x = \blacksquare$

   B. The equation has infinitely many solutions.

   C. The equation has no solution.

10. **Think About the Process**

    a. What is a possible first step in solving $0.4(3x + 18) = 1.2(x + 6)$?

       A. Multiply each side by 10.

       B. Subtract 10 from each side.

       C. Add 10 to each side.

       D. Divide each side by 10.

    b. Solve $0.4(3x + 18) = 1.2(x + 6)$.

       A. $x = \blacksquare$

       B. The equation has infinitely many solutions.

       C. The equation has no solution.

See your complete lesson at MyMathUniverse.com

11. a. Writing Classify the equation $49x + 33 = 49x + 38$ as having one solution, no solution, or infinitely many solutions.

   b. Write an equation that has one solution, an equation that has no solution, and an equation that has infinitely many solutions.

12. a. Reasoning Classify the equation $64x - 16 = 16(4x - 1)$ as having one solution, no solution, or infinitely many solutions.

   b. Of which type of equation are there the greatest number: Equations with no solutions, equations with infinitely many solutions, or equations with exactly one solution? Explain your reasoning.

13. Error Analysis Your friend says the solution to $4x + 24x - 2 = 7(4x + 2)$ is $x = 16$.

   a. Which answer shows the correct solution for $4x + 24x - 2 = 7(4x + 2)$?

     A. $x = $ ■

     B. The equation has infinitely many solutions.

     C. The equation has no solution.

   b. What was your friend's likely error?

     A. Your friend subtracted 2 from each side instead of adding.

     B. Your friend incorrectly applied the Distributive Property.

     C. Your friend combined the like terms incorrectly.

     D. Your friend combined the constant terms incorrectly.

14. Classify the equation, $11,067x - 5,208 = 93(119x - 56)$, as having one solution, no solution, or infinitely many solutions.

15. Cleaning Rates Two rival dry cleaners both advertise their prices. Store A's prices are modeled by the expression $20x - 8$, where x is the number of items brought in. Store B's prices are modeled by the expression $5(4x + 4)$, where x is the number of items brought in. When do the two stores charge the same rate?

   A. The two stores charge the same rate when ■ items are brought in.

   B. The two stores always charge the same rate.

   C. The two stores never charge the same rate.

16. a. Open-Ended Which answer shows the correct solution for $6x + 26x - 10 = 8(4x + 10)$?

     A. $x = $ ■

     B. The equation has infinitely many solutions.

     C. The equation has no solution.

   b. Write a word problem that this equation, or any of its equivalent forms, represents.

17. Which answer shows the correct solution for $3(4x + 2) + 35 = 16x + 2 - 4x + 39$?

   A. $x = $ ■

   B. The equation has infinitely many solutions.

   C. The equation has no solution.

18. a. Challenge Find the correct solution for $38x + 2,522x - 55 = 64(40x + 32)$.

   b. What does it mean if an equation simplifies to $0 = 0$?

19. Challenge Which answer shows the correct solution for $7(6x - 5) + 7 = 42x - 28$?

CCSS: 8.EE.C.7, 8.EE.C.7a

Part 1

Example Solving Two-Step Equations for Real-World Problems

An employee earns $7.25 per hour for the first 40 hours worked in a week and $10.88 for each hour of overtime. One week's paycheck is $344.40.

Write and solve an equation to determine how many hours of overtime the employee worked.

Solution

Know
- Hourly rate for first 40 hours: $7.25 per hour
- Hourly rate for each hour of overtime: $10.88 per hour
- Total paycheck: $344.40

Need
The number of hours of overtime worked

Plan
Write and solve an equation where the variable is the number of hours of overtime worked.

Words

| 40 hours times $7.25 per hour | plus | number of hours of overtime times $10.88 per hour | equals | $344.40 |

Equation

Let v = the number of overtime hours worked.

$$40(7.25) \quad + \quad v(10.88) \quad = \quad 344.40$$

continued on next page >

Part 1

Solution continued

$$40(7.25) + v(10.88) = 344.40$$

Multiply. $$290 + v(10.88) = 344.40$$

Subtract 290 from $$290 - 290 + v(10.88) = 344.40 - 290$$
each side.

Simplify. $$v(10.88) = 54.40$$

Divide each side by 10.88. $$\frac{v(10.88)}{10.88} = \frac{54.40}{10.88}$$

Simplify. $$v = 5$$

The employee worked 5 hours of overtime.

Check

$$40(7.25) + v(10.88) = 344.40$$

$$40(7.25) + 5(10.88) \overset{?}{=} 344.40$$

$$290 + 54.40 \overset{?}{=} 344.40$$

$$340.00 = 340.40 ✔$$

Part 2

Example Writing and Solving Equations with Like Terms

Two friends go out to eat and order the same meal. They pay a 6% tax and a 20% tip on their meals. The total bill, including tax and tip, is $27.72. How much did each meal cost before tax and tip? (Assume that the friends pay a tip on the cost of the meals only.)

Solution

Words | cost of two meals | + | 6% | of | cost of two meals | + | 20% | of | cost of two meals | = | total bill

 to Let m = the cost of one meal.

Equation 2m + 0.06 • 2m + 0.20 • 2m = 27.72

continued on next page >

Part 2

Solution continued

Method 1 Work with the decimals.

$$2m + 0.06(2m) + 0.20(2m) = 27.72$$

Simplify.	$2m + 0.12m + 0.4m = 27.72$
Combine like terms.	$2.52m = 27.72$
Divide each side by 2.52.	$\dfrac{2.52m}{2.52} = \dfrac{27.72}{2.52}$
Simplify.	$m = 11$

Method 2 Remove the decimals from the equation.

$$2m + 0.06(2m) + 0.20(2m) = 27.72$$

Multiply each side by 100.	$100[2m + 0.06(2m) + 0.20(2m)] = 100(27.72)$
Use the Distributive Property.	$200m + 12m + 40m = 2{,}772$
Then multiply. Combine like terms.	$252m = 2{,}772$
Divide each side by 252.	$\dfrac{252m}{252} = \dfrac{2{,}772}{252}$
Simplify.	$m = 11$

Check ·

$$2m + 0.06(2m) + 0.20(2m) = 27.72$$

Substitute 11 for _m_.	$2(11) + 0.06[2(11)] + 0.20[2(11)] \stackrel{?}{=} 27.72$
Simplify.	$22 + 1.32 + 4.4 \stackrel{?}{=} 27.72$
Simplify.	$27.72 = 27.72 \checkmark$

Part 3

Intro

The Think/Write graphic organizer is a tool that can help you make sense of problems.

For example, solve the equation $3(q + 4) = 8$.

Think

8 is not divisible by 3, so start by using the Distributive Property.

Undo addition first. Subtract 12 from each side.

Divide each side by 3.

Write

$$3(q + 4) = 8$$
$$3q + 12 = 8$$

$$3q = -4$$

$$q = -\frac{4}{3}$$

Example Writing and Solving Equations with Infinitely Many Solutions

Your friend tells you the secret to her math trick! She says that she subtracts 3 from the result in Step 5 to get the starting number. Use a math equation to explain the trick.

Step 1 Think of a number.
Step 2 Add 8.
Step 3 Double the result.
Step 4 Subtract 10.
Step 5 Divide by 2.

Solution

Think

Step 1 is to think of a number. Let n represent this number.

Step 2 is to add 8.

Step 3 is to double the result. That means multiply by 2.

Step 4 is to subtract 10.

Step 5 is to divide by 2. Set the result equal to $n + 3$.

Write

n

$n + 8$

$2(n + 8)$

$2(n + 8) - 10$

$$\frac{2(n + 8) - 10}{2} = n + 3$$

continued on next page >

Part 3

Solution continued

$$\frac{2(n + 8) - 10}{2} = n + 3$$

Multiply each side by 2. $\quad 2\left[\dfrac{2(n + 8) - 10}{2}\right] = 2(n + 3)$

Simplify $\quad 2(n + 8) - 10 = 2(n + 3)$

Use the Distributive Property. $\quad 2n + 16 - 10 = 2n + 6$

Simplify. $\quad 2n + 6 = 2n + 6$

Subtract 2n from each side. $\quad 2n - 2n + 6 = 2n - 2n + 6$

Combine like terms. $\quad 6 = 6$

The equation has infinitely many solutions. No matter what number you pick, your friend can quickly determine your number by subtracting 3 from your result in Step 5.

1. A rental car agency charges $240.00 per week plus $0.25 per mile to rent a car. How many miles can you travel in one week for $370.00?

2. Given the perimeter of a rectangle is 98 in. and the width is 22 in., what is the length of the rectangle?

3. An appliance store decreases the price of a 19-in. television set 25% to a sale price of $482.63. What was the original price? Round to the nearest cent.

4. **Reasoning** Jim is paid $25 per hour at his job. He currently has $1,250 in his bank account. In order to go on a trip with his friends he needs to have $2,500.

   a. How many hours over the next few weeks must he work until he reaches the amount needed to go on the trip?

   b. If one of the three given dollar amounts changes, how would that change the number of hours that Jim must work?

5. **Open-Ended** Dan takes an airplane to visit his parents. He pays the airline a total of $450. The cost of the ticket is $315. The airline also charges $15 for every pound that the luggage goes over the 50 pound limit.

   a. How many pounds is Dan's luggage over the 50 pound limit?

   b. Describe another situation using the same numbers.

6. Danielle and Drew are sightseeing for the day. Between the two of them they take 77 pictures. Danielle takes 17 more than twice as many pictures as Drew.

   a. How many pictures does Drew take?

   b. How many pictures does Danielle take?

7. The O'Briens are buying new windows for their house. The company installs the new windows for $2,250. The total cost for buying the windows and having them installed is $4,432.50. If the O'Briens pay $145.50 per window, how many windows did they buy?

8. **Think About the Process** A family of 3 joins a gym. Each person pays $100 to join plus $10 per month. The family decides to stop going after they have paid $600 altogether.

   a. Let x represent the total number of months. How could the equation be written?

   A. $10x + 100 = 600$

   B. $3(10x) + 100 = 600$

   C. $10x + 3(100) = 600$

   D. $3(10x + 100) = 600$

   b. The family went to the gym for ___ months.

9. A rectangular athletic field is twice as long as it is wide. If the perimeter of the athletic field is 72 yards, what are its dimensions?

   a. What is the width?

   b. What is the length?

10. **Think About the Process** Frank works at a company that sells magazine subscriptions. He gets paid $7 per subscription for the first 75 that he sells. After he sells 75 subscriptions he gets paid $12 for each one he sells. Frank makes $861 from selling the subscriptions.

   a. Let x represent the additional subscriptions. Which equation could be used to solve this problem?

   A. $7(75) + 12x = 525$

   B. $7(75) + 12x = 861$

   C. $7x + 12(75) = 525$

   D. $7x + 12(75) = 861$

   b. How many additional subscriptions does Frank sell after the first 75?

11. Think About the Process A family of 5 joins a gym. Each person pays $25 to join plus $15 per month. The family decides to stop going after they have paid $800 all together.

   a. Let x represent the total number of months. How could the equation be written?

   A. $15x + 25 = 800$

   B. $15x + 5(25) = 800$

   C. $5(15x + 25) = 800$

   D. $5(15x) + 25 = 800$

   b. How many months did the family go to the gym?

12. Becky is typing an essay for her politics class. The essay needs to be 5,200 words long. Becky can type 25 words per minute. If Becky has 700 words typed so far, how many hours will it take for Becky to finish typing the essay?

13. Challenge A zoo has a total of 216 tigers, lions, and giraffes combined. One-fourth of these animals are tigers and one-half are lions. Of the giraffes, half are new. How many of the total number of animals are giraffes that are new?

14. Challenge A company has 930 total employees. The company has three departments. There is a marketing department, an accounting department, and a human resources department. The number of employees in the accounting department is 10 more than three times the number of employees in the human resources department. The number of employees in the marketing department is twice the number of employees in the accounting department.

   a. How many employees are in the human resources department?

   b. How many employees are in the accounting department?

   c. How many employees are in the marketing department?

Perfect Squares, Square Roots, and Equations of the form $x^2 = p$

CCSS: 8.EE.A.2

Key Concept

Perfect Squares A number that is the square of an integer is a **perfect square**.

2 squared ⟶ $(2)^2 = (2) \times (2)$, or 4   −2 squared ⟶ $(-2)^2 = (-2) \times (-2)$, or 4

3 squared ⟶ $(3)^2 = (3) \times (3)$, or 9   −3 squared ⟶ $(-3)^2 = (-3) \times (-3)$, or 9

4 squared ⟶ $(4)^2 = (4) \times (4)$, or 16   −4 squared ⟶ $(-4)^2 = (-4) \times (-4)$, or 16

The numbers 4, 9, and 16 are perfect squares.

Square Root The **square root** of a number is another number that when multiplied by itself is equal to the original number.

In this program, $\sqrt{}$ means the positive square root of a number, unless stated otherwise.

$\sqrt{4} = 2$ because $2 \times 2 = 4$

$\sqrt{9} = 3$ because $3 \times 3 = 9$

Relationship Between Squares and Square Roots Squaring a number and taking a square root are inverse operations.

3 squared is 9, so 3 is a square root of 9.

Square

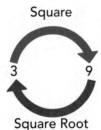

3   9

Square Root

Number of Solutions What does $x^2 = p$ mean?

To solve the equation $x^2 = 4$, think: What number multiplied by itself equals 4?

2 squared = $2 \times 2 = 4$

and

−2 squared = $(-2)^2 = (-2) \times (-2) = 4$

$x = 2$ and $x = -2$, or $x = \pm 2$

continued on next page >

Key Concept

continued

Now, consider the equation $x^2 = p$ for a value of $p > 0$.

$$\sqrt{p} \text{ squared} = \sqrt{p} \times \sqrt{p} = p$$

and

$$-\sqrt{p} \text{ squared} = -\sqrt{p} \times -\sqrt{p} = p$$

$$x = \sqrt{p} \text{ and } x = -\sqrt{p}, \text{ or } x = \pm\sqrt{p}$$

In general, an equation of the form $x^2 = p$, when $p > 0$, will always have two solutions, one positive and one negative, $x = \pm\sqrt{p}$.

Solving Equations Containing Squares To solve an equation of the form $x^2 = p$, you need to take the square root of each side of the equation.

Solve $x^2 = 100$.

Write the equation.	$x^2 = 100$
Take the square root of each side.	$\sqrt{x^2} = \pm\sqrt{100}$
Simplify the square roots.	$x = \pm10$
Write the solutions.	The solutions are 10 and -10.

Check ·

$$10^2 = 10 \times 10 = 100 \;✔$$

$$(-10)^2 = (-10) \times (-10) = 100 \;✔$$

Part 1

Example Solving Equations Using Square Roots

Solve each equation.

a. $x^2 = 4$ **b.** $x^2 = 81$ **c.** $x^2 = 49$ **d.** $x^2 = 16$

continued on next page >

Part 1

Example continued

Solution ·

To solve each equation, take the square root of each side of the equation.

a. $x^2 = 4$

$x = \pm\sqrt{4}$

$x = \pm 2$

The solutions are 2 and −2.

b. $x^2 = 81$

$x = \pm\sqrt{81}$

$x = \pm 9$

The solutions are 9 and −9.

c. $x^2 = 49$

$x = \pm\sqrt{49}$

$x = \pm 7$

The solutions are 7 and −7.

d. $x^2 = 16$

$x = \pm\sqrt{16}$

$x = \pm 4$

The solutions are 4 and −4.

Part 2

Example **Solving Equations Using Square Roots of Fractions**

Solve $a^2 = \frac{64}{81}$.

Solution ·

Think	**Write**
Write the equation.	$a^2 = \frac{64}{81}$
Take the square root of each side.	$a = \pm\sqrt{\frac{64}{81}}$
Simplify the square root.	$a = \pm\frac{8}{9}$
Write the solutions.	The solutions are $\frac{8}{9}$ and $-\frac{8}{9}$.
Check your solutions.	$\left(\frac{8}{9}\right)^2 = \frac{64}{81}$ ✓
	$\left(-\frac{8}{9}\right)^2 = \frac{64}{81}$ ✓

Part 3

Example Using Square Roots to Solve Area Problems

A company makes small custom design stamps that have a square image area. The image area has an area of 1,200 mm².

a. What is the exact length of one side of the image area?

b. If your answer is not a perfect square, approximate your answer to the nearest tenth of a millimeter.

Solution

a. You can find the length of one side by using the formula for the area of a square.

Use the formula for the area of a square. $A = s^2$

Substitute 1,200 for the area. $1,200 = s^2$

Take the square root of each side. $\sqrt{1,200} = s$

> Since we are dealing with a length, you only need to find the positive square root. Length cannot be negative.

The exact length of one side of the square is $\sqrt{1,200}$ millimeters.

b. You can approximate $\sqrt{1,200}$ using two different methods.

Method 1 Start by finding the two closest perfect squares. The perfect squares closest to 1,200 are 1,156 and 1,225.

$$34^2 = 1,156$$

$$\longleftarrow 1,200$$

$$35^2 = 1,225$$

Next, compare 1,200 with 34.5^2, the midpoint of the integers that $\sqrt{1,200}$ falls between.

$$34.5^2 = 1,190.25$$

$$1,200 > 1,190.25$$

$$34.5^2 < 1,200 < 35^2$$

continued on next page >

Part 3

Solution continued

Then, create a table of values to help determine $\sqrt{1,200}$ to the nearest tenth.

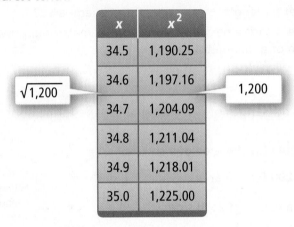

x	x²
34.5	1,190.25
34.6	1,197.16
34.7	1,204.09
34.8	1,211.04
34.9	1,218.01
35.0	1,225.00

$\sqrt{1,200}$ 1,200

Finally, to see if $\sqrt{1,200}$ is closer to 34.6 or 34.7, compare 1,200 with 34.65^2.

- If $1,200 < 34.65^2$, then $34.6 < \sqrt{1,200} < 34.65$; round down to 34.6.
- If $1,200 > 34.65^2$, then $34.65 < \sqrt{1,200} < 34.7$; round down to 34.7.

$34.65^2 = 1,200.6225$ and $1,200 < 34.65^2$; round down to 34.6.

$\sqrt{1,200}$ rounded to the nearest tenth is 34.6. The length of one side of the square is about 34.6 millimeters.

Method 2 Using a calculator.

Use the square root function on your calculator.

$$\sqrt{1,200} \approx 34.641$$

The length of one side of the square is about 34.6 millimeters.

1. Use the fact that 196 is a perfect square to evaluate $\sqrt{196}$.

2. Use the fact that 64 is a perfect square to evaluate $\sqrt{64}$.

3. Solve the equation $z^2 = 4$. Simplify your answer. Use a comma to separate answers as needed.

4. Solve the equation $y^2 = \frac{25}{81}$. Simplify your answer. Use a comma to separate answers as needed.

5. Solve the equation $v^2 = 47$. Round to the nearest tenth. Use a comma to separate answers as needed.

6. The area of a square garden is $\frac{1}{81}$ km². How long is each side?

7. **Mental Math**
   a. Use the fact that 64 is a perfect square to evaluate $\sqrt{64}$.
   b. Without using a calculator or computing on paper, list perfect squares of whole numbers in order. Take the list as far as you can. Then list at least five other perfect squares you know that would be farther out in the list.

8. a. **Writing** Use the fact that 49 is a perfect square to evaluate $\sqrt{49}$.
   b. Describe two situations in which evaluating $\sqrt{49}$ would be useful.

9. **Error Analysis** On a recent homework assignment, Nati needed to solve this equation completely. He incorrectly wrote "$g = -6$."
   a. Solve the equation $g^2 = 36$. Simplify your answer. Use a comma to separate answers as needed.
   b. What error did Nati make?
      A. He did not take the square root of 36 correctly since $(-6)^2 \neq 36$.
      B. He did not solve the equation completely since there is a positive answer as well.
      C. He did not square 36 correctly since $36^2 \neq -6$.

D. He did not solve the equation completely since there are two negative answers.

10. **Think About the Process** You are given the following equation.
$$d^2 = \frac{49}{225}$$
   a. Which of these questions does the equation suggest?
      A. What number when multiplied by 2 is equal to $\frac{49}{225}$?
      B. What number when multiplied by itself is equal to d?
      C. What number when multiplied by itself is equal to either 49 or 225?
      D. What number when multiplied by itself is equal to $\frac{49}{225}$?
   b. Solve the equation for d.

11. a. **Reasoning** Solve the equation $w^2 = \frac{81}{16}$. Simplify your answer. Use a comma to separate answers as needed.
   b. If the square of a number is less than 1, does it follow that the number must be less than 1? If the square of a positive number is greater than 1, does it follow that the number must be greater than 1? Include examples to explain your reasoning.

12. You are given the equation $c^2 = 203$.
   a. Write down two perfect squares you know, one that is less than 203 and one that is greater than 203. Then write down their square roots as two numbers you know c must be between.
   b. Use a calculator to solve for c. Round to the nearest tenth.

13. **Estimation** Solve the equation $b^2 = 77$.
   a. Estimate using the perfect square closest to 77.
   b. Use a calculator. Round to the nearest tenth as needed.

14. **Postage Stamp** A square stamp has area 1,120 mm². About how long is each side?

15. **a. Mental Math** Solve the equation $c^2 = 400$. Simplify your answer. Use a comma to separate answers as needed.

   b. Explain how you can use mental math to find the solution.

16. Solve the equation $k^2 = 1\frac{19}{81}$. Simplify your answer. Use a comma to separate answers as needed.

17. **Think About the Process** The power W (in watts) an electric circuit uses is equal to I^2R, where I is the current (in amperes) and R is the circuit's resistance (in ohms). Suppose a circuit with resistance 40 ohms uses 1,960 watts.

   a. Which of these equations could you solve to find the current in the circuit?

   A. $40 = I^2$

   B. $49 = I^2$

   C. $78{,}400 = I^2$

   D. $1{,}960 = I^2$

   b. The current in the circuit is ■ ampere(s).

18. **Challenge** Yael used to have a square garage with 228 ft² of floor space. She recently built an addition to it. The garage is still a square, but now it has 50% more floor space.

   a. What was the length of one side of the garage originally? Round to the nearest tenth as needed.

   b. What is the length of one side of the garage now?

   c. What was the percent increase in the length of one side?

19. **Challenge** Holly wants to make a frame for a painting. The painting is square and has area 225 square inches. The framing material costs $1.35 per inch. How much will she spend? You may assume that the framing material Holly buys will be the exact amount she needs.

Perfect Cubes, Cube Roots, and Equations of the Form $x^3 = p$

Vocabulary
cube root, perfect cube

CCSS: 8.EE.A.2

Key Concept

Perfect Cubes A number that is a cube of an integer is a **perfect cube**.

2 cubed ⟶ $(2)^3$
= (2) × (2) × (2), or 8

3 cubed ⟶ $(3)^3$
= (3) × (3) × (3), or 27

4 cubed ⟶ $(4)^3$
= (4) × (4) × (4), or 64

−2 cubed ⟶ $(-2)^3$
= (−2) × (−2) × (−2), or −8

−3 cubed ⟶ $(-3)^3$
= (−3) × (−3) × (−3), or −27

−4 cubed ⟶ $(-4)^3$
= (−4) × (−4) × (−4), or −64

The numbers 8, 27, 64, −8, −27, and −64 are perfect cubes. Unlike perfect squares, perfect cubes may be negative.

Cube Root The **cube root** of a number is a number that when used as a factor three times gives the original number.

The symbol $\sqrt[3]{}$ means the cube root of a number.

$\sqrt[3]{27} = 3$ because 3 × 3 × 3 = 27

$\sqrt[3]{-27} = -3$ because −3 × −3 × −3 = −27

Relationship Between Cubes and Cube Roots Raising a number to the third power and taking the cube root of a number are inverse operations.

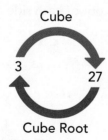

Cube

3   27

Cube Root

3 cubed is 27, so $\sqrt[3]{27} = 3$.

−3 cubed is −27, so $\sqrt[3]{-27} = -3$.

continued on next page >

Key Concept

continued

Solving Equations Containing Cubes To solve an equation of the form $x^3 = p$, take the cube root of each side of the equation.

Solve $x^3 = 125$.

Write the equation.	$x^3 = 125$
Take the cube root of each side.	$\sqrt[3]{x^3} = \sqrt[3]{125}$
Simplify the cube root.	$x = 5$
Write the solutions.	The solution is 5

Check ·

$$5^3 = 5 \times 5 \times 5$$
$$= 125 \checkmark$$

Part 1

Example Solving Equations Using Cube Roots

Solve each equation.

    a. $x^3 = 8$ **b.** $x^3 = -27$ **c.** $x^3 = 64$ **d.** $x^3 = -125$

Solution ·

To solve each equation, take the cube root of each side of the equation.

a. $x^3 = 8$	**b.** $x^3 = -27$	**c.** $x^3 = 64$	**d.** $x^3 = -125$
$x^3 = 2^3$	$x^3 = (-3)^3$	$x^3 = 4^4$	$x^3 = (-5)^3$
$x = \sqrt[3]{2^3}$	$x = \sqrt[3]{(-3)^3}$	$x = \sqrt[3]{4^3}$	$x = \sqrt[3]{(-5)^3}$
$x = 2$	$x = -3$	$x = 4$	$x = -5$
The solution is 2.	The solution is -3.	The solution is 4.	The solution is -5.

Part 2

Example Solving Equations Using Cube Roots of Fractions

Solve $w^3 = \frac{8}{343}$.

Solution ·

Think	**Write**
Write the equation.	$w^3 = \frac{8}{343}$
Take the cube root of each side.	$w = \sqrt[3]{\frac{8}{343}}$
Simplify the cube root.	$w = \frac{2}{7}$
Write the solution.	The solution is $\frac{2}{7}$.
Check the solution.	$\left(\frac{2}{7}\right)^3 = \frac{2}{7} \cdot \frac{2}{7} \cdot \frac{2}{7} = \frac{8}{343}$ ✓

Part 3

Example Using Cube Roots to Solve Volume Problems

An aquarium in the shape of a cube has a volume of 1,256 cubic inches.

  a. What is the exact length of one side of the aquarium?
  b. If your answer is not a perfect cube, approximate your answer to the nearest tenth of an inch.

Solution ·

  a. You can use the formula for the volume of a cube to find the length of one side.

Use the formula for the volume of a cube.	$V = s^3$
Substitute 1,256 for the volume.	$1{,}256 = s^3$
Take the cube root of each side.	$\sqrt[3]{1{,}256} = s$

  The exact length of one side of the aquarium is $\sqrt[3]{1{,}256}$ inches.

continued on next page >

Part 3

Solution continued

b. You can approximate $\sqrt[3]{1{,}256}$ by finding the two closest perfect cubes. The perfect cubes closest to 1,256 are 1,000 and 1,331.

$$10^3 = 1{,}000$$

$$\longleftarrow \quad 1{,}256$$

$$11^3 = 1{,}331$$

Next, compare 1,256 with 10.5^3, the midpoint of the integers that $\sqrt[3]{1{,}256}$ falls between.

$$10.5^3 = 1{,}157.625$$

$$1{,}256 > 1{,}157.625$$

$$10.5^3 < 1{,}256 < 11^3$$

Then, create a table of values to help determine $\sqrt[3]{1{,}256}$ to the nearest tenth.

x	x^3
10.5	1,157.625
10.6	1,191.016
10.7	1,225.043
10.8	1,259.712
10.9	1,295.029
11.0	1,331.000

$\sqrt[3]{1{,}256}$ ⟷ 10.7 / 10.8 ⟷ 1,256

Finally, to see if $\sqrt[3]{1{,}256}$ is closer to 10.7 or 10.8, compare 1,256 with 10.75³.

- If $1{,}256 < 10.75^3$, then $10.7 < \sqrt[3]{1{,}256} < 10.75$; round down to 10.7.
- If $1{,}256 < 10.75^3$, then $10.75 < \sqrt[3]{1{,}256} < 10.8$; round down to 10.8.

$10.75^3 = 1{,}242.296875$ and $1{,}256 > 10.75^3$; round up to 10.8.

$\sqrt[3]{1{,}256}$ rounded to the nearest tenth is 10.8. The length of one side of the aquarium is about 10.8 inches.

1. Use the fact that -512 is a perfect cube to evaluate $\sqrt[3]{-512}$. Write an integer or a simplified fraction.

2. Find the cube root $\sqrt[3]{-64}$.

3. Simplify the expression $\sqrt[3]{125}$.

4. Solve the equation $w^3 = 1{,}000$.

5. Solve the equation $d^3 = \frac{1}{125}$. Simplify your answer. Write an integer, proper fraction, or mixed number.

6. Solve the equation $v^3 = 12$. Use a calculator. Round to the nearest tenth.

7. Find the value of w. Use a calculator. Round to the nearest tenth.
$$w^3 = 3{,}087$$

8. The volume of a cube is 8 in.^{3}. How long is each side?

9. **a. Writing** Evaluate $\sqrt[3]{-216}$. Write an integer or a simplified fraction.

   b. Explain how you can check that your result is correct.

10. **Error Analysis** On a math test, George writes 9 as the solution to the equation $d^3 = 27$.

    a. Find the correct solution. Write an integer or a simplified fraction.

    b. What error did George likely make on the test?

    A. George cubed 27.

    B. George divided 27 by 3.

    C. George multiplied 27 by 3.

    D. George divided 27 by 30.

11. **Think About the Process**

    a. When solving the equation $w^3 = \frac{8}{1{,}331}$, what does the solution look like when you have taken the cube root of each side but have not yet done any calculating?

    A. $w = \frac{\sqrt[3]{8}}{1{,}331}$

    B. $w = \sqrt[3]{\frac{8}{1{,}331}}$

    C. $w = \frac{8}{\sqrt[3]{1{,}331}}$

    D. $w^3 = \sqrt[3]{\frac{8}{1{,}331}}$

    b. Solve for w.

12. **a. Reasoning** Find the value of z in the equation $z^3 = \frac{27}{1{,}000}$. Simplify your answer. Write an integer, proper fraction, or mixed number.

    b. If the cube of a number is less than 1, does it follow that the number must be less than 1? Include examples to explain your reasoning.

    c. If the cube of a positive number is greater than 1, does it follow that the number must be greater than 1? Include examples to explain your reasoning.

13. **Estimation** Solve for c in the equation $c^3 = 55$.

    a. Estimate using the perfect cube closest to 55.

    b. Use a calculator to solve for c. Round to the nearest tenth.

14. **Building Blocks** A company is making building blocks. Each building block is a cube and has volume $\frac{8}{343}$ ft^3. How long is each side of the building block?

15. **a.** Find the value of c for the equation $c^3 = 1{,}728$.

    b. The equation $c^2 = p$ can have zero, one, or two solutions. What can you say about the number of solutions of the equation $c^3 = p$? Explain.

16. Solve the equation $v^3 = 18\frac{26}{27}$ for v. Simplify your answer. Write an integer, proper fraction, or a mixed number.

17. **Think About the Process** The zoo is creating a new tank for some of its fish. The zoo wants the tank to be a cube and be able to hold 3,375 ft^3 of water.

    a. Which of these equations would you solve to find the length of each side of the tank?

    A. $3V = 3{,}375$

    B. $\frac{3{,}375}{3} = s^3$

    C. $V^3 = 3{,}375$

    D. $3{,}375 = s^3$

    b. Each side of the tank is ■ ft long.

18. a. Writing Evaluate $\sqrt[3]{-27}$. Write as an integer or a simplified fraction.

   b. Explain how you can check that your result is correct.

19. Error Analysis On a math test, George writes 243 as the solution to the equation $n^3 = 729$.

   a. Find the correct solution. Write an integer or a simplified fraction.

   b. What error did George likely make on the test?

     A. George divided 729 by 3.

     B. George cubed 729.

     C. George multiplied 729 by 3.

     D. George divided 729 by 30.

20. a. Reasoning Find the value of c in the equation $c^3 = \frac{64}{343}$. Simplify your answer. Write an integer, proper fraction, or mixed number.

   b. If the cube of a number is less than 1, does it follow that the number must be less than 1? Include examples to explain your reasoning.

   c. If the cube of a positive number is greater than 1, does it follow that the number must be greater than 1? Include examples to explain your reasoning.

21. Estimation Solve for g in the equation $g^3 = 208$.

   a. Estimate using the perfect cube closest to 208.

   b. Use a calculator to solve for g. Round to the nearest tenth.

22. Challenge A family is packing their belongings to prepare for a trip. They use a box that has the shape of a cube.

   a. If the box has a volume of 86 ft^3, what is the length of one side? Round to the nearest tenth as needed.

   b. The kids want to bring poster board to draw on. If the poster board is square and has an area of 9 ft^2, will the poster board fit in the box flat against a side?

23. Challenge The Travers are adding a new room to their house. The room will be a cube with volume 6,859 ft^3. They are going to put in hardwood floors, and the contractor charges $10 per square foot. How much will the hardwood floors cost?

CCSS: 8.EE.A.1

Part 1

▶ Intro

Remember that exponents are a shorthand notation that allows you to write expressions containing repeated multiplication more efficiently and precisely.

$$7^2 \cdot 7^3$$

$$7^2 = 7 \cdot 7 \text{ and } 7^3 = 7 \cdot 7 \cdot 7$$

$$7^2 \cdot 7^3 = \underbrace{7 \cdot 7 \cdot 7 \cdot 7 \cdot 7}_{5 \text{ factors of } 7} = 7^5$$

Multiplying Powers with the Same Base To multiply powers with the same base, add the exponents.

Arithmetic: $\quad 7^2 \cdot 7^3 = 7^{2+3} = 7^5$

Algebra: $\quad\;\; a^m \cdot a^n = a^{m+n}$, where $a \neq 0$ and m and n are integers

▶ Example Simplifying Products of Powers

Use the numbers to simplify each expression.

$$8 \qquad 18 \qquad 12 \qquad 3 \qquad 5 \qquad 2 \qquad 10$$

a. $5^2 \cdot 5^8 = 5^{\blacksquare + \blacksquare}$ $\qquad\qquad\qquad = 5^{\blacksquare}$

b. $x^3 \cdot x^5 \cdot x^{10} = x^{\blacksquare + \blacksquare + \blacksquare}$ $\qquad\; = x^{\blacksquare}$

c. $2m^{10} \cdot 5m^2 = (2 \cdot 5) \cdot m^{\blacksquare + \blacksquare}$ $\quad = 10m^{\blacksquare}$

Solution

a. $5^2 \cdot 5^8 = 5^{2+8}$
$\qquad\quad\; = 5^{10}$

b. $x^3 \cdot x^5 \cdot x^{10} = x^{3+5+10}$
$\qquad\qquad\quad\;\; = x^{18}$

c. Remember to multiply the coefficients of m just as you would multiply two numerical expressions. Only the exponents get added.

$$2m^{10} \cdot 5m = (2 \cdot 5) \cdot (m^{10} \cdot m^2)$$
$$= (2 \cdot 5) \cdot m^{10+2}$$
$$= 10m^{12}$$

Part 2

Intro

Some expressions containing exponents include a different relationship, so they require a different property to simplify.

$$(5^2)^3 = (5)^2 \cdot (5^2) \cdot (5^2)$$
$$= (5 \cdot 5) \cdot (5 \cdot 5) \cdot (5 \cdot 5)$$
$$= 5^{2+2+2}$$
$$= 5^6$$

Power of a Power To find the power of a power, multiply the exponents.

Arithmetic: $\quad (5^2)^3 = 5^{2 \cdot 3} = 5^6$

Algebra: $\qquad (a^m)^n = a^{mn}$, where $a \neq 0$ and m and n are integers

Example Simplifying Powers of Powers

Use the numbers to simplify each expression.

$$30 \qquad 3 \qquad 6 \qquad 4 \qquad 12 \qquad 2 \qquad 5$$

a. $(10^3)^2 = 10^{\blacksquare \cdot \blacksquare} \qquad = 10^{\blacksquare}$

b. $(x^3)^4 = x^{\blacksquare \cdot \blacksquare} \qquad = x^{\blacksquare}$

c. $(a^5)^6 = a^{\blacksquare \cdot \blacksquare} \qquad = a^{\blacksquare}$

Solution

a. To find the power of a power, multiply the exponents.
$$(10^3)^2 = 10^{3 \cdot 2}$$
$$= 10^6$$

b. $(x^3)^4 = x^{3 \cdot 4}$
$$= x^{12}$$

c. $(a^5)^6 = a^{5 \cdot 6}$
$$= a^{30}$$

Part 3

Intro

Some algebraic expressions containing exponents include several bases or a combination of numbers and variables, so inspect the expression carefully in order to apply the properties of exponents successfully.

$$(2 \cdot 3)^3 = (2 \cdot 3) \cdot (2 \cdot 3) \cdot (2 \cdot 3)$$
$$= (2 \cdot 2 \cdot 2) \cdot (3 \cdot 3 \cdot 3)$$
$$= 2^3 \cdot 3^3$$
$$(2 \cdot 3)^3 = 2^{1 \cdot 3} \cdot 3^{1 \cdot 3} = 2^3 \cdot 3^3$$

Power of a Product To find the power of a product, raise each factor to the power.

Arithmetic: $(2 \cdot 3)^3 = 2^3 \cdot 3^3$

Algebra: $(ab)^n = a^n b^n$, where $a \neq 0$, $b \neq 0$, and n is an integer

Example Simplifying Expressions with Multiplication and Exponents

Simplify each expression.

    a. $(3cd)^2$ **b.** $(5m^2 n^3)^3$

Solution

    a. $(3cd)^2 = 3^2 \cdot c^2 \cdot d^2$ Raise each factor to the second power.
              $= 9c^2 d^2$

    b. $(5m^2 n^3)^3 = 5^3 \cdot (m^2)^3 \cdot (n^3)^3$ Raise each factor to the third power.
                   $= 5^3 \cdot m^{2 \cdot 3} \cdot n^{3 \cdot 3}$
                   $= 5^3 \cdot m^6 \cdot n^9$ For a power of a power, multiply the exponents.
                   $= 125 m^6 n^9$

Key Concept

You've seen a few multiplication properties of exponents presented in this lesson, so it's a good idea to review and summarize them before learning about more properties in the next lesson.

To multiply powers with the same base, add the exponents.

Arithmetic: $7^2 \cdot 7^3 = 7^{2+3} = 7^5$

Algebra: $a^m \cdot a^n = a^{m+n}$, where $a \neq 0$ and m and n are integers

To find a power of a power, multiply the exponents.

Arithmetic: $(5^2)^3 = 5^{2 \cdot 3} = 5^6$

Algebra: $(a^m)^n = a^{mn}$, where $a \neq 0$ and m and n are integers

To find a power of a product, raise each factor to the power and simplify.

Arithmetic: $(2 \cdot 3)^3 = 2^3 \cdot 3^3 = 8 \cdot 27 = 216$

Algebra: $(ab)^n = a^n b^n$, where $a \neq 0$, $b \neq 0$, and n is an integer

1. Simplify $8^4 \cdot 8^2$ to an equivalent exponential expression.

2. Simplify the expression $(4x^5)(5x^6)$.

3. Simplify the expression.
$$(-7y^3)(5y^2)$$

4. Think About the Process

a. What do you do to find the power of a power?

   A. Divide the exponents.

   B. Subtract the exponents.

   C. Add the exponents.

   D. Multiply the exponents.

b. Simplify the expression $(x^3)^7$.

5. Simplify the expression $(6^9)^8$.

6. Simplify the expression $(x^{17})^2$.

7. Use the properties of exponents to rewrite the expression $(3 \cdot 6)^2$.

8. Simplify the expression $(3x^6)^2$.

9. Think About the Process

a. How do you multiply powers that have the same base?

   A. Divide the exponents.

   B. Subtract the exponents.

   C. Multiply the exponents.

   D. Add the exponents.

b. Simplify the expression $x^7 \cdot x^5 \cdot x^4$.

10. a. Reasoning Simplify $x^{11} \cdot x^9$ and $x^{12} \cdot x^8$ to equivalent exponential expressions.

b. Does $x^{11} \cdot x^9 = x^{12} \cdot x^8$ for all values of x?

c. Give another way to justify your answer without doing any arithmetic.

11. a. Multiple Representations Simplify the expression $3^4 \cdot 3^5$. Write your answer using exponential notation. Simplify your answer.

b. What are three other ways to write the product as the multiplication of two powers?

   A. $3^5 \cdot 3^6, 3^5 \cdot 3^7, 3^2 \cdot 3^4$

   B. $3^4 \cdot 3^4, 3^4 \cdot 3^6, 3^4 \cdot 3^7$

   C. $3^5 \cdot 3^5, 3^2 \cdot 3^5, 3^3 \cdot 3^5$

   D. $3^5 \cdot 3^4, 3^3 \cdot 3^6, 3^2 \cdot 3^7$

12. Simplify the expression. Choose the correct answer below.
$$(3fg)^9$$

   A. $(3fg)^9 = 19{,}683fg^9$

   B. $(3fg)^9 = 59{,}049g^{10}f^{10}$

   C. $(3fg)^9 = 6{,}561g^8f^8$

   D. $(3fg)^9 = 19{,}683f^9g^9$

13. Error Analysis Your teacher asks the class to evaluate the expression $(2^3)^1$. Your classmate gives an incorrect answer of 16.

a. Evaluate the expression.

b. What was the likely error?

   A. Your classmate divided the exponents.

   B. Your classmate multiplied the exponents.

   C. Your classmate added the exponents.

   D. Your classmate subtracted the exponents.

14. a. Writing Use a property of exponents to write $(3b)^5$ as a product of powers.

b. Describe the property of exponents that you used. In words, what does the power of a product equal?

15. Flow Rate A company manufactures faucets. It uses the expression $(4y^6)^3$ mm/s to calculate the maximum flow rate of water flowing out a spout with area y^6 mm². Use a property of exponents to simplify the flow-rate expression. Write your answer using exponential notation. Simplify your answer.

16. a. Simplify the expression $[(-20)^5]^3$.

b. Is the number positive or negative? Explain how you know.

17. a. Simplify the expression $3(x^8)^3 + 3(x^2)^{12}$.

b. Give the values of x for which the expression is positive. Explain how you know.

c. Give the values of x for which the expression is negative. Explain how you know.

See your complete lesson at MyMathUniverse.com

18. Think About the Process

a. How do you multiply powers that have the same base?

  A. Multiply the exponents.

  B. Subtract the exponents.

  C. Divide the exponents.

  D. Add the exponents.

b. Simplify the expression $x^8 \cdot x^4 \cdot x^3$.

19. a. Reasoning Simplify $x^{11} \cdot x^3$ and $x^8 \cdot x^6$ to equivalent exponential expressions.

b. Does $x^{11} \cdot x^3 = x^8 \cdot x^6$ for all values of x?

c. Give another way to justify your answer without doing any arithmetic.

20. Error Analysis Your teacher asks the class to evaluate the expression $(5^2)^1$. Your classmate gives an incorrect answer of 125.

a. Evaluate the expression.

b. What was the likely error?

  A. Your classmate divided the exponents.

  B. Your classmate added the exponents.

  C. Your classmate subtracted the exponents.

  D. Your classmate multiplied the exponents.

21. a. Writing Use a property of exponents to write $(3x)^4$ as a product of powers.

b. Describe the property of exponents that you used. In words, what does the power of a product equal?

22. Challenge You are given the equation $bx^6 \cdot cx^9 \cdot 5x^d = 195x^{25}$. If b and c are both integers greater than 1 and $b < c$, find the values of b, c, and d that make the equation true for all values of x.

23. Challenge You are given the equation $(3d^n g^4)^m = 9d^6 g^8$. Find the two positive integers, m and n, that make the equation true.

CCSS: 8.EE.A.1

Part 1

► Intro

Exponents allow you to write expressions containing repeated multiplication more efficiently and precisely.

Simplify the expression $\frac{7^8}{7^3}$.

$$\frac{7^8}{7^3} = \frac{{}^1 7 \cdot {}^1 7 \cdot {}^1 7 \cdot 7 \cdot 7 \cdot 7 \cdot 7 \cdot 7}{{}_1 7 \cdot {}_1 7 \cdot {}_1 7}$$

$$= \frac{7 \cdot 7 \cdot 7 \cdot 7 \cdot 7}{1}$$

$$= 7^5$$

Dividing Powers with the Same Base

Arithmetic: $\frac{7^8}{7^3} = 7^{8-3} = 7^5$

Algebra: $\frac{a^m}{a^n} = a^{m-n}$, where $a \neq 0$ and m and n are integers

► Example Simplifying Quotients of Powers

Use the numbers from the box to simplify each expression.

| 20 | 9 | 7 | 3 | 4 | 10 | 13 |

a. $\frac{8^{10}}{8^7} = 8^{\blacksquare - \blacksquare} = 8^{\blacksquare}$ **b.** $\frac{y^{13}}{y^9} = y^{\blacksquare - \blacksquare} = y^{\blacksquare}$ **c.** $\frac{d^{20}}{d^{13}} = d^{\blacksquare - \blacksquare} = d^{\blacksquare}$

Solution

a. $\frac{8^{10}}{8^7} = 8^{10-7}$ ⟵ To divide numbers with the same base, subtract the exponents.

$= 8^3$

b. $\frac{y^{13}}{y^9} = y^{13-9}$

$= y^4$

c. $\frac{d^{20}}{d^{13}} = d^{20-13}$

$= d^7$

Part 2

Intro

Some expressions containing exponents include a different relationship, so they require a different property to simplify.

Simplify the expression $\left(\dfrac{3}{5}\right)^4$.

$$\left(\frac{3}{5}\right)^4 = \frac{3}{5} \cdot \frac{3}{5} \cdot \frac{3}{5} \cdot \frac{3}{5}$$

$$= \frac{3 \cdot 3 \cdot 3 \cdot 3}{5 \cdot 5 \cdot 5 \cdot 5}$$

$$= \frac{3^4}{5^4}$$

$$\left(\frac{3}{5}\right)^4 = \frac{3^{1 \cdot 4}}{5^{1 \cdot 4}} = \frac{3^4}{5^4}$$

Power of a Quotient To find the power of a quotient, raise the numerator and the denominator to the power and simplify.

Arithmetic: $\left(\dfrac{3}{5}\right)^4 = \dfrac{3^4}{5^4} = \dfrac{81}{625}$

Algebra: $\left(\dfrac{a}{b}\right)^n = \dfrac{a^n}{b^n}$, where $a \neq 0$, $b \neq 0$, and n is an integer

Example Simplifying Expressions with Division and Exponents

Simplify each expression.

a. $\left(\dfrac{a^7}{5}\right)^3$ **b.** $\left(\dfrac{2x^3}{3y}\right)^2$

Solution

a. Raise the numerator and the denominator to the third power.

$\left(\dfrac{a^7}{5}\right)^3 = \dfrac{(a^7)^3}{5^3}$

Multiply the exponents in the numerator.

$= \dfrac{a^{7 \cdot 3}}{5^3}$

Simplify.

$= \dfrac{a^{21}}{125}$

So, $\left(\dfrac{a^7}{5}\right)^3 = \dfrac{a^{21}}{125}$.

continued on next page >

Part 2

Solution continued

b. Raise the numerator and the denominator to the second power.

$$\left(\frac{2x^3}{3y}\right)^2 = \frac{(2x^3)^2}{(3y)^2}$$

Use the Power to a Product Property in the numerator and denominator.

$$= \frac{2^2(x^3)^2}{3^2y^2}$$

Multiply the exponents in the numerator.

$$= \frac{2^2 x^{3\cdot2}}{3^2 y^2}$$

Simplify.

$$= \frac{4x^6}{9y^2}$$

So, $\left(\frac{2x^3}{3y}\right)^2 = \frac{4x^6}{9y^2}$.

Key Concept

You've seen a few division properties of exponents in this lesson, so it's a good idea to review and summarize them before moving on to the next lesson.

To divide numbers or variables with the same nonzero base, subtract the exponents.

Arithmetic: $\dfrac{7^6}{7^2} = 7^{6-2} = 7^4$

Algebra: $\dfrac{a^m}{a^n} = a^{m-n}$, where $a \neq 0$ and m and n are integers

To find a power of a quotient, raise the numerator and the denominator to the power and simplify.

Arithmetic: $\left(\dfrac{3}{5}\right)^2 = \dfrac{3^2}{5^2}$

Algebra: $\left(\dfrac{a}{b}\right)^n = \dfrac{a^n}{b^n}$, where $a \neq 0$, $b \neq 0$, and n is an integer

1. **Think About the Process** You want to simplify the following expression.
$$\frac{13^{11}}{13^8}$$
   a. Which equation shows the property to use?

   A. $\frac{a^m}{a^n} = a^{m+n}$ **B.** $\frac{a^m}{a^n} = a^{m-n}$

   C. $\frac{a^m}{a^n} = a^{m-a}$ **D.** $\frac{a^m}{a^n} = a^{n-m}$

   b. Simplify the expression. Your answer should have only positive exponents.

2. Use a property of exponents to simplify $\frac{3^9}{3^5}$.

3. Use a property of exponents to simplify $\frac{y^{12}}{y^2}$.

4. **Think About the Process** You want to simplify the following expression.
$$\left(\frac{5}{c}\right)^3$$
   a. Which equation shows the property to use?

   A. $\left(\frac{a}{b}\right)^n = \frac{n^a}{n^b}$ **B.** $\left(\frac{a}{b}\right)^n = \frac{b^n}{a^n}$

   C. $\left(\frac{a}{b}\right)^n = \frac{n^b}{n^a}$ **D.** $\left(\frac{a}{b}\right)^n = \frac{a^n}{b^n}$

   b. Simplify the expression. Your answer should have only positive exponents.

5. Use a property of exponents to express $\left(\frac{y}{2}\right)^3$ as a fraction.

6. Use properties of exponents to simplify $\left(\frac{x^4}{7}\right)^2$.

7. **a. Error Analysis** Gino incorrectly said that $\frac{9^{11}}{9^7} = \frac{0^{11}}{0^7}$. Use a property of exponents to simplify $\frac{9^{11}}{9^7}$ correctly.

   b. What was Gino's likely error?

   A. He added the exponents.

   B. He subtracted the exponents incorrectly.

   C. He subtracted the bases instead of the exponents.

   D. He subtracted the bases and the exponents.

8. **a. Reasoning** Use a property of exponents to simplify $\frac{30y^{12}}{15y^2}$.

   b. For what values of y will the expression be negative?

9. **a. Writing** Use a property of exponents to express $\left(\frac{x}{9}\right)^2$ as a fraction.

   b. If you had to do more work with this expression, would it be better to leave the denominator in exponential form or to expand it? Justify your answer.

10. Use a property of exponents to simplify $\frac{-42x^5}{14x^2}$.

11. **Bacteria** The amount of bacteria in an infection n hours after taking medication is $\left(\frac{13}{x}\right)^n$. Write a simplified expression that represents the amount of bacteria in an infection 3 hours after taking medication. Write your answer using exponential notation. Simplify your answer.

12. Use properties of exponents to simplify $\left(\frac{5z^6}{6}\right)^2$.

13. **a.** Use properties of exponents to simplify $\frac{7^{13}}{7^8}$.

   b. Suppose the exponent in the denominator is greater than the exponent in the numerator. Describe a new property of exponents you could use to simplify the expression. Give two examples.

14. **a.** Use properties of exponents to simplify $\left(\frac{x^6}{7}\right)^3$.

   b. Evaluate when $x = 1$.

15. a. Error Analysis Gino incorrectly said that $\frac{6^{10}}{6^8} = \frac{0^{10}}{0^8}$. Use a property of exponents to simplify $\frac{6^{10}}{6^8}$ correctly.

    b. What was Gino's likely error?

        A. He subtracted the bases instead of the exponents.

        B. He subtracted the bases and the exponents.

        C. He subtracted the exponents incorrectly

        D. He added the exponents.

16. a. Reasoning Use a property of exponents to simplify $\frac{42y^{13}}{7y^5}$.

    b. For what values of y will the expression be negative?

17. a. Writing Use a property of exponents to express $\left(\frac{y}{6}\right)^2$ as a fraction.

    b. If you had to do more work with this expression, would it be better to leave the denominator in exponential form or to expand it? Justify your answer.

18. a. Use properties of exponents to simplify $\frac{-50y^9}{10y^5}$.

    b. Suppose the exponent in the denominator is greater than the exponent in the numerator. Describe a new property of exponents you could use to simplify the expression. Give two examples.

19. a. Challenge Use properties of exponents to simplify $\frac{c^5d^6}{c^3d^3}$.

    b. Evaluate when $c = 2$ and $d = 4$. Simplify your answer.

20. Challenge Use properties of exponents to simplify the expression $\left(\frac{(x^2yz^4)^3(xy^3z^2)^4}{xy^3z^2}\right)^2$. Show how to simplify the expression in two different ways.

CCSS: 8.EE.A.1

Part 1

Intro

In an earlier lesson, you learned how to divide expressions with the same base. You can use that property to examine and justify a special case.

Simplify the expression $\frac{4^3}{4^3}$.

$$\frac{4^3}{4^3} = \frac{4 \cdot 4 \cdot 4}{4 \cdot 4 \cdot 4}$$

$$= \frac{64}{64}$$

$$= 1$$

$$\frac{4^3}{4^3} = 4^{3-3}$$

$$= 4^0$$

$$\frac{4^3}{4^3} = 4^0 = 1$$

Zero Exponent Property

Arithmetic

$(-3)^0 = 1$

Algebra

For every nonzero number a, $a^0 = 1$.

Example Simplifying Expressions Using the Zero Exponent Property

Simplify each expression. Assume all variables $\neq 0$.

a. $\frac{18x^{20}}{18x^{20}}$ **b.** $\frac{w^8z^{15}}{w^8z^8}$ **c.** $\frac{9x^5y^{12}}{3x^2y^{12}}$ **d.** $5x^0$

Solution

> Divide the coefficients.
> $18 \div 18 = 1$

a. $\frac{18x^{20}}{18x^{20}} = 1x^{20-20}$

> To divide powers with the same base, subtract the exponents.

$$= x^0$$

$$= 1$$

> $x^0 = 1$

b. $\frac{w^8z^{15}}{w^8z^8} = w^{8-8}z^{15-8}$

$$= w^0z^7$$

$$= z^7$$

continued on next page >

Part 1

Solution continued

c. $\dfrac{9x^5y^{12}}{3x^2y^{12}} = 3x^{5-2}y^{12-12}$

$\qquad\qquad\quad = 3x^3$

d. $5x^0 = 5 \cdot 1$

$\qquad\quad = 5$

Part 2

Intro

You can also use the property for dividing powers with the same base to examine and justify another special case.

Simplify the expression $\dfrac{8^3}{8^5}$.

$$\dfrac{8^3}{8^5} = \dfrac{8 \cdot 8 \cdot 8}{8 \cdot 8 \cdot 8 \cdot 8 \cdot 8}$$

$$= \dfrac{{}^1\!\!8 \cdot {}^1\!\!8 \cdot {}^1\!\!8}{{}_1 8 \cdot {}_1 8 \cdot {}_1 8 \cdot 8 \cdot 8}$$

$$= \dfrac{1}{8^2}$$

$$\dfrac{8^3}{8^5} = 8^{3-5}$$

$$= 8^{-2}$$

$$\dfrac{8^3}{8^5} = 8^{-2} = \dfrac{1}{8^2}$$

Negative Exponent Property

Arithmetic

$8^{-5} = \dfrac{1}{8^5}$

Algebra

For every nonzero number a and integer n, $a^{-n} = \dfrac{1}{a^n}$.

Example Simplifying Expressions Using the Negative Exponent Property

Simplify each expression using positive exponents.

a. $\dfrac{2^8}{2^{11}}$

b. $\dfrac{100b^{50}}{200b^{75}}$

c. $\dfrac{a^{-3}b^7c^5}{a^5b^2c^7}$

d. $(2x^3y^{-5})^{-2}$

continued on next page >

Part 2

Example continued

Solution ·

a. Simplify $\frac{2^8}{2^{11}}$.

Subtract exponents when dividing powers with the same base.	$\frac{2^8}{2^{11}} = 2^{8-11}$
Simplify the exponents.	$= 2^{-3}$
Rewrite using the definition of negative exponents.	$= \frac{1}{2^3}$

b. Simplify $\frac{100b^{50}}{200b^{75}}$.

Subtract exponents when dividing powers with the same base.	$\frac{100b^{50}}{200b^{75}} = \frac{100}{200} \cdot b^{50-75}$
Simplify the coefficients and the exponents.	$= \frac{1}{2} \cdot b^{-25}$
Rewrite using the definition of negative exponents.	$= \frac{1}{2} \cdot \frac{1}{b^{25}}$
	$= \frac{1}{2b^{25}}$

c. Simplify $\frac{a^{-3}b^7c^5}{a^5b^2c^7}$.

Subtract exponents when dividing powers with the same base.	$\frac{a^{-3}b^7c^5}{a^5b^2c^7} = a^{-3-5}b^{7-2}c^{5-7}$
Simplify the exponents.	$= a^{-8}b^5c^{-2}$
Rewrite using the definition of negative exponents.	$= \frac{b^5}{a^8c^2}$

d. Simplify $(2x^3y^{-5})^{-2}$.

Raise each factor to the −2 power.	$(2x^3y^{-5})^{-2} = 2^{-2} \cdot (x^3)^{-2} \cdot (y^{-5})^{-2}$
Multiply the exponents.	$= 2^{-2} \cdot x^{-6} \cdot y^{10}$
Rewrite using the definition of negative exponents.	$= \frac{1}{2^2} \cdot \frac{1}{x^6} \cdot y^{10}$
Simplify.	$= \frac{y^{10}}{2^2x^6}$

Part 3

Example Comparing Powers with Positive, Negative, and Zero Exponents

Classify each expression as *greater than 1*, *equal to 1*, or *less than 1*.

a. 3^{-2} **b.** 2^3 **c.** 3^2

d. 2^{-3} **e.** 3^0 **f.** 2^0

Solution

a. $3^{-2} = \dfrac{1}{3^2} = \dfrac{1}{3 \cdot 3} = \dfrac{1}{9}$, which is less than 1.

b. $2^3 = 2 \cdot 2 \cdot 2 = 8$, which is greater than 1.

c. $3^2 = 3 \cdot 3 = 9$, which is greater than 1.

d. $2^{-3} = \dfrac{1}{2^3} = \dfrac{1}{2 \cdot 2 \cdot 2} = \dfrac{1}{8}$, which is less than 1.

e. $3^0 = 1$

f. $2^0 = 1$

Key Concept

You've seen the properties of zero and negative exponents in this lesson, so it's a good idea to review and summarize them before moving on to the next lesson.

Zero Exponent Property For every nonzero number a, $a^0 = 1$.

Examples:

$$4^0 = 1 \qquad (-3)^0 = 1 \qquad x^0 = 1$$

Negative Exponent Property For every nonzero number a and integer n, $a^{-n} = \dfrac{1}{a^n}$.

Examples:

$$8^{-5} = \dfrac{1}{8^5} \qquad (-3)^{-2} = \dfrac{1}{(-3)^2} \qquad x^{-3} = \dfrac{1}{x^3}$$
$$= \dfrac{1}{9}$$

1. Simplify the expression 11^0.

2. Simplify the expression $\frac{5w^4}{w^4}$. Assume that w is nonzero.

3. Simplify this expression. Assume that x is nonzero. Your answer should have only positive exponents.
$$x^{-10} \cdot x^6$$

4. Simplify the expression 5^{-3}.

5. Simplify the expression $\frac{8^3}{8^7}$.

6. Is the value of the expression 3^{-2} greater than 1, equal to 1, or less than 1?

7. Is the value of the expression $\left(\frac{1}{4}\right)^0$ greater than 1, equal to 1, or less than 1?

8. Is the value of the expression greater than 1, equal to 1, or less than 1?
$$\left(\left(\frac{1}{4}\right)^{-2}\right)^0$$

9. a. **Writing** Simplify the expression $9y^0$. Assume that y is nonzero.

   b. Describe how the values of the expression vary with the values chosen for y. Give examples.

10. a. **Multiple Representations** Simplify the expression $(-3.2)^0$.

    b. Write at least two expressions equivalent to this one. Explain why they are equivalent.

11. a. **Reasoning** Simplify $(-3)^{-8}$.

    b. Is the result the same as the result of simplifying -3^{-8}? Do $(-3)^{-9}$ and -3^{-9} simplify to the same value? Explain.

12. **Think About the Process** In the expression below, assume that x is nonzero.
$$7x^{-3}$$

    a. First find the base of the exponential term.

    b. Simplify the expression. Your answer should have only positive exponents.

13. **Error Analysis** Alexander simplifies the expression $\frac{100y^{41}}{600y^{71}}$ to $\frac{1}{6y^{30}}$. Hope simplifies it to $\frac{y^{30}}{6}$. If y is nonzero, which student is incorrect? Why?

    A. Alexander is incorrect. He can simplify the expression further.

    B. Hope is incorrect. She can simplify the expression further.

    C. Alexander is incorrect. He wrote the difference of the exponents in the denominator, not the numerator.

    D. Hope is incorrect. She wrote the difference of the exponents in the numerator, not the denominator.

14. **Choosing an Activity** Julia has to classify the expression $\frac{4^2}{4^5}$ for her math homework before she can join her classmates outside. She decides to use the value of the expression to help choose which activity to do. If the value is greater than 1, she will play basketball. If the value is equal to 1, she will play soccer. If the value is less than 1, she will play tennis. Which activity is Julia going to do today?

15. **Think About the Process**

    a. Simplify this expression. Assume that b and d are nonzero.
$$\frac{b^9 d^{20}}{b^9 d^9}$$

    b. Which rule(s) for exponents did you use? Select all that apply.

       A. Power of a Product

       B. Power of a Quotient

       C. Zero Exponent Property

       D. Multiplying Powers with the Same Base

       E. Dividing Powers with the Same Base

       F. Power of a Power

16. Simplify the expression $\frac{2c^7 g^8}{38c^7 g^6}$. Assume that c and g are both nonzero.

17. **Choosing an Activity** Julia has to classify the expression $\frac{2^3}{2^3}$ for her math homework before she can join her classmates outside. She decides to use the value of the expression to help choose which activity to do. If the value is greater than 1, she will play basketball. If the value is equal to 1, she will play soccer. If the value is less than 1, she will play tennis. Which activity is Julia going to do today?

18. **Think About the Process**

   a. Simplify this expression. Assume that c and y are nonzero.

   $\dfrac{c^8 y^{12}}{c^8 y^8}$

   b. Which rule(s) for exponents did you use? Select all that apply.

   A. Power of a Quotient

   B. Zero Exponent Property

   C. Dividing Powers with the Same Base

   D. Power of a Product

   E. Power of a Power

   F. Multiplying Powers with the Same Base

19. **Think About the Process** In the expression below, assume that x is nonzero.

   $5x^{-2}$

   a. First find the base of the exponential term.

   b. Simplify the expression. Your answer should have only positive exponents.

20. **a.** Is the value of the expression $((-3)^2)^{-3}$ greater than 1, equal to 1, or less than 1?

   b. Describe a situation when you would use an exponent that is negative.

21. **Challenge** Simplify the expression $\left(\dfrac{162w^6 x^2}{-18w^9 x^{-9}}\right)^{-1}$. Assume that w and x are both nonzero.

22. **a. Challenge** Is the value of the expression $\left(\dfrac{1}{4^{-3}}\right)^{-2}$ greater than 1, equal to 1, or less than 1?

   b. If the value of the expression is greater than 1, show how you can change one sign to make the value less than 1. If the value is less than 1, show how you can change one sign to make the value greater than 1. If the value is equal to 1, show how you can make one change to make the value not equal to 1.

Comparing Expressions with Exponents

CCSS: 8.EE.A.1

Part 1

Intro

Throughout this topic you have studied the properties of exponents. You can use the properties of exponents to write equivalent expressions.

Example Writing Equivalent Expressions Using Properties of Exponents

Write four expressions equivalent to 2^{13}. Explain your reasoning for each expression.

Solution

Answers will vary. Sample answers:

Use $2^{13} = 2^m \cdot 2^n$, where $m + n = 13$, to find some equivalent expressions.

$$2^{13} = 2^{10+3}$$
$$= 2^{10} \cdot 2^3$$

$$2^{13} = 2^{8+5}$$
$$= 2^8 \cdot 2^5$$

Use $2^{13} = \dfrac{2^m}{2^n}$, where $m - n = 13$, to find some equivalent expressions.

$$2^{13} = 2^{20-7}$$
$$= \dfrac{2^{20}}{2^7}$$

$$2^{13} = 2^{30-17}$$
$$= \dfrac{2^{30}}{2^{17}}$$

So, $2^{10} \cdot 2^3$, $2^8 \cdot 2^5$, $\dfrac{2^{20}}{2^7}$, and $\dfrac{2^{30}}{2^{17}}$ are equivalent to 2^{13}.

Part 2

Example Comparing Expressions Using Properties of Exponents

Use $<$, $>$, or $=$ to complete each statement.

a. $3^6 \; \blacksquare \; 3^2 \cdot 3^3$
b. $7^4 \; \blacksquare \; \dfrac{7^8}{7^4}$
c. $\left(\dfrac{1}{4}\right)^{16} \; \blacksquare \; \left(\dfrac{1}{4}\right)^8 \cdot \left(\dfrac{1}{4}\right)^2$

Solution

a. $3^6 \; \blacksquare \; 3^2 \cdot 3^3$

Write the original problem.	$3^6 \; \blacksquare \; 3^2 \cdot 3^3$
Rewrite $3^2 \cdot 3^3$ using the properties of exponents.	$3^6 \; \blacksquare \; 3^{2+3}$
Simplify.	$3^6 \; \blacksquare \; 3^5$
Compare the exponents, $6 > 5$.	$3^6 \; \blacksquare \; 3^5$
Complete the statement.	$3^6 > 3^5$

b. $7^4 \; \blacksquare \; \dfrac{7^8}{7^4}$

Write the original problem.	$7^4 \; \blacksquare \; \dfrac{7^8}{7^4}$
Rewrite $\dfrac{7^8}{7^4}$ using the properties of exponents.	$7^4 \; \blacksquare \; 7^{8-4}$
Simplify.	$7^4 \; \blacksquare \; 7^4$
Compare the exponents, $4 = 4$.	$7^4 \; \blacksquare \; 7^4$
Complete the statement.	$7^4 = 7^4$

c. $\left(\dfrac{1}{4}\right)^{16} \; \blacksquare \; \left(\dfrac{1}{4}\right)^8 \cdot \left(\dfrac{1}{4}\right)^2$

Write the original problem.	$\left(\dfrac{1}{4}\right)^{16} \; \blacksquare \; \left(\dfrac{1}{4}\right)^8 \cdot \left(\dfrac{1}{4}\right)^2$
Rewrite the expression on the right using the properties of exponents.	$\left(\dfrac{1}{4}\right)^{16} \; \blacksquare \; \left(\dfrac{1}{4}\right)^{8+2}$
Simplify.	$\left(\dfrac{1}{4}\right)^{16} \; \blacksquare \; \left(\dfrac{1}{4}\right)^{10}$
Compare the exponents, 16 and 10, given a base that is between 0 and 1.	$\dfrac{1}{4^{16}} \; \blacksquare \; \dfrac{1}{4^{10}}$
Complete the statement.	$\dfrac{1}{4^{16}} < \dfrac{1}{4^{10}}$

Remember that the larger the denominator, the smaller the fraction.

Part 3

Intro

You can compare numerical expressions with exponents that do not have the same base as long as you can rewrite one or both of the expressions using the same base.

5^{28} and 25^{19}

> Look at 25^{19}. You can write 25 as 5^2.

$25^{19} = (5^2)^{19}$

> Rewriting may also involve applying properties of exponents.

$\quad = 5^{2 \cdot 19}$

$\quad = 5^{38}$

5^{28} and 5^{38}

> Since the bases are the same, you can compare the exponents.

5^{28} and 5^{38}

$28 < 38$

$5^{28} < 5^{38}$, so $5^{28} < 25^{19}$

Example Comparing Expressions by Rewriting Terms as Powers With the Same Base

Use $<$, $>$, or $=$ to complete each statement.

a. $3^{18} \blacksquare 9^{10} \cdot 3^3$

b. $4^{21} \blacksquare 2^{28} \cdot 8^4$

Solution

a. $3^{18} \underline{\quad ? \quad} 9^{10} \cdot 3^3$

$3^{18} \underline{\quad ? \quad} (3^2)^{10} \cdot 3^3$

> Rewrite 9 as a power with base 3. $9 = 3^2$.

$3^{18} \underline{\quad ? \quad} 3^{2 \cdot 10} \cdot 3^3$

$3^{18} \underline{\quad ? \quad} 3^{20} \cdot 3^3$

$3^{18} \underline{\quad ? \quad} 3^{20+3}$

$3^{18} \underline{\quad ? \quad} 3^{23}$

> Compare the exponents

$3^{18} < 3^{23}$

So, $3^{18} < 9^{10} \cdot 3^3$.

b. $4^{21} \underline{\quad ? \quad} 2^{28} \cdot 8^4$

$(2^2)^{21} \underline{\quad ? \quad} 2^{28} \cdot (2^3)^4$

> Rewrite 4 and 8 as powers with base 2. $4 = 2^2$ and $8 = 2^3$.

$2^{2 \cdot 21} \underline{\quad ? \quad} 2^{28} \cdot 2^{3 \cdot 4}$

$2^{42} \underline{\quad ? \quad} 2^{28} \cdot 2^{12}$

$2^{42} \underline{\quad ? \quad} 2^{28+12}$

$2^{42} \underline{\quad ? \quad} 2^{40}$

> Compare the exponents

So, $4^{21} > 2^{28} \cdot 8^4$.

Digital Resources

1. Use properties of exponents to write an expression equivalent to 3^{14}.

2. Which expressions are equivalent to 2^{11}? Select all that apply.

   A. $2^7 \cdot 2^4$ **B.** $\dfrac{2^{24}}{2^{13}}$

   C. $\dfrac{2^9}{2^2}$ **D.** $2^9 \cdot 2^2$

3. Which expressions are equivalent to $\left(\dfrac{1}{6}\right)^{16}$?

   Select all that apply.

   A. $\left(\dfrac{1}{6}\right)^2 \cdot \left(\dfrac{1}{6}\right)^8$ **B.** $\left(\dfrac{1}{6}\right)^{10} \cdot \left(\dfrac{1}{6}\right)^6$

   C. $\left[\left(\dfrac{1}{6}\right)^8\right]^2$ **D.** $\left[\left(\dfrac{1}{6}\right)^5\right]^6$

4. Use the properties of exponents to compare 3^9 and $3^3 \cdot 3^2$.

5. Use the properties of exponents to compare $\left(\dfrac{7}{9}\right)^{12}$ and $\left[\left(\dfrac{7}{9}\right)^2\right]^4$.

6. Use the properties of exponents to compare 49^4 and $(7^3)^2$.

7. Compare 9^{-17} and $3^{-25} \cdot 27^{-5}$.

8. **a.** **Writing** Use the properties of exponents to compare 5^{-9} and $\dfrac{5^{19}}{5^{22}}$.

   b. Explain how you could find another exponential expression that is greater than one of the expressions and less than the other.

9. Is 16^{-16} less than or greater than $\dfrac{64^6}{64^{11}}$?

10. **a.** **Reasoning** Use properties of exponents to compare 64^{14} and $16^7 \cdot 16^9$.

    b. What common base did you use to compare the expressions? What other common base could you have used? Explain.

11. **Error Analysis** Your friend says that $5^9 \cdot 5^3$ is equivalent to 5^{27}.

    a. Which expression is equivalent to $5^9 \cdot 5^3$?

       A. 5^{12} **B.** 5^6

       C. 5^{-6}

    b. What mistake did your friend likely make?

       A. Your friend multiplied the exponents instead of adding them.

       B. Your friend added the exponents instead of subtracting them.

       C. Your friend subtracted the exponents instead of adding them.

       D. Your friend added the exponents instead of multiplying them.

12. **Think About the Process** You are given the equation below, with a missing exponent.
    $5^{24} = 5^9 \cdot 5^?$

    a. How can you find the value of the missing exponent?

       A. Subtract 24 from 9.

       B. Add 5 and 24.

       C. Subtract 9 from 24.

       D. Add 9 and 24.

    b. Complete the equation.
       $5^{24} = 5^9 \cdot 5^{\blacksquare}$

13. **Construction Materials** The weight of a stack of bricks is 9^4 pounds. The weight of a stack of lumber is $\dfrac{27^9}{3^{10}}$ pounds. Which stack is heavier?

    A. The stack of bricks is heavier.

    B. The stack of lumber is heavier.

    C. The stacks have equal weight.

14. **a.** **Open-Ended** Write an expression equivalent to 2^{12}.

    b. Name the property of exponents you used to write the equivalent expression. For each of the other properties of exponents, write one expression that is equivalent to the given expression because of that property.

15. **Error Analysis** Your friend says that $8^{10} \cdot 8^3$ is equivalent to 8^{30}.

   a. Which expression is equivalent to $8^{10} \cdot 8^3$?

   A. 8^7

   B. 8^{13}

   C. 8^{-7}

   b. What mistake did your friend likely make?

   A. Your friend added the exponents instead of multiplying them.

   B. Your friend added the exponents instead of subtracting them.

   C. Your friend multiplied the exponents instead of adding them.

   D. Your friend subtracted the exponents instead of adding them.

16. **Construction Materials** The weight of a stack of bricks is 9^5 pounds. The weight of a stack of lumber is $\frac{27^9}{3^6}$ pounds. Which stack is heavier?

   A. The stack of lumber is heavier.

   B. The stack of bricks is heavier.

   C. The stacks have equal weight.

17. **a. Open-Ended** Write an expression equivalent to 4^{16}.

   b. Name the property of exponents you used to write the equivalent expression. For each of the other properties of exponents, write one expression that is equivalent to the given expression because of that property.

18. **Think About the Process** Use the properties of exponents to compare $\left(\frac{1}{6}\right)^{12}$ and $\left[\left(\frac{1}{6}\right)^3\right]^2$.

   a. After you have used the properties of exponents to rewrite the second expression, what should you do to compare the expressions?

   A. Subtract the lesser exponent from the greater exponent.

   B. Compare the exponents and decide which is least.

   C. Multiply the base times each exponent.

   b. Which expression is greater, the first or the second?

19. Use the properties of exponents to compare $\left(\frac{1}{6}\right)^{-5}$ and $\left(\frac{1}{6}\right)^3 \cdot \left(\frac{1}{6}\right)^8$.

20. Use the properties of exponents to compare $\left(\frac{1}{5}\right)^{-4}$ and $\frac{5^{12}}{5^7}$.

21. **Challenge** Use the properties of exponents to compare $\frac{2^4 \cdot 5^8}{2^{-1} \cdot 5^2}$ and $\frac{2^3 \cdot 5^5 \cdot 2^2 \cdot 3^4}{3^4}$.

22. **a. Challenge** Compare 27^9 and $9^{10} \cdot 81^2$.

   b. Show how you compared the expressions using one base. Then show how you can compare the expressions using a base different from the one you used.

CCSS: 8.EE.A.1

---Part 1---

Example Applying Properties of Exponents to Area Problems

The length and width of a rectangle are described using algebraic expressions as shown in the diagram.

a. Write an algebraic expression to represent the area of the rectangle.

b. What must be true about the value of x in order for the expression you wrote in part (a) to make sense for the problem situation? Explain your reasoning.

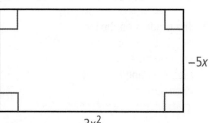

$-5x$

$3x^2$

Solution ·

a. The area of a rectangle is given by

Area = base · height

So, the expression that represents the area of the rectangle is,

$(3x^2)(-5x) = -15x^3$.

b. Since area is always positive, the value of the algebraic expression representing the area must be positive.

$-15x^3$ is the product of two factors, -15 and x^3. The product of two negative factors is positive. So, x^3 must represent a negative number. x^3 is negative when x is negative.

So, any number $x < 0$ will make the algebraic expression $-15x^3$ reasonable for a problem that involves area.

Part 2

Example Analyzing Algebraic Expressions Using Properties of Exponents

For what values of a, if any, does $(ab)^2 = ab^2$? Explain your reasoning.

Solution ·

Apply the properties of exponents to rewrite $(ab)^2$.

> The product on the left side has an exponent 2. So raise each of the factors, a and b, to the exponent 2.

$$(ab)^2 = ab^2$$
$$a^2b^2 = ab^2$$

Now examine each variable.

$$a^2b^2 = ab^2$$

Both expressions contain b^2, but the a parts of each expression are different. Check the possible values for a.

So, when would $a^2 = a$? In other words, what number has the same value as its square?

> $0^2 = 0$ and $1^2 = 1$.

$0^2 = 0$	$5^2 = 25$
$1^2 = 1$	$6^2 = 36$
$2^2 = 4$	$7^2 = 49$
$3^2 = 9$	$8^2 = 64$
$4^2 = 16$	$9^2 = 81$

Looks like two possible values for a are 0 and 1.

Better check for any negative numbers.

> There are no negative numbers that have the same value as their squares.

$(-1)^2 = 1$	$(-5)^2 = 25$
$(-2)^2 = 4$	$(-6)^2 = 36$
$(-3)^2 = 9$	$(-7)^2 = 49$
$(-4)^2 = 16$	$(-8)^2 = 64$

No additional values for a come from studying the negatives.

Positive and negative fractions will not result in any additional values for a.

$a^2 = a$ only when $a = 0$ or $a = 1$.

So, $(ab)^2 = ab^2$ when $a = 0$ or $a = 1$.

1. For what values of x is it reasonable to use the expression $-4x^5$ to represent the following situation? **The distance Wendell bikes to the library.**

 A. for integer values of x

 B. for any value of x except zero

 C. for negative values of x

 D. for positive values of x

2. For what value of x will $5^x = 5$?

3. For what value(s) of x will $-2x^2 = -32$?

 A. 4 **B.** 4 and -4

 C. 16 and -16 **D.** 16

4. An expression representing the volume of an aquarium is $11m^5$.

 a. For what values of m is the expression $11m^5$ reasonable?

 A. positive numbers

 B. any number other than zero

 C. negative numbers

 D. any integer

 b. What values of m are reasonable if the expression representing the volume is $-11m^5$? Explain.

5. An expression representing the area of a square is $7n^4$. For what value(s) of n is the expression $7n^4$ reasonable?

 A. The value of n can be any number other than zero.

 B. The value of n must be a positive number.

 C. The value of n must be zero.

 D. The value of n must be a negative number.

6. Think About the Process You need to find the value(s) of t for which it is reasonable for the expression $6t^{11}$ to represent the area of a rectangle.

 a. What is a reasonable way to make sure that the area of a rectangle is always positive?

 A. For the area to be positive, both dimensions should be negative.

 B. For the area to be positive, the dimensions should have different signs.

 C. For the area to be positive, both dimensions should be positive.

 b. For what value(s) of t is it reasonable for the expression $6t^{11}$ to represent area?

 A. The value of t must be zero.

 B. The value of t must be a positive number.

 C. The value of t must be a negative number.

 D. The value of t can be any number.

7. Carie drives $-5x$ miles in the morning and $2x^2$ miles in the afternoon.

 a. Which expression represents the total distance Carie drives?

 A. $-5x \div 2x^2$ **B.** $5x - 2x^2$

 C. $-5x + 2x^2$ **D.** $-5x(2x^2)$

 b. What must be true about the value of x in order for the expression to make sense for the situation?

 A. The value of x must be an integer.

 B. The value of x must be a positive number.

 C. The value of x must be a negative number.

 D. The value of x can be any number.

8. A playground is in the shape of a square that measures $5n$ meters on each side. The area of the new playground is 225 square meters.

 a. For what value(s) of n will $25n^2 = 225$?

 A. 3 and -3 **B.** -3

 C. 9 **D.** 9 and -9

 b. Which of these values of n make sense for this situation? Use a comma to separate answers as needed.

9. a. For what value(s) of k will $-189 = -7k^3$? Use a comma to separate answers as needed.

 b. How would you write an equation using $(-k)^3$ that you can solve with a positive value of k? A negative value of k?

See your complete lesson at MyMathUniverse.com

10. For what value(s) of x will $4^{13} = 2^x$? Use a comma to separate answers as needed.

11. **Think About the Process**
    a. How would you find values of y that make $(2y)^2 = 4y$ true?
       A. Use the fact that $(a^2)^2 = a^{2 \cdot 2}$ to rewrite $(2y)^2$. Then solve for y.
       B. Use the fact that $(ab)^2 = a^2 b^2$ to rewrite $(2y)^2$. Then solve for y.
       C. Use the fact that $a^2 \cdot a^2 = a^{2+2}$ to rewrite $(2y)^2$. Then solve for y.
    b. Find these values of y.

12. A playground is in the shape of a square that measures $6n$ meters on each side. The area of the new playground is 324 square meters.
    a. For what value(s) of n will $36n^2 = 324$?
       A. 9 and -9
       B. 3 and -3
       C. -3
       D. 9
    b. Which of these values of n make sense for this situation? Use a comma to separate answers as needed.

13. a. For what value(s) of k will $-56 = -7k^3$? Use a comma to separate answers as needed.
    b. How would you write an equation using $(-k)^3$ that you can solve with a positive value of k? A negative value of k?

14. For what value(s) of x will $3^x = 3$? Use a comma to separate answers as needed.

15. **Think About the Process** You need to find the value(s) of t for which it is reasonable for the expression $-3t^{11}$ to represent the area of a rectangle.
    a. What is a reasonable way to make sure that the area of a rectangle is always positive?
       A. For the area to be positive, both dimensions should be positive.
       B. For the area to be positive, the dimensions should have different signs.
       C. For the area to be positive, both dimensions should be negative.
    b. For what value(s) of t is it reasonable for the expression $-3t^{11}$ to represent area?
       A. The value of t must be zero.
       B. The value of t must be a positive number.
       C. The value of t must be a negative number.
       D. The value of t can be any number.

16. **Challenge** Renee picks out clothes for work. She has $-9x$ shirts, $-4x$ pairs of shoes, and $-7x$ pairs of pants.
    a. Write an expression that represents the number of possible combinations of shirts, pairs of shoes, and pairs of pants.
    b. For what value of x is the expression reasonable?
       A. The value of x must be a positive integer.
       B. The value of x must be a negative integer.
       C. The value of x must be an integer.
       D. The value of x can be any number.

17. **Challenge** For what value(s) of m is $2 \cdot \sqrt{m} + \left(\frac{1}{6}\right)^{-2} = 44$ true? Use a comma to separate answers as needed.

See your complete lesson at MyMathUniverse.com

CCSS: 8.EE.A.3, 8.EE.A.4

Part 1

▶ Intro

You can express numbers as products using powers of 10.

Number	Powers of 10	Exponent
5000	5×10^3	3
500	5×10^2	2
50	5×10^1	1
5	5×10^0	0
0.5	5×10^{-1}	−1
0.05	5×10^{-2}	−2
0.005	5×10^{-3}	−3

▶ Example Understanding Powers of Ten

Look for patterns in the table. Decide whether each statement is *true* or *false*.

a. As the exponent of 10 increases, the number becomes greater.

b. A negative exponent of 10 makes the number negative.

c. 5×10^3 is greater than 5×10^2.

d. 5×10^{-3} is greater than 5×10^{-2}.

Number	Powers of 10
5000	5×10^3
500	5×10^2
50	5×10^1
5	5×10^0
0.5	5×10^{-1}
0.05	5×10^{-2}
0.005	5×10^{-3}

continued on next page >

Solution ··

a. As the exponent of 10 increases, the number becomes greater.

Number	Powers of 10
5000	5×10^3
500	5×10^2
50	5×10^1
5	5×10^0
0.5	5×10^{-1}
0.05	5×10^{-2}
0.005	5×10^{-3}

Numbers become greater

Exponent of 10 increases

The statement is true.

b. A negative exponent of 10 makes the number negative.

0.5	5×10^{-1}
0.05	5×10^{-2}
0.005	5×10^{-3}

Numbers are *not* negative

Exponents are negative

Remember that negative exponents indicate a reciprocal.

$10^{-1} = \frac{1}{10^1}$ and $10^{-2} = \frac{1}{10^2}$. The statement is false.

c. 5×10^3 is greater than 5×10^2.

5000	5×10^3
500	5×10^2

5000 is greater than 500.

3 is greater than 2. As the exponent of 10 increases, the number increases. The statement is true.

d. 5×10^{-3} is greater than 5×10^{-2}.

0.05	5×10^{-2}
0.005	5×10^{-3}

0.005 is *not* greater than 0.05.

Remember that -3 is less than -2. As the exponent of 10 decreases, the number decreases. The statement is false.

Key Concept

Some numbers are so large or so small that they are difficult to write. You can use *scientific notation* to express such numbers so they are easy to write and compare.

A number in **scientific notation** is written as the product of two factors, one greater than or equal to 1 and less than 10, and the other a power of 10.

| The first factor is greater than or equal to one and less than 10. | $6.92 \times \mathbf{10^5}$ | The exponent is an integer. |

Standard Form   Scientific Notation
692,000   = 6.92×10^5

Part 2

Example Identifying Numbers Expressed in Scientific Notation

Which of the following numbers is expressed in scientific notation? For numbers not in scientific notation, explain why each is *not* expressed in scientific notation.

20×10^3	5×2^{10}	4×10^{-3}	2.7×10^{120}
4.22	7.5×10^0	10×10^6	0.5×10^2

Solution ·

Numbers expressed in scientific notation:

| 4 is greater than or equal to 1 and less than 10. | 4×10^{-3} | 10^{-3} is an integer power of 10. |

| 7.5 is greater than or equal to 1 and less than 10. | 7.5×10^0 | 10^0 is an integer power of 10. |

| 2.5 is greater than or equal to 1 and less than 10. | 2.7×10^{120} | 10^{120} is an integer power of 10. |

continued on next page >

Part 2

Solution continued

Other numbers:

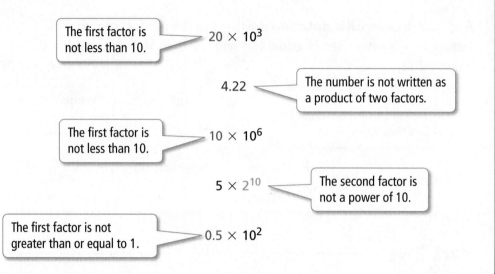

The first factor is not less than 10. → 20×10^3

4.22 ← The number is not written as a product of two factors.

The first factor is not less than 10. → 10×10^6

5×2^{10} ← The second factor is not a power of 10.

The first factor is not greater than or equal to 1. → 0.5×10^2

Part 3

Intro

Suppose you multiply two large numbers using paper and pencil or mental math.

$$800{,}000 \cdot 7{,}000{,}000 = 5{,}600{,}000{,}000{,}000$$

The product is an even larger number with many zeros.

Now suppose you use a calculator to multiply the numbers.

$$800{,}000 \cdot 7{,}000{,}000 = 5.6\mathrm{E}{+}12$$

What happened to all the zeros? Most calculator displays do not have enough space to show that many digits. So they use special notation. You can interpret this notation as scientific notation.

The "+" means the exponent of 10 is positive. You can read $5.6\mathrm{E}{+}12$ as "five and six tenths times ten to the twelfth power."

$$5.6\mathrm{e}{+}12$$
$$\downarrow \qquad \downarrow$$
$$5.6 \times 10^{12}$$

Part 3

> **Example Relating Calculator Displays to Scientific Notation**

Match each calculator result with the calculation that produced it. Then write the calculator results in scientific notation.

5.2E+17	5.2E−7	5.2E−10	5.2E+15

a. 52,000,000 · 100,000,000   **b.** 520,000,000 · 1,000,000,000

c. 52 ÷ 100,000,000   **d.** 52 ÷ 100,000,000,000

Solution ·

Products of large numbers are even larger. On a calculator, large numbers in scientific notation are represented by a positive number after the E.

  a. 52,000,000 · 100,000,000 = 5.2E+15
  $$= 5,200,000,000,000,000$$

You can also express this number in scientific notation as 5.2×10^{15}.

As the number of zeros increases, the product increases.

  b. 52,000,000 · 100,000,000 = 5.2E+17
  $$= 520,000,000,000,000,000$$

You can also express this number in scientific notation as 5.2×10^{17}.

When you divide a number by a greater number, the quotient is less than 1. On a calculator, small numbers (less than 1) in scientific notation are represented by a negative number after the E.

  c. 52 ÷ 100,000,000 = 5.2E−7
  $$= 0.00000052$$

You can also express this number in scientific notation as 5.2×10^{-7}.

As the divisor increases, the quotient decreases.

  d. 52 ÷ 100,000,000,000 = 5.2E−10
  $$= 0.00000000052$$

You can also express this number in scientific notation as 5.2×10^{-10}.

1. Which of the following is a pattern in the table?

Number	Powers of 10
1,830	1.83×10^3
183.0	1.83×10^2
18.3	1.83×10^1
1.83	1.83×10^0
0.183	1.83×10^{-1}
0.0183	1.83×10^{-2}
0.00183	1.83×10^{-3}

A. As the exponent of 10 increases, the number decreases.

B. As the exponent of 10 decreases, the number decreases.

C. The exponents that are less than 0 cause the number to become negative.

D. The exponents that are greater than 0 cause the number to decrease.

2. Which list shows the numbers in order from least to greatest?

A. 3.18×10^{-3}, 3.18×10^5, 3.18×10^6

B. 3.18×10^6, 3.18×10^5, 3.18×10^{-3}

C. 3.18×10^{-3}, 3.18×10^6, 3.18×10^5

D. 3.18×10^5, 3.18×10^{-3}, 3.18×10^6

3. Which of the following numbers is written in scientific notation?

A. 20×10^7 B. 20

C. 8.66   D. 8.66×10^7

4. Is the number 4.74×14^2 in scientific notation?

A. No, it is not in scientific notation. The first factor is not less than 10.

B. No, it is not in scientific notation. The first factor is not greater than or equal to 1.

C. No, it is not in scientific notation. The second factor is not a power of 10.

D. The number is in scientific notation.

5. a. Which of these calculations produces the calculator result 8.1E+12?

A. $81 \times 100{,}000{,}000{,}000$

B. $81 \div 100{,}000{,}000{,}000$

C. $81 \div 10{,}000{,}000{,}000{,}000$

D. $81 \times 10{,}000{,}000{,}000{,}000$

b. Write the calculator result in scientific notation.

6. a. **Writing** After doing a calculation, your calculator display shows 4.5E−11. Express this result in scientific notation.

b. Give three reasons why your calculator shows this result instead of 0.000000000045.

7. **Reasoning** Is 23×10^{-6} in scientific notation?

A. No, it is not in scientific notation. The second factor is not a power of 10.

B. No, it is not in scientific notation. The number is not written as a product of 2 factors.

C. No, it is not in scientific notation. The first factor is not less than 10.

D. The number is in scientific notation.

8. **Error Analysis** Fred's math teacher asks, "Which of the following numbers are written in scientific notation?" Fred says, "4.75×10^8 is written in scientific notation."

a. What is the correct answer? Select all that apply.

A. 8.87×10^8 B. 4.75×10^8

C. 17   D. 4.75

b. What error did Fred make?

A. The number 17 is also written in scientific notation.

B. The number 8.87×10^8 is also written in scientific notation.

C. The number 4.75×10^8 is not written in scientific notation.

D. The number 4.75 is also written in scientific notation.

9. **Astronomy** In a science fiction book, the distances from four planets to another planet are given in light years. Which list shows the distances in order from least to greatest?

   A. 6.35×10^6, 6.35×10^{-2}, 6.35×10^4, 6.35×10^7

   B. 6.35×10^{-2}, 6.35×10^7, 6.35×10^4, 6.35×10^6

   C. 6.35×10^7, 6.35×10^6, 6.35×10^4, 6.35×10^{-2}

   D. 6.35×10^{-2}, 6.35×10^4, 6.35×10^6, 6.35×10^7

10. Pierre evaluates an expression on his calculator, and the calculator display shows 5.7E−11. Express this result in scientific notation.

11. **a.** Which number is not written in scientific notation?

    A. 9.91×10^6 **B.** 1.51×18^3

    C. 3.27×10^6 **D.** 1.51×10^3

    E. 9.91×10^3 **F.** 3.27×10^3

    b. Why is this number not in scientific notation?

    A. The first factor is not less than 10.

    B. The second factor is not a power of 10.

    C. The first factor is not greater than or equal to 1.

    D. The number is not written as a product of 2 factors.

    c. Show two other ways that numbers can look like they are written in scientific notation, but really are not. Ask a classmate or family member why the numbers are not in scientific notation.

12. Which list shows the numbers in order from least to greatest?

    A. 9.07×10^{-7}, 7.74×10^{-7}, 7.03×10^{-8}, 3.35×10^{-4}, 1.99×10^{-9}

    B. 3.35×10^{-4}, 9.07×10^{-7}, 7.74×10^{-7}, 7.03×10^{-8}, 1.99×10^{-9}

    C. 1.99×10^{-9}, 3.35×10^{-4}, 7.03×10^{-8}, 7.74×10^{-7}, 9.07×10^{-7}

    D. 1.99×10^{-9}, 7.03×10^{-8}, 7.74×10^{-7}, 9.07×10^{-7}, 3.35×10^{-4}

13. **a. Challenge** Which list shows the numbers in order from least to greatest?

    A. 4.51×10^{-8}, 5.66×10^{-8}, 6.31×10^{-7}, 6.53×10^{-7}, 9.45×10^{-5}

    B. 9.45×10^{-5}, 6.53×10^{-7}, 6.31×10^{-7}, 5.66×10^{-8}, 4.51×10^{-8}

    C. 5.66×10^{-8}, 4.51×10^{-8}, 6.53×10^{-7}, 6.31×10^{-7}, 9.45×10^{-5}

    D. 9.45×10^{-5}, 6.31×10^{-7}, 6.53×10^{-7}, 4.51×10^{-8}, 5.66×10^{-8}

    b. Explain how the order would change if all the exponents were zero. Then change the exponents to their opposites and list the numbers in order from least to greatest.

14. **a. Challenge** Which number is expressed in scientific notation?

    A. 3.42×18^9 **B.** 18×18^9

    C. 0.99×18^9 **D.** 0.99×10^9

    E. 3.42×10^9 **F.** 18×10^9

    b. When a number is written in scientific notation, could zero ever be in the ones place of the first factor? Which digits, if any, would never be in the ones place?

Using Scientific Notation to Describe Very Large Quantities

CCSS 8.EE.A.3

Key Concept

When you are working with large numbers in standard form, it is helpful to express them in scientific notation.

Method 1

3.84,000.

> Move the decimal point to get a factor greater than or equal to 1 but less than 10.

$384,000 = 3.84 \times 100,000$

> Write the number as a product of 2 factors.

$384,000 = 3.84 \times 10^5$

> Write 100,000 as a power of 10.

Method 2

3.84,000.

> The decimal point moves 5 places to the left.

$384,000 = 3.84 \times 10^5$

> Use 5 as the exponent of 10.

You can also rewrite numbers expressed in scientific notation in standard form.

Method 1

$7.32 \times 10^6 = 7.32 \times 1,000,000$

> Write as a product of 2 factors.

$= 7,320,000$

> Multiply the factors.

Method 2

$7.32 \times 10^6 = 7.320000.$

> The exponent is 6. Move the decimal 6 places to the right. Insert zeros as necessary.

$= 7,320,000$

See your complete lesson at MyMathUniverse.com

Part 1

Example Writing Large Numbers in Scientific Notation

One astronomical unit (AU) is the average distance between Earth and the sun. It is approximately 93 million miles. Express this distance in scientific notation.

Solution ·

Method 1

93 million = 93,000,000

9.3,000,000

> Move the decimal point to get a factor greater than or equal to 1 but less than 10.

$93,000,000 = 9.3 \times 10,000,000$

> Write as a product of 2 factors.

$= 9.3 \times 10^7$

> Write 10,000,000 as a power of 10.

1 AU is 9.3×10^7 miles.

Method 2

93 million = 93,000,000

9.3,000,000

> Move the decimal point to get a factor greater than or equal to 1 but less than 10.

> The decimal point moves 7 places to the left.

$93,000,000 = 9.3 \times 10^7$

> Use 7 as the exponent of 10.

1 AU is 9.3×10^7 miles.

Part 2

Example Rewriting Numbers From Scientific Notation To Standard Form

The estimated age of the universe is 1.37×10^{10} years. Express this age in standard form.

Solution ·

$1.37 \times 10^{10} = 1.3700000000.$

> The exponent is 10. Move the decimal 10 places to the right. Insert zeros as necessary.

$= 13,700,000,000$

The estimated age of the universe is 13,700,000,000 years.

Part 3

> **Example** **Writing Very Large Numbers in Standard Form**

The list below shows numbers of bacteria in four colonies in a microbiology lab. Estimate each number in scientific notation using a single digit for the first factor. Then determine whether each statement is *true* or *false*.

Colony A: 79,854,000

Colony B: 2,124,000

Colony C: 6,180,000

Colony D: 397,000

    a. Colony A has about 40 times as many bacteria as Colony B.

    b. Colony C has about 30 times as many bacteria as Colony B.

    c. Colony B has about 5 times as many bacteria as Colony D.

Solution

Estimate the numbers in scientific notation.

Colony A: 8×10^7
Colony B: 2×10^6
Colony C: 6×10^6
Colony D: 4×10^5

    a. Colony A has about 40 times as many bacteria as Colony B.

        Colony A: 8×10^7

        Colony B: 2×10^6

Since $\frac{8}{2} = 4$ and the numbers differ by one power of 10, Colony A has about 4×10 or 40 times as many bacteria as Colony B. The statement is true.

    b. Colony C has about 30 times as many bacteria as Colony B.

        Colony C: 6×10^6

        Colony B: 2×10^6

Since $\frac{6}{2} = 3$ and the numbers have the same power of 10, Colony C has about 3 times as many bacteria as Colony B. The statement is false.

    c. Colony B has about 5 times as many bacteria as Colony D.

        Colony B: 2×10^6

        Colony D: 4×10^5

Since $\frac{2}{4} = 0.5$ and the numbers differ by one power of 10, Colony B has about 0.5×10 or 5 times as many bacteria as Colony D. The statement is true.

1. Express the number 80,000 in scientific notation.

2. Express the number 60,000 in scientific notation.

3. **Think About the Process** You want to express 437,000 in scientific notation.

   a. What is the first step?

   A. Move the decimal point 5 places to the left to get 4.37.

   B. Move the decimal point 4 places to the left to get 4.37.

   C. Move the decimal point 4 places to the left to get 43.7.

   D. Move the decimal point 5 places to the left to get 43.7.

   b. What is the result?

4. Express the number 8.5×10^5 in standard form.

5. The diameter of a certain star is about 9.3×10^6 km. Express this diameter in standard form.

6. Which number is greater?
   A. 6×10^6 **B.** 7×10^9

7. A rectangle has length 8×10^4 mm and width 4×10^4 mm. The rectangle's length is how many times its width?

8. **a.** **Writing** Express the number 5.2×10^6 in standard form.

   b. Describe two advantages that scientific notation has over standard form. Describe two advantages of standard form. Give examples for each.

9. Two space probes, Pilgrim 4 and Titan 2, were launched several decades ago. Today, they are about 6.93×10^9 km and 2.31×10^{11} m from Earth, respectively. Which probe is farther from Earth today?

10. **a.** **Reasoning** Which number is less, 6.9×10^6 or 630,000?

    b. When you compare two numbers in scientific notation, which do you compare first, the first factors or the exponents? Explain.

11. **Error Analysis** Owen incorrectly claims that because $20,000 = 20 \times 1,000$, he can express 20,000 in scientific notation as 20×10^3.

    a. What was Owen's error?

    A. The product he found is correct, but 20×10^3 is not in scientific notation since 20 is not less than 10.

    B. The product he found is correct, but 20×10^3 is not in scientific notation since 20 is not less than 1.

    C. He found the power of 10 incorrectly since $1,000 \neq 10^3$.

    D. He found the product incorrectly since $20,000 \neq 20 \times 1,000$.

    b. Express 20,000 in scientific notation correctly.

12. **Population** An historian predicts that by 2050, about 1.56×10^7 people will live in a certain country. Express this prediction in standard form.

13. **a.** Express the number 586,400,000 in scientific notation.

    b. Describe a situation in which this number might arise. Explain why it would be easier to use scientific notation in that situation.

14. **a.** **Multiple Representations** Express the mass 6,200,000 kilograms using scientific notation in two ways, first with kilograms and then with grams.

    b. List some other scientific-notation forms for this mass using other metric prefixes.

15. Express the number 4.3076×10^8 in standard form.

16. At the end of 2002, the population of Cities A and B were 670,000 and 6.8×10^5, respectively.

    a. Which city had the greater population at the end of 2002?

    b. In 2003, the populations became equal while the total population stayed the same. What was each city's population at the end of 2003?

17. **Think About the Process** A scientist has two colonies of bacteria, A and B. Colony A has 6.6×10^7 bacteria. Colony B has 3,300,000 bacteria.

    a. Express the number of bacteria in Colony B in scientific notation.

    b. The number of bacteria in Colony A is how many times the number of bacteria in Colony B?

    c. Describe the steps you take when comparing two numbers written in scientific notation without changing them to standard form.

18. **Challenge** A scientist is growing bacteria in three colonies, A, B, and C. At the moment, there are 3.5×10^6 bacteria in Colony A, 2.6×10^6 bacteria in Colony B, and 9.3×10^6 bacteria in all.

    a. Express each of these numbers in standard form.

    b. Use those results to find the number of bacteria in Colony C by evaluating the expression $9.3 \times 10^6 - (3.5 \times 10^6 + 2.6 \times 10^6)$.

19. **Challenge** The populations of Cities A and B are 2.6×10^5 and 1,560,000, respectively. The population of City C is two times the population of City B. The population of City C is how many times the population of City A?

Using Scientific Notation to Describe Very Small Quantities

CCSS: 8.EE.A.3

Key Concept

When you are working with small numbers in standard form, it is helpful to express them in scientific notation.

Method 1

0.0002.34

> Move the decimal point to get a factor greater than or equal to 1 but less than 10.

$0.000234 = 2.34 \times 0.0001$

> Write the number as a product of 2 factors.

$0.000234 = 2.34 \times 10^{-4}$

> Write 0.0001 as a power of 10.

Method 2

0.0002.34

> Move the decimal point to get a factor greater than or equal to 1 but less than 10.

> The decimal point moves 4 places to the right.

$0.000234 = 2.34 \times 10^{-4}$

> Use −4 as the exponent of 10.

You can also rewrite numbers expressed in scientific notation in standard form.

Method 1

$1.32 \times 10^{-3} = 1.32 \times 0.001$

> Write the number as a product of 2 factors.

$= 0.00132$

> Multiply the factors.

Method 2

$1.32 \times 10^{-3} = 0.001.32$

> The exponent is −3. Move the decimal 3 places to the left. Insert zeros as necessary.

$= 0.00132$

Example Expressing Small Numbers in Scientific Notation

Human eyes are sensitive to only a very small region of the electromagnetic spectrum called visible light. Express the wavelength of violet light in scientific notation.

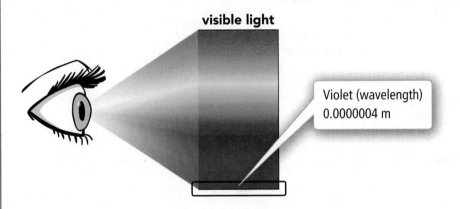

visible light

Violet (wavelength)
0.0000004 m

Solution

Method 1

0.0000004.0

> Move the decimal point to get a factor greater than or equal to 1 but less than 10.

$0.0000004 = 4.0 \times 0.0000001$

> Write the number as a product of 2 factors.

$0.0000004 = 4.0 \times 10^{-7}$

> Write 0.0000001 as a power of 10.

Violet light has a wavelength of 4.0×10^{-7} m.

Method 2

0.0000004.0

> Move the decimal point to get a factor greater than or equal to 1 but less than 10.

> The decimal point moves 7 places to the right.

$0.0000004 = 4.0 \times 10^{-7}$

> Use −7 as the exponent of 10.

Violet light has a wavelength of 4.0×10^{-7} m.

Part 2

Example Rewriting Small Numbers Expressed in Scientific Notation in Standard Form

The rate at which Earth's tectonic plates move varies around the world. One of Earth's plates moves about 1.23×10^{-2} cm per day. Express this rate in standard form.

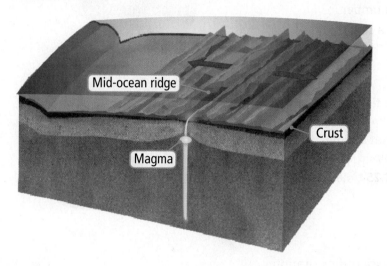

Mid-ocean ridge

Crust

Magma

Solution ·

$$1.23 \times 10^{-2} = 0.01.23$$

> The exponent of 10 is −2. Move the decimal 2 places to the left.

$$= 0.0123$$

This plate moves at a rate of 0.0123 cm per day.

Part 3

Example Comparing Small Numbers in Scientific Notation

The diameters of human cells photographed with a microscope in one lab are shown (photos not to scale). Estimate each number in scientific notation using a single digit for the first factor. Then fill in the blanks.

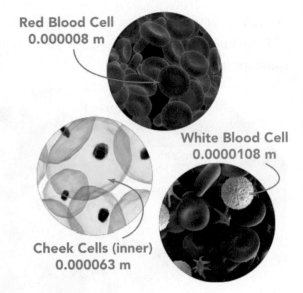

Red Blood Cell
0.000008 m

White Blood Cell
0.0000108 m

Cheek Cells (inner)
0.000063 m

   a. A ■ cell is about 6 times as large as a white blood cell.

   b. A cheek cell is about ■ times as large as a red blood cell.

   c. A ■ cell is about 1.25 times as large as a ■ cell.

Solution

Estimate the numbers in scientific notation.

Cheek cell: $0.000063 \approx 6 \times 10^{-5}$

Red blood cell: $0.000008 = 8 \times 10^{-6}$

White blood cell: $0.0000108 \approx 1 \times 10^{-5}$

a. A cheek cell is about 6 times as large as a white blood cell.

Cheek cell: 6×10^{-5}

White blood cell: 1×10^{-5} — The number have the same power of 10.

Since $\frac{6}{1} = 6$ and the numbers have the same power of 10, a cheek cell is about 6 times as large as a white blood cell.

b. A cheek cell is about 7.5 times as large as a red blood cell.

Cheek cell: 6×10^{-5}

Red blood cell: 8×10^{-6} — The number differ by one power of 10.

Since $\frac{6}{8} = 0.75$ and the numbers differ by one power of 10, a cheek cell is about 0.75×10 or 7.5 times as large as a red blood cell.

c. A white blood cell is about 1.25 times as large as a red blood cell.

White blood cell: 1×10^{-5}

Red blood cell: 8×10^{-6} — The number differ by one power of 10.

Since $\frac{1}{8} = 0.125$ and the numbers differ by one power of 10, a white blood cell is about 0.125×10 or 1.25 times as large as a red blood cell.

1. Express the number 0.0073 in scientific notation.

2. Express 0.5 in scientific notation by counting decimal places.

3. Write 3.91×10^{-2} in standard form.

4. The length of a bacterial cell is 6.2×10^{-6} m. Express the length of the cell in standard form.

5. Which number is greater, 7×10^{-9} or 6×10^{-4}?

6. Write 0.00000734 in scientific notation by counting decimal places.

7. A plant cell has length 5.8×10^{-6} m and width 2.9×10^{-6} m. What is the ratio of the plant cell's length to its width?

8. **a. Writing** Express 0.000000298 in scientific notation.

   b. Explain how negative powers of 10 make small numbers easier to write and compare.

9. **Think About the Process**

   a. What should you do first to write 5.871×10^{-7} in standard form?

   A. Move the decimal point 7 places to the right.

   B. Move the decimal point 6 places to the right.

   C. Move the decimal point 6 places to the left.

   D. Move the decimal point 7 places to the left.

   b. Write 5.871×10^{-7} in standard form.

10. **Reasoning** A nanometer is one-billionth of a meter. A centimeter is one-hundredth of a meter, and a kilometer is 1,000 meters. An X-ray can have a wavelength of 0.000000036 meter.

    a. Express this wavelength in scientific notation.

    b. Which unit is most appropriate for measuring the wavelength of an X-ray?

A. meter

B. nanometer

C. kilometer

D. centimeter

11. **Error Analysis** Your teacher asks you to write 3.92×10^{-6} in standard form. Your classmate gives an incorrect answer of 0.000000392.

    a. Write 3.92×10^{-6} in standard form.

    b. What was your classmate's likely error?

    A. Your classmate moved the decimal point 1 extra place to the left.

    B. Your classmate moved the decimal point 1 extra place to the right.

    C. Your classmate moved the decimal point 2 extra places to the left.

    D. Your classmate moved the decimal point 2 extra places to the right.

12. **Hair Growth** Human hair grows at a rate of 2.33×10^{-6} m per minute or 1.398×10^{-4} m per hour.

    a. Express each rate in standard form.

    b. Explain how you would find the rate at which hair grows per day.

13. **Mental Math** Express this number in scientific notation.

    0.0000000004

14. **Multiple Representations** The numbers below represent 0.002 as a product of two factors. Which product is written in scientific notation?

    A. 2×10^{-3}

    B. 20×10^{-4}

    C. 0.2×10^{-2}

    D. 200×10^{-5}

15. **Mental Math** Write 8×10^{-3} in standard form.

16. The diameter of a cheek cell is 4.6×10^{-6} m. The diameter of a red blood cell is 2.3×10^{-6} m. The diameter of a white blood cell is 9.2×10^{-5} m.

a. What is the ratio of the diameter of a cheek cell to the diameter of a red blood cell? Write the ratio as a simplified fraction.

b. What is the ratio of the diameter of a white blood cell to the diameter of a red blood cell? Write the ratio as a simplified fraction.

17. Think About the Process The length of cell A is 8×10^{-5} m. The length of cell B is 0.000004 m.

a. What is the ratio of cell A's length to cell B's length?

b. Is it easier to find the ratio when the numbers are expressed in scientific notation or in standard form? Explain your reasoning.

18. Challenge One nanometer, nm, is equal to 1×10^{-6} millimeters, mm, and 1×10^{-3} micrometers, μm. The rate at which your fingernails grow is 1.58 nm/s which is the same as 1.58×10^{-6} mm/s and 1.58×10^{-3} μm/s.

a. Express each number in standard form to find the rates in mm/s and μm/s.

b. Explain how expressing a number in standard form helps you decide which units you should use when describing a measurement.

19. Challenge You are given the numbers 0.00000156, 6.17×10^{-6}, 0.00000000617, and 1.56×10^{-9}.

a. Which number is the greatest?

   A. 1.56×10^{-9}

   B. 0.00000000617

   C. 6.17×10^{-6}

   D. 0.00000156

b. Which number is the least?

   A. 0.00000000617

   B. 0.00000156

   C. 1.56×10^{-9}

   D. 6.17×10^{-6}

Part 1

Intro

Adding, subtracting, multiplying, or dividing large or small numbers in scientific notation is easier and more efficient than operating on the same numbers in standard form.

To add or subtract numbers in scientific notation, they must have the same power of 10. Add or subtract the first factors of the numbers and keep the same power of 10.

$$(6 \times 10^4) + (2 \times 10^4) = (6 + 2) \times 10^4$$
$$= 8 \times 10^4$$

Sometimes sums or differences of numbers in scientific notation are numbers that are not in scientific notation. In those cases, you need to rewrite the sum or difference in the correct form.

$$(2.5 \times 10^{-9}) - (2.1 \times 10^{-9}) = (2.5 - 2.1) \times 10^{-9}$$
$$= 0.4 \times 10^{-9}$$
$$= 4.0 \times 10^{-10}$$

> This number is not in scientific notation because 0.4 is less than 1. Move the decimal one place to the right and rewrite.

To add or subtract numbers in scientific notation, make sure they have the same power of 10, then add or subtract the first factors.

Addition of Numbers in Scientific Notation

Arithmetic: $(6 \times 10^4) + (2 \times 10^4) = (6 + 2) \times 10^4 \times 10^4$

Algebra: $(a \times 10^n) + (b \times 10^n) = (a + b) \times 10^n, = 8$

where $1 \le a < 10$ and $1 \le b < 10$ and n is an integer.

Subtraction of Numbers in Scientific Notation

Arithmetic: $(9 \times 10^{-2}) - (3 \times 10^{-2}) = (9 - 3) \times 10^{-2} = 6 \times 10^{-2}$

Algebra: $(a \times 10^n) - (b \times 10^n) = (a - b) \times 10^n,$

where $1 \le a < 10$ and $1 \le b < 10$ and n is an integer.

Part 1

Example Subtracting Numbers in Scientific Notation

Deuterium and tritium are hydrogen atoms. Deuterium contains one proton and one neutron. Tritium has a mass of 5.0224×10^{-24} g. What is the difference of the mass of tritium and the mass of deuterium?

Proton mass:
1.6726×10^{-24} g

Neutron mass:
1.6749×10^{-24} g

Solution

Know
- Deuterium has 1 proton and 1 neutron.
- The masses of a proton and neutron
- The mass of tritium

Need
The difference of the masses of tritium and deuterium

Plan
Add the masses of the proton and neutron to find the mass of deuterium. Then subtract the mass of deuterium from the mass of tritium.

Step 1 Find the mass of deuterium.

Mass of deuterium = proton mass + neutron mass

$$= (1.6726 \times 10^{-24}) + (1.6749 \times 10^{-24})$$

$$= (1.6726 + 1.6749) \times 10^{-24}$$

Use the Distributive Property and then add.

$$= 3.3475 \times 10^{-24}$$

Step 2 Find the difference of the masses of the two atoms.

Difference in mass = mass of tritium − mass of deuterium

$$= (5.0224 \times 10^{-24}) - (3.3475 \times 10^{-24})$$

$$= (5.0224 - 3.3475) \times 10^{-24}$$

Use the Distributive Property and then subtract.

$$= 1.6749 \times 10^{-24}$$

The difference in mass between deuterium and tritium is 1.6749×10^{-24} g.

Part 2

Intro

You can use what you know about multiplying powers with the same base to multiply numbers in scientific notation.

To multiply numbers in scientific notation, use the commutative and associative properties to group the first factors together and to group the powers of 10 together. Then find both products. Since the powers are both base 10, you can add the exponents.

> Group the first factors together.

> Group the powers of 10 together.

$$(2 \times 10^{-5})(3 \times 10^{11}) = (2 \cdot 3) \times (10^{-5} \cdot 10^{11})$$
$$= 6 \times 10^{(-5+11)}$$
$$= 6 \times 10^{6}$$

> Multiplying powers of 10 is the same as adding the exponents.

Sometimes products of numbers in scientific notation are numbers that are not in scientific notation. In those cases, you need to rewrite the product in the correct form.

> Group the first factors together.

> Group the powers of 10 together.

$$(6 \times 10^{4})(4 \times 10^{-7}) = (6 \cdot 4) \times (10^{4} \cdot 10^{-7})$$
$$= 24 \times (10^{4} \cdot 10^{-7})$$
$$= 24 \times 10^{(4-7)}$$
$$= 24 \times 10^{-3}$$
$$= 2.4 \times 10^{-2}$$

> Multiplying powers of 10 is the same as adding the exponents.

> This number is not in scientific notation because 24 is greater than 10. Move the decimal one place to the left.

Multiplication of Numbers in Scientific Notation

Arithmetic: $(2 \times 10^{-5})(3 \times 10^{11}) = (2 \cdot 3) \times 10^{(-5+11)} = 6 \times 10^{6}$

Algebra: $(a \times 10^{m}) + (b \times 10^{n}) = (a \cdot b) \times 10^{(m+n)}$

where $1 \le a < 10$ and $1 \le b < 10$ and m and n are an integers.

Part 2

Example Multiplying Numbers in Scientific Notation

A carpet can contain millions of dust mites. Suppose the length of a dust mite is 2.5×10^{-4}m. If a carpet has one million dust mites and they all crawled away single file, how long would the line be?

Solution ·

1 million = 1,000,000 = 1×10^6

length of dust mite $\times$ number of dust mites = total length

$$(2.5 \times 10^{-4})(1 \times 10^6) = (2.5 \cdot 1) \times (10^{-4} \cdot 10^6)$$

$$= 2.5 \times 10^{-4+6}$$

$$= 2.5 \times 10^2$$

> Use the Associative Property to group factors together.

> To multiply exponents with the same base, add their powers together.

The line of dust mites would be 2.5×10^2 or 250 meters long.

Part 3

Intro

You can use what you know about dividing powers with the same base to divide numbers in scientific notation.

To divide numbers in scientific notation, write the expression as a product of quotients. Then find both quotients. Since the powers are both base 10, you can subtract the exponents.

> Divide the first factors.

> Divide the powers of 10.

$$\frac{7 \times 10^4}{2 \times 10^9} = \frac{7}{2} \times \frac{10^4}{10^9}$$

$$= 3.5 \times \frac{10^4}{10^9}$$

$$= 3.5 \times 10^{(4-9)}$$

$$= 3.5 \times 10^{-5}$$

> Dividing powers of 10 is the same as subtracting the exponents.

Sometimes quotients of numbers in scientific notation are numbers that are not in scientific notation. In those cases, you need to rewrite the quotient in the correct form.

continued on next page >

Part 3

Intro continued

> Divide the first factors.

> Divide the powers of 10.

$$\frac{3 \times 10^2}{5 \times 10^{-8}} = \frac{3}{5} \times \frac{10^2}{10^{-8}}$$

$$= 0.6 \times \frac{10^2}{10^{-8}}$$

> Dividing powers of 10 is the same as subtracting the exponents.

$$= 0.6 \times 10^{(2-(-8))}$$

$$= 0.6 \times 10^{10}$$

> This number is not in scientific notation because 0.6 is less than 1. Move the decimal one place to the right.

$$= 6.0 \times 10^9$$

To divide numbers in scientific notation, divide the first factors and subtract the exponents of the powers of 10.

Division of Numbers in Scientific Notation

Arithmetic: $\dfrac{7 \times 10^4}{2 \times 10^9} = \dfrac{7}{2} \times 10^{(4-9)} = 3.5 \cdot 10^{-5}$

Algebra: $\dfrac{a \times 10^m}{b \times 10^n} = \dfrac{a}{b} \times 10^{(m-n)}$

where $1 \leq a < 10$ and $1 \leq b < 10$ and m and n are integers.

Example Dividing Numbers in Scientific Notation

If beetles of the size shown stood end-to-end to make a line 1.25×10^2 m long, how many beetles would there be?

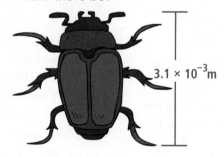

3.1×10^{-3}m

Solution

$$\frac{\text{lenght of line}}{\text{length of one beetle}} = \text{number of beetles}$$

Group factors together.

$$\frac{1.25 \times 10^2}{3.1 \times 10^{-3}} = \frac{1.25}{3.1} \times \frac{10^2}{10^{-3}}$$

To divide exponents with the same base, subtract their powers.

$$\approx 0.4 \times 10^{2-(-3)}$$

Rewrite in scientific notation.

$$= 0.4 \times 10^5$$

Simplify.

$$= 0.4 \times 10^4$$

There would be about 4×10^4 or 40,000 beetles.

1. Add $3.6 \times 10^7 + 5.1 \times 10^7$ and write your answer in scientific notation.

2. Subtract $8.4 \times 10^8 - 3.2 \times 10^8$ and write your answer in scientific notation.

3. **Think About the Process**

   a. Describe the procedure for multiplying two numbers in scientific notation.

   A. Multiply the first factors, then add the exponents of the powers of 10.

   B. Multiply the first factors, then subtract the exponents of the powers of 10.

   C. Add the first factors, then multiply the exponents of the powers of 10.

   D. Add the first factors, then add the exponents of the powers of 10.

   b. Find the product of $(8.1 \times 10^{-5})(6 \times 10^{-5})$.

4. Simplify the expression $(7 \times 10^{-6})(7 \times 10^{-6})$. Write the answer in scientific notation.

5. A certain star is 4.3×10^2 light years from the Earth. One light year is about 5.9×10^{12} miles. How far from the earth (in miles) is the star?

6. Divide $\frac{7.2 \times 10^{-8}}{3 \times 10^{-2}}$. Express your answer in scientific notation.

7. **Estimation** You are given the following expression and asked to find the sum.

   $$3.4 \times 10^4 + 2.58 \times 10^5$$

   a. Round each decimal to the nearest integer. Use these rounded numbers to estimate the sum.

   A. 3×10^4

   B. 6×10^5

   C. 3×10^5

   D. 6×10^4

   b. Find the sum. Write your answer in scientific notation.

8. In one year, the total amount of garbage generated in a certain country was 6.958×10^{10} pounds. In the same year, the country's population was 4.57×10^6 people. Determine the pounds of garbage produced per person in that country in one year.

9. **Think About the Process**

   a. Find the quotient of the first factors of $\frac{2.2 \times 10^5}{4.4 \times 10^{-3}}$. What do you notice?

   A. The quotient of the first factors is greater than 1 but less than 10.

   B. The quotient of the first factors is greater than 10.

   C. The quotient of the first factors is less than 1.

   b. Find $\frac{2.2 \times 10^5}{4.4 \times 10^{-3}}$.

   c. How does this affect the exponent of the quotient?

10. **Writing** Subtract $2.4 \times 10^5 - 5 \times 10^4$. Describe the process of rewriting the numbers in this problem with the same power of 10.

11. a. **Reasoning** Subtract $3.95 \times 10^{-2} - 3.36 \times 10^{-2}$ and write your answer in scientific notation.

    b. Can you write the result using different exponents? Explain.

12. On a certain planet, Continent X has area 6.23×10^6 square miles and Continent Y has area 6.36×10^6 square miles. Which continent is larger? By how many square miles is its area greater?

    A. The area of Continent X is ▇ square miles greater than the area of Continent Y.

    B. The area of Continent Y is ▇ square miles greater than the area of Continent X.

13. **Error Analysis** Your friend says that the product of 4.8×10^8 and 2×10^{-3} is 9.6×10^{-5}.

 a. What is the correct product?

 b. What mistake did your friend likely make?

   A. Your friend subtracted the exponents instead of adding.

   B. Your friend added the numbers instead of multiplying.

   C. Your friend incorrectly calculated the exponent of the product.

   D. Your friend multiplied the exponents instead of adding.

14. **Grocery Shopping** A research study reports than an average person purchases 180 granola bars per year. If there are 280 million people in the country, how many granola bars are purchased by the whole country in one year?

15. **Open-Ended** Total consumption of fruit juice in a particular country in 2006 was about 2.28 billion gallons. The population of that country in 2006 was 300 million.

 a. What was the average number of gallons of fruit juice consumed per person in the country in 2006?

 b. Using the per person amount from this problem, about how many gallons would your class consume?

16. Find the sum of $4.87 \times 10^6 + 3.52 \times 10^6 + 3.61 \times 10^6$.

17. **Estimation** The mass of Planet X is 6.486×10^{25} kg. The mass of Planet Y is 5.063×10^{25} kg.

 a. Round the first factor of each mass to the nearest integer. Use scientific notation.

 b. Estimate the sum of the masses.

   A. 1.1×10^{25} kg

   B. 11×10^{26} kg

   C. 1.1×10^{26} kg

 c. Find the combined mass of the planets.

18. **Challenge** The mass of one oxygen molecule is 5.3×10^{-23} grams.

 a. Find the mass of 30,000 molecules of oxygen in grams.

 b. What is the mass of 30,000 molecules of oxygen in kilograms? Express your answers in scientific notation.

19. **Challenge** According to a survey, there are approximately 179.3 million pet birds, dogs, and cats in a particular country. The same survey reports there are about 50.1 million pet dogs in the country. What percent of the pet birds, dogs, and cats in the country are dogs?

CCSS: 8.EE.A.4, Also 8.EE.A.1 and 8.EE.A.3

Part 1

Example Converting Units in Scientific Notation

Polaris, also called the North Star, is commonly used for navigation due to its alignment with the North Pole. It is approximately 2.53×10^{15} miles from Earth. Express this distance in scientific notation using an appropriate unit from the given list. Explain your choice of units.

$$1 \text{ AU} = 9.3 \times 10^7 \text{ mi}$$

$$1 \text{ light-year} = 63{,}241.1 \text{ AU}$$

$$1 \text{ mile} = 1{,}760 \text{ yards}$$

Solution

Distance in Astronomical Units (AU)

$$2.53 \times 10^{15} \text{ mi} \times \frac{1 \text{ AU}}{9.3 \times 10^7 \text{ mi}} = \frac{2.53 \times 10^{15}}{9.3 \times 10^7} \text{ AU}$$

> To calculate distance in AU set up the product so that the unit mi cancels.

$$2.53 \times 10^{15} \text{ mi} \times \frac{1 \text{ AU}}{9.3 \times 10^7 \text{ mi}} = \frac{2.53 \times 10^{15}}{9.3 \times 10^7} \text{ AU}$$

> To divide powers of ten, subtract the exponents.

$$= \frac{2.53}{9.3} \times 10^{(15-7)} \text{ AU}$$

$$\approx 0.272 \times 10^8 \text{ AU}$$

> Convert to scientific notation.

$$\approx 0.2.72 \times 10^8 \text{ AU}$$

> The decimal point moves 1 place to the right, so subtract 1 from the exponent of 10.

continued on next page >

Solution continued

Polaris is 2.72×10^7 AU away from Earth. AU are appropriate units for large distances in space since an AU covers a much greater distance than a mile. The use of AU is useful for expressing distances within our solar system.

Distance in Light-Years

$$2.72 \times 10^7 \text{ AU} \times \frac{1 \text{ light–year}}{63{,}241.1 \text{ AU}} = 2.72 \times 10^7 \times \frac{1 \text{ light–year}}{6.3{,}241.1}$$

> Convert to scientific notation.

> To calculate distance in light-years set up the product so that the unit AU cancel.

> The decimal point moves 4 places to the left, so the power of ten is 10^4.

$$= \frac{2.72 \times 10^7}{6.324 \times 10^4} \text{ light–years}$$

$$= \frac{2.72}{6.324} \times 10^{(7-4)} \text{ light–years}$$

$$\approx 0.430 \times 10^3 \text{ light–years}$$

> To divide powers of ten, subtract the exponents.

> The decimal point moves 1 place to the right, so subtract 1 from the exponent of 3

$$\approx 0.4.30 \times 10^3 \text{ light–years}$$

> Convert to scientific notation.

Polaris is about 4.30×10^2, or 430 light-years away from Earth. Light-years are also appropriate units for large distances in space since light-years cover greater distances than miles or AU. The use of light-years would be quite useful for expressing distances beyond our solar system.

Distance in Yards

It does not make sense to express the distance to Polaris in yards. The distances in space are so large that a small unit, such as a yard, seems trivial.

Part 2

Example Solving for Exponents in Scientific Notation Equations

What is the value of n?

$$1.2 \times 10^7 = (3 \times 10^8)(4 \times 10^n)$$

Solution

Think	**Write**
Rewrite the product using the commutative and associative properties.	$1.2 \times 10^7 = (3 \times 10^8)(4 \times 10^n)$ $= (3 \cdot 4) \times (10^8 \cdot 10^n)$
When you multiply powers with the same base, you add the exponents.	$= 12 \times 10^{(8 + n)}$
Write 12 in scientific notation.	$= (1.2 \times 10^1) \times 10^{(8 + n)}$
When you multiply powers with the same base, you add the exponents.	$= 1.2 \times 10^{(8 + n + 1)}$ $= 1.2 \times 10^{(9 + n)}$
Set the given expression equal to the simplified expression.	$1.2 \times 10^7 = 1.2 \times 10^{(9 + n)}$
Divide each side by 1.2.	$\dfrac{1.2 \times 10^7}{1.2} = \dfrac{1.2 \times 10^{(9 + n)}}{1.2}$
If equal powers have the same base, then their exponents must be equal.	$10^7 = 10^{(9 + n)}$ $7 = 9 + n$
Subtract 9 from each side to solve for n.	$7 - 9 = 9 + n - 9$ $-2 = n$ The value of n is -2.

1. A star is 3.822×10^{16} miles from Earth. Express this distance in scientific notation using an appropriate unit from the given list. What is the most appropriate unit for expressing the distance from Earth? How far from Earth is the star?

1 light-year ≈ 5.88×10^{12} miles
1 mile = 5,280 feet
1 foot = 12 inches

A. The most appropriate unit is the inch. The star is ■ inches from Earth.

B. The most appropriate unit is the foot. The star is ■ feet from Earth.

C. The most appropriate unit is the light-year. The star is ■ light-years from Earth.

D. The most appropriate unit is the mile. The distance in miles is given.

2. What is the value of n in the equation $1.9 \times 10^7 = (1 \times 10^5)(1.9 \times 10^n)$?

3. What is the value of n?
$4.2 \times 10^n = (3 \times 10^5)(1.4 \times 10^7)$

4. A whale has a mass of 1.3×10^5 kilograms. Express the mass in scientific notation using an appropriate unit from the given list.

1 metric ton = 1×10^3 kilograms
1 kilogram ≈ 2.2 pounds
1 kilogram = 1×10^4 decigrams

What is the most appropriate unit for expressing the mass? What is the mass of the whale?

A. The most appropriate unit is the metric ton. The mass of the whale is ■ metric tons.

B. The most appropriate unit is the decigram. The mass of the whale is ■ decigrams.

C. The most appropriate unit is the pound. The mass of the whale is ■ pounds.

D. The most appropriate unit is the kilogram. The mass of the whale in kilograms is given.

5. Two stars are 9.996×10^{16} miles apart. Express this distance in scientific notation using an appropriate unit from the given list. What is the most appropriate unit for expressing the distance between the two stars? How far apart are the two stars?

1 mile ≈ 1,609 meters
1 kilometer = 1,000 meters
1 light-year ≈ 5.88×10^{12} miles

A. The most appropriate unit is the meter. The stars are ■ meters apart.

B. The most appropriate unit is the kilometer. The stars are ■ kilometers apart.

C. The most appropriate unit is the light-year. The stars are ■ light-years apart.

D. The most appropriate unit is the mile. The distance in miles is given.

6. The depth of the deepest part of a body of water is 190,080 inches. Express this depth in scientific notation using an appropriate unit from the given list. What is the most appropriate unit for expressing the depth? What is the depth?

1 centimeter = 10 millimeters
1 meter = 100 centimeters
1 inch = 2.54 centimeters

See your complete lesson at MyMathUniverse.com

7. For the equation
$4.2 \times 10^6 = (6 \times 10^n)(7 \times 10^3)$, your friend incorrectly says the value of n is 3.

  a. What is the correct value of n?

  b. What was your friend's likely error?

   A. He solved the equation
   $6 \div n = 3$.

   B. He solved the equation $3n = 6$.

   C. He solved the equation
   $n + 3 - 1 = 6$.

   D. He solved the equation
   $n + 3 = 6$.

8. a. What is the value of n in the equation
$1.5 \times 10^{12} = (5 \times 10^5)(3 \times 10^n)$?

  b. Explain why the exponent on the left side of the equation is not equal to the sum of the exponents on the right side.

9. What is the value of n in the equation
$3.2 \times 10^n = (-4 \times 10^{14})(8 \times 10^{-8})$?

10. Think About the Process The speed of sound is about 13,504 inches per second. Use the conversion
1 meter $\approx$ 39.37 inches.

  a. Express the speed of sound using scientific notation to complete the following sentence.

   The speed of sound is about ■ meters per second, ■ centimeters per second, and ■ millimeters per second.

  b. What is the most appropriate way to express the speed of sound?

   A. Millimeters per second

   B. Centimeters per second

   C. Meters per second

  c. How many minutes does it take to hear a sound 12,348 meters, 1,234,800 centimeters, and 12,348,000 millimeters away?

11. Challenge Lake A has volume
1.35×10^2 mi^3. Lake B has volume
1.5288×10^{13} ft^3. These volumes could also be expressed in cubic kilometers, liters, or cubic meters using conversions from the list.

1 mi$^3 \approx 4.17$ km^3
1 mi$^3 \approx 1.47 \times 10^{11}$ ft^3
1 km$^3 = 1 \times 10^{12}$ L
1 km$^3 = 1 \times 10^9$ m^3

  a. Express the volume of each lake using scientific notation and the most appropriate metric unit.

   A. The most appropriate unit is the liter. Lake A has the volume ■ L. Lake B has volume ■ L.

   B. The most appropriate unit is the cubic kilometer. Lake A has volume ■ km^3. Lake B has volume ■ km^3.

   C. The most appropriate unit is the cubic meter. Lake A has volume ■ m^3. Lake B has volume ■ m^3.

  b. Which lake is larger?

12. Think About the Process You are given the following equation.
$1.8 \times 10^n = (6 \times 10^8)(3 \times 10^6)$

  a. Which equation relates the value of n to the other two exponents?

   A. $6 = n + 8$

   B. $n = 1 + 8 + 6$

   C. $18 = 8 + n - 1$

   D. $n = 8 + 6 - 1$

  b. What is the value of n?

13. Challenge What is the value of n in the equation
$-5.4 \times 10^{-16} = (6 \times 10^n)(-9 \times 10^{-6})$?

Graphing Proportional Relationships

CCSS: 8.EE.B.5

Part 1

Example Graphing Proportional Relationships

A video game store has a frequent shopper program. You earn 4 points for every video game you buy. Draw a graph to model this situation.

You need 48 points for a free game. How many video games do you need to buy to have enough points for a free game?

Solution ·

For every game you buy, you earn 4 points. Since you can only buy entire games, it only makes sense to plot points with *x*-coordinates that are whole numbers. For each point on the graph, the *y*-coordinate should be four times the *x*-coordinate.

Since you need 48 points for a free game, look for a point on the graph until you reach a *y*-coordinate of 48.

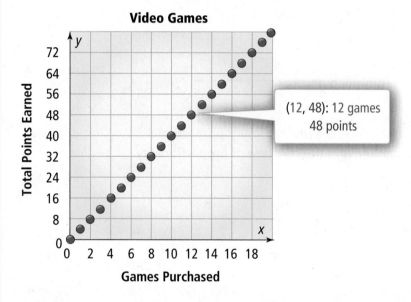

You need to buy 12 games to have enough points for a free game.

Key Concept

Proportional Relationships

Proportional relationships can be shown using tables, graphs, and equations. Each model below shows a proportional relationship where y is twice x.

Table A table shows a proportional relationship when one quantity is a constant multiple of the other quantity.

x	y
0	0
1	2
2	4
3	6

Each y-value is twice the x-value.

Graph A graph shows points with a proportional relationship if a line that passes through the origin can be drawn through the points. For each point, the y-coordinate is a constant multiple of the x-coordinate.

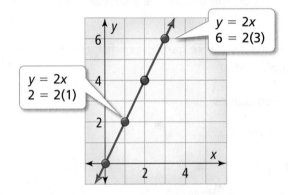

$y = 2x$
$6 = 2(3)$

$y = 2x$
$2 = 2(1)$

Equation Equations in the form $y = mx$ represent proportional relationships. In the equation, m is the constant of proportionality, or the constant multiple $\frac{y}{x}$.

The constant of proportionality is 2.

The equation of the line is $y = 2x$.

Part 2

Example Graphing Proportional Relationships in Quadrant I

A salesperson earns a 10% commission on sales of energy efficient appliances. Draw a graph to model this situation. Is the amount of the commission proportional to the amount of sales? How do you know?

Solution

Step 1 Make a table of values.

Commission Earned

Sales ($)	Commission ($)
100	10
200	20
300	30
400	40

> The commission amount is 10% or 0.1, of the sales amount.

Step 2 Draw the graph.

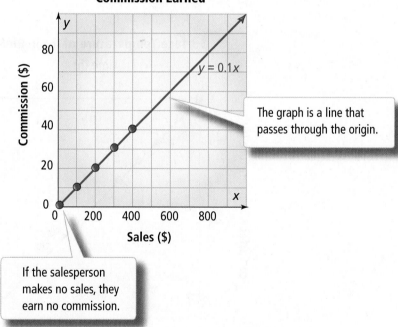

Commission Earned

> The graph is a line that passes through the origin.

> If the salesperson makes no sales, they earn no commission.

The graph shows a proportional relationship between the amount of the sales and the amount of the commission. The graph is a line that passes through the origin.

The graph shows for every $100 of sales, the salesperson earns $10 in commission, or for every $10 of sales, the salesperson earns $1 in commission.

Part 3

Example Graphing Proportional Relationships in Quadrant IV

Ice forms at 0°C. The surface temperature of the ice on an ice rink decreases 0.5°C every hour. Draw a graph to model this situation. Start when the surface temperature of the ice is 0°C.

Is the surface temperature of the ice proportional to time? How do you know?

Solution

Step 1 Make a table of values.

Time (h)	Temperature (°C)
1	− 0.5
2	−1
3	−1.5
4	−2

The temperature decreases by 0.5°C every hour, starting from 0°C at time 0.

Step 2 Draw the graph.

The surface temperature is 0°C at time 0.

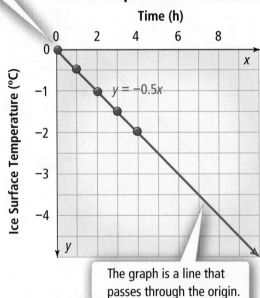

Surface Temperature of Ice in Rink

$y = -0.5x$

The graph is a line that passes through the origin.

The graph shows a proportional relationship between time and the temperature of the ice. The graph is a line that passes through the origin.

The graph shows for each hour that passes, the ice gets 0.5°C colder.

1. An electronics store has a frequent shopper program. The buyer earns 4 points for every movie purchased. Draw a graph which models this situation.

2. An airline company rewards the customers who fly often with a frequent flyer program. The airline will give their customers 550 points for every 2 flights that they take. Draw a graph which models this situation.

3. A class is having a bake sale. The class earns 12 cents for each cookie sold.

   a. Draw a graph which models this situation.

   b. How many cookies does the class need to sell to earn 36 cents?

4. **Think About the Process** A dry cleaning company charges $14 to clean and press 2 jackets.

   a. Draw a graph of the relation.

   b. How can you find the cost to clean and press 4 jackets using a graph?

   A. Locate 4 on the *y*-axis then move to the right to find the corresponding *x*-value.

   B. Locate 4 on the *x*-axis then move down to find the corresponding *y*-value.

   C. Locate 4 on the *x*-axis then move up to find the corresponding *y*-value.

   D. Locate 4 on the *y*-axis then move to the left to find the corresponding *x*-value.

   c. Find the cost to clean and press 4 jackets.

5. A clothing store has an 18% sales tax on all items purchased.

   a. Draw a graph which models this situation.

   b. Is the amount of taxes proportional to the purchase?

6. A salesperson earns a commission that is a percent of the sales. The graph shows the proportional relationship between sales and commission. What percent commission does the salesperson earn?

Commission per Sales

Commission Earned / *Sales (in Thousands)*

7. A submarine dives at 130 feet per minute. Draw a graph which models this situation. Start when the submarine is at sea level (0 feet).

8. A 12-inch candle burns at a rate of 1 inch per hour.

   a. Draw a graph which models this situation.

   b. How long will the candle last?

9. **Error Analysis** A tree grows 5 inches each year. Angela is asked to find when the tree will be $1\frac{2}{3}$ feet tall. Angela incorrectly says 20 years.

   a. Draw a graph which models the situation.

   b. How many years will it take for the tree to be $1\frac{2}{3}$ feet tall?

   c. Which mistake might Angela have made?

   A. Angela did not convert the height of the tree correctly.

   B. Angela gave the height of the tree in inches not the number of years.

   C. Angela gave the height of the tree in feet not the number of years.

   D. Angela drew a graph with a negative relationship instead of a positive relationship.

See your complete lesson at MyMathUniverse.com

10. Mental Math Leonid is saving for a video game. Leonid earns $350 a week but he saves $330 a week for other expenses.

   a. Draw a graph which models the situation.

   b. If the video game costs $60, how many weeks will it take before Leonid can afford the video game?

11. Writing The price of a certain clothing item in the year 2000 was $7.25. Due to inflation the price increased 9% each year.

   a. Draw a graph which represents the price of the item since 2000.

   b. Is the relationship proportional? If the relationship is proportional what would make the relationship not proportional? If the relationship is not proportional what would make the relationship proportional?

12. The Water Cycle Suppose that for a certain lake the same percent of water that evaporates from it is replaced every time it rains. The graph models the proportional relationship between water evaporated and rainfall. What percent of water lost is replaced when it rains?

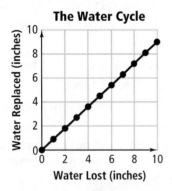

The Water Cycle

13. Reasoning Jimmy pays $3.69 for every gallon of gas he puts in his car. Draw a graph which models the change in the amount of money Jimmy has.

14. As an incentive to drive carefully, an insurance company lowers the cost of a driver's insurance by $16 a month every 2 years that the driver does not have an accident or get a speeding ticket.

   a. Draw a graph that models the change in the amount of insurance.

   b. If the driver is currently paying $86 a month, how many years will it be before the driver is paying $54 a month?

15. Think About the Process At the speed of 50 miles per hour (mph), a car's fuel efficiency is 45 miles per gallon (mpg) of gasoline. For every mile per hour over 50, the car loses 2% of its fuel efficiency.

   a. Draw a graph of the situation.

   b. What is one way to tell if the graph represents a proportional relationship?

      A. The graph will pass through the origin.

      B. The graph will be a line.

      C. The graph will be a curve not a line.

      D. The graph will be a line that passes through the origin.

   c. Is the change in the car's fuel efficiency proportional to the car's speed?

16. Challenge Every week a rowing team improves their time for a 2,000-m course by 1.1 seconds.

   a. Draw a graph which models the change in the team's time.

   b. How many seconds will the team improve after 5 weeks? How long will it take the team to finish the course after 5 weeks if it currently takes the team 12 minutes?

CCSS: 6.NS.A.1

Part 1

Example Writing Linear Equations from Graphs

The graph shows the distance d a car travels in time t at a constant speed r.

  a. What is the constant speed of the car?
  b. How far will the car travel in 2 h?
  c. How long will it take the car to travel 120 mi?
  d. Write an equation in $d = rt$ form to model the situation shown.

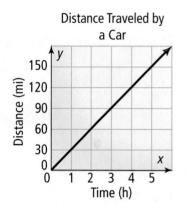

Distance Traveled by a Car

Solution

  a. The car is traveling at a constant speed r of 30 mi/h.
  b. The car will travel 60 mi in 2 h.
  c. It will take 4 h to travel 120 mi.
  d. The equation $d = 30t$ models this situation.

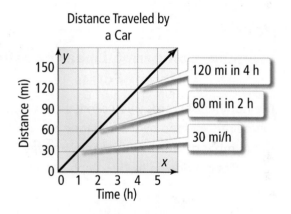

Distance Traveled by a Car

120 mi in 4 h
60 mi in 2 h
30 mi/h

Key Concept

Recall that the graph of a proportional relationship is a line that passes through the origin. An equation that models a proportional relationship can be written in the form $y = mx$. The equation $y = mx$ shows y is always a constant multiple m of x.

An equation in the form $y = mx$ is an example of a linear equation.

An equation is a **linear equation** if the graph of all of its solutions is a line.

Part 2

Example **Writing Linear Equations from Verbal Descriptions**

A restaurant is running a lunch special. All prices are $\frac{1}{3}$ off. Write an equation that models the lunch price y based on the original price x.

Solution ·

The lunch special price y is $\frac{1}{3}$ off the original price x.

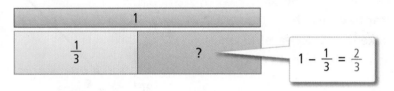

The lunch price y is $\frac{2}{3}$ the original price x. This situation can be modeled by the equation $y = \frac{2}{3}x$.

Part 3

Example **Comparing Linear Equations in Different Forms**

The number of words y you can type in x minutes can be represented by the equation $y = 55x$. The number of words your friend can type in x minutes is modeled by the graph. Which of you can type faster?

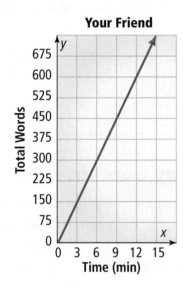

Solution ·

The equation and the graph each show a proportional relationship between the number of words and time. Compare the constants of proportionality.

You: The equation $y = 55x$ represents the number of words y you can type in x minutes. The equation shows a constant of proportionality of 55 words per minute.

continued on next page >

Part 3

Solution continued

Your friend:

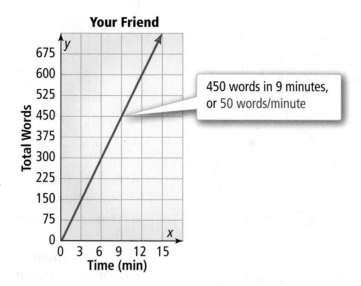

Your Friend

450 words in 9 minutes, or 50 words/minute

The graph shows a constant of proportionality of 50 words per minute.

You can type 55 words per minute. Your friend can type 50 words per minute. You can type faster.

1. The graph shows a proportional relationship between a family's distance from home, *y*, and the time they spend driving, *x*. Write an equation for the relationship shown by the graph.

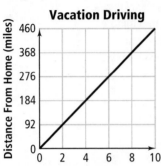

Vacation Driving

2. Michael is having a yard sale. For each item, he is asking for nine-tenths of the price for which he bought the item. Write an equation for the situation, where *y* is the price he is asking and *x* is the original price of the item.

3. The number of miles Catalina walks is represented by the equation $y = 7x$, where *x* is the number of hours spent walking and *y* is the number of miles walked. The number of miles Jake walks in *x* hours is modeled by the equation $y = 5x$. Who walks faster?

4. **Writing** The graph shows a proportional relationship between the variables *y* and *x*.

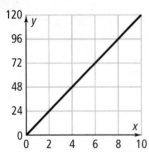

   a. Write an equation to model the relationship.

   b. Explain how you know there is a proportional relationship if you are given either an equation or a graph.

5. **Think About the Process** The graph shows a proportional relationship between *y* and *x*.

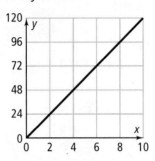

   a. Find the value of the constant of proportionality *m*.

   b. Write an equation that models the line.

6. **Money** The graph shows a proportional relationship between a person's total savings in dollars and the number of weeks they have been saving. Write an equation that models the savings.

Money

7. Write an equation for the proportional relationship below. *y* is one-eleventh of *x*.

8. The middle school is going to have a walkathon. Elena raises $225 for walking 9 laps. Bentley raises $120 for walking 5 laps. Let *y* represent the number of dollars raised and *x* the number of laps walked. Who raises more money per lap?

9. Error Analysis Students have to compare the height of two plants to see which plant grows more per day. The table shows the height of plant 1, in cm, over 5 days. The graph shows the height of plant 2, in cm, over 10 days. Guillermo incorrectly says that since plant 1 grows 6 cm per day and plant 2 grows 4 cm per day, plant 1 grows more per day.

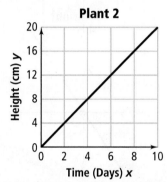

Plant 2

Plant 1				
Days	2	3	4	5
Height (cm)	6	9	12	15

a. Which plant grows more per day?

b. What error might Guillermo have made?

10. Multiple Representations Erin goes to the mall to buy jeans. The equation $y = 24x$ models the total cost, y, of x pairs of jeans at store Z. The table shows the relationship between the total cost and the number of pairs of jeans at store V.

Store V				
Pairs of Jeans	2	3	4	5
Total Cost ($)	36	54	72	90

a. Which store charges more per pair of jeans?

b. Show each of the relationships two other ways.

11. Think About the Process The tables show the relationship between the number of pages read, y, and the number of hours spent reading, x.

Parker				
Hours	1	3	5	7
Pages Read	42	126	210	294

Avery				
Hours	2	4	6	8
Pages Read	78	156	234	312

a. Which word expression below represents the constant of proportionality?

A. $\dfrac{\text{Pages Read}}{\text{Hours}}$

B. Pages Read $\times$ Hours

C. $\dfrac{\text{Hours}}{\text{Pages Read}}$

D. Pages Read $-$ Hours

b. Find the constant of proportionality for each person.

c. Which person reads more pages per hour?

12. Challenge A movie theater sends out a coupon for 70% off the price of a ticket.

a. Write an equation for the situation, where y is the price of the ticket with the coupon, and x is the original price of the ticket. Use integers or decimals for any numbers in the expression.

b. Draw a graph of the equation and explain why the line should only be in the first quadrant.

Vocabulary
slope, slope of a line

CCSS: 8.EE.B.5

Part 1

Intro

Slope describes the steepness of lines in the coordinate plane. The **slope of a line** is the ratio of the vertical change to the horizontal change.

$$\text{slope} = \frac{\text{vertical change}}{\text{horizontal change}} \begin{matrix} \longleftarrow \text{rise} \\ \longleftarrow \text{run} \end{matrix}$$

$$= \frac{3}{2}$$

The slope of the line is $\frac{3}{2}$.

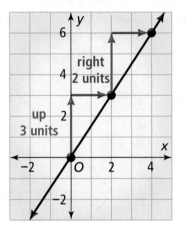

Example Identifying Slopes from Graphs

Find the slope of each line.

a.

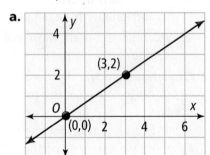

b.

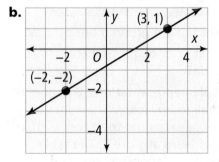

c.

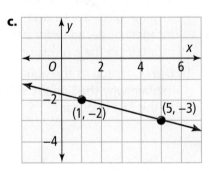

continued on next page >

Solution

a. The graph shows a rise of 2 and a run of 3.

As the *x*-coordinates increase by 3, the *y*-coordinates increase by 2.

The slope of the line is $\frac{2}{3}$.

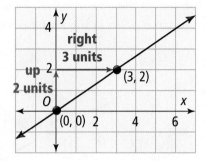

b. The graph shows a rise of 3 and a run of 5.

As the *x*-coordinates increase by 5, the *y*-coordinates increase by 3.

The slope of the line is $\frac{3}{5}$.

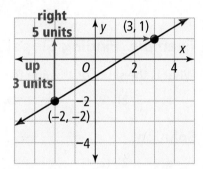

c. The graph shows a rise of −1 and a run of 4.

As the *x*-coordinates increase by 4, the *y*-coordinates decrease by 1.

The slope of the line is $-\frac{1}{4}$.

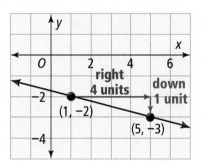

Part 2

Intro

You can find the slope of the line by subtracting the coordinates of any two points on the line. The first *y*-coordinate you use for the rise must belong to the same point as the first *x*-coordinate you use for the run.

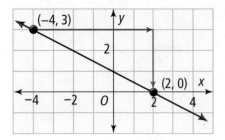

$$\text{slope} = \frac{\text{change in } y\text{–coordinates}}{\text{change in } x\text{–coordinates}}$$

$$= \frac{3 - 0}{-4 - 2}$$

$$= \frac{3}{-6}, \text{ or } -\frac{1}{2}$$

Example Finding Slopes from Pairs of Points

What is the slope of the line that passes through each pair of points?

   a. $(-3, 2)$, $(2, 4)$ **b.** $(6, 1)$, $(8, -5)$ **c.** $(-2, 4)$, $(1, 4)$

Solution ···

a. $(-3, 2)$, $(2, 4)$

$$\text{slope} = \frac{\text{change in } y\text{–coordinates}}{\text{change in } x\text{–coordinates}}$$

$$= \frac{2 - 4}{-3 - 2}$$

$$= \frac{-2}{-5}$$

$$= \frac{2}{5}$$

The slope of the line is $\frac{2}{5}$.

b. $(6, 1)$, $(8, -5)$

$$\text{slope} = \frac{\text{change in } y\text{–coordinates}}{\text{change in } x\text{–coordinates}}$$

$$= \frac{-5 - 1}{8 - 6}$$

$$= \frac{-6}{2}$$

$$= -3$$

The slope of the line is -3.

continued on next page >

Part 2

Solution continued

c. $(-2, 4), (1, 4)$

$$\text{slope} = \frac{\text{change in } y\text{–coordinates}}{\text{change in } x\text{–coordinates}}$$

$$= \frac{4 - 4}{-2 - 1}$$

$$= \frac{0}{-3}$$

$$= 0$$

The slope of the line is 0.

Check

You can also check the slope $\frac{2}{5}$ by using a graph.

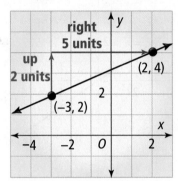

The graph shows a rise of 2 and a run of 5.

The slope of the line is $\frac{2}{5}$. ✔

You can use this method to check the other slopes as well.

Key Concept

$$\text{slope} = \frac{\text{change in } y\text{-coordinates}}{\text{change in } x\text{-coordinates}} \xleftarrow{\text{rise}} \xleftarrow{\text{run}}$$

A line with positive slope slants upward from left to right.

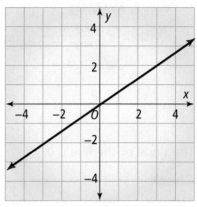

A line with negative slope slants downward from left to right.

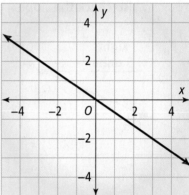

A line with a slope of 0 is horizontal.

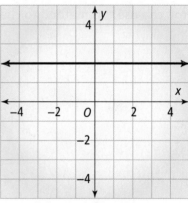

A line with an undefined slope is vertical.

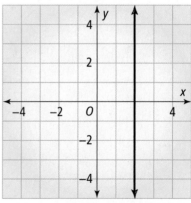

See your complete lesson at MyMathUniverse.com

Part 3

Example Finding Slopes from Rise and Run

The building code for a ramp recommends the ramp should rise no more than 1 in. for every 12 in. of length. Does the ramp shown meet the building code? How do you know?

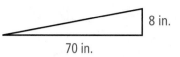

8 in.
70 in.

Solution ·

Know	**Need**	**Plan**
• The ramp is 8 in. high and 70 in. long. • The ramp should rise no more than 1 in. high for every 12 in. in length.	Determine if the ramp meets the building code.	• Find the $\frac{\text{rise}}{\text{run}}$ ratio for the ramp. • Find the $\frac{\text{rise}}{\text{run}}$ ratio recommended by the building code. • Compare the ratios.

Step 1 Find the $\frac{\text{rise}}{\text{run}}$ ratio for the ramp.

The ramp has a rise of 8 in. and a run of 70 in.

$$\frac{\text{rise}}{\text{run}} = \frac{8 \text{ in.}}{70 \text{ in.}}$$
$$= \frac{4}{35}$$

Step 2 Find the $\frac{\text{rise}}{\text{run}}$ ratio recommended by the building code.

According to the building code, the ramp should have a $\frac{\text{rise}}{\text{run}}$ ratio of no more than $\frac{1 \text{ in.}}{12 \text{ in.}}$, or $\frac{1}{12}$.

Step 3 Compare the ratios.

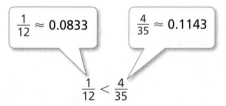

$\frac{1}{12} \approx 0.0833$ $\frac{4}{35} \approx 0.1143$

$$\frac{1}{12} < \frac{4}{35}$$

The $\frac{\text{rise}}{\text{run}}$ ratio of the ramp is greater than the recommended $\frac{\text{rise}}{\text{run}}$ ratio.

The ramp does *not* meet the building code.

1. Think About the Process

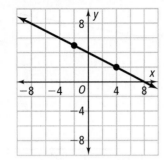

a. Write the expression for the slope of a line using any two points.

   A. $\dfrac{\text{horizontal change}}{\text{vertical change}}$

   B. $\dfrac{\text{vertical change}}{\text{horizontal change}}$

   C. vertical change × horizontal change

   D. vertical change − horizontal change

b. Find the slope of the line to the right.

2. Find the slope of the line.

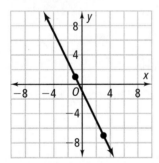

3. Think About the Process

  a. Find the expression that will correctly find the slope of a line that goes through the points (−5, 3) and (5, 7).

   A. $\dfrac{3 - 7}{5 - (-5)}$

   B. $\dfrac{7 - 3}{-5 - 5}$

   C. $\dfrac{3 - (-5)}{7 - 5}$

   D. $\dfrac{7 - 3}{5 - (-5)}$

  b. Find the slope of the line.

4. Find the slope of the line through the points (−2, 3) and (1, −3).

5. Line 1 passes through the points (−2, −7) and (3, 3). Line 2 passes through the points (5, 1) and (9, 1).

  a. Find the slope of each line.

  b. Which line has the greater slope?

6. A contractor is roofing a house. The contractor considers a roof to be steep when the roof rises 7 in. or more for every 12 in. it runs. The following graph is a model of how steep the roof is. Does the contractor believe the roof is steep? What is the slope of the roof?

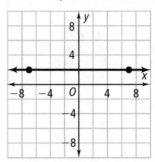

  a. No, the contractor does not believe the roof is steep because the slope of the roof is ■.

  b. Yes, the contractor believes the roof is steep because the slope of the roof is ■.

7. The science teacher is showing students a model rocket. The teacher says for the rocket to be shot correctly the $\frac{\text{rise}}{\text{run}}$ should be from $\frac{11 \text{ in.}}{4 \text{ in.}}$ up to straight up (vertical) before the launch. The graph shows the slope of the rocket before the launch.

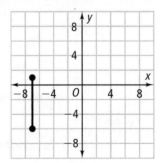

  a. Find the slope at which the rocket is being shot.

  b. Will the rocket be shot correctly?

8. Flying The graph represents an airplane descending. The *y*-axis represents the number of feet the plane has descended, and the *x*-axis represents elapsed time in minutes. Each *y* unit represents 1,000 ft. Find the slope of the line.

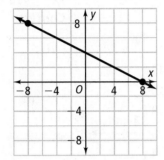

9. a. Writing What is the slope of the line which goes through the points $(-2, -5)$ and $(1, 7)$?

  b. Explain how the formula for the slope of a line relates to the graph.

10. a. Mental Math Using the slope formula, find the slope of the line through the points $(0, 0)$ and $(2, 4)$.

  b. Explain how you can use mental math to find the slope of the line.

11. Error Analysis A problem asks the students to find the slope of the line that passes through the points $(-5, 13)$, and $(5, -7)$. Joy says that the slope of the line is $-\frac{1}{2}$.

  a. Find the slope of the line.

  b. What error might Joy have made?

  A. Joy chose the wrong first *y*-coordinate after selecting the first *x*-coordinate.

  B. Joy set the formula up as $\frac{\text{change in } x\text{–coordinates}}{\text{change in } y\text{–coordinates}}$.

  C. Joy subtracted *x*-coordinates from *y*-coordinates.

  D. Joy chose the wrong first *x*-coordinate after selecting the first *y*-coordinate.

12. a. Reasoning Find the slope of each line of the graphs.

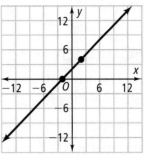

Line 1

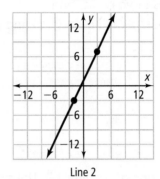

Line 2

  b. Which graph has the greater slope?

  c. Explain how you know which graph has the greater slope without doing any calculations.

13. a. Use the slope formula to find the slope of the line passing through the points $(-2, 3)$ and $(6, -1)$. Write an integer or an improper fraction.

  b. Find two or more points that the line passes through.

14. Challenge One line, Line 1, passes through the points $(-1, 3)$ and $(-1, 5)$. Another line, Line 2, passes through the points $(4, 14)$ and $(7, 23)$. Which line has undefined slope? Find the slope of the other line.

15. Challenge A factory has a conveyor belt, Conveyor 1, which brings the supplies into the factory. The conveyor belt rises 25 ft for every 5 ft it runs. The factory has another conveyor belt, Conveyor 2, which sends the products out of the factory. This conveyor belt descends 12 ft for every 3 ft it runs.

  a. Find the slope of each conveyor belt.

  b. Which is the steeper conveyor belt?

See your complete lesson at MyMathUniverse.com

5-4 | Unit Rates and Slope

Key Concept

A rate is a ratio that describes how one quantity changes as the other quantity changes.

You can find a unit rate from a graph in the same way that you find slope.

Choose two points on the graph to find the slope. Use the points (0, 2) and (3, 6).

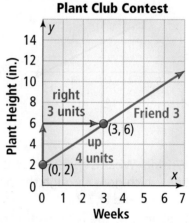

Plant Club Contest

$$\text{slope} = \frac{\text{change in } y\text{-coordinates}}{\text{change in } x\text{-coordinates}}$$

$$= \frac{6 - 2}{3 - 0}$$

$$= \frac{4}{3}$$

The slope of the line is $\frac{4}{3}$. The slope can be interpreted as a rate or a unit rate.

The plant grew at a rate of $\frac{4 \text{ in.}}{3 \text{ weeks}}$ or $\frac{4}{3}$ in. per week.

Part 1

Example Finding Unit Rates from Graphs

The graph shows the amount of milk used to make a particular cheddar cheese. How many ounces of cheese can you make per gallon of milk?

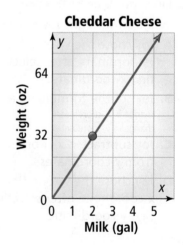

Cheddar Cheese

continued on next page >

Part 1

Example continued

Solution ·

The amount of cheese you can make depends on the amount of milk you have. The unit rate of ounces of cheese per gallon of milk is equivalent to the slope of the line.

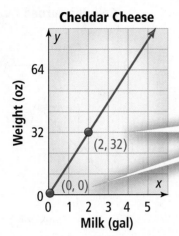

Cheddar Cheese

Find the slope of the line using the points (0, 0) and (2, 32).

Find the slope using the points (0, 0) and (2, 32).

$$\text{slope} = \frac{\text{change in } y\text{-coordinates}}{\text{change in } x\text{-coordinates}}$$

$$= \frac{32 - 0}{2 - 0}$$

$$= \frac{32}{2}$$

$$= 16$$

The graph has a slope of 16. The slope represents $\frac{16 \text{ oz cheddar cheese}}{1 \text{ gal milk}}$, or 16 oz of cheddar cheese per gallon of milk.

You can make 16 oz of cheese per gallon of milk.

Part 2

Example Relating Unit Rates and Slopes of Graphs

Your neighbor burns 88 Calories in 8 min cross-country skiing. There is a proportional relationship between Calories burned and time.

a. What is the unit rate of Calories per min?

b. Use the unit rate to draw a graph that models this situation, where the horizontal axis shows time and the vertical axis shows the total Calories burned. What is the slope of the line?

continued on next page >

Part 2

Example continued

Solution ·

a. Your neighbor burns 88 Calorie in 8 min. The unit rate is

$\dfrac{88 \text{ Calories}}{8 \text{ min}} = \dfrac{11 \text{ Calories}}{1 \text{ min}}$, or 11 Calories per minute.

b. Since there is a proportional relationship between Calories burned and time, the graph is a line that passes through the origin. The line should show a unit rate of 11 Calories per minute. The unit rate is equivalent to the slope of the line.

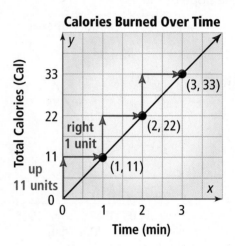

Calories Burned Over Time

You can use the unit rate to draw the graph. Start at the origin and then use the unit rate to find another point on the line.

The slope of the line is 11.

Part 3

Example Using Slopes as Unit Rates to Solve Problems

Your friend borrows $200 from her parents. The graph shows how much money she owes her parents. How much is she repaying her parents per week? How long will it take your friend to repay her loan?

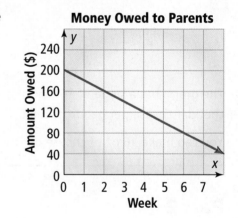

Money Owed to Parents

continued on next page >

Example continued

Solution ·

Choose two points on the graph to find the slope.

Use the points (0, 200) and (4, 120).

$$\text{slope} = \frac{\text{change in } y\text{-coordinates}}{\text{change in } x\text{-coordinates}}$$

$$= \frac{200 - 120}{0 - 4}$$

$$= \frac{80}{-4}$$

$$= -20$$

The slope of the line is −20.

The slope represents a unit rate of −$20 per week. The y-axis shows the amount owed, so that unit rate is showing the amount owed decreasing by $20 per week.

Your friend is repaying her parents $20 per week.

You friend needs to repay $200.

$$\frac{\$20}{1 \text{ week}} = \frac{\$20}{1 \text{ week}} \cdot \frac{10}{10}$$

$$= \frac{\$200}{10 \text{ weeks}}$$

> Multiply the numerator and denominator by 10 to find an equivalent rate with a numerator of $200, the total amount owed.

It will take your friend 10 weeks to repay her parents.

1. The points (15,21) and (25,35) form a proportional relationship.

  a. Find the slope of the line through the points.

  b. Draw a graph which represents this relationship.

2. Your neighbor burns 117 Calories in 13 minutes cross-country skiing. There is a proportional relationship between Calories burned and time.

  a. Find the unit rate.

  b. Draw a graph which represents the relationship between time and Calories burned.

3. The graph represents an object slowing to a stop. Find two points on the line and use them to find the slope of the line.

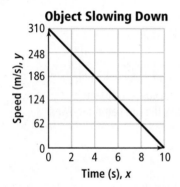

4. **Think About the Process** The graph shows the relationship between the cost in dollars of the taxi ride and the distance in miles the taxi travels.

  a. How can you find the slope of the line?

  b. What is the slope?

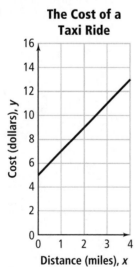

5. **Error Analysis** A question on a test asks students to find the speed at which a car travels. The graph shows a proportional relationship between the distance traveled in miles and time in hours. Anna incorrectly says that the speed of the car is $\frac{1}{64}$ mile per hour.

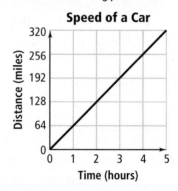

  a. What is the speed of the car?

  b. What error might Anna have made?

6. **Writing** The graph shows a proportional relationship between the number of workers and weekly cost in dollars for a company.

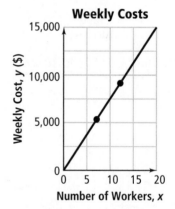

  a. Use the points (7,5250) and (12,9000) to find the weekly cost for the company for each worker.

  b. Describe what a unit rate is used for.

7. **Reasoning** Assume that Car *X* and Car *Y* are both traveling at constant speeds. Car *X* has traveled 186 miles in 3 hours. Car *Y* has traveled 142 miles in 2 hours.

   a. Draw a graph which represents the relationship between distance and time for Car *X*.

   b. Draw a graph which represents the relationship between distance and time for Car *Y*.

   c. Explain your reasoning.

8. The graph shows the number of Calories burned running. How many Calories do you burn per minute?

Calories Burned

9. **Open-Ended** The graph shows a relationship that is not proportional.

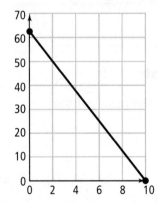

   a. Use the points (0,63) and (10,0) to find the slope.

   b. Describe a situation this graph could model.

10. **Think About the Process** At the beginning of summer, a maintenance crew refills the swimming pool at a city park. The relationship between time and the amount of water in the pool is proportional. After 4 hours, the pool holds 5,200 gallons of water.

   a. How could you graph this relationship?

   b. Draw a graph which represents the relationship between time and the volume of water in the pool.

11. The relationship between the number of gallons of water in a tank and number of hours is proportional. One point on the line modeling the relationship is (2,7200).

   a. Find the slope of the line.

   b. Draw a graph which represents the relationship between time and the volume of water in the tank.

   c. Use the graph to find how long it will take to fill the tank if it holds 72,000 gallons.

12. **Challenge** The relationship between the number of parts a machine can manufacture and time is proportional. Suppose that the machine manufactures 24,900 parts in 3 hours.

   a. Find the unit rate.

   b. Draw a graph which represents the relationship between time and the number of parts made.

   c. How long will it take the machine to make 199,200 parts?

13. **Challenge** These graphs show the relationship between growth and time for two different plants.

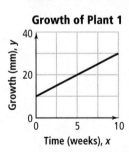 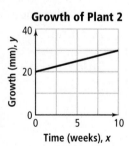

   a. Find the slope of the line for each graph.

   b. Compare the slopes.

CCSS: 8.EE.B.6

Key Concept

The **y-intercept** of a graph is the *y*-value at which the graph crosses the *y*-axis.

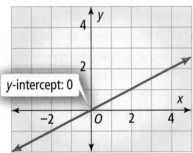

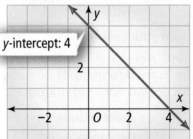

Part 1

Example Graphing Lines to Find *y*-Intercepts

Graph the equation $y = x + 3$. What is the *y*-intercept of the graph of the equation?

Solution ·

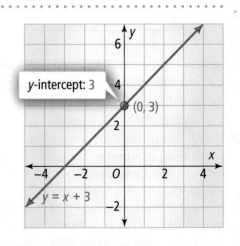

The *y*-intercept of the graph of the equation is 3.

Part 2

Example Finding y-Intercepts of Lines

For each graph or the graph of each equation, find the y-intercept.

a.
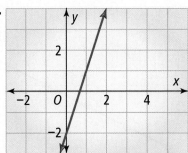

b.
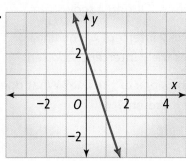

c. $y = 4x - 3$

d. $y = -4x + 3$

Solution

a.
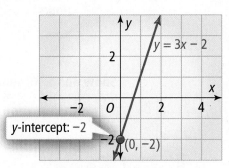

b.
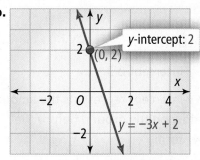

c.
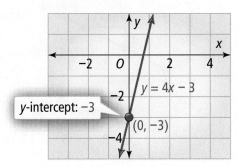

d.
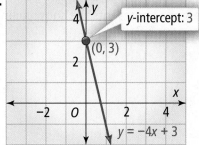

Part 3

Example Understanding Slopes and *y*-Intercepts

The line models the total amount of snow on the ground during a snowstorm.

What is the *y*-intercept of the line? What does the *y*-intercept represent?

What is the slope of the line? What does the slope represent?

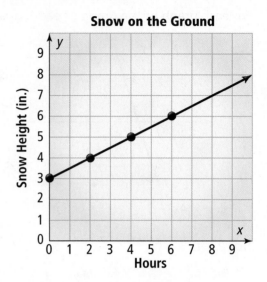

Snow on the Ground

Solution

The *y*-intercept is 3.

The *y*-intercept represents the amount of snow on the ground before the snowstorm.

The slope of the line is $\frac{1}{2}$.

The slope represents the snow falling at a rate of $\frac{1}{2}$ in. per hour.

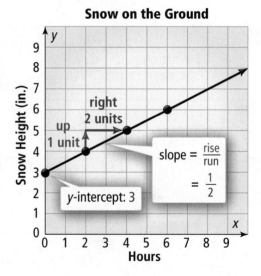

Snow on the Ground

$$\text{slope} = \frac{\text{rise}}{\text{run}}$$

$$= \frac{1}{2}$$

y-intercept: 3

1. Graph the equation $y = 2x - 4$ and find the y-intercept.

2. What is the y-intercept of the graph shown below?

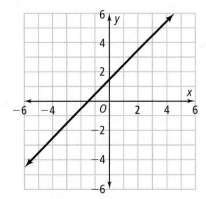

3. Think About the Process

   a. Before graphing, describe where on the graph of the line $y = x - 7$ the y-intercept will be located.

      A. The y-intercept will be located where the x-value is 1.

      B. The y-intercept will be located where the graph crosses the y-axis.

      C. The y-intercept will be located where the graph crosses the x-axis.

      D. The y-intercept will be located where the x-value is -1.

   b. Graph the equation.

   c. What is the y-intercept of the graph of the equation?

4. The line in the graph models the growth of a plant in the past 10 years.

   Growth of a Plant

   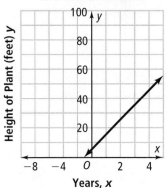

   a. What is the y-intercept of the line?

   b. What does the y-intercept represent?

      A. The height of the plant 10 years ago

      B. The growth of the plant each year

      C. The tallest the plant will grow

      D. How many years ago the plant was planted

   c. How many years ago did the plant start to grow?

5. Think About the Process

   a. How does the slope affect the graph of a line?

      A. The slope affects where the line ends.

      B. The slope affects the steepness of the line.

      C. The slope affects where the line starts.

      D. The slope affects where the line will cross the y-axis.

   b. Graph the equation $y = \frac{3}{4}x - 6$ and identify the y-intercept.

6. Error Analysis Jamal's notes say to let $x = 0$ and solve for y to find the y-intercept of an equation. He incorrectly says the y-intercept of this equation is 5.

   a. Graph the equation $y = x - 5$.

   b. Find the y-intercept using Jamal's method.

   c. Which mistake might Jamal have made?

      A. He let $x = 1$ and solved for y.

      B. He let $y = 0$ and solved for x.

      C. He let $y = 1$ and solved for x.

      D. He let $x = 0$ and solved for y.

See your complete lesson at MyMathUniverse.com

7. a. Writing What is the *y*-intercept of the graph?

b. Describe a situation for the graph of the line.

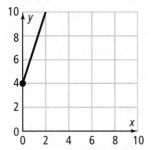

8. Cell Phones A cell phone company charges a $35 startup fee and then $0.50 for every minute used. The equation $y = 0.50x + 35$ models this situation. Graph the equation and find the *y*-intercept.

9. Reasoning Each question on an 88-point test is worth 2 points. Partial answers receive partial credit. The line models this situation.

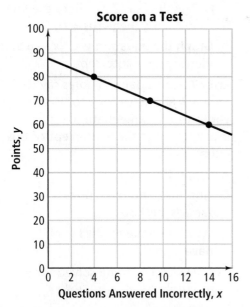

Score on a Test

a. What is the *y*-intercept?

b. What does the *y*-intercept represent?

c. What is the slope of the line?

d. What does the slope of the line represent?

e. Describe how you could use the graph to find the maximum number of incorrect answers allowed for a passing mark of 60 points.

10. a. Graph the equation $y + 14 = x$.

b. Identify the *y*-intercept.

11. A line passes through the *y*-axis at a *y*-value of -2. For every 4 units up, the line moves 5 units to the right.

a. Graph the equation described.

b. What is the *y*-intercept?

12. Challenge The line in the graph models the total cost of an engraved watch. The watch costs $12 plus $1.25 for each engraved letter.

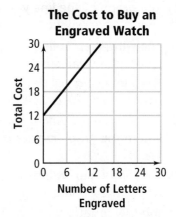

The Cost to Buy an Engraved Watch

a. What is the *y*-intercept of the line?

b. What does the *y*-intercept represent?

c. If you have $17, what is the maximum number of letters you can engrave?

CCSS: 8.F.B.4

Part 1

Intro

The equation of a non-vertical line can be written in the form $y = mx + b$, where m is the slope and b is the y-intercept.

$$y = mx + b$$

slope y-intercept

An equation written in the form $y = mx + b$ is in **slope-intercept form**.

You can use the slope-intercept form to write and graph the equation of a non-vertical line.

Example Writing Equations in Slope-Intercept Form

Write an equation in slope-intercept form for each line.

a.

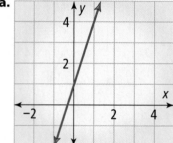

b.

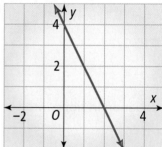

c.

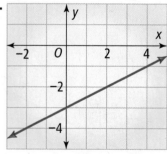

continued on next page >

See your complete lesson at MyMathUniverse.com

Solution ·

a. Find the slope. Two points on the line are (0, 1) and (1, 4).

$$\text{slope} = \frac{4 - 1}{1 - 0}$$

$$= 3$$

The *y*-intercept is 1.

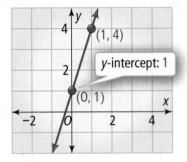

Write an equation in slope-intercept form.

$$y = mx + b$$

Substitute 3 for *m* and 1 for *b*. $y = 3x + 1$

b. Find the slope. Two points on the line are (0, 4) and (1, 2).

$$\text{slope} = \frac{2 - 4}{1 - 0}$$

$$= -2$$

The *y*-intercept is 4.

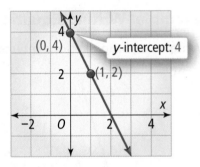

Write an equation in slope-intercept form.

$$y = mx + b$$

Substitute −2 for *m* and 4 for *b*. $y = -2x + 4$

c. Find the slope. Two points on the line are (0, −3) and (2, −2).

$$\text{slope} = \frac{-3 - (-2)}{0 - 2}$$

$$= \frac{-1}{-2}$$

$$= \frac{1}{2}$$

The *y*-intercept is −3.

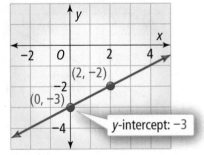

Write an equation in slope-intercept form.

$$y = mx + b$$

$$y = \frac{1}{2}x + (-3)$$

Substitute $\frac{1}{2}$ for *m* and −3 for *b*. $y = \frac{1}{2}x - 3$

Part 2

Example Using Linear Equations in Slope-Intercept Form

The line models the relationship between a temperature in degrees Celsius and degrees Fahrenheit.

a. What is the *y*-intercept of the line?

b. What is the slope of the line?

c. Write an equation for the line where *x* is the temperature in degrees Celsius and *y* is the temperature in degrees Fahrenheit.

d. Use your equation to find the Fahrenheit equivalent for 18°C.

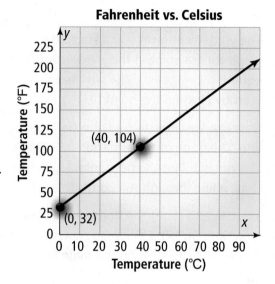

Fahrenheit vs. Celsius

Solution ···

a. The *y*-intercept is 32.

b. Use the points (0, 32) and (40, 104) to find the slope of the line.

$$\text{slope} = \frac{104 - 32}{40 - 0}$$

$$= \frac{72}{40}$$

$$= \frac{9}{5}$$

c. An equation for the line is $y = \frac{9}{5}x + 32$.

d. To find the Fahrenheit equivalent for 18°C, use the equation $y = \frac{9}{5}x + 32$.

$$y = \frac{9}{5}x + 32$$

Substitute 18 for *x*. $= \frac{9}{5}(18) + 32$

Multiply. $= \frac{162}{5} + 32$

Rewrite the fraction as a decimal. $= 32.4 + 32$

Simplify. $= 64.4$

So, 18°C is equivalent to 64.4°F.

Part 3

Intro

You can use an equation in slope-intercept form to graph a linear equation.

The y-intercept gives you a starting point. Start by plotting a point at the y–intercept for the equation $y = \frac{4}{3}x - 1$. The y-intercept is -1. Start by plotting the point $(0, -1)$.

Next use the slope to find another point on the line. The slope of the equation is $\frac{4}{3}$. The rise is 4. The run is 3. Plot the new point $(3, 3)$. Then draw a line through the points.

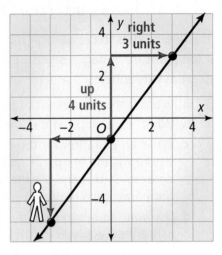

You can also count the slope in the other direction. Go left 3 units. Go down 4 units. The point $(-3, -5)$ is on the same line.

Example Graphing Equations in Slope-Intercept Form

Graph the equation $y = \frac{1}{4}x - 5$.

Solution

Graph the equation $y = \frac{1}{4}x - 5$.

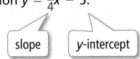

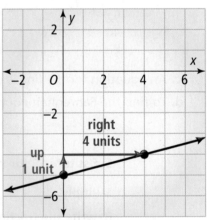

The y–intercept is -5. Start by plotting the point $(0, -5)$.

The slope is $\frac{1}{4}$. The rise is 1. Start at $(0, -5)$ and go 1 unit up.

The run is 4. So then go 4 units right. Plot the new point $(4, -4)$.

Now draw a line through the points $(0, -5)$ and $(4, -4)$.

Key Concept

Equations in the form $y = mx + b$ and $y = mx$ are both examples of linear equations.

Characteristics of the Graph of the Equation	$y = mx$	$y = mx + b, b \neq 0$
Slope	m	m
y-intercept	0	b
$\dfrac{\text{change in } y}{\text{change in } x}$ is constant	yes	yes
Shows a proportional relationship between x and y	yes	no

1. Write an equation for the line in slope-intercept form. Use integers or fractions for any numbers in the equation.

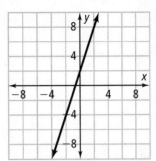

2. Write an equation for the line in slope-intercept form.

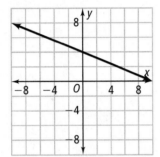

3. The line models Danny's savings account. He started with $6 in his account. He saves $3 each day. Write an equation for the line in slope-intercept form where x is the number of days he saves and y is the total amount in his account.

Danny's Savings Account

4. Graph the equation $y = 2x + 4$. Use the slope and y-intercept when drawing the line.

5. Think About the Process
  a. Find the y-intercept of the line.
  b. Write an equation for the line in slope-intercept form.

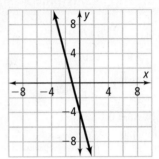

6. Juice Sales The graph represents the decrease of the sales of apple juice.

Sales of Apple Juice

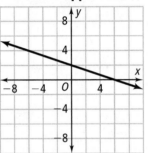

  a. Write an equation for the line in slope-intercept form to represent this situation.
  b. Explain how you know the sales of apple juice are decreasing.

7. Think About the Process
  a. What should you do first to graph the equation $y = \frac{3}{4}x + 2$?
  b. Graph the equation $y = \frac{3}{4}x + 2$.

8. a. Reasoning What is the graph of the equation $y = \frac{1}{5}x - 3$?
  b. Is it possible to find the value for y when x equals 6 without substituting 6 in the same equation? Explain.

9. Error Analysis Amy began with $30 in her bank account and spent $5 each day. She incorrectly wrote an equation for the line in slope-intercept form as $y = -5x + 6$.

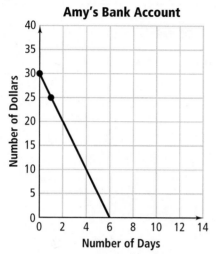

Amy's Bank Account

a. What is the correct equation for the line in slope-intercept form?

b. What mistake might Amy have made?

10. Writing The line models the cost of trail mix. It costs $3 per pound plus 50¢ for the storage container.

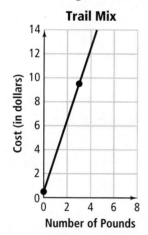

Trail Mix

a. Write an equation in slope-intercept form for the line, where x is the number of pounds and y is the total cost. Use integers or decimals for any numbers in the equation.

b. How much does it cost for 1 pound of trail mix?

c. Describe another situation that uses the same equation.

11. The line models the cost of ordering concert tickets online. The tickets cost $21 per person plus a $12.25 processing fee.

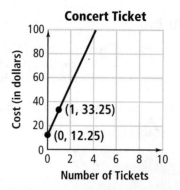

Concert Ticket

(1, 33.25)
(0, 12.25)

a. Write an equation for the line in slope-intercept form, where x is the number of tickets and y is the total cost. Use integers or decimals for any number in the equation.

b. Explain how you can write an equation for this situation without using a graph at all.

12. Challenge The line models a recipe for chicken pie. The recipe calls for 16 ounces of chicken for the first 4 people. The recipe calls for 6 ounces of chicken for each additional person.

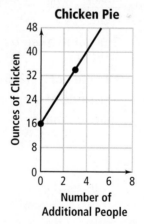

Chicken Pie

a. Write an equation for the line in slope-intercept form, where x is the number of additional people and y is the total number of ounces. Use integers or fractions for any numbers in the equation.

b. If you have 40 ounces of chicken, how many people can you feed?

CCSS: 8.EE.B.5, 8.EE.B.6

Part 1

Example Comparing Rates in Different Forms

Which of the three sea animals is the fastest? How do you know?

A Bottlenose Dolphin can travel 8.5 mi every $\frac{1}{2}$ h.

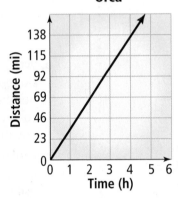

Sea Lion

Time (min)	Distance (mi)
12	5
24	10
36	15
48	20
60	25

Orca

Solution

Find each speed in miles per hour and compare.

Dolphin: $\dfrac{8.5\text{mi}}{\frac{1}{2}\text{h}} = \dfrac{17\text{mi}}{1\text{h}}$.

The dolphin can travel at a speed of 17 mi/h.

Orca: Use the points (2, 69) and (0, 0) to find the slope of the line. The slope of the line is equivalent to the speed of an orca in miles per hour.

$$\text{slope} = \frac{69 - 0}{2 - 0}$$

$$= \frac{69}{2}$$

$$= 34.5$$

The orca has a speed of 34.5 mi/h.

Sea lion: The ratio $\dfrac{\text{distance (mi)}}{\text{time (min)}}$ shown in each row of the table is equivalent to 2.4 mi/min. The table shows sea lions can travel 25 mi in 60 min.

Since 60 min = 1 h, a sea lion can travel at a speed of 25 mi/h.

The orca is the fastest of the three sea animals.

Part 2

Example Comparing Linear Equations

An 8th grade class wants to hire a DJ for their end-of-the-year party.

DJ A

$20 per hour plus
a $75 set-up fee

DJ B

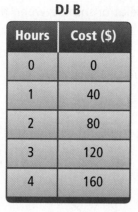

Hours	Cost ($)
0	0
1	40
2	80
3	120
4	160

DJ C

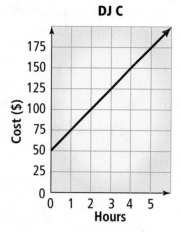

a. Write an equation that represents the total cost y of hiring each DJ for x hours.

b. Which DJ charges the highest hourly rate?

c. Which equation(s) show a proportional relationship between the number of hours x and the total cost y?

d. If you only have $150 to spend, which DJ can you hire for the longest period of time?

Solution

a. Each equation shows the total cost y for x hours.

DJ A:

Words   Cost equals $20 times number of hours plus $75 set-up fee

to

Let x = the number of hours.

Let y = the total cost, in dollars.

Equation y = 20 • x + 75

The cost of hiring DJ A can be represented by the equation
$y = 20x + 75$.

continued on next page >

DJ B:

The table shows a proportional relationship between the number of hours and the total cost.

$$\frac{\text{total cost}}{\text{number of hours}} = \frac{\$40}{1 \text{ hour}}$$

The table shows a cost per hour of $40/h.

The cost of hiring DJ B can be represented by the equation $y = 40x$.

DJ C:

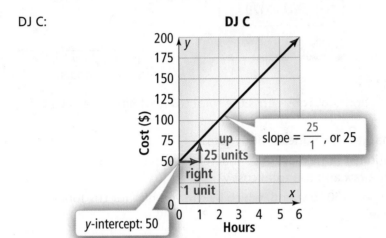

The cost of hiring DJ C can be represented by the equation $y = 25x + 50$.

b. The slope of each equation represents the costs per hour.

DJ A   DJ B   DJ C

$y = 20x + 75$ $y = 40x$ $y = 25x + 50$

DJ A charges $20 per hour, DJ B charges $40 per hour, and DJ C charges $25 per hour. DJ B charges the most per hour.

c. Equations of the form $y = mx$ show a proportional relationship between x and y. Only the equation $y = 40x$ shows a proportional relationship between the number of hours and the total cost.

d. In each equation, y represents the total cost for x hours. You need to find the x-value that corresponds to a y-value of 150. Substitute 150 for y and solve for x.

continued on next page >

Part 2

Solution continued

DJ A:

Write the original equation.	$y = 20x + 75$
Substitute 150 for y.	$150 = 20x + 75$
Subtract 75 from both sides.	$150 - 75 = 20x + 75 - 75$
Divide both sides by 20.	$\dfrac{75}{20} = \dfrac{20x}{20}$
Simplify.	$3.75 = x$

DJ B:

Write the original equation.	$y = 40x$
Substitute 150 for y.	$150 = 40x$
Divide both sides by 40.	$\dfrac{150}{40} = \dfrac{40x}{40}$
Simplify.	$3.75 = x$

DJ C:

Write the original equation.	$y = 25x + 50$
Substitute 150 for y.	$150 = 25x + 50$
Subtract 50 from both sides.	$150 - 50 = 25x + 50 - 50$
Divide both sides by 25.	$\dfrac{100}{25} = \dfrac{25x}{25}$
Simplify.	$4 = x$

You can hire DJ A for 3.75 h, DJ B for 3.75h, or DJ C for 4 h. You can hire DJ C for the longest period of time.

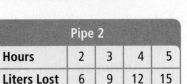

1. Caitlin, Sam, and Bobby are trying to see who runs the fastest. Caitlin says she can run 7 miles every hour. The table below shows the relationship between total miles Sam ran and time. The graph below shows the relationship for Bobby. Who runs the fastest?

Sam				
Hours	2	3	4	5
Distance (miles)	20	30	40	50

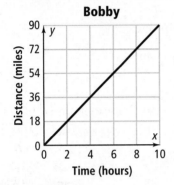

Bobby

2. Bailey is counting how much money she has in change. There are nickels, dimes, and quarters. She has a total of $3 in quarters and nickels.

a. Write an equation for how much money Bailey has in change, where y is the total amount of money in dollars and x is the number of dimes she has.

b. If Bailey has $10 in change, how many dimes does she have?

3. There are three pipes that are leaking, Pipe 1, Pipe 2, and Pipe 3. The rate at which Pipe 1 loses water is represented by the equation $y = 8x$, where y is the total amount of water in liters lost and x is the number of hours. The table shows the relationship between the liters lost and the number of hours for Pipe 2. The graph shows the relationship for Pipe 3.

Pipe 2				
Hours	2	3	4	5
Liters Lost	6	9	12	15

Pipe 3

(3, 14.73)

a. Which of the following is a good estimate for the slope of the line for Pipe 3?

A. 5   **B.** 4

C. 6   **D.** 7

b. Which pipe loses more water per hour?

4. Think About the Process There are three beaches in a town, Beach 1, Beach 2, and Beach 3. The equation $y = 101x$ represents the total number of people at Beach 1 after x hours. The table below shows the relationship between hours since Beach 2 opened and the total number of people. The graph that represents the number of people at Beach 3 passes through the points (0,0) and (4,404), where y is the total number of people and x is the number of hours since the opening.

Beach 2				
Hours	2	3	4	5
Total People	202	303	404	505

a. In order to compare the proportional relationships for each beach, what expression should you use to represent the slope of the graph for Beach 3?

b. Which beach has a greater number of people arriving per hour?

See your complete lesson at MyMathUniverse.com

5. A math problem on a test asks the students to write and solve an equation for the following scenario. A town plants a tree in the park on the 300th anniversary of the town. The tree is 5 feet tall when it is planted. The local nursery says that the tree will grow 4 feet every year. Audrey says the equation is $y = 5x + 4$ and after 7 years the tree will be 33 feet tall.

a. Write an equation for the height of the tree, where y is the total height of the tree and x is the number of years that have passed since it was planted. Use integers or fractions for any numbers in the equation.

b. How many years will have passed when the tree is 33 feet tall?

c. What error might Audrey have made?

   A. Audrey did not find the correct number of years that have passed.

   B. Audrey switched the m and b terms of the equation.

   C. Audrey switched the m and b terms of the equation and did not find the correct number of years that have gone by.

6. Two friends are going on a vacation. The hotel room they are staying in is $150 per night. The total cost for both tickets to the theme park they are going to is $100.

a. Write an equation for how much money the friends will spend on the vacation, where y is the total cost of the vacation and x is the total number of nights.

b. How many nights are the friends going on vacation if they plan on spending $550? Draw algebra tiles to solve for the number of nights that the friends are on vacation.

7. Think About the Process A bakery is making muffins to bring to the town picnic. They have already made 200 muffins. The bakery can make 40 muffins in an hour.

a. Write an equation for the total number of muffins the bakery will make, where y is the total number of muffins made and x is the number of additional hours spent making the muffins.

   A. $y = 200x + 40$

   B. $200 = 40x + y$

   C. $y = 40x + 200$

   D. $x = 40y + 200$

b. How many additional hours would the bakery spend making muffins if they make 640 muffins?

8. Challenge Gavin is interested in getting a new phone. One phone company, Phone 1, charges a monthly fee of $5. They also charge $0.10 per minute. Another company, Phone 2, charges $3 for a monthly fee and $0.25 per minute.

a. Write an equation for the total cost of each phone bill, where y is the total cost and x is the total number of minutes on the phone. Use integers or decimals for any numbers in the expression.

b. Which phone company will allow Gavin to talk the longest if he only wants to spend $24 a month?

What is a System of Linear Equations in Two Variables?

Vocabulary
solution of a system of linear equations, system of linear equations

CCSS: 8.EE.C.8, 8.EE.C.8, Also 8.EE.C.8c

Key Concept

One pencil and one marker cost $1.50. Two pencils and one marker cost $2.00. What are the cost of one pencil and the cost of one marker?

A **system of linear equations** is two or more linear equations with the same two variables that are solved simultaneously.

$$/ \quad + \quad / \quad = \$1.50$$

$$p \quad + \quad m \quad = \quad 1.5$$

$$// \quad + \quad / \quad = \$2.00$$

$$2p \quad + \quad m \quad = \quad 2$$

The **solution of a system of linear equations** is any ordered pair (x, y) that is a solution of every equation in the system.

The solution of the system is $(0.5, 1)$, the values for the variables p and m that make both equations true.

$$p + m = 1.5 \qquad\qquad 2p + m = 2$$
$$0.5 + 1 \stackrel{?}{=} 1.5 \qquad\quad 2(0.5) + 1 \stackrel{?}{=} 2$$
$$1.5 = 1.5 ✔ \qquad\qquad 2 = 2 ✔$$

The **solution of a system of linear equations** is the point of intersection of the graphs of the lines defined by the equations.

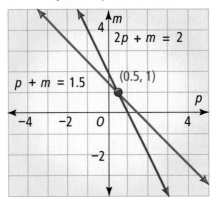

See your complete lesson at MyMathUniverse.com

Part 1

Example Identifying Systems of Linear Equations

Determine whether each of the following represents a system of linear equations.

a. $y = 1.5x$ **b.** $x = 2$ **c.** $14x - 24y$
    $y = 2x - 1$ $y = -3$

d. $2x + 3y = 6$ **e.** $5x - 7y$ **f.** $y = x$
                                                            $y = x + 5$

g. $2.5x - 3.75y = 5.5$

Solution ···

A system of linear equations is formed by two or more linear equations, so the systems are given in parts (a), (b), and (f):

$y = 1.5x$ $x = 2$ $y = x$
$y = 2x - 1$ $y = -3$ $y = x + 5$

Expressions and single equations are not systems, so parts (c), (d), (e), and (g) are not systems:

$14x - 24y$ $2x + 3y = 6$ $5x - 7y$ $2.5x - 3.75y = 5.5$

Part 2

Example **Determining if Coordinate Pairs are Solutions of Systems of Equations**

Is (2, 4) a solution of each system of equations? Explain your reasoning.

a. $y = 2x$
$y = 6x - 8$

b. $x - y = -1$
$2x - y = 1$

Solution ·

Determine whether (2, 4) is a solution of each system.

a. $y = 2x$
$4 \overset{?}{=} 2(2)$
$4 = 4$ ✓

Substitute 2 for x and 4 for y.

$y = 6x - 8$
$4 \overset{?}{=} 6(2) - 8$
$4 \overset{?}{=} 12 - 8$
$4 = 4$ ✓

Since (2, 4) is a solution of each equation, it is a solution of the system.

b. $x - y = -1$
$2 - 4 \overset{?}{=} -1$
$-2 \neq -1$ ✗

Substitute 2 for x and 4 for y.

$2x - y = 1$
$2(2) - 4 \overset{?}{=} 1$
$4 - 4 \overset{?}{=} 1$
$0 \neq 1$ ✗

Since (2, 4) is not a solution of each equation, it is not a solution of the system.

Part 3

Example Writing Systems of Equations to Represent Problems

Wildlife biologists studied the weights of two alligators over a period of 12 months. The initial weight and growth rate of each alligator are shown in the table. Write a system of equations the biologists could use to compare the weights of the alligators.

	Alligator 1	Alligator 2
Initial Weight	4 lb	6 lb
Rate of Growth	1.5 lb per month	1 lb per month

Solution

Write an equation for the weight of Alligator 1.

Words   weight   equals   initial weight   plus   growth rate   times   time

to

Let w = alligator weight.

Let t = time in months.

Equation w = 4 + 1.5 · t

Write an equation for the weight of Alligator 2.

Words   weight   equals   initial weight   plus   growth rate   times   time

to

Let w = alligator weight.

Let t = time in months.

Equation w = 6 + 1 · t

The system is $w = 4 + 1.5t$.
$$w = 6 + t$$

1. Which of the following represents a system of linear equations?

I $b = c + 24$
$b = 2c^2 + 3c$

II $15b + 4d$
$6.7d - c$

III $b = 7c - 24$
$c = b - 6$

IV $b = -6c$
$c = 9$

V $8b + 7cd = 57$
$b = 5.4c - d$

VI $b = 0.63c$
$b = c$

Select all that apply.

A. I
B. II
C. III
D. IV
E. V
F. VI

2. Why isn't $4y - 5z = 3.2$ a system of linear equations?

3. Is (2, 1) a solution of the following system of linear equations?

$-2x + y = -3$
$x + y = 3$

4. Which of the ordered pairs, (6,4), (6,3), or (1,3), is a solution of the system of equations? Select all that apply.

$-3x + 5y = 12$
$7x + 4y = 19$

A. (6,3)
B. (1,3)
C. (6,4)
D. None of the ordered pairs are solutions of the system.

5. Writing You open two bank accounts. In one bank account, your initial deposit is $560 and you deposit $105 each month. Your initial deposit in the other bank account is $1,160 and you deposit $55 each month. Let d represent the total number of dollars in an account. Let t represent the time in months.

a. Which of the following systems can you use to compare how much is in each account?

A. $d = 560 + 55t$
$d = 1,160 + 105t$

B. $d = 560t + 1,160$
$d = 105t + 55$

C. $d = 560 + 105t$
$d = 1,160 + 55t$

D. $d = 560t + 105$
$d = 1,160t + 55$

b. How can using a system of equations be helpful in this situation?

6. a. Reasoning Is the following a system of linear equations?

$z = 4x + 4y$
$4x = 8y + 8z$

A. No, because there are more than two variables.

B. No, because only one of the equations is linear.

C. No, because there is only one equation.

D. No, because they are expressions.

E. Yes, it is a system of linear equations.

b. Does a system of linear equations always have two variables? Do you have to use the same variables in all of the equations? Explain.

7. Error Analysis A company has two branches that are growing rapidly. Branch 1 opened with 16 clients and they get 4 new clients each week. Branch 2 opened with 42 clients and they get 11 new clients each week. A manager of the company wants to compare the number of clients each branch has, n, with respect to the number of weeks since the company opened, w. The manager incorrectly uses the system of equations below to compare the number of clients for each branch.

$n = 16w + 4$
$n = 42w + 11$

a. Write a system that the manager can use to compare the number of clients for each branch.

b. What error might the manager have made?

See your complete lesson at MyMathUniverse.com

8. **Hydrology** Scientists observe the depth of two lakes for three months. The initial depth of the lakes and the rate of change in depth of each lake are shown in the table in figure 1. Let d represent the initial depth of a lake and t represent the number of weeks.

   a. Write a system of equations you could use to compare the depths of the lakes over that time period.

   b. Which lake is deeper after 5 weeks?

9. **Think About the Process**

   a. What is the first step in deciding if the ordered pair $(6, -13)$ is a solution of the given system of linear equations?

   $$3x = -34 - 4y$$
   $$52 = -2y + 13x$$

   b. Is $(6, -13)$ a solution of the system?

10. Is the ordered pair $(3, 2)$ a solution of the following system of linear equations?

    $$-8x - 4y + 3x = -35 + 6y$$
    $$5x - 2y + 2y = 6 + 3x$$

    A. Yes, because it is a solution of one of the equations.

    B. No, because it is only a solution of one of the equations.

    C. Yes, because it is a solution of both equations.

    D. No, because it is not a solution of either equation.

11. The length of one rectangle is 4 more than three times the width. The length of a second rectangle is 28 inches. Which two systems of equations could you use to compare the lengths? Let L represent length and w represent the width.

    A. $L = 4w$ **B.** $L + 3w = 4$
    $L = 28w$ $L = 28$

    C. $L = 4 + 3w$ **D.** $L + 3w = 4$
    $L = 28$ $L - 3w = 28$

    E. $L - 3w = 4$ **F.** $L = 4 + 28w$
    $L = 28$ $L = 4 + 3w$

12. **Challenge** Which ordered pair is a solution of the system of linear equations?

    $$-4y - 2x = 4 - 6y - 7x$$
    $$6y + 5y = -29 - 5x + 3x$$

    A. $(-5, -3)$ **B.** $(2, -3)$

    C. $(-5, 2)$

13. **Think About the Process** A family is renting a car for a trip. Company F charges an initial price of $25 plus $0.35 per mile. Company G charges an initial price of $13 plus $0.40 per mile.

    a. What variables do you need to write a system of equations to compare the costs to rent a car from the two companies?

    A. The initial price c and the cost per mile m

    B. The initial price c and the number of miles driven m

    C. The total cost to rent the car c and the number of miles driven m

    D. The cost per mile c and the number of miles driven m

    E. The total cost to rent the car c and the cost per mile m

    b. Write a system of equations that models this situation.

14. **Challenge** The cost of renting a bike from Shop M is $42 for the day. The cost of renting a bike from Shop N is $8 per hour plus a $10 fee. Let c represent the cost, and t represent time in hours.

    a. Write a system of equations you could use to compare the costs.

    b. Which shop offers a better deal if you rent for 3 hours?

(Figure 1)

	Lake 1	Lake 2
Initial Depth	58 feet	53 feet
Rate of Change	0 feet per week	3 feet per week

See your complete lesson at MyMathUniverse.com

CCSS: 8.EE.C.8, 8.EE.C.8b

Key Concept

When you solve two-variable systems of linear equations, you are finding intersections of lines. Solving a two-variable system has three possible outcomes.

One solution The lines intersect. The equations have different slopes.

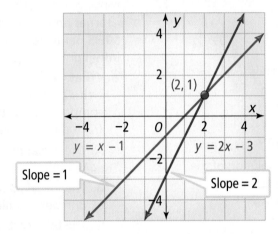

No solution The lines are parallel. The equations have the same slope but different *y*-intercepts.

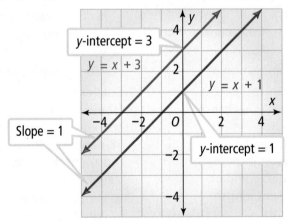

continued on next page >

See your complete lesson at MyMathUniverse.com

Key Concept

continued

Infinitely many solutions The lines are the same. The equations have the same slope and the same y-intercept.

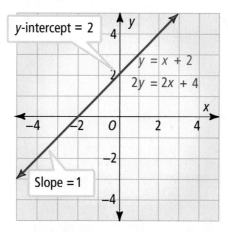

y-intercept = 2

$y = x + 2$

$2y = 2x + 4$

Slope = 1

Part 1

Intro

Inspecting the equations before you try to solve a system is a strategic way to handle these types of problems.

Example Inspecting Linear Systems to Find the Number of Solutions

Without graphing, decide whether the system of linear equations has *one solution*, *no solution*, or *infinitely many solutions*.

a. $y = 4x - 1$
$y = 4x + 2$

b. $y = 2x + 4$
$y = -x + 1$

c. $y = 5x + 4$
$2y = 10x + 8$

d. $x = 3$
$y = 4$

e. $2x + 3y = 6$
$8x + 12y = 24$

f. $x + y = -1$
$x + y = 1$

Solution

a.

The slopes are the same.

The y-intercepts are different.

$y = 4x - 1$

$y = 4x + 2$

continued on next page >

The system has no solution.

b.

> The slopes are different, so the lines intersect.

$y = 2x + 4$
$y = -1x + 1$

The system has exactly one solution.

c. $y = 5x + 4$
$2y = 10x + 8$

> If you solve the second equation for y, you get $y = 5x + 4$.

The lines are the same. They have the same slope and y-intercept. So there are infinitely many solutions.

d. $x = 3$ — Vertical line

$y = 4$ — Horizontal line

The lines intersect, so the system has only one solution.

e. $2x + 3y = 6$
$8x + 12y = 24$

> You can rewrite the second equation as $4(2x + 3y) = 4(6)$, so the lines are the same.

The system has infinitely many solutions.

f.

> The slopes are the same.

> The y-intercepts are different.

$1x + y = -1$
$1x + y = 1$

The system has no solution.

Part 2

Intro

You can also apply previous understandings of number sense when working with systems of equations.

Solve the system of equations.

$$x + y = 8$$
$$x + y = 25$$

This system has no solution because $x + y$ cannot equal 8 and 25 simultaneously.

Example Knowing When Equations Are the Same Using Inspection

By inspecting the equations, what can you determine about the solution(s) to this system?

$$3x - y = 6$$
$$6x - 2y = 12$$

Solution

$3x - y = 6$ and $6x - 2y = 12$ are the same line because $6x - 2y = 12$ can be written as $2(3x - y) = 2(6)$.

Therefore, this system has infinitely many solutions.

1. Without graphing, decide whether the system of equations has one solution, no solution, or infinitely many solutions.

$y = 3x + 14$
$y = -3x + 14$

2. Without graphing the equations, decide whether the system has one solution, no solution, or infinitely many solutions.

$5y = x - 9$ $4x - 10y = 18$

3. Does this system have one solution, no solution, or an infinite number of solutions?

$3x + 2y = 7$
$27x + 18y = 5$

4. Decide if the system of equations has one solution, no solution, or infinitely many solutions.

$3x + 18y = 252$
$6x - 36y = 128$

5. How many solutions does this system have?

$x + 5y = 0$
$25y = -5x$

6. a. **Writing** How many solutions does the system of equations have?

$8x + 10y = 21$

$$y = -\frac{4}{5}x + 24$$

  b. Write a situation you could model using this system of equations. Then interpret the number of solutions in the context of your situation.

7. **Reasoning** How many solutions are there for this system of equations?

$y = 9x + 1$
$y = 7x + 1$

  A. Exactly one solution, because the slopes are not equal.

  B. No solution, because the slopes are equal and the y-intercepts are not equal.

  C. No solution, because the y-intercepts are not equal.

  D. Exactly one solution, because the slopes are equal but the y-intercepts are not equal.

  E. Infinitely many solutions, because the slopes are equal and the y-intercepts are equal.

8. **Mental Math** By inspecting the equations, what can you determine about the solution(s) of this system?

$y = 6x + 16$
$4y = 24x + 68$

  A. The system has exactly one solution.

  B. The system has infinitely many solutions.

  C. The system has no solution.

9. **Error Analysis** Charlene says that this system of equations has infinitely many solutions.

$13x + 4y = 33$ $26y + 8x = 66$

  a. How many solutions does the system have?

  b. What error might Charlene have made?

  A. Charlene compared the slope in the first equation to the y-intercept in the second.

  B. Charlene found the y-intercept incorrectly.

  C. Charlene compared the y-intercept in the first equation to the slope in the second.

  D. Charlene found the slope incorrectly.

10. **Space Exploration** Two rovers are exploring a planet. The system of equations shows each rover's elevation, y, at time x.

    Rover A: $y = 1.9x - 6$

    Rover B: $3y = 5.7x - 18$

    a. Without graphing these equations, what conclusion can you make about the system of equations?

    b. Interpret your results in the context of the problem.

11. **Think About the Process** Consider the following system of equations.

    $$y = \frac{5}{4}x - 5 \qquad y = \frac{1}{3}x - 5$$

    a. What must be true for a system of equations to have infinitely many solutions?

    A. The slopes must be equal and the y-intercepts must be equal.

    B. The slopes must be equal and the y-intercepts must not be equal.

    C. The slopes must not be equal.

    b. How many solutions does the system of equations above have?

12. **Mental Math** By inspecting the equations, what can you determine about the solution(s) of this system?

    $20y = 35x + 90$

    $12y = 21x + 54$

13. You plant two flowers in a garden. The equations $y = 13.7x + 16$ and $y = 7.8x + 16$ model the heights of y of the flowers, in millimeters, after x days.

    a. What does the y-intercept of each equation represent?

    A. the height of the flower when planted

    B. the height of the flower after 10 days

    C. the rate of growth of the flower

    D. the difference of the flowers' heights

    b. Will the flowers ever be the same height?

    A. The flowers are the same height when they are planted.

    B. The flowers are always the same height.

    C. The flowers will never be the same height.

14. **Think About the Process**

    a. Under what circumstances does the system of equations $Qx + Ry = S$ and $y = Tx + S$ have infinitely many solutions?

    A. When $T = -Q$ and $R = 1$

    B. When $T = Q$ and $R = -1$

    C. When $T = Q$ and $R = S$

    D. When $T = -Q$ and $R = S$

    b. Use your result to make a conclusion about the system of equations $-5x + y = 8$ and $y = 5x + 8$.

15. **a.** **Challenge** Decide if the system of equations has one solution, no solution, or infinitely many solutions.

    $27x + 39y = 186$

    $-18x - 26y = -124$

    b. Write another system of equations with the same number of solutions that uses the first equation.

16. **Challenge** Without graphing, what can you determine about the solution(s) of this system?

    $-16x + 56y = 184$

    $12x - 42y = -132$

Solving Systems of Linear Equations by Graphing

CCSS: 8.EE.C.8a, 8.EE.C.8b, Also 8.EE.C.8, 8.EE.C.8c

Part 1

Example Identifying Solutions of Systems of Linear Equations from a Graph

What are the coordinates of the solution of the system represented by the graph?

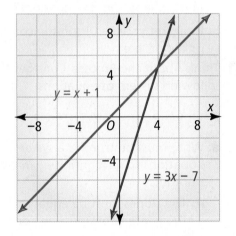

$y = x + 1$

$y = 3x - 7$

Solution

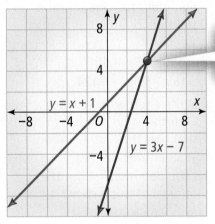

$y = x + 1$

$y = 3x - 7$

The solution is the point of intersection, (4, 5).

The lines intersect at (4, 5), so (4, 5) is the solution of the system.

Part 2

Example Estimating Solutions of Systems of Linear Equations by Graphing

Estimate the solution of the system by graphing the equations.

$$y = 2x$$

$$y = -6x + 4$$

Solution ·

Graph the equations and then estimate the point of intersection visually.

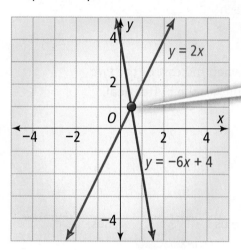

The point of intersection is (0.5, 1).

The solution of the system is (0.5, 1).

Part 3

Example Writing and Graphing Systems of Equations to Solve Problems

A photographer offers two portrait packages.

Package A

$25 for 12 photos

+ $.40 for each extra print.

Package B

$30 for 12 photos

+ $.15 for each extra print.

Write and graph a system of equations to find when the cost of the two packages will be the same. Explain when Package A is the better deal.

Solution

Step 1 Write a system of equations.

Package A:

Words	total cost	equals	cost of 12 photos	plus	cost per print	times	number of prints

 Let c = the total cost.

Let p = the number of extra prints.

Equation	c	=	25	+	0.4	•	p

Package B:

Words	total cost	equals	cost of 12 photos	plus	cost per print	times	number of prints

Let c = the total cost.

Let p = the number of extra prints.

Equation	c	=	30	+	0.15	•	p

The system is $c = 25 + 0.4p$.

$c = 30 + 0.15p$

continued on next page >

Part 3

Solution continued

Step 2 Graph the system to find the solution.

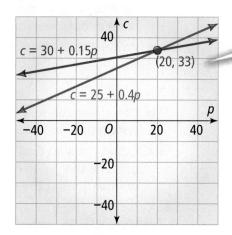

$c = 30 + 0.15p$

$(20, 33)$

$c = 25 + 0.4p$

The two lines intersect at the point (20, 33).

The cost of the two packages will be the same if you order the 12 photos and 20 extra prints. The total cost will be $33.

Package *A* is best for fewer than 20 extra prints. Package *B* is best for more than 20 extra prints.

1. a. Graph each equation.

$x + 4y = 8$

$3x + 4y = 0$

b. Determine the solution of the system of equations.

2. a. Graph each equation.

$y = 3x - 4$

$y = -3x + 5$

b. Estimate the solution of the system of equations.

A. (1.5, 0.5) **B.** (−1.5, −0.5)

C. (0.5, 1.5) **D.** (−1.5, 0.5)

3. Renting a canoe to use on River Y costs $33. Renting a canoe to use on River Z costs $5 per hour plus a $13 deposit. The total cost, *c*, of renting a canoe, for *n* hours can be represented by a system of equations.

a. Which system of equations could be used to find out how many hours the canoe can be rented?

A. River Y $c = 33$

River Z $c = 5n + 13$

B. River Y $c = 5n - 33$

River Z $c = 13$

C. River Y $c = 33$

River Z $c = 5n - 13$

D. River Y $c = 5n + 13$

River Z $c = 13$

b. On a separate piece of paper, graph the system of equations.

c. How many hours could you rent the canoe for the cost to be the same on both rivers?

4. The cost of endless chicken wings at Restaurant X is $10. The cost of chicken wings at Restaurant Z is 60¢ per wing plus a $2 charge for sauce. The total cost, *c*, of *n* chicken wings can be represented by a system of equations.

a. Write the system of equations.

b. Graph the system of equations.

c. How many chicken wings do you have to have for the cost to be the same at both restaurants?

5. a. Writing Graph each equation.

$x = y$

$2x = y - 3$

b. Determine the solution of the system of equations.

c. Explain how to find the equation of a line that intersects the system of equations at the same point.

6. Reasoning The cost of making copies at Store W is $5 regardless of the number of copies. The cost of making copies at Store Z is 20¢ per copy plus a $2 charge for the use of the machine. The total cost, *c*, of making *n* copies can be represented by a system of equations.

a. Which system of equations could be used to find out the cost of making copies?

b. Which graph shows the system of equations correctly?

c. How many copies do you have to make for the cost to be the same at both stores?

d. If you have to make a smaller number of copies which store should you go to? If you have to make a large number of copies which store should you go to? Explain.

7. **Think About the Process** You are given the following system of equations.

$$y = -3x + 6$$
$$y + 3 = 3(x - 3)$$

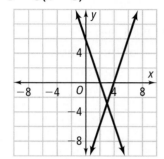

   a. Which point on the graph is the solution of the system of equations?

   b. What is the solution of the system of equations?

8. **Error Analysis** Holly was asked to estimate the solution of the system of equations. She incorrectly said the solution is $(-5, -2.5)$.

$$y - 2x = 0$$
$$y = 6x + 10$$

   a. Graph the equations.

   b. Estimate the solution of the system of equations.

   A. $(2.5, 5)$ **B.** $(2.5, -5)$

   C. $(-5, 2.5)$ **D.** $(-2.5, -5)$

   c. What mistake might Holly have made?

9. **a. Open-Ended** Estimate the solution of the system by graphing the equations.

$$y - 5x = 0$$
$$y = 15x + 16$$

   A. $(-1.6, -8)$ **B.** $(1.6, 8)$

   C. $(-8, 1.6)$ **D.** $(1.6, -8)$

   b. Find an example of a system of equations with infinitely many solutions. Describe what the graph would look like for that system.

10. **a.** Graph each equation.

$$x + y = 10$$
$$x = y + 4$$

   b. Determine the solution of the system of equations.

11. When buying tickets to a play online, they cost $12.75 per ticket plus a $12.00 fee per order. When buying tickets at the box office, they cost $15.75 per ticket. The total cost, c, of going to the play, for n people can by represented by a system of equations.

   a. Which system of equations could be used to find how many tickets you have to buy for the cost to be the same?

   b. Which is the correct graph for the system of equations?

12. **Challenge a.** Graph each equation.

$$y = 0.5x - 4$$
$$y = -2.5x - 2.5$$

   b. Estimate the solution of the system of equations.

   c. Find a system of equations that has no solutions and graph that system.

Solving Systems of Linear Equations Using Substitution

CCSS: 8.EE.C.8b, 8.EE.C.8c, Also 8.EE.C.8

Key Concept

You can solve linear systems using an algebraic method called the **substitution method**. Solve one of the equations for one of the variables. Then substitute the expression for the variable into the other equation and solve for the second variable.

Solve the system by substitution.

$$y = 3x$$
$$2x + y = 15$$

Step 1 Solve for the first variable.

Since $y = 3x$, you can substitute $3x$ for y in $2x + y = 15$.

Write the second equation.	$2x + y = 15$
Substitute 3x for y.	$2x + 3x = 15$
Simplify.	$5x = 15$
Divide each side by 5.	$x = 3$

Step 2 Solve for the second variable.

Since $x = 3$, substitute 3 for x in either equation and solve for y.

Write either equation.	$y = 3x$
Substitute 3 for x.	$y = 3(3)$
Simplify	$y = 9$

Step 3 Write the solution.

Since $x = 3$, and $y = 9$, the solution is $(3, 9)$.

Step 4 Check your solution.

Substitute the solution $(3, 9)$ into each equation.

$y = 3x$ $2x + y = 15$

$9 \stackrel{?}{=} 3(3)$ Substitute 3 for x and 9 for y. $2(3) + 9 \stackrel{?}{=} 15$

$9 = 9 ✔$ $6 + 9 \stackrel{?}{=} 15$

                                        $15 = 15 ✔$

Part 1

Example Solving Systems of Linear Equations Using Substitution

Solve the system using substitution. Check your answer.

$$y = x + 3$$
$$2x + 2y = 38$$

Solution

Step 1 Estimate the solution by graphing the equations.

Graph the equations $2x + 2y = 38$ and $y = x + 3$.

Estimate: The lines intersect so there is one solution. The solution falls in Quadrant 1, so both values should be positive.

Now start solving the system using substitution.

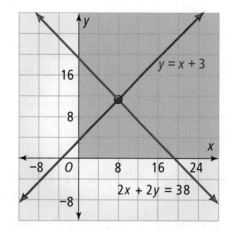

Step 2 Solve for the first variable.

Since $y = x + 3$, substitute $x + 3$ for y in $2x + 2y = 38$ and solve for x.

Write the second equation.	$2x + 2y = 38$
Substitute $x + 3$ for y. Use parentheses.	$2x + 2(x + 3) = 38$
Use the Distributive Property.	$2x + 2x + 6 = 38$
Simplify.	$4x + 6 = 38$
Subtract 6 from each side.	$4x = 32$
Divide each side by 4.	$x = 8$

Step 3 Solve for the second variable.

Since $x = 8$, substitute 8 for x in either equation and solve for y.

Write either equation.	$2x + 2y = 38$
Substitute 8 for x.	$2(8) + 2y = 38$
Simplify.	$16 + 2y = 38$
Subtract 16 from each side.	$2y = 22$
Divide each side by 2.	$y = 11$

continued on next page >

Part 1

Solution continued

  Step 4 Write the solution.

  Since $x = 8$ and $y = 11$, the solution is (8, 11).

  Step 5 Check your solution.

  Check your solution by substituting (8, 11) into each equation.

  $y = x + 3$ $\qquad\qquad\qquad\qquad\qquad\qquad\qquad$ $2x + 2y = 38$

  $11 \overset{?}{=} 8 + 3$ $\qquad$ Substitute 8 for x $\qquad$ $2(8) + 2(11) \overset{?}{=} 38$

  $\qquad\qquad\qquad\qquad$ and 11 for y.

  $11 = 11 \checkmark$ $\qquad\qquad\qquad\qquad\qquad\qquad\qquad$ $16 + 22 \overset{?}{=} 38$

  $\qquad\qquad\qquad\qquad\qquad\qquad\qquad\qquad\qquad\qquad\qquad\qquad$ $38 = 38 \checkmark$

  Since (8, 11) is a solution of each equation, it is a solution of the system.

Part 2

Example Writing Systems of Linear Equations to Solve By Substitution

Wildlife biologists studied the weights of two alligators over a period of 12 months. The initial weight and growth rate of each alligator are shown in the table. After how many months did the alligators weigh the same amount? What is the amount that they weighed?

	Alligator 1	Alligator 2
Initial Weight	4 lbs	6 lbs
Rate of Growth	1.5 lbs per month	1 lb per month

Solution

Write an equation for the weight of Alligator 1.

Words	weight	equals	initial weight	plus	growth rate	times	time

to

Let w = alligator weight.

Let t = time in months.

Equation	w	=	4	+	1.5	·	t

continued on next page >

Part 2

Solution continued

Write an equation for the weight of Alligator 2.

Words | weight | equals | initial weight | plus | growth rate | times | time |

 to

Let w = alligator weight.

Let t = time in months.

Equation $\quad w \quad = \quad 6 \quad + \quad 1 \quad \cdot \quad t$

Write the solution to the system in the form (t, w).

$$w = 4 + 1.5t$$
$$w = 6 + t$$

Solve the system using substitution.

Step 1 Solve for the first variable.

Substitute $6 + t$ for w in the other equation and solve for t.

Write the other equation.	$w = 4 + 1.5t$
Substitute $6 + t$ for w.	$6 + t = 4 + 1.5t$
Subtract 6 from each side.	$t = -2 + 1.5t$
Subtract $1.5t$ from each side.	$-0.5t = -2$
Divide each side by -0.5.	$t = 4$

$t = 4$ means that after 4 months, the alligators will weigh the same amount. Now, find that amount.

Step 2 Solve for the second variable.

Substitute 4 for t in either equation and solve for w.

Write either equation.	$w = 6 + t$
Substitute 4 for t.	$w = 6 + 4$
Simplify.	$w = 10$

$w = 10$ means that after 4 months, both alligators will weigh 10 pounds.

Step 3 Write the solution.

The solution is $(4, 10)$.

continued on next page >

Part 2

Solution continued

Step 4 Check your solution.

Check your solution by substituting (4, 10) into each equation.

$w = 4 + 1.5t$ $\qquad\qquad\qquad\qquad\qquad$ $w = 6 + t$

$10 \overset{?}{=} 4 + 1.5(4)$ $\qquad$ Substitute 4 for t and 10 for w. $\qquad$ $10 \overset{?}{=} 6 + 4$

$10 \overset{?}{=} 4 + 6$ $\qquad\qquad\qquad\qquad\qquad\qquad$ $10 = 10\ \checkmark$

$10 = 10\ \checkmark$

So, (4, 10) is the solution to the system.

1. Solve the system of equations by substitution.

    $$y = 3x - 10$$
    $$3x + 2y = 16$$

2. Find the solution to the system of equations by substitution.

    $$p = q + 2$$
    $$2p + 3q = -26$$

3. Together, teammates Pedro and Ricky got 2,666 base hits last season. Pedro had 276 more hits than Ricky. How many hits did each player have?

4. River C is 100 miles longer than River D. If the sum of their lengths is 5,500 miles, what is the length of each river?

5. **Writing** A seed company planted a floral mosaic of a national flag. The perimeter of the flag is 420 feet.

    a. Determine the flag's length and width if the length is 110 feet greater than the width.

    b. Write three situations to which you could apply the resulting system of equations.

6. a. **Reasoning** Solve the system of linear equations using substitution.

    $$x = 8y - 4$$
    $$x + 8y = 6$$

    b. Which expression would be easier to substitute into the other equation, in order to solve the problem? Explain your reasoning.

7. **Error Analysis** Tim incorrectly says that the solution of the system of equations is $(-9, -4)$.

    $$6g - 2h = -6$$
    $$11 = h - 5g$$

    a. What is the correct solution?

    b. What error might Tim have made?

    A. Tim made a mistake calculating the h-value.

    B. Tim made a mistake calculating the g-value.

    C. Tim switched the values of g and h.

    D. Tim used opposite signs for g and h.

8. **Swimming Pool** On a certain hot summer day, 481 people used the public swimming pool. The daily prices are $1.25 for children and $2.25 for adults. The receipts for admission totaled $865.25. How many children and how many adults swam at the public pool that day?

9. **Multiple Representations** You are given the following system of equations.

    $$2x - 5y = 26$$
    $$x = 3y + 15$$

    a. Find the solution of the system of equations by substitution.

    b. Draw a picture using algebra tiles to show the substitution.

10. **Multiple Representations** Find the solution of the system of equations by substitution.

    $$3g - 11k = 17$$
    $$2g = 4k + 8$$

    b. Draw a picture using algebra tiles to show the substitution.

11. An airplane encountered a head wind during a flight between Joppetown and Jawsburgh, which took 4 hours and 42 minutes. The return flight took 4 hours. If the distance from Joppetown to Jawsburgh is 1400 miles, find the airspeed of the plane (the speed of the plane in still air) and the speed of the wind, assuming both remain constant.

12. Farmer Brown planted corn and wheat on his 370 acres of land. The cost of planting and harvesting corn (which includes seed, planting, fertilizer, machinery, labor, and other costs) is $280 per acre. The cost of planting and harvesting wheat is $135 per acre. If Farmer Brown's total cost was $83,300, how many more acres of corn than wheat did the farmer plant?

See your complete lesson at MyMathUniverse.com

13. Think About the Process Consider the following system of equations.

$$\frac{2}{5}r + \frac{5}{2}s = -3$$
$$r = \frac{2}{5}s + \frac{29}{5}$$

a. What should you substitute to solve the system of equations by substitution?

A. Substitute $\frac{2}{5}s + \frac{29}{5}$ for r in the equation $r = \frac{2}{5}s + \frac{29}{5}$.

B. Substitute $\frac{2}{5}s + \frac{29}{5}$ for r in the equation $\frac{2}{5}r + \frac{5}{2}s = -3$.

C. Substitute $\frac{2}{5}r + \frac{29}{5}$ for s in the equation $\frac{2}{5}r + \frac{5}{2}s = -3$.

D. Substitute $\frac{2}{5}r + \frac{29}{5}$ for s in the equation $r = \frac{2}{5}s + \frac{29}{5}$.

b. Solve the system of equations by substitution.

14. Challenge Solve the system of equations by the substitution method. Then use the solution to evaluate the expression $4x(-5 + y)$.

$$8x + 2y + 3 = 19 + 12y - x$$
$$2x = y + 26 - 5x$$

15. Think About the Process Tim's piggy bank contains dimes and nickels worth $5.50. He has 70 coins in all.

a. Let x represent the number of dimes and let y represent the number of nickels. Which system of equations models this problem?

A. $x + y = 70$
$0.10x + 0.05y = 5.50$

B. $x + y = 70$
$0.10y + 0.05x = 5.50$

C. $x + y = 5.50$
$0.10x + 0.05y = 70$

D. $x + y = 5.50$
$0.10y + 0.05x = 70$

b. How many of each coin does Tim have?

16. Challenge The members of the city cultural center have decided to put on a play once a night for a week. Their auditorium holds 500 people. By selling tickets, the members would like to raise $2,050 every night to cover all expenses. Let d represent the number of adult tickets sold at $6.50. Let s represent the number of student tickets sold at $3.50 each.

a. If all 500 seats are filled for a performance, how many of each type of ticket must have been sold for the members to raise exactly $2,050?

b. At one performance there were three times as many student tickets sold as adult tickets. If there were 480 tickets sold at that performance, how much below the goal of $2,050 did ticket sales fall?

Solving Systems of Linear Equations Using Addition

CCSS: 8.EE.C.8b, 8.EE.C.8c, Also 8.EE.C.8, 8.EE.C.8a

Key Concept

You can solve linear systems using an algebraic method called the **addition method**.

In the addition method, you solve the system by adding the equations to eliminate one of the variables.

Solve the system by addition.

$$x + y = -1$$
$$3x - y = 5$$

Step 1 Solve for the first variable.

$$x + 1y = -1$$
$$3x - 1y = 5$$

> Since the sum of the coefficients of the y-terms is 0, add the equations to eliminate y.

Write the original equations.	$x + y = -1$
Add the equations.	$\dfrac{3x - y = 5}{4x + 0 = 4}$
Simplify.	$4x = 4$
Solve for x.	$x = 1$

Step 2 Solve for the second variable.

Since $x = 1$, substitute 1 for x in either equation and solve for y.

Write either equation.	$x + y = -1$
Substitute 1 for x.	$1 + y = -1$
Solve for y.	$y = -2$

Step 3 Write the solution.

Since $x = 1$ and $y = -2$, the solution is $(1, -2)$.

Step 4 Check your solution.

Substitute the solution $(1, -2)$ into each equation.

$$x + y = -1 \qquad\qquad\qquad 3x - y = 5$$
$$1 + (-2) \stackrel{?}{=} -1 \qquad\qquad 3(1)-(-2) \stackrel{?}{=} 5$$

> Substitute 1 for x and -2 for y.

$$-1 = -1 ✔ \qquad\qquad\qquad 3 + 2 \stackrel{?}{=} 5$$
$$5 = 5 ✔$$

Part 1

Example **Selecting Substitution or Addition to Solve Systems**

Inspect the equations. Decide whether the Addition Method or Substitution Method would be the most efficient algebraic method to solve each system.

$$7x + 2y = 10$$
$$-7x + y = -16$$

$$2a + 5b = 17$$
$$6a - 5b = -9$$

$$y = x + 3$$
$$2x - y = 7$$

$$p + q = 7$$
$$p - q = -10$$

Solution ·

In the following three systems, the coefficients of the highlighted terms are additive inverses, so use the addition method.

$$2a + 5b = 17$$
$$6a - 5b = -9$$

$$7x + 2y = 10$$
$$-7x + y = -16$$

$$p + 1q = 7$$
$$p - 1q = -10$$

In the system below, the first equation is in slope-intercept form, so use the substitution method.

$$y = x + 3$$
$$2x - y = 7$$

Example **Solving a System of Equations by Addition**

Solve the system of equations by addition.

$$2x + 5y = 17$$
$$6x - 5y = -9$$

Solution ·

Step 1 Solve for the first variable.

Write the original equation.	$2x + 5y = 17$
Add the equations.	$\dfrac{6x - 5y = -9}{8x + 0 = 8}$
Simplify.	$8x = 8$
Solve for x.	$x = 1$

Since the sum of the coefficients of the *y*-terms is 0, add the equations to eliminate *y*.

continued on next page >

Solution continued

Step 2 Solve for the second variable.

Since $x = 1$, substitute 1 for x in either equation and solve for y.

Write either equation.	$2x + 5y = 17$
Substitute 1 for x.	$2(1) + 5y = 17$
Simplify.	$2 + 5y = 17$
Subtract 2 from each side.	$5y = 15$
Divide each side by 5.	$y = 3$

Step 3 Write the solution.

Since $x = 1$ and $y = 3$, the solution is $(1, 3)$.

Step 4 Check your solution.

Check your solution by substituting $(1, 3)$, into each question.

$2x + 5y = 17$ $6x - 5y = -9$

$2(1) + 5(3) \stackrel{?}{=} 17$ (Substitute 1 for x and 3 for y.) $6(1) - 5(3) \stackrel{?}{=} -9$

$2 + 15 \stackrel{?}{=} 17$ $6 - 15 \stackrel{?}{=} -9$

$17 = 17 ✔$ $-9 = -9 ✔$

Since $(1, 3)$ is a solution each equation, it is a solution of the system.

Part 3

Example **Writing Systems of Equations to Solve Using Addition**

Two runways at an airport, Runway A and Runway B, have a combined length of 20,500 feet. The difference of their lengths is 5,500 feet. What is the length of each runway?

continued on next page >

Solution ·

Write an equation for the combined length of the runways.

Words

| length of Runway A | plus | length of Runway B | equals | total length |

 to

Let x = the length of Runway A.

Let y = the length of Runway B.

Equation x + y =   20,500

Write an equation for the difference of the lengths of the runways.

Words

| length of Runway A | minus | length of Runway B | equals | difference of lengths |

 to

Let x = the length of Runway A.

Let y = the length of Runway B.

Equation x – y =   5,500

The system is $x + y = 20{,}500$

$x - y = 5{,}500$

Solve the system using addition.

Step 1 Solve for the first variable.

Eliminate one variable because the sum of the coefficients of the y-terms is 0, and the equations to eliminate y.

Write the original equations.	$x + y = 20{,}500$
Add the equations.	$\dfrac{x - y = 5{,}500}{2x + 0 = 26{,}000}$
Simplify.	$2x = 26{,}000$
Divide each side by 2.	$x = 13{,}000$

continued on next page >

Part 3

Solution continued

Step 2 Solve for the second variable.

Substitute 13,000 for x in either equation and solve for y.

Write either equation.	$x + y = 20{,}500$
Substitute 13,000 for x.	$13{,}000 + y = 20{,}500$
Subtract 13,000 from each side.	$y = 7{,}500$

Step 3 Write the solution.

The solution is (13,000, 7,500). Runway A is 13,000 feet long, and Runway B is 7,500 feet long.

Step 4 Check your solution.

Check your solution by substituting (13,000, 7,500) into each equation.

$$x + y = 20{,}500$$

$$13{,}000 + 7{,}500 \stackrel{?}{=} 20{,}500$$

$$20{,}500 = 20{,}500 \checkmark$$

Substitute 13,000 for x and 7,500 for y.

$$x - y = 5{,}500$$

$$13{,}000 - 7{,}500 \stackrel{?}{=} 5{,}500$$

$$5{,}500 = 5{,}500 \checkmark$$

1. Find the most efficient algebraic method to solve each system of equations.

   I. $-2x + 5y = 10$
       $5x - 5y = -10$

   II. $y = 2x + 10$
       $5x - 5y = -10$

2. Which system of equations is best solved using addition?

   A. $-3x + 5y = 9$
        $3x - 2y = -9$

   B. $x = 5y + 9$
     $-3x - 2y = -9$

   C. $x = 5y + 9$
     $-3x - 2y = 9$

3. Solve the system of equations using addition.

$$x + y = 6$$
$$x - y = 2$$

4. Which systems of equations are best solved using addition? Select all that apply.

   A. $x = -3y + 9$
     $5.1x - 5.1y = 9$

   B. $5.1x + 5.1y = 9$
     $5.1x - 5.1y = -9$

   C. $3x + 3y = 9$
     $-3x - 5y = -9$

   D. $x = 3y + 9$
     $3x - 5y = -9$

5. Think About the Process Suni needs to solve the system of equations using addition.

$$-5x + 3y = 15$$
$$2x - 3y = -15$$

  a. What variable should Suni solve for first?

    A. y **B.** x

  b. Find the solution.

6. Solve the system using addition.

$$7x + 2y = -13$$
$$-7x + y = 25$$

7. Think About the Process Two friends spent $47 at the mall. The first friend spent less than the second friend. The difference between the amount each friend spent was $31. To find the amount each friend spent, solve a system of equations using the addition method.

  a. What is the next step after writing the system of equations?

    A. Graph the system of equations.

    B. Add the equations to eliminate a variable.

    C. Solve one of the equations for one of the variables.

    D. Substitute an expression for one of the variables into the other equation.

  b. Find the amount each friend spent.

8. The sum of two numbers is 23. When the second number is subtracted from the first number, the difference is 9. Find the two numbers.

9. There are two red jars of marbles and one blue jar of marbles. Jars of the same color marbles contain the same number of marbles in them. There are 35 marbles in total. The difference between the number of marbles in a red jar and the number of marbles in a blue jar is 4. Find the number of marbles in each type of jar.

10. a. Writing Solve the system using addition.

$$x - 3.1y = 11.5$$
$$-x + 3.5y = -13.5$$

  b. Explain why the addition method is a good choice for solving the system. If you wanted to solve for x first, is the addition method still a good choice? Explain.

See your complete lesson at MyMathUniverse.com

11. On a team, 6 girls and 3 boys scored a total of 72 points. The difference between the number of points scored by the 6 girls and the number of points scored by the 3 boys is 36. Each girl scored the same number of points and each boy scored the same number of points. Find the number of points scored by each girl and each boy.

12. **Reasoning** Which method is the most efficient algebraic method to solve the system of equations?

$$x = 4y + 12$$
$$-3x - 3y = -12$$

 A. The substitution method, because one of the equations is in "$y =$" form.

 B. The substitution method, because one of the equations is in "$x =$" form.

 C. The addition method, because the x-terms are additive inverses.

 D. The addition method, because the y-terms are additive inverses.

13. **Error Analysis** Lois claims the solution to the system of equations is $(-1, -4)$.

$$5.5x + 5.3y = -27.3$$
$$4.1x - 5.3y = -11.1$$

 a. Solve the system of equations using addition.

 b. What mistake might Lois have made?

 A. She used the opposite sign for y in the answer.

 B. She used the opposite sign for x in the answer.

 C. She exchanged x and y in the answer.

 D. She used the opposite sign for x and y.

14. **Trains** Two trains, Train A and Train B, weigh a total of 312 tons. Train A is heavier than Train B. The difference of their weights is 170 tons. What is the weight of each train?

15. **Multiple Representations** Solve the system of equations using addition.

$$x - 7y = 11$$
$$x + 7y = {}^-17$$

 a. Which of the following shows the correct solution, written two ways?

 A. $(-3, -2)$, $x = -2$ and $y = -3$

 B. $(-2, -3)$, $x = -2$ and $y = -3$

 C. $(-3, -2)$, $x = -3$ and $y = -2$

 D. $(11, -17)$, $x = -17$ and $y = 11$

 E. $(11, -17)$, $x = 11$ and $y = -17$

 F. $(-7, 7)$, $x = 7$ and $y = -7$

 b. Draw a graph to show the solution in a third way.

16. Two balloons, Balloon A and Balloon B, have a total volume of $\frac{3}{5}$ gallons. Balloon A has a greater volume than Balloon B. The difference of their volumes is $\frac{1}{5}$ gallons. What is the volume of each balloon? Simplify your answers.

17. Solve the system using addition.

$$6x + 9y = 6\frac{3}{5}$$
$$-6x + y = -\frac{3}{5}$$

18. a. **Challenge** Use addition to solve the system. Then solve the system again, this time using the substitution method.

$$1\frac{3}{4}x + y = 2\frac{3}{16}$$
$$\frac{1}{4}x - y = -1\frac{11}{16}$$

 b. Was one method easier than another? Explain.

19. **Challenge** On a fishing trip, Reba catches two types of fish. Each of Fish A weighs $\frac{7}{9}$ pound and each of Fish B weighs $\frac{1}{9}$ pound. The total weight of all the fish is $5\frac{7}{9}$ pounds. The difference in weight of all of Fish A and all of Fish B is $5\frac{1}{9}$ pounds. Find how many fish of each type Reba caught.

See your complete lesson at MyMathUniverse.com

Solving Systems of Linear Equations Using Subtraction

CCSS: 8.EE.C.8, 8.EE.C.8b, 8.EE.C.8c, Also 8.EE.C.8a

Key Concept

Just as you can use addition to solve systems of linear equations, you can also use subtraction.

In the **subtraction method,** you solve the system by subtracting the equations to eliminate one of the variables.

Solve the system by subtraction.

$$2x + 1y = 10$$
$$x + 1y = 7$$

Step 1 Solve for the first variable.

$$2x + 1y = 10$$
$$x + 1y = 7$$

Since the coefficients of the y-terms are the same, subtract the equations to eliminate y.

Write the original equations.	$2x + y = 10$
Subtract the equations.	$\dfrac{x + y = 7}{x + 0 = 3}$
Simplify.	$x = 3$

Step 2 Solve for the second variable.

Since $x = 3$, substitute 3 for x in either equation and solve for y.

Write either equation.	$x + y = 7$
Substitute 3 for x.	$3 + y = 7$
Solve for y.	$y = 4$

Step 3 Write the solution.

Since $x = 3$ and $y = 4$, the solution is (3, 4).

Step 4 Check your solution.

Substitute the solution (3, 4) into each equation.

$$2x + y = 10 \qquad\qquad\qquad x + y = 7$$

$$2(3) + 4 \stackrel{?}{=} 10 \qquad\qquad 3 + 4 \stackrel{?}{=} 7$$

Substitute 3 for x and 4 for y.

$$6 + 4 \stackrel{?}{=} 10 \qquad\qquad\qquad 7 = 7 ✔$$

$$10 = 10 ✔$$

See your complete lesson at MyMathUniverse.com

Part 1

Example Selecting the Most Efficient Method to Solve Systems

Inspect the equations. Decide whether the Addition Method, Subtraction Method, or Substitution Method would be the most efficient algebraic method to solve each system.

$$5p + q = 4 \qquad y = x + 3 \qquad 7x + 2y = 10$$
$$4p - q = 5 \qquad y = 2x - 9 \qquad 7x + y = -16$$

$$2a + 5b = 17 \qquad 3x + 2y = 10$$
$$6a - 5b = -9 \qquad x + 2y = -8$$

Solution ·

In the following two systems, the coefficients of the highlighted terms are additive inverses, so use the addition method.

$$2a + 5b = 17 \qquad 5p + 1q = 4$$
$$6a - 5b = -9 \qquad 4p - 1q = 5$$

In the following two systems, the coefficients of the highlighted terms are the same, so use the subtraction method.

$$3x + 2y = 10 \qquad 7x + 2y = 10$$
$$x + 2y = -8 \qquad 7x + y = -16$$

In the system below, the equations are in slope-intercept form, so use the substitution method.

$$y = x + 3$$
$$y = 2x - 9$$

Part 2

Example Solving a System of Equations by Subtraction

Solve the system by subtraction.

$$3x - y = 4$$
$$2x - y = 1$$

continued on next page >

Part 2

Example continued

Solution ·

Step 1 Solve for the first variable.

Write the original equations. $3x - 1y = 4$

Subtract the equations.
$$\begin{array}{r} 2x - 1y = 1 \\ \hline x + 0 = 3 \end{array}$$

Since the coefficients of the y-terms are the same, subtract the equations to eliminate y.

Simplify. $x = 3$

Step 2 Solve for the second variable.

Since $x = 3$, substitute 3 for x in either equation and solve for y.

Write either equation.	$3x - y = 4$
Substitute 3 for x.	$3(3) - y = 4$
Simplify.	$9 - y = 4$
Subtract 9 from each side.	$-y = -5$
Divide each side by -1.	$y = 5$

Step 3 Write the solution.

Since $x = 3$ and $y = 5$, the solution is $(3, 5)$.

Step 4 Check your solution.

Check your solution by substituting $(3, 5)$ into each equation.

$3x - y = 4$ $\quad\quad\quad\quad\quad\quad\quad$ $2x - y = 1$

$3(3) - 5 \stackrel{?}{=} 4$ $\quad$ Substitute 3 for x and 5 for y. $\quad$ $2(3) - 5 \stackrel{?}{=} 1$

$9 - 5 \stackrel{?}{=} 4$ $\quad\quad\quad\quad\quad\quad\quad$ $6 - 5 \stackrel{?}{=} 1$

$4 = 4 ✔$ $\quad\quad\quad\quad\quad\quad\quad\quad\quad$ $1 = 1 ✔$

Since $(3, 5)$ is a solution of each equation, it is a solution of the system.

Part 3

Example Writing Systems of Equations to Solve by Subtraction

All together, 292 tickets were sold for a school basketball game. An adult ticket costs \$3. A student ticket costs \$1. Ticket sales were \$470.

Write and solve a system of equations to find the number of each type of ticket sold.

Solution

Write an equation for the total number of tickets sold.

Words	total tickets	equals	number of adult tickets	plus	number of student tickets

Let a = the number of adult tickets.

Let s = the number of student tickets.

Equation	292	=	a	+	s

Write an equation for the total ticket sales.

Words	total sales	equals	price of adult ticket • number of adult tickets	plus	price of student ticket • number of student tickets

Let a = the number of adult tickets.

Let s = the number of student tickets.

Equation	470	=	$3 • a$	+	$1 • s$

The system is $a + s = 292$

$3a + s = 470$

Solve the system using subtraction.

Step 1 Solve for the first variable.

Eliminate one variable. Because the coefficients of the s-terms are the same, subtract the equations to eliminate s.

Write the original equations.	$a + s = 292$
Subtract the equations.	$\dfrac{3a + s = 470}{-2a + 0 = -178}$
Solve for a.	$a = 89$

continued on next page >

Part 3

Solution continued

Step 2 Solve for the second variable.

Substitute 89 for *a* in either equation and solve for *s*.

Write either equation.	$a + s = 292$
Substitute 89 for *a*.	$89 + s = 292$
Subtract 89 from each side.	$s = 203$

Step 3 Write the solution.

The solution is (89, 203). There were 89 adult tickets sold and 203 student tickets sold.

Step 4 Check your solution.

Check your solution by substituting (89, 203) into each equation.

$$a + s = 292 \qquad\qquad 3a + s = 470$$

$$89 + 203 \stackrel{?}{=} 292 \qquad\qquad 3(89) + 203 \stackrel{?}{=} 470$$

Substitute 89 for *a* and 203 for *s*.

$$292 = 292 \checkmark \qquad\qquad 267 + 203 \stackrel{?}{=} 470$$

$$470 = 470 \checkmark$$

1. Find the best algebraic method to solve the given system by inspecting the equations.

   $2x - 4y = -2$
   $-6x + 4y = -14$

   A. subtraction   **B.** addition
   C. substitution

2. Which of these systems of equations would be best solved using the subtraction method? Select all that apply.

   I. $3x - 4y = 0$
           $-9x + 4y = -36$

   II. $2y = x - 2$
           $y = 3x - 7$

   III. $-4x + 3y = 0$
           $-4x - 9y = -36$

   A. System III   **B.** System II
   C. System I

3. Which of these systems of equations would be best solved using the subtraction method? Select all that apply.

   I. $3x - 8y + 4y = -2$
          $-9x - 4y = -50$

   II. $2y = -7x + 8x - 1$
           $y = 3x - 7$

   III. $-8x + 4x + 3y = -2$
            $4x - 9y = -50$

   A. System I   **B.** System III
   C. System II

4. Solve the system of equations using subtraction.

   $2x - 7y = -13$
   $8x - 7y = 11$

5. Solve the system of equations using subtraction.

   $2x - 2y = -4$
   $2x + y = 11$

6. At a basketball game, a team made 56 successful shots. They were a combination of 1- and 2-point shots. The team scored 94 points in all. Write and solve a system of equations to find the number of each type of shot.

7. Yesterday, a movie theater sold 279 bags of popcorn. A large bag of popcorn costs $4. A small bag of popcorn costs $1. In all, the movie theater made $567 from popcorn sales. Write and solve a system of equations to find how many bags of each size of popcorn were sold.

8. **a. Writing** Solve the system of equations using subtraction.

   $x + y = 3$
   $x - y = 1$

   b. Describe two different ways to solve the system.

9. **a. Reasoning** Which is the best algebraic method to solve the given system by inspecting the equations?

   $3x - 6y + 2y = -1$
   $3x + 3x + 4y = 46$

   A. substitution   **B.** addition
   C. subtraction

   b. Explain your reasoning.

10. **Error Analysis** A student incorrectly claimed the solution of this system of equations is (4, −2).

    $4x - 5y = 6$
    $6x - 5y = 14$

    a. What is the correct solution?

    b. What mistake might the student have made?

    A. The signs on the *x*- and *y*-coordinates are incorrect.

    B. The sign on the *x*-coordinate is correct, but the sign on the *y*-coordinate is incorrect.

    C. The student switched the *x*- and *y*-coordinates.

    D. The sign on the *y*-coordinate is correct, but the sign on the *x*-coordinate is incorrect.

11. **Age** If you add Natalie's age and Fred's age, the result is 44. If you add Fred's age to 3 times Natalie's age, the result is 70. Write and solve a system of equations to find how old Fred and Natalie are.

See your complete lesson at MyMathUniverse.com

12. A credit card company offers a cash-back program on transactions. For every transaction over $100 the customer gets $3 back. For every transaction $100 or less, the customer gets $1 back. The customer made 18 transactions in all, and the total number of dollars given back was $24. Write and solve a system of equations to find the number of transactions of each type.

> There were ■ transactions over $100 and ■ transactions of $100 or less.

13. Estimation The perimeter of a rectangle is about 19.8 cm. If you double the width of the rectangle the perimeter is about 26.2 cm. Find the dimensions of the smaller rectangle. Round the given values to the nearest integer. Use the rounded values to write and solve a system of equations to find the length and the width of the rectangle.

14. Two airplanes are carrying food and medical supplies to a country in need. One airplane is carrying 61 meals and 59 medical kits. The total cost for the supplies on that airplane is $777. The other airplane is carrying 75 meals and 59 medical kits. The total cost for the supplies on that airplane is $847.

  a. Write and solve a system of equations to find the price of one meal and the price of one medical kit.

  b. If a third airplane is carrying 70 meals and 63 medical kits, what is the total cost of supplies?

15. Solve the system of equations using subtraction.

$-8x + 4x + 2y = -6$
$-4x + 2y - 8y = -54$

16. Think About the Process You want to solve this system of equations using subtraction. The first step is to subtract the equations to eliminate y.

$4x - 5y = 11$
$8x - 5y = 27$

a. What should be your next step?

  A. Add -16 and -4.

  B. Add -16 and 4.

  C. Divide -16 by 4.

  D. Divide -16 by -4.

b. Solve the system.

17. Think About the Process Two groups of people went shopping for camping supplies. They went to the same store. The first group spent $299 on 7 flashlights and 11 sleeping bags. The second group spent $304 on 8 flashlights and 11 sleeping bags. Let x be the price of one flashlight and y be the price for one sleeping bag. Which of these systems could you solve to find the price of one flashlight and the price of one sleeping bag?

  A. $7x + 11y = 304$
     $8x + 11y = 299$

  B. $11x + 7y = 299$
     $11x + 8y = 304$

  C. $7x + 11y = 299$
     $8x + 11y = 304$

  D. $11x + 7y = 304$
     $11x + 8y = 299$

18. Challenge Solve the system of equations using subtraction.

$3x - 8y = 7 - 6y$
$6x - 2y = 31 - 3x$

19. Challenge A car repair shop charges $1 for mounting a tire purchased from the shop. The repair shop charges $7 for mounting a tire that was purchased from another shop. Last month, the total charges for mounting tires were $812. The number of tires mounted and purchased from the shop was 440 less 3 times the number of tires mounted that were purchased from other shops. Write and solve a system of equations to find the number of tires purchased from the shop and from other shops.

CCSS: 8.EE.C.8b, 8.EE.C.8c, Also 8.EE.C.8

Key Concept

In this Topic, you have learned how to solve systems of linear equations in two variables in a variety of ways. Use the following steps to choose the most efficient method.

Step 1 Analyze the system.

Check whether the system has a solution by comparing the slopes and the *y*-intercepts of the equations.
- If the system has a solution, solve it using one of the four methods that you have studied.
- If the system does not have a solution, write "no solution." You are done.

Step 2 Decide on a method.

Choose the Graphing Method when
- the equations are in the form $y = mx + b$,

or
- you want to estimate the solution

Choose the Substitution Method when
- it is easy to isolate one of the variables on one side of an equation,

or
- the equations are in the form $y = mx + b$

Choose the Addition Method when
- the equations have both variables on one side of the equal sign,

and
- the coefficients of the same variable in each equation are additive inverses

Choose the Subtraction Method when
- the equations have both variables on one side of the equal sign,

and
- the coefficients of the same variable in each equation are the same number

continued on next page >

See your complete lesson at MyMathUniverse.com

Key Concept

continued

Step 3 Apply your method.
- Solve for one of the variables.
- Substitute to solve for the second variable.
- Write your solution.

Step 4 Check your solution.
- The solution must produce a true equation when you substitute the values for the variables in both original equations of the system.
- Make sure your answer makes sense in the original problem.

Part 1

Example Choosing Methods to Solve Systems of Linear Equations

Which method would be the most efficient method to use to solve each system? Explain your reasoning.

a. $5x + y = 12$
$8x - y = 14$

b. $-3x = 18$
$6x + 4y = 20$

c. $2x + 3y = 8$
$x + 3y = 12$

Solution $\cdots\cdots\cdots\cdots\cdots\cdots\cdots\cdots\cdots\cdots\cdots\cdots\cdots\cdots\cdots\cdots\cdots\cdots\cdots$

a. $5x + 1y = 12$
$8x - 1y = 14$
The coefficients of the y-terms are additive inverses, so use the addition method.

b. $-3x = 18$ ⟵ You can solve the first equation for x.
$6x + 4y = 20$
Use the substitution method.

c. $2x + 3y = 8$
$x + 3y = 12$
The coefficients of the y-terms are the same, so use the subtraction method.

Intro

Sometimes it is not easy to isolate one of the variables in a linear system. In that case, it may be easier to solve the system by multiplying one or both equations by a constant, if necessary, and then adding or subtracting the resulting equations.

Solve the system.

$$2a + 5b = 4$$
$$3a - 2b = 6$$

Step 1 Analyze the system and decide on a method.

$$2a + 5b = 4$$
$$3a - 2b = 6$$

Notice the coefficients of the b-terms have opposite signs. If you can make them additive inverses, then you can use addition to solve the system.

Step 2 Change the equations to eliminate one variable.

Multiply by 2. $\quad 2a + 5b = 4 \longrightarrow 4a + 10b = 8$

Multiply by 5. $\quad 3a - 2b = 6 \longrightarrow 15a - 10b = 30$

Additive inverses

Step 3 Apply your method.

When you add the equations, you get $19a = 38$. So $a = 2$.

Write either equation.	$2a + 5b = 4$
Substitute 2 for a.	$2(2) + 5b = 4$
Multiply.	$4 + 5b = 4$
Subtract 4 from each side.	$5b = 0$
Solve for b.	$b = 0$

Step 4 Write the solution.

Since $a = 2$ and $b = 0$, the solution is $(2, 0)$.

continued on next page >

Intro continued

Step 5 Check your solution.

Substitute the solution (2, 0) into each equation.

$$2a + 5b = 4 \qquad\qquad\qquad\qquad 3a - 2b = 6$$

$$2(2) + 5(0) \stackrel{?}{=} 4 \qquad\qquad\qquad 3(2) - 2(0) \stackrel{?}{=} 6$$

> Substitute 2 for a
> and 0 for b.

$$4 = 4 \checkmark \qquad\qquad\qquad\qquad\qquad 6 = 6 \checkmark$$

Example Eliminating a Variable to Solve Systems of Linear Equations

Solve the linear system.
$$2x - 3y = 0$$
$$3x - 2y = 5$$

Solution

Step 1 Analyze the system and decide on a method.

> You can choose to eliminate either variable.

$$2x - 3y = 0$$
$$3x - 2y = 5$$

If you use the addition method, you will need to multiply one of the equations by a negative number to make the coefficients of one of the variables additive inverses.

Step 2 Change the equations to eliminate one variable.

Multiply the first equation by 2 and the second equation by -3 to get coefficients of y that are opposites.

> Multiply by 2.

$$2x - 3y = 0 \longrightarrow 4x - 6y = 0$$

> Multiply by -3.

$$3x - 2y = 5 \longrightarrow -9x + 6y = -15$$

> Additive inverses

Step 3 Apply your method.

$$
\begin{array}{r}
4x - 6y = 0 \\
-9x + 6y = -15 \\
\hline
-5x + 0 = -15
\end{array}
$$

Add the equations.

Solve for x.
$$x = 3$$

continued on next page >

Part 2

Solution continued

Substitute 3 for x in either equation and solve for y.

Write either equation.	$2x - 3y = 0$
Substitute 3 for x.	$2(3) - 3y = 0$
Multiply.	$6 - 3y = 0$
Subtract 6 from each side.	$-3y = -6$
Solve for y.	$y = 2$

Step 4 Write the solution.

The solution is (3, 2).

Step 5 Check your solution.

Check your solution in both equations.

$$2x - 3y = 0 \qquad\qquad 3x - 2y = 5$$
$$2(3) - 3(2) \stackrel{?}{=} 0 \qquad\qquad 3(3) - 2(2) \stackrel{?}{=} 5$$

Substitute 3 for x and 2 for y.

$$6 - 6 \stackrel{?}{=} 0 \qquad\qquad 9 - 4 \stackrel{?}{=} 5$$
$$0 = 0 \checkmark \qquad\qquad 5 = 5 \checkmark$$

Part 3

Example **Choosing Methods and Solving Systems of Equations**

A piece of glass with an initial temperature of 99°C is cooled at a rate of 3.5°C per minute. At the same time, a piece of copper with an initial temperature of 0°C is heated at a rate of 2.5°C per minute. Let $t =$ the temperature in degrees Celsius and $m =$ the time in minutes.

a. Which method would be the most efficient to use to solve the system?

$$t = 99 - 3.5m$$
$$t = 0 + 2.5m$$

b. When will both objects reach the same temperature? What is the temperature?

Solution ·

Step 1 Analyze the system and decide on a method. Since both equations are in "$t =$" form, use the Substitution Method.

$$t = 99 - 3.5m$$
$$t = 0 + 2.5m$$

continued on next page >

Part 3

Solution continued

Step 2 Apply your method.

Write the first equation.	$t = 99 - 3.5m$
Substitute 2.5m for t.	$2.5m = 99 - 3.5m$
Add 3.5m to each side.	$6m = 99$
Divide each side by 6.	$m = 16.5$

Substitute 16.5 for m in either equation and solve for t.

Write either equation.	$t = 0 + 2.5m$
Substitute 16.5 for m.	$t = 2.5(16.5)$
Simplify.	$t = 41.25$

Step 3 Write the solution.

The solution is (16.5, 41.25). Both objects will have a temperature of 41.25°C in 16.5 minutes.

Step 4 Check your solution.

Check your solution in both equations.

$t = 99 - 3.5m$ $t = 0 + 2.5m$

$41.25 \stackrel{?}{=} 99 - 3.5(16.5)$ — Substitute 16.5 for m and 41.25 for t. → $41.25 \stackrel{?}{=} 2.5(16.5)$

$41.25 \stackrel{?}{=} 99 - 57.75$ $41.25 = 41.25 \checkmark$

$41.25 = 41.25 \checkmark$

1. Why would the subtraction method be the most efficient method to use to solve this system?

$5x + 3y = 13$
$7x + 3y = 17$

   A. The y-terms are additive inverses.

   B. The first equation can be solved easily for x.

   C. The y-terms are the same.

2. Solve the system of equations.

$2p + 5q = 1$
$5p + 13q = 2$

3. The perimeter of a standard-sized rectangular rug is 36 ft. The length is 2 ft greater than the width. Find the dimensions using the following system.

$2 + W = L$
$2W + 2L = 36$

4. **a.** Solve the system of equations.

$2p + 5q = 9$
$5p + 13q = 23$

   b. Explain what method you used and why. What other method could you have used?

5. Solve the system of equations.

$5x - 13 = 5y + 7x$
$4x + 15y = -10$

6. A math problem asks the student to solve this system using the subtraction method. When Noreen uses the subtraction method, her equation is $47x = -207$.

$2x + 5y = 58$
$7x + 6y = 111$

   a. Solve the given system of linear equations.

   b. What error might Noreen have made?

   A. Noreen subtracted the coefficients of x when they should be added.

   B. Noreen should have eliminated x instead of y to be more efficient.

   C. Noreen added the coefficients of x when they should be subtracted.

7. A seed company planted a floral mosaic of a national flag. The perimeter of the flag is 2,060 ft. Determine the flag's width and length if the length is 390 ft greater than the width.

8. **a.** Why would the addition method be the most efficient method to use to solve the following system?

$3x + 5y = 26$
$-3x + 6y = 18$

   A. The first equation can be solved easily for y.

   B. The x-terms are the same.

   C. The x-terms are additive inverses.

   b. Solve the system using another method. Explain why using the other method helps justify why the addition method is the most efficient method.

9. **a.** Find two numbers whose sum is 31 and whose difference is 1.

   b. Explain how you could solve for the two numbers using mental math.

10. **Think About the Process**

   a. If you solve the linear system by adding to eliminate x, which step could you do first?

$2x + 5y = -23$
$5x + 13y = -60$

   A. Multiply the first equation by -5 and the second equation by 2.

   B. Multiply the first equation by -5 and the second equation by -2.

   C. Multiply the first equation by -2 and the second equation by 5.

   D. Multiply the first equation by 5 and the second equation by 2.

   b. Solve for x and y.

11. a. What method would be the most efficient to use to solve the following system?

$4x + 5y = 40$

$7x + 5y = 55$

    A. the substitution method

    B. the addition method

    C. the subtraction method

b. Why is this method the most efficient to use to solve the system?

    A. The first equation can be solved easily for x.

    B. The y-terms are the same.

    C. The y-terms are additive inverses.

12. Challenge Solve the system of equations.

$$\frac{x + 6}{2} - \frac{y + 4}{3} = 5$$

$$\frac{x + y}{2} = \frac{1}{6} + \frac{x - y}{3}$$

13. Think About the Process A deli has two platters of sandwiches. The first platter costs $31 for 2 roast beef sandwiches and 3 turkey sandwiches. The other platter costs $29 for 3 roast beef sandwiches and 2 turkey sandwiches. Let x represent the cost of each roast beef sandwich and y represent the cost of each turkey sandwich.

a. What is the system of linear equations for the given scenario?

    A. $3x + 2y = 31$
       $3x + 2y = 29$

    B. $2x + 3y = 29$
       $3x + 2y = 31$

    C. $2x + 3y = 31$
       $2x + 3y = 29$

    D. $2x + 3y = 31$
       $3x + 2y = 29$

b. What is the cost of each sandwich?

14. a. Challenge An airplane is preparing to land at an airport. It is 36,000 feet above the ground and is descending at the rate of 3,300 feet per minute. At the same airport, another airplane is taking off and will ascend at the rate of 2,700 feet per minute. When will the two airplanes be at the same altitude and what will that altitude be?

b. Use two other methods to solve the problem. Explain which methods are easier to use and which are more difficult to use for the situation.

Vocabulary
function, mapping diagram, relation, vertical-line test

CCSS: 8.F.A.1

Part 1

Intro

Any set of ordered pairs is called a **relation**.

{(0, 0), (1, 8), (2, 16), (3, 24), (4, 32)}

The input values are the *x*-coordinates.

The output values are the *y*-coordinates.

Input	Output
0	0
1	8
2	16
3	24
4	32

A **mapping diagram** describes a relationship by linking the input values to the corresponding output values using arrows.

Input   **Output**

Input	Output
0	0
1	8
2	16
3	24
4	32

Example   Matching Ordered Pairs and Mapping Diagrams

Write the set of ordered pairs that corresponds to each mapping diagram.

a.
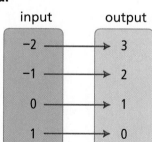

b.
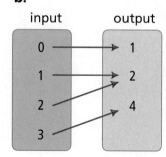

c.
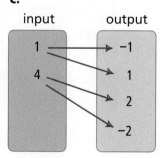

Solution ·

    a. {(−2, 3), (−1, 2), (0, 1), (1, 0)}
    b. {(0, 1), (1, 2), (2, 2), (3, 4)}
    c. {(1, −1), (1, 1), (4, 2), (4, −2)}

Key Concept

A **function** is a rule for taking each input value and producing exactly one output value.

Function

input   output

Not a Function

input   output

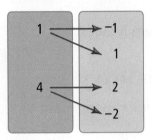

Part 2

Example **Using Mapping Diagrams to Identify Functions**

Which relations are functions? Use a mapping diagram to explain your reasoning.

    a. {(0, 1), (1, 4), (2, 5), (3, 7)}
    b. {(−2, 0,), (−1, 0), (0, 0), (1, 0)}
    c. {(0, −1), (0, 3), (1, 2), (3, 2)}

Solution ·

    a. This relation is a function because each input value produces exactly one output value.

input   output

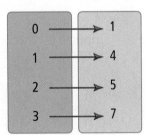

continued on next page >

Part 2

Solution continued

b. This relation is a function because each input value produces exactly one output value.

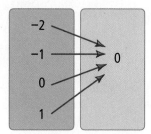

c. This relation is not a function because the input value 0 produces two different output values, −1 and 3.

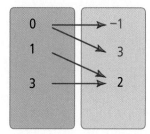

Part 3

Intro

You can describe data from a table using ordered pairs, so a relation can be also defined using a table of values.

Hours Worked	Pay ($)
0	0
1	12
2	24
3	36

Ordered Pairs
(0, 0)
(1, 12)
(2, 24)
(3, 36)

Part 3

Example Recognizing Functions

Is each relation a function? Explain.

a.

input	output
1	3
1	2
2	-4
3	2

b.

input	output
-3	-5
-2	-5
-1	-5
0	-5

c.

input	output
0	12
1	14
2	16
3	18

Solution

a. This relation is not a function because the input value 1 produces two different output values, 3 and 2.

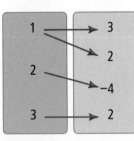

b. This relation is a function because each input value produces exactly one output value.

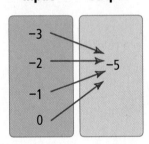

c. This relation is a function because each input value produces exactly one output value.

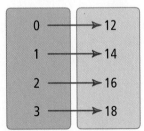

Part 4

Intro

A two-variable relationship is often represented by a graph. So, it makes sense that a relation can be defined by a graph.

If the graph of a relation displays points with coordinates that are easily read, you can write the ordered pairs and then use a mapping diagram to determine whether the relation is a function.

There is a way other than mapping diagrams to inspect a relation and determine if it is a function.

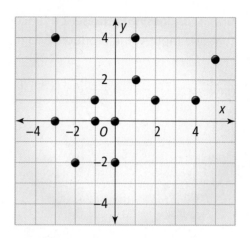

You can use a pencil or a straight edge to represent a vertical line. Place the pencil at the left of the graph. Move it to the right across the graph. If, for each input value, it passes through exactly one point on the graph, then the graph represents a function. Remember to keep the pencil vertical at all times as you move it across the graph.

Example Using the Vertical Line Test

Use the vertical line test to determine if each graph represents a function.

a.
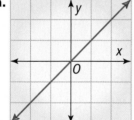

b.
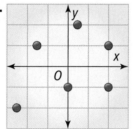

c.
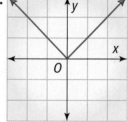

Solution

Graph (a) represents a function because each input value produces exactly one output value.

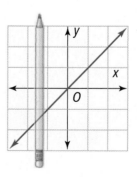

continued on next page >

Solution continued

Graph (b) does not represent a function because the vertical line test reveals that one input value produces two different output values here.

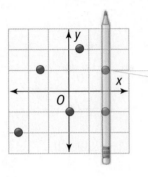

The pencil touches the relation in two places here. The relation is not a function.

Graph (c) represents a function because each input value produces exactly one output value.

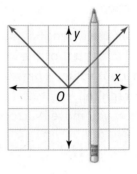

1. Write a set of ordered pairs represented by the mapping diagram shown.

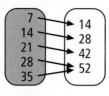

A. {(14,7), (28,14), (21,42), (52,28), (35,52)}

B. {(7,14), (28,14), (21,42), (52,28), (35,52)}

C. {(14,7), (28,14), (42,21), (52,28), (52,35)}

D. {(7,14), (14,28), (21,42), (28,52), (35,52)}

2. Draw a mapping diagram of the ordered pairs {(3,17), (5,19), (7,19), (11,23), (13,29)}.

3. a. Draw a mapping diagram which represents the relation {(1,6), (2,5), (2,7), (7,9), (4,10), (1,1)}.

b. Is the relation a function?

4. Does the relation {(5,−2), (5,−8), (4,−6), (7,−1)} represent a function?

5. a. Draw a mapping diagram of the relation shown.

b. Is the relation a function?

Input	Output
5	10
9	32
13	10
16	32

6. Is the relation shown in the table a function?

Input	Output
4	1
8	3
4	3
8	4

7. Is the graph that of a function?

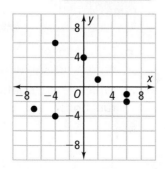

8. a. Writing Write a set of ordered pairs is represented by the mapping diagram.

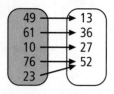

b. Describe the relation.

9. Reasoning Does the relation {(−2,2), (−7,1), (−3,9), (−8,4), (−9,5), (−6,8)} represent a function? Explain your reasoning.

10. Error Analysis On a recent math test, students had to use a graph to decide if the relation represented by the ordered pairs {(1,2), (6,12), (12,24), (18,36)} is a function. Bobby drew the graph shown and said the relation was not a function. Part of his answer was incorrect.

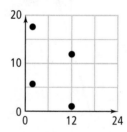

a. Draw a graph which represents the relation.

b. Is the relation a function?

c. What error did Bobby most likely make?

A. Bobby drew the incorrect graph. The correct graph of the relation is a function. Bobby's graph is not a function.

B. Bobby drew the incorrect graph. The correct graph of the relation is not a function. Bobby's graph is a function.

C. Bobby drew the correct graph but said that the relation was not a function. The relation is a function.

See your complete lesson at MyMathUniverse.com

11. Multiple Representations The ordered pairs of four relations are listed in the table.

Relation 1		Relation 2		Relation 3		Relation 4	
x	y	x	y	x	y	x	y
3	3	5	31	2	3	7	10
4	5	6	28	3	3	8	20
5	7	7	25	4	3	9	30
5	9	8	22	5	3	9	40
6	11	9	19	6	3	10	50

a. Select each relation that is a function.

b. Write out the ordered pairs and draw a graph for each relation.

12. Use the vertical line test to determine whether the relation is also a function. Is the relation also a function?

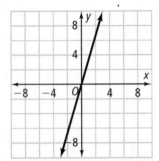

13. a. Draw a graph which represents the relation shown.

b. Is the relation a function? Use the vertical line test to decide.

Input	Output
3	2
3	4
6	1
6	3

14. Think About the Process

Input	Output
−3	−24
2	−42
12	−24
14	−42

a. Draw a mapping diagram of the relation shown in the table.

b. Is the relation a function?

c. Describe how a mapping diagram can be helpful when you need to decide whether a relation is a function.

15. Think About the Process

a. How does a mapping diagram describe a relation?

A. A mapping diagram describes a relation by linking the input values to the corresponding output values using arrows.

B. A mapping diagram describes a relation by linking the output values to the corresponding input values using arrows.

b. Draw a mapping diagram which represents the relation shown.

{(3,39), (6,39), (9,78), (15,117)}

16. a. Challenge Draw a mapping diagram of the ordered pairs {(5,10), (10,20), (15,30), (20,40), (25,40)}.

b. Is the relation a function?

c. Describe how you can use different representations of a relation to analyze a situation.

17. a. Challenge Draw a mapping diagram which represents Relation P.

Relation P		Relation Q	
Input	Output	Input	Output
3	6	6	7
7	14	6	16
15	6	14	3
16	14	14	15

b. Draw a mapping diagram which represents Relation Q.

c. Which of the relations are functions?

CCSS: 8.F.A.1

Key Concept

Recall that a function is a relationship between two quantities, called the input and the output, where for each input, there is exactly one output.

You can represent functions in four ways. Each of these ways may be considered a "view" of the relationship. When you know one view, you can usually determine the remaining three views.

Ordered Pairs A set of ordered pairs identifies specific values that satisfy the function.

Suppose a car gets 28 miles per gallon. In this situation, distance is a function of the number of gallons of gasoline.

The input is the number of gallons of gas.
The output is the distance.

(input, output)
(x, y)
(1, 28)
(2, 56)
(3, 84)

Table of Values A table identifies specific values that satisfy the function.

Input, x (number of gallons)	Output, y (distance in miles)
1	28
2	56
3	84
4	112

Graph A graph gives a visual picture of the function.

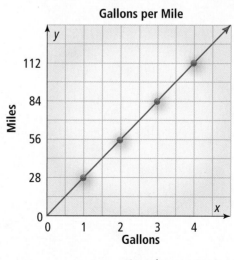

Gallons per Mile

continued on next page >

Key Concept

continued

Rule A function is a rule for taking each input value and producing exactly one output value.

$$y = 28x$$

Input variable, number of gallons of gas

output variable, distance (in miles)

Part 1

Example Representing Functions in Different Ways

During one hour of walking, you burn about 257 Calories. The total number of Calories burned is a function of the number of hours you walked. How can you represent this situation in four different ways?

Solution

The total number of Calories burned is a function of the number of hours you walked. Since the Calories burned depends on the hours walked, the input is time (in hours) and the output is the number of Calories burned.

View 1: Ordered pairs

(input, output)
(0, 0)
(1, 257)
(2, 514)
(3, 771)
(4, 1,028)

View 2: Table of values

Calories Burned Walking

Time (hours)	Calories Burned
0	0
1	257
2	514
3	771
4	1,028

continued on next page >

Part 1

Solution continued

View 3: Graph

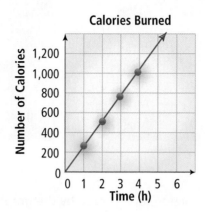

View 4: Rule

During one hour of walking, you burn about 257 Calories.

Words

| Total Calories burned | equals | Calories burned per hour | times | Time |

Let x = the number of hours walked.

Let y = the total number of Calories burned.

Equation

| y | = | 257 | • | x |

$$y = 257x$$

The function rule is $y = 257x$.

Part 2

Example Relating Graphs and Tables of Functions

Which table could be a view of the function represented by the graph?

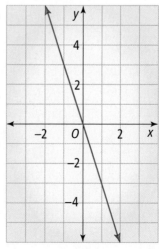

continued on next page >

Part 2

Example continued

A.

x	y
0	0
1	3
2	6
3	9

B.

x	y
0	0
1	−3
2	−6
3	−9

C.

x	y
−3	6
−2	2
−1	1
0	0

Solution

Table B is another view of the function represented by the graph.

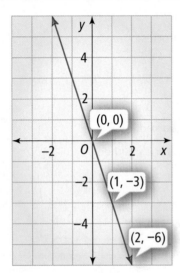

B.

x	y
0	0
1	−3
2	−6
3	−9

1. The value of y is one more than x.

a. Represent this relationship by completing the table.

x	y	Ordered Pair (x, y)
0	1	(0, 1)
1	■	■
2	■	■
3	■	■

b. Represent the relationship using an equation. Simplify your answer. Write an expression using x as the variable.

c. Draw a graph to represent the relationship.

2. You can make 7 gal of liquid fertilizer by mixing 8 tsp of powdered fertilizer with water.

a. Represent the relationship between the teaspoons of powder used and the gallons of fertilizer by completing the table.

x	y	Ordered Pair (x, y)
0	■	■
8	7	(8, 7)
16	■	■
24	■	■

b. Represent the relationship using an equation. Simplify your answer. Write an expression using x as the variable.

c. Draw a graph to represent the relationship.

3. Estimation A train leaves the station at time $x = 0$. Traveling at a constant speed, the train travels 242 km in 1.7 h.

a. Round to the nearest 10 km and the nearest whole hour.

The train travels about ■ km in about ■ h.

b. Represent the relationship using a table. For 2, 3, and 4 hours, give values for distance traveled and the corresponding ordered pair.

c. Represent the relationship using an equation. Write an expression using x as the variable.

d. Graph the relationship.

4. Mental Math Make a table of values for the function $y = \frac{2}{5}x + 1$. Complete the table.

x	y
10	■
5	■
−5	■
−10	■

5. a. Writing Complete the table of values that matches the graph.

x	y
■	1
4	■
8	■
■	7

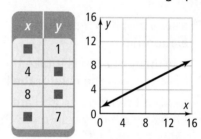

b. Describe a situation you could model using this graph and table of values. Interpret the meaning of the point (80,38) in your situation.

6. a. Reasoning Without completing the table, which equation could match this table?

A. $y = 2x + 3$
B. $y = 3x + 2$
C. $y = x + 3$
D. $y = 2x - 3$

x	y
−8	■
−4	■
0	3
4	11
8	■

b. Complete the table.

7. Estimation While exploring a planet, a robot descends at a rate of 267 feet every 3.3 hours from a hill peak 1,620 feet above sea level.

  a. Estimate the robot's rate of descent by rounding to the nearest 10 feet and the nearest whole hour.

  b. In the table below, represent the robot's elevation, y, after x hours.

Hours, x	Elevation, y (feet)	Ordered Pair (x, y)
3	■	■
4	■	■
10	■	■

  c. Represent the relationship using an equation. Simplify your answer. Write an expression using x as the variable.

  d. Draw a graph to represent the relationship.

  e. How many hours will it take the robot to reach the base of the hill?

8. Think About the Process You are given the function "y is six more than x divided by three."

  a. Which form is best to find first? A table, an equation, or a graph?

  b. Represent the relationship using an equation. Write an expression using x as the variable.

  c. Represent the relationship using a table. Complete the table below.

x	y	Ordered Pair (x, y)
−3	5	(−3, 5)
0	■	■
3	■	■
6	■	■

  d. Graph the relationship.

9. Think About the Process

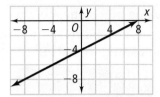

  a. What do you notice about the graph that could help you make a table of values?

    A. The y-values are always greater than the x-values.

    B. As the x-values increase, the y-values always increase.

    C. The y-values are always less than the x-values.

    D. As the x-values increase, the y-values always decrease.

  b. Use the graph to complete the table.

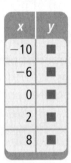

x	y
−10	■
−6	■
0	■
2	■
8	■

10. Challenge The value of y is eight more than one-half x.

  a. Represent the relationship by completing the table.

x	y	Ordered Pair (x, y)
0	8	(0, 8)
2	■	■
4	■	■
6	■	■

  b. Represent the relationship using an equation. Simplify your answer.

  c. Draw a graph to represent the relationship.

Vocabulary
linear function,
rate of change

CCSS: 8.F.A.3, 8.F.B.5

Key Concept

A **linear function** is a function that has a constant rate of change. Its graph is a straight line.

In an earlier lesson, you learned that the slope of a line is a ratio that compares a vertical change to the corresponding horizontal change.

$$\text{slope} = \frac{\text{vertical change}}{\text{horizontal change}}$$

You can also describe slope as a rate of change. A **rate of change** is a comparison between two quantities that are changing. If you draw a graph of the quantities, then

$$\text{rate of change} = \frac{\text{vertical change}}{\text{horizontal change}}$$

Consider the following set of ordered pairs.

{(2, 1), (5, 3), (8, 5), (11, 7)}

Using the vertical line test, you can see that the graph represents a function. Since the graph is a straight line, the ordered pairs represent a linear function.

$$\text{rate of change} = \frac{\text{vertical change}}{\text{horizontal change}}$$

$$= \frac{2}{3}$$

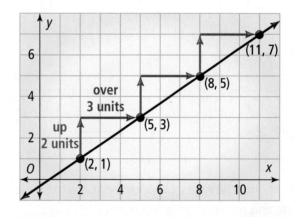

Part 1

Example Graphing Ordered Pairs to Identify Linear Functions

Graph each set of ordered pairs to determine if it represents a linear function. If it does, find the rate of change.

    a. {(1, 5), (2, 7), (3, 9), (4, 11), (5, 13),}
    b. {(0, 0), (1, 1), (2, 4), (3, 9)}

continued on next page >

Part 1

Example continued

Solution

a. Make a graph of the ordered pairs.

You can connect the points with a straight line and each input has only one output, so the ordered pairs represent a linear function.

The rate of change is $\frac{2}{1}$ or 2.

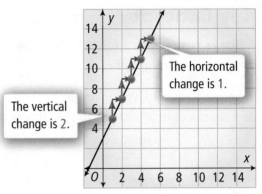

The vertical change is 2.

The horizontal change is 1.

b. Make a graph of the ordered pairs.

You can't connect the points with a straight line, so the ordered pairs do not represent a linear function.

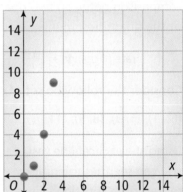

Part 2

Intro

You can find the rate of change from a table by finding the change in the inputs and the change in the outputs.

$$\text{rate of change} = \frac{\text{change in output}}{\text{change in input}}$$

Does the following table represent a linear function?

Input	Output
1	5
2	8
3	11
4	14
5	17

1 ⟩ 3
1 ⟩ 3
1 ⟩ 3
1 ⟩ 3

$$\text{rate of change} = \frac{\text{change in output}}{\text{change in input}}$$

$$= \frac{3}{1}, \text{ or } 3$$

continued on next page >

Part 2

Since the rate of change is constant and each input has only one output, the table represents a linear function.

Example Identifying Linear Functions from Tables

Does the relation defined by each table represent a linear function? Explain.

a.

Input	Output
0	2
1	4
2	7
3	8
4	10

b.

Input	Output
0	0
3	1
6	3
9	6
12	10

Solution ·

a. Find the change in the inputs and the change in the outputs.

Input	Output
0	2
1	4
2	7
3	8
4	10

rate of change $= \frac{\text{change in output}}{\text{change in input}}$

The rate of change from the first pair of values to the second pair of values is $\frac{2}{1}$. However, the rate of change from the second pair of values to third is $\frac{3}{1}$.

Since the rate of change is not constant, this relation is not a linear function.

b. Find the change in the inputs and the change in the outputs.

Input	Output
0	0
3	1
6	3
9	6
12	10

rate of change $= \frac{\text{change in output}}{\text{change in input}}$

The rate of change from the first pair of values to the second pair of values is $\frac{1}{3}$. However, the rate of change from the second pair of values to third is $\frac{2}{3}$.

Since the rate of change is not constant, this relation is not a linear function.

Part 3

Intro

You can use linear functions to analyze situations, make predictions, or draw conclusions.

Example Using Rate of Change of Linear Functions

When a scuba diver goes under water, the weight of the water puts pressure on the diver. The table shows how the water pressure on the diver increases as the diver's depth increases.

Water Pressure on a Diver

Diver's Depth (ft)	Water Pressure (lb/in.^{2})
10	4.4
20	8.8
30	13.2
40	17.6

a. What is the rate of charge of this linear function? What does this rate of change represent in this situation?

b. Use the rate of change to predict the water pressure on a diver at a depth of 60 feet and at a depth of 100 feet.

Solution

a. Find the change in the inputs and the change in the outputs.

The rate of change is $\frac{4.4}{10}$.

This means that the water pressure increases 4.4 pounds per square inch of pressure for each increase of 10 feet in depth.

Water Pressure on a Diver

Diver's Depth (ft)	Water Pressure (lb/ in.^{2})
10	4.4
20	8.8
30	13.2
40	17.6

10) 10) 10)   ) 4.4) 4.4) 4.4

continued on next page >

Part 3

Solution continued

b. Use the rate of change to extend the table.

The water pressure at 60 feet is 26.4 lb/in.²

The water pressure at 100 feet is 44 lb/in.²

Water Pressure on a Diver

Diver's Depth (ft)	Water Pressure (lb/ in.²)
10	4.4
20	8.8
30	13.2
40	17.6
50	22.0
60	26.4
70	30.8
80	35.2
90	39.6
100	44.0

10 ... 4.4 (repeated for each interval)

1. a. Draw a graph which shows the set of ordered pairs {(1,5), (2,7), (3,9), (4,11), (5,13)}.

   b. Does the set of ordered pairs represent a linear function?

2. The graph of the set of ordered pairs below represents a linear function. Find the rate of change.

   {(1, 6.1), (2, 9.1), (3, 12.1), (4, 15.1)}

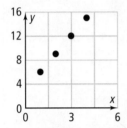

3. Does the relation defined by the table represent a linear function?

Input	Output
1	10
2	13
3	16
4	19
5	22

   A. Yes, because the rate of change is not constant.

   B. Yes, because the rate of change is 3.

   C. No, because the rate of change is 3.

   D. No, because the rate of change is not constant.

4. Determine whether the relation defined by the table represents a linear function. Explain your answer.

Input	Output
4	14.4
7	24.2
10	35.0
13	32.8
16	45.6

   A. Yes, because the rate of change is 2.6.

   B. No, because the rate of change is not constant.

   C. No, because the rate of change is 2.6.

   D. Yes, because the rate of change is not constant.

5. A student is completing a homework assignment. Each minute, the student records the number of problems left to complete. The table shows the data.

Homework Assignment						
Time (minutes)	0	1	2	3	4	5
Problems Left	23	20	17	14	11	8

   a. What is the rate of change of this linear function?

   b. What does the rate of change represent in this situation?

6. a. **Reasoning** Does the relation represent a linear function?

Input	Output
1	54
2	162
3	486
4	1,458
5	4,374

   A. Yes, because the rate of change is not constant.

   B. No, because the rate of change is not constant.

   C. Yes, because the rate of change is 18.

   D. No, because the rate of change is 18.

   b. If the change in outputs for a relation is not constant, does that mean the relation is not linear? Explain your reasoning.

See your complete lesson at MyMathUniverse.com

7. Estimation The graph of the set of ordered pairs represents a linear function.

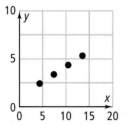

a. Estimate the rate of change.

b. Suppose that the ordered pair $(20, y)$ is also part of the linear function. Estimate the value of y.

8. The set of ordered pairs {(22,18), (17,14), (12,10), (7,6)} represents a linear function.

a. Draw a graph which shows the set of ordered pairs.

b. What is the rate of change?

9. Think About the Process A highway maintenance crew uses a special hydroseeding liquid to grow grass along the sides of the highway. One worker measures the depth of the liquid in the holding tank and the area of the land sprayed. The table shows the data. **(Figure 1)**

a. Which data points can you use to find the rate of change? Select all that apply.

A. (0, 14.4) and (3, 13.5)

B. (0, 14.4) and (0, 13.5)

C. (3, 13.5) and (5, 12.9)

D. (0, 14.4) and (14.4, 0)

E. (0, 14.4) and (11, 11.1)

F. (14.4, 3) and (13.5, 3)

b. What is the rate of change of this linear function?

c. What does the rate of change represent in this situation?

For every square foot of land sprayed, the depth of the tank decreases by ■ inch.

10. Think About the Process Below is a set of ordered pairs.

{(1, 1.0), (1, 1.3), (1, 1.6), (1, 1.9), (1, 2.2)}

a. What are the requirements for a set of ordered pairs to represent a linear function?

b. Graph the set of ordered pairs.

c. Does the set of ordered pairs represent a linear function?

11. Challenge You use a faucet to fill a watering can that holds 85.8 ounces of water. You measure the amount of the water in the can every 4 seconds. The table shows the data. **(Figure 2)**

a. What is the rate of change of the amount of the water in the watering can?

b. What does the rate of change mean in this situation?

c. How many seconds after the last measurement in the table will the watering can be full?

(Figure 1)

Growing Grass					
Area Sprayed (square feet)	0	3	5	8	11
Depth of Liquid (inches)	14.4	13.5	12.9	12.0	11.1

(Figure 2)

Filling a Watering Can					
Time (seconds)	0	4	8	12	16	20
Ounces of Water	0	8.8	17.6	26.4	35.2	44.0

See your complete lesson at MyMathUniverse.com

CCSS: 8.F.A.3, 8.F.B.5, Also 8.F.A.1

Key Concept

Think of a juggler's ball being tossed in the air and falling back down. The relationship between speed and time is not always the same:

- As the ball rises, the speed decreases.
- As the ball falls, the speed increases.

The table shows the height of a juggling ball at a given time. You can plot the data from the table on a graph.

Input Time (s)	Output Height (ft)
0	3
1	5
2	6
3	5
4	3

Left differences: 1, 1, 1, 1
Right differences: 2, 1, −1, −2

The rate of change is not constant.

Height of a Juggling Ball

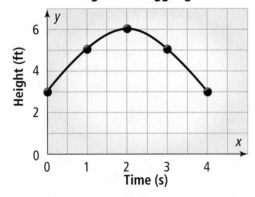

Rate of change is the change in the outputs divided by the change in the inputs. The rate of change is not constant. In cases like these, nonlinear functions are needed to describe how the variables are related. **Nonlinear functions** are functions that do not have a constant rate of change. The graph of a nonlinear function is not a straight line.

Part 1

Example Identifying Graphs as Linear or Nonlinear Functions

Identify whether each graph is a linear function or a nonlinear function.

a. 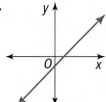   b.   c.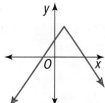

Solution

Linear Function

a.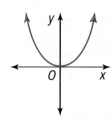

This graph is a straight line, so it represents a linear function.

Nonlinear Functions

b. 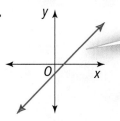   c.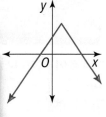

These graphs are not straight lines, so they do not represent linear functions.

Part 2

Example Recognizing Nonlinear Functions from Tables

Identify the tables that represent nonlinear functions. Explain your reasoning.

a.

Input	Output
1	−8
2	−16
3	−24
4	−32
5	−40

b.

Input	Output
1	1.5
2	2.5
3	5.5
4	8.5
5	10.5

c.

Input	Output
1	1
2	3
3	6
4	10
5	15

Solution

a.

Input	Output
1	−8
2	−16
3	−24
4	−32
5	−40

1 ⟶)−8
1 ⟶)−8
1 ⟶)−8
1 ⟶)−8

The rate of change is constant, $-\frac{8}{1}$ or −8, so this function is a linear function.

b.

Input	Output
1	1.5
2	2.5
3	5.5
4	8.5
5	10.5

1 ⟶)1
1 ⟶)3
1 ⟶)3
1 ⟶)2

Since the rate of change is not constant, this function is a nonlinear function.

c.

Input	Output
1	1
2	3
3	6
4	10
5	15

1 ⟶)2
1 ⟶)3
1 ⟶)4
1 ⟶)5

The rate of change is not constant so this is a nonlinear function.

Part 3

Example Analyzing Nonlinear Relationships

Suppose there are 20 rabbits on an island and that the rabbit population can triple every six months.

a. Make a table of values to find how many rabbits there would be after 2 years.

b. Does this relationship represent a nonlinear function? Explain.

c. Using the table, when would you expect the rabbit population to reach 1,000,000 rabbits?

Solution

a. After two years, there would be 1,620 rabbits.

Rabbit Population

Time (yr)	Number of Rabbits
0	20
$\frac{1}{2}$	20 × 3 = 60
1	60 × 3 = 180
$1\frac{1}{2}$	180 × 3 = 540
2	540 × 3 = 1,620

b. Find the rate of change. Since the rate of change is not constant, this relationship represents a nonlinear function.

Rabbit Population

Time (yr)	Number of Rabbits
0	20
$\frac{1}{2}$	20 × 3 = 60
1	60 × 3 = 180
$1\frac{1}{2}$	180 × 3 = 540
2	540 × 3 = 1,620

$\frac{1}{2}$) 40
$\frac{1}{2}$) 120
$\frac{1}{2}$) 360
$\frac{1}{2}$) 1,080

continued on next page >

Solution continued

c. After 5 years, the rabbit population will be over 1,000,000.

Rabbit Population

Time (yr)	Number of Rabbits
0	20
$\frac{1}{2}$	$20 \times 3 = 60$
1	$60 \times 3 = 180$
$1\frac{1}{2}$	$180 \times 3 = 540$
2	$540 \times 3 = 1,620$
$2\frac{1}{2}$	$1,620 \times 3 = 4,860$
3	$4,860 \times 3 = 14,580$
$3\frac{1}{2}$	$14,580 \times 3 = 43,740$
4	$43,740 \times 3 = 131,220$
$4\frac{1}{2}$	$131,220 \times 3 = 393,660$
5	$393,660 \times 3 = 1,180,980$

1. Justin opens a savings account with $4. He saves $2 each week. The table represents his account balance. Decide whether the table represents a linear function or a nonlinear function.

Justin's Savings Account						
Week	0	1	2	3	4	5
Money in Account	4	6	8	10	12	14

2. **a.** Which function or functions are linear?

   b. Which function or functions are nonlinear?

Function I

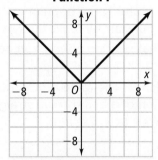

Function II

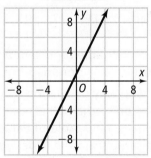

Function III

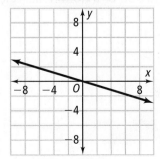

3. **Error Analysis** A student was asked to decide which table or tables represent a linear function. She incorrectly said that only Table II represents a linear function.

Table I					
Input	4	8	12	16	20
Output	10	2	−6	−14	−22

Table II					
Input	2	4	6	8	10
Output	9	16	25	36	49

Table III					
Input	−4	−8	−12	−16	−20
Output	−23	−35	−47	−59	−71

a. Decide which table or tables represent a linear function.

b. What mistake might the student have made?

   A. She found the function that decreases instead of increases.

   B. She found a nonlinear function instead of a linear function.

   C. She found the function that represents a straight line.

   D. She found the function with a constant rate of change.

4. **a. Multiple Representations** Does the table represent a linear function or a nonlinear function?

Input	Output
0	3
1	4
2	11
3	30
4	67

b. Use separate graph paper to plot the points from the table.

See your complete lesson at MyMathUniverse.com

5. a. Which of these tables represents a linear function?

Table I

Input	Output
0	9
1	4
2	1
3	0
4	1

Table II

Input	Output
0	27
1	22
2	17
3	12
4	7

b. Explain your reasoning.

6. Think About the Process

Input	Output
0	2
1	1
2	0
3	−1
4	0

a. What is the first step to decide whether the table represents a linear or a nonlinear function?

A. Calculate the slope using two points.

B. Find the y-intercept.

C. Find the x-intercept.

D. Find the rate of change.

b. Does the table represent a linear or a nonlinear function?

7. Think About the Process The population of an endangered species declines by a factor of 4 every 10 years. The table represents the population of the species over 50 years. (**Figure 1**)

a. Decide whether the table represents a linear function or a nonlinear function.

b. How would you find the population after 60 years?

A. Add 4 to the population after 50 years.

B. Divide the population after 50 years by 4.

C. Subtract 4 from the population after 50 years.

D. Multiply the population after 50 years by 4.

c. What will the population be after 60 years?

8. Challenge The table represents the position of a ball thrown straight up in the air over 5 seconds.

Position of a Ball					
Time (seconds)	1	2	3	4	5
Position (inches)	12.5	17	20.5	23	24.5

a. Does the table represent a linear function or a nonlinear function?

b. Explain why you cannot find the position of the ball after 6 seconds. Create a new table of values for the same situation. Does your table of values represent a linear function or a nonlinear function?

(Figure 1)

Population of an Endangered Species					
Years	10	20	30	40	50
Population	92,160	23,040	5,760	1,440	360

See your complete lesson at MyMathUniverse.com

CCSS: 8.F.B.5

Part 1

Intro

An interval is a period of time between two points of time or events.

A jogger begins her run around a park by increasing her speed until she reaches her normal jogging speed. She then jogs at a constant speed for most of her run. Finally, she begins her cool-down by jogging at a slower rate until she stops.

There are 3 distinct intervals for this situation: the interval where the jogger's speed is *increasing*, the interval where she runs at a constant speed, and the interval where her speed is decreasing.

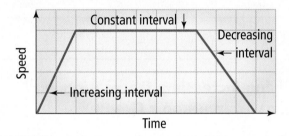

Example Identifying Intervals From Graphs

Label each interval as *increasing, constant,* or *decreasing*.

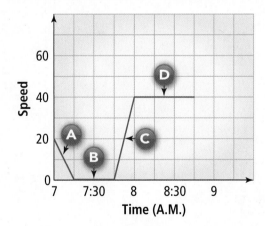

continued on next page >

Part 1

Example continued

Solution

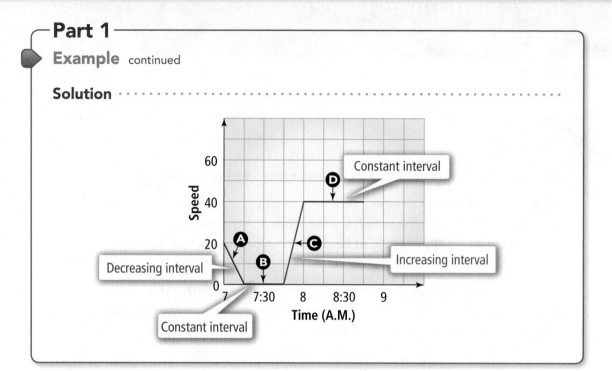

Constant interval

Decreasing interval

Increasing interval

Constant interval

Part 2

Example **Identifying Increasing, Decreasing, and Constant Intervals on a Graph**

Label the graphs to indicate which intervals are increasing, decreasing, or constant.

a.

b.

Solution

a.

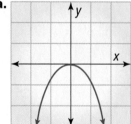

Increasing interval

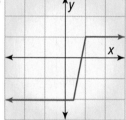
Decreasing interval

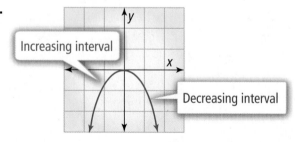

continued on next page >

Part 2

Solution continued

b.

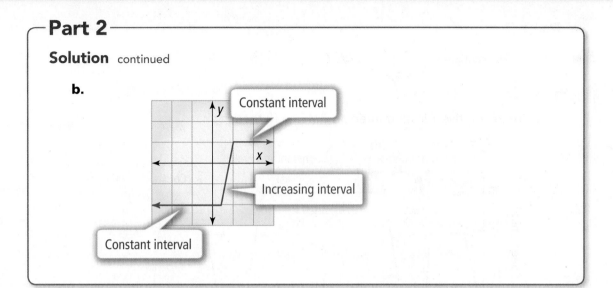

Part 3

Example Comparing Intervals on Graphs

The graph shows the speed of a commuter boat as it makes an evening trip.

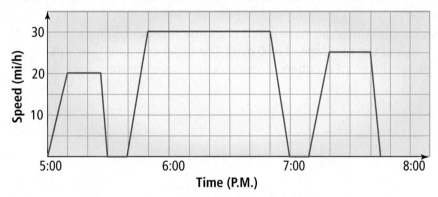

a. How many constant intervals are defined in the graph?

b. How are the constant intervals alike?

c. How are the constant intervals different?

continued on next page >

Part 3

Example continued

Solution ·

a. There are five constant intervals defined in the graph.

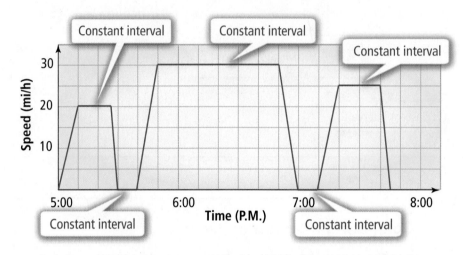

b. All of the constant intervals indicate lengths of time when the speed is constant.

c. Two constant intervals have about the same number of minutes in length and the same speed of 0 mi/h. The other constant intervals occur for different numbers of minutes and have different speeds.

1. You have a device that monitors the voltage across a lamp in a certain circuit. The results are shown in the graph. Use the graph to classify intervals of behavior of the given function.

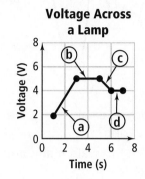

Voltage Across a Lamp

2. **a.** Which intervals, if any, are increasing?

   b. Which intervals, if any, are decreasing?

   c. Which intervals, if any, are constant?

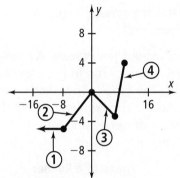

3. The graph shows the speed of a bus during the morning commute.

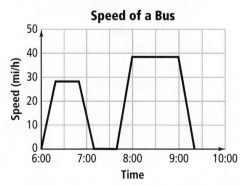

Speed of a Bus

   a. How many increasing intervals are defined in the graph?

   b. How are the increasing intervals alike?

   c. How are the increasing intervals different?

4. **Writing** You have a device that monitors the sound pressure level of a normal conversation located 1 meter away. The results are shown in the graph.

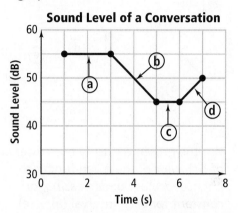

Sound Level of a Conversation

   a. Use the graph to classify intervals of behavior of the given function.

   b. Explain what a constant interval represents in this situation.

5. **Think About the Process** The graph shows the speed of your neighbor's car on his way back home last Friday. You want to find the number of constant intervals defined in the graph.

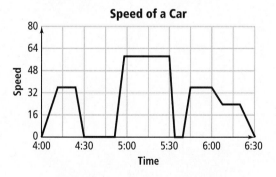

Speed of a Car

   a. What should be your first step?

   b. How many constant intervals are defined in the graph?

See your complete lesson at MyMathUniverse.com

6. Temperature Yesterday, your friend used a thermometer to measure the temperature in degrees Fahrenheit inside the refrigerator between 5:00 P.M. and 7:00 P.M. The results are shown in the graph. Use the graph to classify intervals of behavior of the given function.

Temperature Inside a Refrigerator

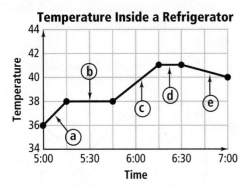

7. Use the graph to classify each interval of behavior of the given function. Choose *increasing*, *decreasing*, or *constant* for each interval (a) − (e).

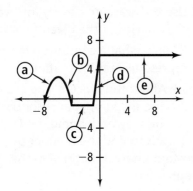

8. You are given the following graph.

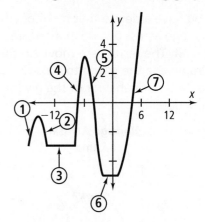

a. Which intervals, if any, are increasing?

b. Which intervals, if any, are decreasing?

c. Which intervals, if any, are constant?

9. Think About the Process A runner went out for a run in the park last night. The graph shows her speed during the run. You want to find the number of decreasing intervals defined in the graph.

Speed of a Runner

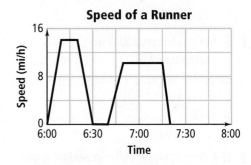

a. What should be your first step?

   A. Identify the lines that have negative slope.

   B. Identify the lines that have positive slope.

   C. Identify the lines that have a slope of zero.

b. How many decreasing intervals are defined in the graph?

CCSS: 8.F.B.5

Part 1

Intro

When you draw a graph without actual data, you are making a sketch. A sketch can help you to visualize relationships. Consider the following situation.

An athlete measures her pulse rate during a 50-minute workout. The workout includes a 10-minute warm-up period and a 5-minute cool-down period. Sketch and label a graph showing her pulse rate during her workout.

Step 1 Identify the two variables being related.

Time, t

Pulse Rate, r

Step 2 Look for key words that describe the relationship.

Warm-up means pulse rate is increasing.

Cool-down means pulse rate is decreasing.

Step 3 Sketch and label the graph.

Total time − (warm up + cool-down)

50 − (10 + 5)

50 − 15

35

35-minute steady rate.

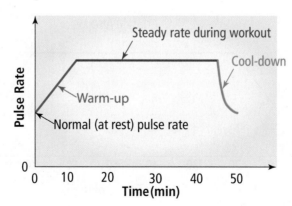

See your complete lesson at MyMathUniverse.com

Part 1

> ### Example Sketching Graphs from Verbal Descriptions

An airplane flew from Melbourne, Australia to Sydney, Australia in 85 minutes. The plane took 20 minutes to reach its cruising altitude and 15 minutes to descend into Sydney. Sketch a graph that shows the plane's altitude during the flight.

Solution ·

Step 1 Identify the two variables being related.

The variables being related are Time, t, and Altitude, a.

Step 2 Look for key words that describe the relationship.

To reach its cruising altitude means the plane was going up or increasing its altitude.

Cruising altitude is the height where the plane levels off and flies parallel to the ground. The plane will maintain this altitude for a major portion of its flight. Passengers are free to walk around during this part of the flight.

Descend means that the plane is coming down or decreasing its altitude.

Step 3 Sketch and label the graph.

Define the parts of the flight:

    A 20-minute ascent or climb.
    A 50-minute period at cruising altitude.
    A 15-minute descent.

> cruising time = total time − (20 + 15)
>   = 85 − 35
>   = 50

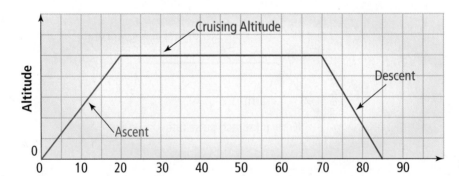

Part 2

Example Matching Verbal Descriptions to Their Graphs

These two situations describe actions that take place after school.

Match each description with its corresponding graph.

a. You leave home and ride your bicycle to the library, where you stay for a while doing research for your science report. Then you ride to your friend's house.

b. You ride your bicycle home from soccer practice. On the way, you stop at your friend's house for a while and then go straight home.

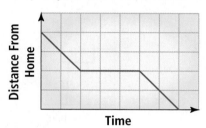 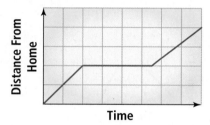

Solution

a. As you ride from home to the library and then to your friend's house, the distance from your home increases as you get farther away from your home. So this graph matches the description.

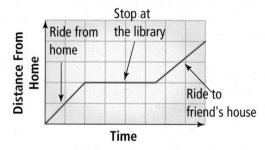

b. As you ride your bike home from soccer practice, the distance to your home is decreasing as you get closer to your home. So this graph matches this description.

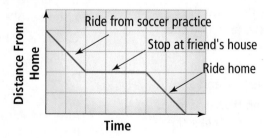

1. Aaron left the theatre, drove toward his workplace, got gas, and then continued driving to his workplace. Let *g* be the amount of gas (in gallons) in the gas tank at *t* minutes after he left the theatre. Draw a graph which shows the relationship between *g* and *t*.

2. Which of the following is a good description of the given graph?

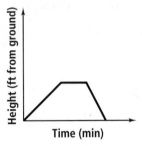

Height (ft from ground) vs. Time (min)

   A. A jet is flying at the same height the whole time.

   B. A jet is going up the whole time.

   C. A jet is coming down from the sky. It reaches a height and stays at that height for a certain period of time. Finally the jet goes higher into the sky.

   D. A jet is going up in the air. It reaches its necessary height and stays at that height for a period of time. Finally the jet is coming down to the ground.

3. **Open-Ended** Ricardo starts at his house and drives for 10 minutes to a friend's house. He stays there for 60 minutes. Let *T* be the time since Ricardo left the house, and *S* be the distance in miles from his house.

   a. Draw a graph that shows the relationship between *T* and *S*.

   b. Describe a situation that would also have a similar graph like the given situation.

4. **Writing** Let *D* be the temperature (in degrees Fahrenheit) at a specific outdoor location at *T* hours after 6 A.M. on a specific day. The temperature rose for 5 hours. Then it

dropped for 12 hours before it rose again for another 7 hours.

   a. Draw a graph which shows the relationship between *D* and *T*.

   b. Explain in words what the highest point on the graph represents and what the lowest point on the graph represents.

5. **a.** **Reasoning** Write a description of the given graph.

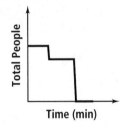

Total People vs. Time (min)

   b. Explain how you know whether an interval is increasing, decreasing, or constant.

6. Which of the following is a good description of the given graph?

Distance from home vs. Time (hours)

   A. Gail is at a friend's house for a few hours. She then drives farther away from her house.

   B. Gail is at a friend's house for a few hours. She then drives to her house.

   C. Gail is at her house and does not leave.

   D. Gail is at her house. She then drives to her friend's house.

7. **Airplane** An airplane begins to ascend. It takes about 33 minutes to reach the highest altitude. The airplane is at this altitude for 22 minutes. Then it descends for 15 minutes. Let *T* be the time in minutes, and *H* be the altitude of the plane. Draw a graph which shows the relationship between *T* and *H*.

8. Error Analysis A math question asks the students to write a scenario for the given graph. Ashley writes that the number of cars in the parking lot for a mall increases for the entire day.

a. Write a description of the given graph.

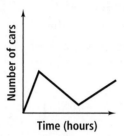

b. What error might Ashley have made?

9. Open-Ended A baseball team scores a steady number of runs in each of the first 4 innings. After that they do not score a run the rest of the game, which lasts 10 innings. Let x represent the inning of the game, and y represent the total number of runs.

a. Draw a graph which shows the relationship between x and y.

b. What would happen to the graph if the innings in which they score runs changes?

10. Think About the Process Elliot has extra spending money in a bank account. He spends some money each month for 9 months. Elliot decides to stop spending for 8 months because he wants to save the money for something else. Let M represent the amount of money Elliot has in his account, and T represent the time in months. Sketch a graph that shows the relationship between M and T.

a. What should the beginning of the graph look like?

b. Draw a graph that shows the relationship between M and T.

11. Challenge A company is looking over how many sales are made during the year. The first 2 months the sales for the company go up every month. Then for the next 4 months the sales go down. Then for 3 months the sales remain constant. For the last 3 months sales go up. Let T represent the time of the year in months, and S represent the sales.

a. Draw a graph which shows the relationship between T and S.

b. Explain why the sales might have gone up, down, or remained constant for the company.

12. Think About the Process

a. What does the horizontal line represent for the given graph?

b. Write a description of the given graph.

13. a. Challenge Write a description of the given graph.

b. Explain what you know about the function from the given graph.

CCSS: 8.F.B.5

Part 1

Example Sketching Graphs of Nonlinear Functions

A model rocket rises quickly, and then slows to a stop as it reaches its maximum height as its fuel burns out. It begins to fall quickly until the parachute opens, after which it falls slowly back down. Sketch a graph of the height of the rocket during its flight. Label each section.

Solution ·

Step 1 Identify the two variables being related.

The variables being related are time and height.

A model rocket rises quickly, and then slows to a stop as it reaches its maximum height as its fuel burns out. It begins to fall quickly until the parachute opens, after which it falls slowly back down.

Step 2 Look for key words that describe the relationship.

rises quickly ⟶ the height of the rocket is increasing quickly.

slows to a stop ⟶ the rocket has reached its maximum height.

falls quickly ⟶ the rocket's height is decreasing quickly.

falls slowly ⟶ the rocket's height is decreasing quickly.

Step 3 Sketch and label the graph.

rises quickly

slows to a stop

falls quickly

falls slowly

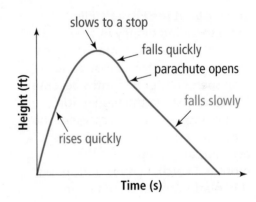

Part 2

Example Showing Functions are Linear Using Tables and Graphs

Explain why $y = 2x + 3$ is a linear function using both a table and a graph.

Solution ·

Step 1 Make a table of values and find the rate of change of $y = 2x + 3$.

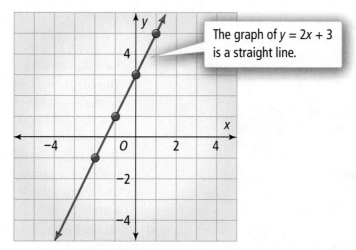

Rate of change = $\frac{2}{1}$, or 2

x	y
−2	−1
−1	1
0	3
1	5

The rate of change is 2 and is constant.

Step 2 Plot the points and draw a line through the points to graph $y = 2x + 3$.

The graph of $y = 2x + 3$ is a straight line.

$y = 2x + 3$ is a linear function since it has a constant rate of change and its graph is a straight line.

1. a. Complete the table of values for the function $y = 4x + 1$.

x	y
−2	■
−1	■
0	■
1	■
2	■

b. Draw a graph for the function.

c. Is the function linear or nonlinear?

A. The function is nonlinear because the rate of change is not constant and the graph of the function is not a line.

B. The function is linear because the rate of change is constant and the graph of the function is a line.

C. The function is linear because the rate of change is not constant and the graph of the function is not a line.

D. The function is nonlinear because the rate of change is constant and the graph of the function is a line.

2. Decide whether the function is linear or nonlinear using both a table and a graph.

$$y = (x + 2)^2 - 4$$

a. Complete the table of values for the function.

x	y
−4	■
−3	■
−2	■
−1	■
0	■

b. Graph the function.

c. Decide whether the function is linear or nonlinear. Explain.

A. The function is nonlinear because the rate of change is not constant and the graph of the function is not a line.

B. The function is linear because the rate of change is not constant and the graph of the function is not a line.

C. The function is nonlinear because the rate of change is constant and the graph of the function is a line.

D. The function is linear because the rate of change is constant and the graph of the function is a line.

3. A student was asked to decide whether the function $y = -5x^2$ is linear or nonlinear using both a table and a graph. He said the function is nonlinear because the rate of change is constant and the graph of the function is not a line.

x	y
−2	■
−1	■
0	■
1	■
2	■

a. Complete the table of values for the function.

b. Draw a graph for the function.

c. Is the function linear or nonlinear?

A. The function is nonlinear because the rate of change is constant and the graph of the function is a line.

B. The function is linear because the rate of change is not constant and the graph of the function is not a line.

C. The function is nonlinear because the rate of change is not constant and the graph of the function is not a line.

D. The function is linear because the rate of change is constant and the graph of the function is a line.

d. What mistake might the student have made?

A. He said the rate of change is constant, but the rate of change is not constant.

B. He said the function is nonlinear, but the function is linear.

C. He said the graph of the function is not a line, but it is a line.

4. You are canoeing 11 miles down a river. After 5.5 miles you stop to eat lunch for 1 hour. You canoe at a speed of 4 miles per hour.

   a. Draw a graph which describes the total distance you canoed.

   b. About how many hours did it take you to canoe 11 miles?

     A. 6 hours   **B.** 1 hour

     C. 2 hours   **D.** 4 hours

5. You are going for an 8-mile run. After 4 miles there is a big hill that causes you to slow down by 3 miles per hour. After the hill you return to your average speed of 8 miles per hour.

   a. Draw a graph which describes the total distance you ran.

   b. Describe another situation that has the same graph.

6. A ball is thrown straight up in the air. The ball's altitude increases until it reaches an altitude of 75 feet and stops momentarily. The ball then falls back toward the ground. It takes the ball 10 seconds to land on the ground.

   a. Draw a graph which describes the altitude of the ball over time.

   b. How many seconds does it take for the ball to stop before falling back toward the ground?

7. Think About the Process In a 13-mile bike race you bike at an average speed of 9 miles per hour. Once you begin the last 4 miles you begin increasing your speed steadily until you reach the finish line.

   a. What part of this situation makes the shape of the graph change?

     A. When your speed remains constant during the first 9 miles

     B. When you stop before the last 4 miles

     C. When your speed begins decreasing during the last 4 miles

     D. When your speed begins increasing during the last 4 miles

   b. Sketch a graph to describe the total distance you biked.

8. Challenge After taking off, an airplane rises for 2 hours. When it reaches an altitude of 3,000 feet, it stays at that altitude for 2 hours. Then it descends for 3 hours until it reaches the ground and slowly comes to a stop.

   a. Draw a graph which describes the altitude of the airplane during its flight.

   b. About how long was the airplane in the air?

9. Think About the Process You are given the following function.

$$y = \frac{1}{2}x + 3$$

   a. What do you need to determine from the table and the graph to decide whether the function is linear or nonlinear?

     A. Whether the y-intercept is positive or negative and whether the x-intercept is positive or negative

     B. Whether the function is increasing or decreasing

     C. Whether the rate of change is constant or not and whether the function is a line

     D. Whether the y-intercept is positive or negative and whether the slope is positive or negative

   b. Complete the table of values for the function.

   c. Graph the function.

   d. Decide whether the function is linear or nonlinear. Explain.

x	y
−2	■
−1	■
0	■
1	■
2	■

     A. The function is nonlinear because it is increasing.

     B. The function is linear because the y-intercept and the slope have the same sign.

     C. The function is nonlinear because the x- and y-intercepts have different signs.

     D. The function is linear because the rate of change is constant and the graph of the function is a line.

CCSS: 8.F.A.3, 8.F.B.4, Also 8.F.A.1 and 8.F.B.5

Part 1

Intro

A linear function is a function whose graph is a straight line.

A **linear function rule** is an equation that describes a linear function.

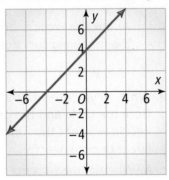

$y = x + 4$, linear, function

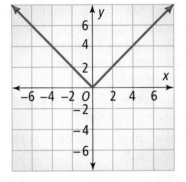

$y = |x|$, nonlinear, function

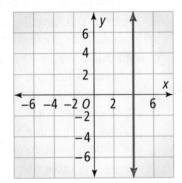

$x = 4$, linear, not a function

Example Matching Linear Function Rules to Their Graphs

Describe each linear function using one of the following rules:

$y = x$ $y = 2x$ $y = x + 2$ $y = -x$ $y = 2$

a.

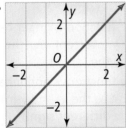

b.

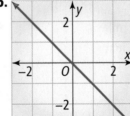

c.

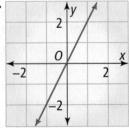

continued on next page >

See your complete lesson at MyMathUniverse.com

Example continued

Solution ·

Method 1 Choose at least three points on each graph and check to see which equation the points satisfy.

a. You can choose points $(-1, -1)$, $(0, 0)$, and $(1, 1)$.

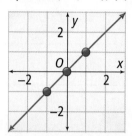

Point	$y = x + 2$	$y = 2x$	$y = x$	$y = -x$	$y = 2$
$(-1, -1)$	$-1 \stackrel{?}{=} -1 + 2$ $-1 \neq 1$	$-1 \stackrel{?}{=} 2(-1)$ $-1 \neq -2$	$-1 = -1$	$-1 \stackrel{?}{=} -(-1)$ $-1 \neq 1$	$-1 \neq 2$
$(0, 0)$	$0 \stackrel{?}{=} 0 + 2$ $0 \neq 2$	$0 \stackrel{?}{=} 2(0)$ $0 = 0$	$0 = 0$	$0 \stackrel{?}{=} -0$ $0 = 0$	$0 \neq 2$
$(1, 1)$	$1 \stackrel{?}{=} 1 + 2$ $1 \neq 3$	$1 \stackrel{?}{=} 2(1)$ $1 \neq 2$	$1 = 1$	$1 \neq -1$	$1 \neq 2$

> All three points satisfy **y = x**, so the equation of the first graph is $y = x$.

b–c. Repeat the process for the other two functions.

Method 2 Graph each equation choice and match the graphs.

a.

> You can make a table of values to help you graph each function.

x	y = x
0	0
1	1
2	2

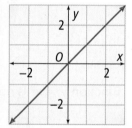

b.

x	y = -x
0	0
−1	1
−2	2

continued on next page >

See your complete lesson at MyMathUniverse.com

Part 1

Solution continued

c.

x	y = 2x
−1	−2
0	0
1	2

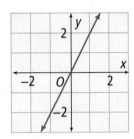

Part 2

Intro

Linear function rules look different from other function rules.

These Are *Linear* Function Rules	These Are *Nonlinear* Function Rules
$b = 7 - a$	$y = |x|$
$d = 3t$	$A = s^2$
$y = 4x - 1$	$y = \dfrac{5}{x}$
$z = \dfrac{y}{2}$	

Example Identifying Linear and Nonlinear Function Rules

Is each function rule *linear* or *nonlinear*?

a. $y = x^2$ **b.** $y = 4x$ **c.** $y = -3x$

d. $y = \dfrac{8}{x}$ **e.** $y = x - 2$

Solution ·

Check by graphing.

a. The function $y = x^2$ is not linear.

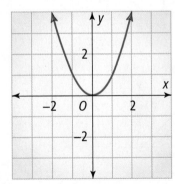

x	y = x²
−2	4
−1	1
0	0
1	1
2	4

> You can make a table of values to help you graph each function.

continued on next page >

Solution continued

b. The function $y = 4x$ is linear.

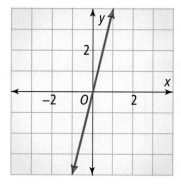

x	y = 4x
−1	−4
0	0
1	4

c. The function $y = -3x$ is linear.

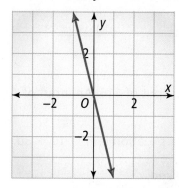

x	y = −3x
−1	3
0	0
1	−3

d. The function $y = \frac{8}{x}$ is not linear.

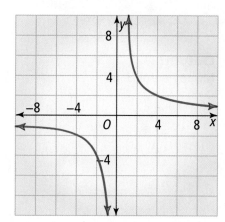

x	$y = \frac{8}{x}$
−8	−1
−4	−2
−1	−8
1	8
4	2
8	1

continued on next page >

Part 2

Solution continued

e. The function $y = x - 2$ is linear.

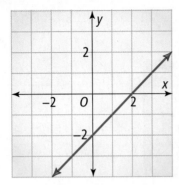

x	y = x − 2
−1	−3
0	−2
1	−1

Key Concept

A dog walker earns $10 plus $3 per dog.

Inputs and Outputs An input of 2 dogs gives an output of $16. An input of 3 dogs gives an output of $19.

Linear Function Rule A linear function rule for the situation is $m = 10 + 3d$.

Input: Number of dogs being walked, **d**

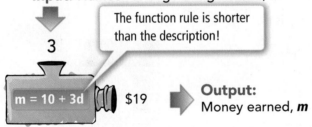

The function rule is shorter than the description!

3

m = 10 + 3d $19

Output: Money earned, **m**

Part 3

Example Matching Verbal Descriptions to Their Function Rules

A swimmer burns 8.8 Calories per minute while swimming laps. Which function rule describes how many Calories c the swimmer burns during any number of minutes m?

$$c = m + 8.8 \qquad c = 8.8m \qquad c = 8.8 - m \qquad c = \frac{8.8}{m}$$

Solution

A swimmer burns 8.8 Calories per minute while swimming laps.

Words | number of Calories burned | is | number of Calories burned per minute | times | number of minutes spent swimming laps

to

Let c = the number of Calories burned.

Let m = the number of minutes spent swimming.

Equation | c | = | 8.8 | • | m

The function rule is $C = 8.8m$.

1. Which rule describes the linear function for the graph? (Hint: You can graph points for each equation.)

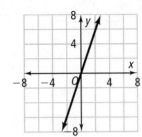

A. $y = x - 3$ **B.** $y = 3x$

C. $y = -3x$ **D.** $y = x + 3$

2. Which rule represents a linear function? Select all that apply.

A. $y = x^3$ **B.** $y = \frac{x}{5}$

C. $y = \frac{2}{x}$

3. Nichole is 2 years older than Ben. What function rule describes Nichole's age for any given age of Ben? Let b represent Ben's age, and let n represent Nichole's age.

A. $n = 2 + b$ **B.** $n = b \div 2$

C. $n = 2b$ **D.** $n = 2 - b$

4. a. Writing Which rule is the function rule for the graph?

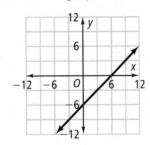

A. $y = 6x$ **B.** $y = x - 6$

C. $y = -6x$ **D.** $y = x + 6$

b. Describe a situation that you could represent with the function.

5. a. Reasoning How can you tell which equation below is a linear function rule?

$y = 6x$ $y = 6x^2$

b. Which rule represents a linear function?

c. Explain the similarities and the differences between the two functions and their graphs.

6. a. Which rule(s) represent(s) a linear function? Select all that apply.

A. $A = s^3$

B. $x = 3.6 - y$

C. $z = -3t$

b. Show or describe the steps you take to answer the question.

7. Error Analysis The students had to decide whether each rule below represents a linear function. Kelly drew the graph. Then she concluded that $y = \frac{3}{x}$ represents a linear function because the graph is a straight line.

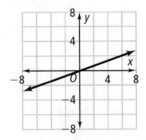

a. Which rule represents a linear function? Select all that apply.

A. $y = \frac{3}{x}$ **B.** $y = x + 3$

C. $y = 3x$ **D.** $y = \frac{x}{3}$

b. How could Kelly have made an error?

8. Yearly Profit A company's profit is equal to revenue minus cost. For one company, the yearly revenue is $35 million. What function rule describes the yearly profit for any yearly cost? Let c represent the yearly cost and p represent the yearly profit, both in millions of dollars.

A. $p = 35c$ **B.** $p = c - 35$

C. $p = 35 - c$ **D.** $p = 35 + p$

9. The table shows the costs of some items at a grocery store. Which function rule describes the cost of any number of pounds of meat? Let p represent the number of boxes of pasta, b represent the number of loaves of bread, m represent the number of pounds of meat, and c represent the cost.

Grocery Store Prices

Item	Price
Pasta (1 box)	$2.00
Bread (1 loaf)	$3.00
Meat (1 pound)	$5.00

A. $c = 2p$ **B.** $c = 5m$

C. $c = 10m$ **D.** $c = 3b$

E. $c = m + 10$ **F.** $c = m + 2$

10. Think About the Process

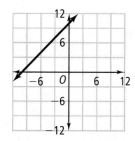

a. Which points could you choose to help you find the function rule for the graph shown? Select all that apply.

A. (0,0)   **B.** (−5,5)

C. (−10,0)   **D.** (10,0)

E. (0,10)   **F.** (0,−10)

b. Explain how you can use the points on the graph to help you.

c. Which rule describes the linear function for the graph?

A. $y = 10x$ **B.** $y = x - 10$

C. $y = x + 10$ **D.** $y = -10x$

11. What is the function rule for the graph?

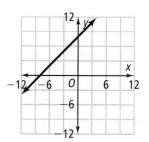

A. $y = x + \frac{17}{2}$ **B.** $y = x - \frac{17}{2}$

C. $y = x - \frac{7}{2}$ **D.** $y = x + \frac{7}{2}$

12. Think About the Process

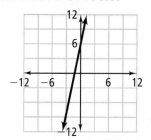

a. The point (0,5) satisfies which rules shown below? Select all that apply.

A. $y = 5x + 5$ **B.** $y = -5x + 5$

C. $y = -5x$ **D.** $y = 5x$

b. What is the function rule for the graph?

A. $y = -5x + 5$ **B.** $y = -5x$

C. $y = 5x + 5$ **D.** $y = 5x$

c. How can points help you choose the correct rule?

d. Why is it important to graph more than one point to find the correct rule?

13. Challenge A train moves at a constant speed of 3.1 miles per minute. Let t represent the time in hours and d represent the distance traveled in miles.

a. What function rule describes the number of miles the train travels during any number of hours?

A. $d = 194t$ **B.** $d = 186t$

C. $d = t + 11{,}160$ **D.** $d = 186 + t$

E. $d = 3.1t$ **F.** $d = t + 3.1$

b. Find a function rule that describes the number of hours the train takes to travel any number of miles.

CCSS: 8.F.B.4, Also 8.F.B.5

Key Concept

As you ride a bike up a hill, both your vertical distance (the rise) and your horizontal distance (the run) from the bottom of the hill change. You can measure the steepness of the hill by its slope, the ratio that compares the rise and run between two points on the hill.

$$\text{slope} = \text{rate of change} = \frac{\text{vertical change}}{\text{horizontal change}}$$

$$= \frac{\text{rise}}{\text{run}}$$

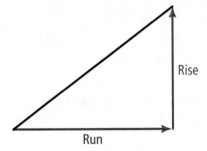

Rise

Run

The slope is also called the rate of change of the linear function that models the hill.

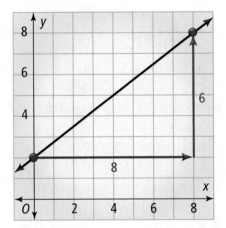

$$\text{rate of change} = \frac{\text{vertical change}}{\text{horizontal change}}$$

$$= \frac{6}{8}, \text{ or } \frac{3}{4}$$

The rate of change of a linear function is constant.

Part 1

Example Finding Rates of Change from Graphs

Find the rate of change of the linear function that models the height of the zip line.

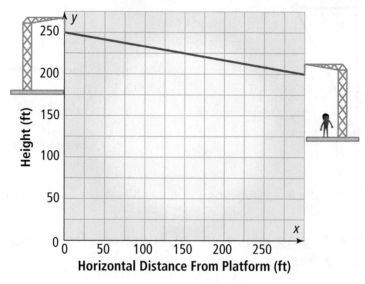

Height (ft)

Horizontal Distance From Platform (ft)

Solution

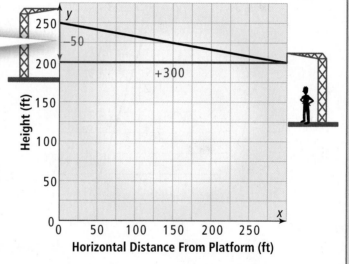

The vertical change is negative since you can only go down, not up, on a zip line.

−50

+300

Height (ft)

Horizontal Distance From Platform (ft)

$$\text{Rate of change} = \frac{\text{vertical change}}{\text{horizontal change}}$$

$$= \frac{-50}{300}$$

$$= -\frac{1}{6}$$

Part 2

Intro

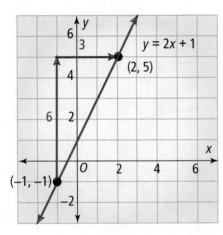

Rate of change $= \dfrac{\text{vertical change}}{\text{horizontal change}}$

$= \dfrac{6}{3}$

$= 2$

The rate of change between $(-1, -1)$ and $(2, 5)$ is 2.

$$y = 2x + 1$$

↑

rate of change

The rate of change of a linear function $y = mx + b$ is m, the coefficient of x.

Example Identifying Equations of Functions from Graphs or Tables

Identify the equation of each linear function shown from the choices given. Then state the rate of change of the function.

$y = 3x + 3$ $y = -3x + 3$ $y = \frac{1}{3}x$ $y = 3x$

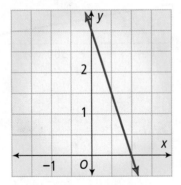

x	y
−2	$-\frac{2}{3}$
0	0
2	$\frac{2}{3}$

continued on next page >

Solution

To find the equation of the linear function in the graph, find three points on the line and test them in each equation.

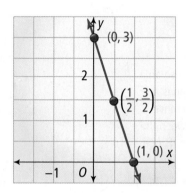

$y = 3x + 3$	
x	y
0	3
$\frac{1}{2}$	$\frac{9}{2}$
1	6

$y = -3x + 3$	
x	y
0	3
$\frac{1}{2}$	$\frac{3}{2}$
1	0

$y = \frac{1}{3}x$	
x	y
0	0
$\frac{1}{2}$	$\frac{1}{6}$
1	$\frac{1}{3}$

Only one point satisfies this equation.

All three points satisfy this equation.

The equation of the linear function shown in the graph is

$$y = -3x + 3$$

The rate of change is -3.

To find the equation of the linear function described by the table of values, test each point in each equation.

x	y
-2	$-\frac{2}{3}$
0	0
2	$\frac{2}{3}$

$y = 3x + 3$	
x	y
-2	-3
0	3
2	9

$y = -3x + 3$	
x	y
-2	9
0	3
2	-3

$y = \frac{1}{3}x$	
x	y
-2	$-\frac{2}{3}$
0	0
2	$\frac{2}{3}$

All three points satisfy this equation.

The equation of the linear function described by the table of values is

$$y = \frac{1}{3}x$$

The rate of change is $\frac{1}{3}$.

Example Finding Rates of Change from Tables

An employee at a candle-making company collected data about the burn time of a new candle.

Find the rate of change of the candle's height between hour 1 and hour 4. What does the rate of change mean in this situation?

Hours Candle Burns	Height of Candle (cm)
0	25
1	22
2	19
3	16
4	13
5	10
6	7

The run on a graph is the difference between the inputs in a table.

The rise on a graph is the difference between the outputs in a table.

Solution

To find the rate of change between hours 1 and 4, find the change in height and the change in time between hours 1 and 4.

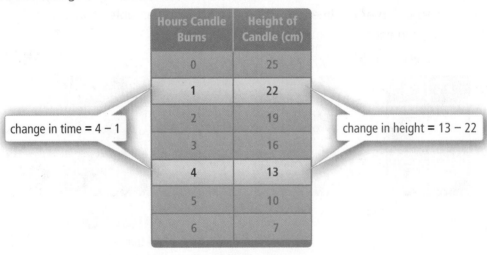

change in time = 4 − 1

change in height = 13 − 22

Hours Candle Burns	Height of Candle (cm)
0	25
1	22
2	19
3	16
4	13
5	10
6	7

$$\text{Rate of change} = \frac{\text{change in height}}{\text{change in time}}$$

$$= \frac{13 - 22}{4 - 1}$$

$$= \frac{-9}{3}, \text{ or } -\frac{3}{1}$$

The rate of change is $-\frac{3}{1}$. This means that the candle's height decreases by 3 cm each hour.

1. Find the rate of change of the linear function from the point (0,6) to the point (20,14). Simplify your answer.

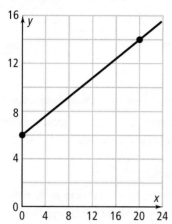

2. a. Identify the equation of the linear function through the points $(-1,-5)$ and $(2,1)$.

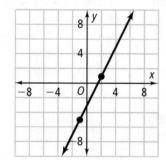

b. What is the rate of change?

3. Think About the Process

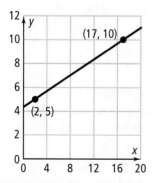

a. How can you use the graph to find the vertical change between the two points?

b. What is the rate of change?

c. Explain why graphs sometimes have positive vertical change and sometimes have negative vertical change.

4. The owner of a bicycle repair shop makes a graph of the number of bicycles repaired in one 8-hour work day. Note that the shop repaired 12 bicycles after 3 hours and 28 bicycles after 7 hours.

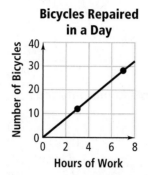

a. What is the equation of the linear function that models the graph?

b. The rate of change is ■, meaning that this many bicycles are repaired per hour.

5. Error Analysis A machinist measured the thickness of a grinding pad every 3 weeks. The table shows the data. The machinist incorrectly calculates that the rate of change of the thickness is -12.

Thickness of Grinding Pad

Time (weeks)	Thickness (mm)
0	73
3	61
6	49
9	37
12	25
15	13
6	41

a. What is the correct rate of change of the thickness? Simplify your answer.

b. What could be the machinist's error?

See your complete lesson at MyMathUniverse.com

6. Estimation Estimate the rate of change of the linear function from the point (24,27) to the point (48,178). (Hint: Round the coordinates to use points on the grid lines.)

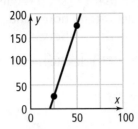

7. Multiple Representations

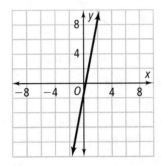

a. What is the equation of the linear function that models the graph?

    A. $y = 4x - 3$ **B.** $y = 5x - 1$

    C. $y = 5x + 1$ **D.** $y = 4x + 3$

b. What is the rate of change of the function?

c. Complete the table.

x	0	1	2	3	4
y	■	■	■	■	■

8. Find the rate of change for the linear function $4y = -3x - 32$.

9. Think About the Process A highway maintenance crew used a special machine to repaint the lines on a highway. One worker measured the depth of the paint in the holding tank and the length of the lines painted. The table shows the data.

Painting Highway Lines

Length of Lines Painted (meters)	Depth of Paint (centimeters)
0	20.6
3	18.2
6	15.8
8	14.2
11	11.8

a. Which data point would be most helpful to use to find the rate of change of the depth of paint in the tank?

b. The rate of change is ■, meaning there is this much less depth, in centimeters, of paint in the tank for each meter of highway line painted.

10. Challenge A bakery uses a large bin to feed flour to the bread-making machines. One day, a worker measures the depth of flour in the bin every 4 minutes. The table shows the data.

Amount of Flour Available

Time (minutes)	Depth of Flour (cm)
0	89.7
4	82.5
8	75.3
12	68.1
16	60.9
20	53.7
24	46.5

a. What is the rate of change of the depth of flour? Simplify your answer.

b. When the level of flour in the bin falls to 10 cm, the machines automatically shut down. If there is 24.4 cm of flour in the bin now, how long until the machines shut down?

See your complete lesson at MyMathUniverse.com

CCSS: 8.F.B.4, Also 8.F.A.3 and 8.F.B.5

Key Concept

Equation A linear function can be written in the form $y = mx + b$.

You can see both the rate of change and the **initial value** of the function in the equation.

$$y = mx + b$$

initial value

rate of change

Graph You can also see both the rate of change and the **initial value** of the function in the graph.

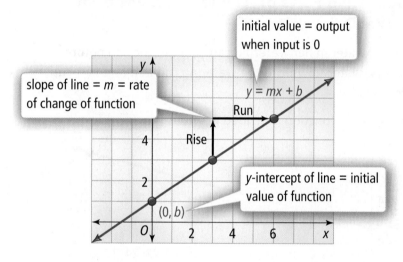

initial value = output when input is 0

slope of line = m = rate of change of function

$y = mx + b$

Run

Rise

y-intercept of line = initial value of function

$(0, b)$

Part 1

Example Identifying Initial Values of Linear Functions from Equations

Match each function below with an initial value.

	−3	⁻2	2	3

a. $y = 3x - 2$
b. $y = 3 - 3x$
c. $y = 2x + 3$
d. $y = -3x + 2$

continued on next page >

Part 1

Example continued

Solution ·

The initial value of a function is the output when the input is 0.

Substitute 0 for x in each equation to find the corresponding value of y.

    a. The function $y = 3x - 2$ has an initial value of -2.

    b. The function $y = 3 - 3x$ has an initial value of 3.

    c. The function $y = 2x + 3$ has an initial value of 3.

    d. The function $y = -3x + 2$ has an initial value of 2.

$y = 3(0) - 2$
$y = 0 - 2$
$y = -2$

Part 2

Example Identifying Parts of Linear Functions from Verbal Descriptions

Josie has 1.5 cups of water in her watering can. She fills the can before watering her plants. Water flows into the watering can at a rate of 1 cup every 4 seconds.

The graph represents the function described in words.

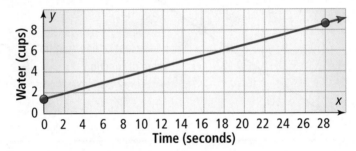

Write each value or equation for the linear function.
- rate of change of the function
- slope of the line
- y-intercept of the line
- initial value of the function
- function rule

continued on next page >

Part 2

Example continued

Solution

Step 1 Find the slope of the line.

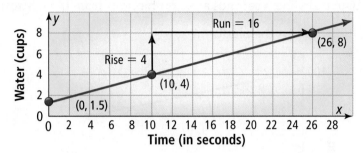

$$\text{slope} = m = \frac{\text{rise}}{\text{run}}$$

> The rate of change of the function is the slope.

$$= \frac{4}{16}$$

$$= \frac{1}{4}$$

The slope of the line is $\frac{1}{4}$.

Step 2 Find the *y*-intercept of the line.

The *y*-intercept is the point where the graph crosses the *y*-axis.

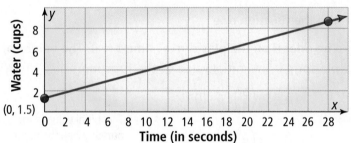

$$y\text{-intercept} = 1.5$$

> The initial value of the function is the *y*-intercept.

The *y*-intercept of the line is 1.5.

Step 3 Find the function rule.

A linear function can be written in the form

$$y = mx + b$$

where m = rate of change, and b = initial value.

Use what you found in the previous steps to find the function rule.

$$y = \left(\frac{1}{4}\right)x + 1.5$$

The function rule is $y = \left(\frac{1}{4}\right)x + 1.5$.

Example Identifying Initial Values in
Real-World Problems

The linear function in the graph models the height off the ground, in feet, of a person riding a zip line, *t* seconds after pushing off from the platform.

How high off the ground is the platform?

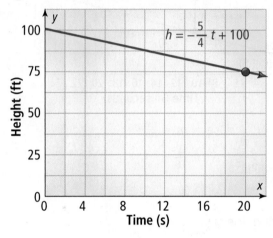

$$h = -\frac{5}{4}t + 100$$

Solution ···

Method 1 Use the function rule.

The rider is on the platform at time *t* = 0. The height of the platform is the initial value of the function.

$$h = -\left(\frac{5}{4}\right)t + 100$$

$$h = -\left(\frac{5}{4}\right)0 + 100$$

> The initial value is the output when the input is 0.

$$h = 0 + 100$$

$$h = 100$$ ◁ initial value

The person started at a height of 100 ft, so the platform is 100 ft off the ground.

continued on next page >

Solution continued

> **Method 2** Use the graph.
>
> The rider is on the platform at the time $t = 0$. The height of the platform is the initial value of the function, or the *y*-intercept of the graph.

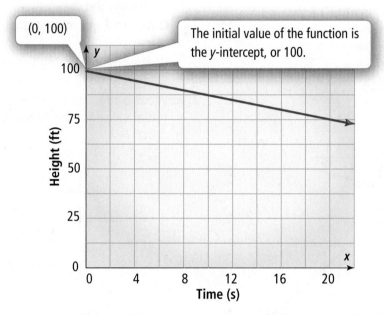

(0, 100)

The initial value of the function is the *y*-intercept, or 100.

The person started at a height of 100 ft, so the platform is 100 ft off the ground.

1. Find the initial value of the linear function $y = 3x + 5$.

2. Which linear function has initial value 2?

$y = -2x + 7$ $y = 7x - 2$

$y = 2x - 7$ $y = 7x + 2$

3. a. Find the rate of change of the linear function shown in the graph. Simplify your answer.

  b. Find the initial value.

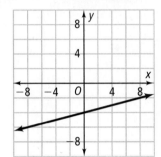

4. a. Find the rate of change and initial value for the linear function. Simplify your answer.

  b. Find the initial value.

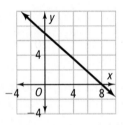

5. The graph models the height h, in meters, of a hot air balloon, t minutes after beginning to descend. How high was the balloon when it began its descent?

Height of a Hot Air Balloon

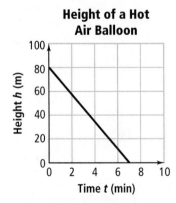

6. The function $y = 0.24x + 37$ models the cost y, in dollars, of driving a rental car x miles.

  a. What is the initial value of this function?

  b. What does the initial value represent in this function?

  A. the miles driven

  B. the total cost of renting and driving the car

  C. the cost per mile of driving the car

  D. the cost of renting the car and driving no miles

7. a. What is the rate of change and the initial value for the function in the graph?

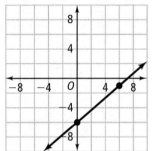

  b. Explain how you can tell, without doing any calculating, whether the rate of change is a positive value or a negative value.

8. Corporate Revenue Let y be a company's revenue in millions of dollars. From 2002 to 2005, the function $y = 1{,}302x + 6{,}535$ approximates the revenue y when x is the number of years after 2002.

  a. Find the initial value of this linear function.

  b. What does the initial value mean?

  A. The initial value is the maximum revenue between 2002 and 2005.

  B. The initial value is the difference in revenue between 2005 and 2002.

  C. The initial value is the revenue in 2002.

  D. The initial value is the difference in revenue between 2002 and 2005.

See your complete lesson at MyMathUniverse.com

9. While riding a bike, you slow down to stop at an intersection. The function $y = -\frac{7}{5}x + 10$ models your speed y, in feet per second, after x seconds. What is your speed when you begin to slow down?

10. Think About the Process

a. Which property do you need to use to write the equations for these linear functions in the form $y = mx + b$?

$y = \frac{3}{2}(x - 9)$ $y = \frac{3}{2}(x + 6)$

$y = \frac{3}{2}(x - 6)$ $y = \frac{3}{2}(x + 9)$

A. The Distributive Property

B. The Identity Property

C. The Associative Property

D. The Commutative Property

b. Which function has initial value -9?

A. $y = \frac{3}{2}(x - 9)$

B. $y = \frac{3}{2}(x - 6)$

C. $y = \frac{3}{2}(x + 9)$

D. $y = \frac{3}{2}(x + 6)$

11. The function shown in the graph models the height, h, of a glider at time t. Find the initial height of the glider and the rate of change of its height. Simplify your answer.

Height of a Glider

12. Challenge Which graph represents a function with initial value -3?

A.
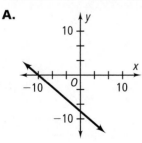

B.
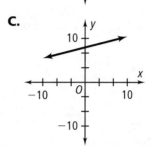

C.
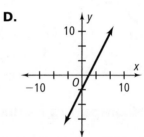

D.

13. Think About the Process The linear function $y = 50 + \frac{3}{5}x$ models y, the height of an elevator in feet, after x seconds.

a. Which property lets you rewrite the equation in $y = mx + b$ form?

A. The Commutative Property

B. The Identity Property

C. The Associative Property

D. The Distributive Property

b. What is the initial value?

c. What does the initial value represent?

A. The height where the elevator starts

B. The floor where the elevator starts

C. The floor where the elevator ends

D. The speed of the elevator

CCSS: 8.F.A.2

Part 1

Intro

The graphs of two linear functions intersect if the functions have different rates of change.

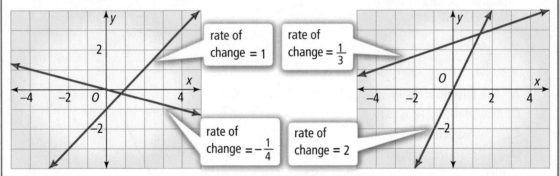

rate of change = 1

rate of change = $\frac{1}{3}$

rate of change = $-\frac{1}{4}$

rate of change = 2

Example Comparing Rates of Change of Linear Functions

For each city, there is a linear function that describes the temperature, in degrees Fahrenheit, in terms of the number of hours since 8:00 A.M.

Which function has the greatest rate of change? What does that mean in this situation?

Eastberry

At 8:00 A.M., the temperature was 62°F. Between 8:00 and noon, the temperature increased by 3°F per hour.

Topperville

$t = 54 + 2h$, where t is the temperature in degrees Fahrenheit and h is the number of hours since 8:00 A.M.

Hilltown	
Time	**Temp. (°F)**
6:00 A.M.	58
7:00 A.M.	60
8:00 A.M.	62
9:00 A.M.	64
10:00 A.M.	66
11:00 A.M.	68
12 noon	70

continued on next page >

Part 1

Example continued

Solution ·

Eastberry

At 8:00 A.M., the temperature was 62°F. Between 8:00 and noon, the temperature increased by 3°F per hour.

In Eastberry, the rate of change is 3.

Hilltown

Time	Temp. (°F)
6:00 A.M.	58
7:00 A.M.	60
8:00 A.M.	62
9:00 A.M.	64
10:00 A.M.	66
11:00 A.M.	68
12 noon	70

In Hilltown, the rate of change is 2.

Topperville

$t = 54 + 2h$, where t is the temperature in degrees Fahrenheit and h is the number of hours since 8:00 A.M.

In Topperville, the rate of change is also 2.

Eastberry has the greatest rate of change. This means that, in Eastberry, the temperature is warming up faster than in Hilltown or Topperville.

Part 2

Example Comparing Initial Values of Linear Functions

For each city, there is a linear function that describes the temperature, in degrees Fahrenheit, in terms of the number of hours since 8:00 A.M.

Compare the initial values of the temperature functions for the three cities. What do the initial values means in this situation?

Eastberry

At 8:00 A.M., the temperature was 62°F. Between 8:00 and noon, the temperature increased by 3°F per hour.

Topperville

$t = 54 + 2h$, where t is the temperature in degrees Fahrenheit and h is the number of hours since 8:00 A.M.

Hilltown

Time	Temp. (°F)
6:00 A.M.	58
7:00 A.M.	60
8:00 A.M.	62
9:00 A.M.	64
10:00 A.M.	66
11:00 A.M.	68
12 noon	70

continued on next page >

Example continued

Solution ·

In Eastberry, the initial value is 62.

Eastberry

At 8:00 A.M., the temperature was 62°F. Between 8:00 and noon, the temperature increased by 3°F per hour.

In Hilltown, the initial value is also 62.

Hilltown

Time	Temp. (°F)
6:00 A.M.	58
7:00 A.M.	60
8:00 A.M.	62
9:00 A.M.	64
10:00 A.M.	66
11:00 A.M.	68
12 noon	70

Topperville

$t = 54 + 2h$, where t is the temperature in degrees Fahrenheit and h is the number of hours since 8:00 A.M.

In Topperville, the initial value is 54.

Eastberry and Hilltown

Topperville

62 – 54 = 8

At 8:00 A.M., it was 8°F warmer in Eastberry and Hilltown than it was in Topperville.

Key Concept

Different rates of change, different initial values

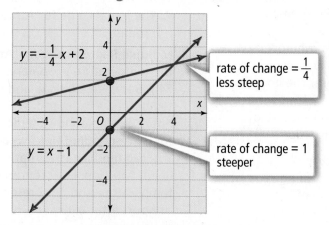

$y = -\frac{1}{4}x + 2$

$y = x - 1$

rate of change $= \frac{1}{4}$
less steep

rate of change $= 1$
steeper

Different rates of change, same initial value

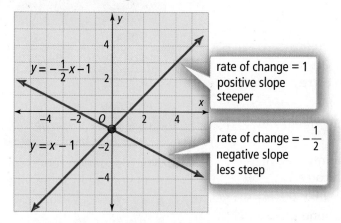

$y = -\frac{1}{2}x - 1$

$y = x - 1$

rate of change $= 1$
positive slope
steeper

rate of change $= -\frac{1}{2}$
negative slope
less steep

Same rate of change, different initial values

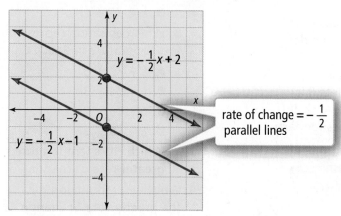

$y = -\frac{1}{2}x + 2$

$y = -\frac{1}{2}x - 1$

rate of change $= -\frac{1}{2}$
parallel lines

1. Linear functions model the scores in the second round of a trivia game. The linear function $y = 4x + 3$ describes Player A's scores, where x is the number of questions answered correctly, and y is the score. The linear function described by the table shows Player B's scores. What do the rates of change tell you for this situation?

Player B's Trivia Score

Correct Answers	Score
1	4
2	5
3	6
4	7

A. Player A gains more point than Player B does for each correct answer in this round.

B. Player A has gained more points in this round.

C. Player B gains more points than Player A does for each correct answer in this round.

D. The score before this round shows Player B is leading.

2. Two athletes are training over a two-week period to increase the number of pushups each can do consecutively. Athlete A can do 16 pushups to start, and increases his total by 2 each day. Athlete B is charting his progress in the table. Compare the initial values for each.

Daily Pushups

Day	Number of Pushups
Start	12
1	15
2	18
3	21

A. The initial value for Athlete B is greater.

B. The initial values are equal.

C. The initial value for Athlete A is greater.

3. **Multiple Representations** At 8:00 A.M. the temperature in Somerville was 74°F. Between 8:00 A.M. and noon, the temperature increased by 3°F per hour. The table shows temperatures for corresponding times in Beech City. You can model each situation with a linear function. Let t represent temperature and h represent number of hours after 8:00 A.M.

Beech City Temperatures

Time	Temperature (°F)
8:00 A.M.	70
9:00 A.M.	72
10:00 A.M.	74
11:00 A.M.	76
12:00 P.M.	78

a. Which equation represents the temperature in Somerville?

A. $t = 74 - 5h$

B. $t = 74 - 3h$

C. $t = 74 + 3h$

D. $t = 70 + 2h$

b. Which equation represents the temperature in Beech City?

A. $t = 70 + 5h$

B. $t = 74 + 3h$

C. $t = 70 + 2h$

D. $t = 70 - 2h$

c. Which city's temperature had the greater rate of change?

4. Which linear function has the greater rate of change, the one described by the equation $y = 2.5x + 6$ or the one described by the table?

x	y
2	−4
4	−1
6	2
8	5

5. Think About the Process You are comparing the rates of change of two linear functions represented in different forms.

x	y
1	9
2	4
3	−1
4	−6

a. For a linear function $y = mx + b$, how can you tell the rate of change of the function?

 A. Find the value of m.

 B. Find the value of x when $y = 0$.

 C. Find the value of y when $x = 1$.

 D. Find the value of $−b$.

b. How can you tell the rate of change of a linear function from a table?

 A. Find the change in y when x increases by 1.

 B. Find the change in x when y increases by 1.

 C. Find the value of x when $y = 1$.

 D. Find the value of y when $x = 1$.

c. Which function has the greater absolute rate of change, the one described by the equation $y = −4x + 8$ or the one described by the table above?

 A. the function described by the table

 B. the function described by $y = −4x + 8$

6. Think About the Process

x	y
1	11
2	12
3	13
4	14

a. For a linear function $y = mx + b$, how can you tell the initial value of the function?

 A. Find the value of x when $y = 1$.

 B. Find the value of y when $x = 1$.

 C. Find the value of m.

 D. Find the value of $−b$.

 E. Find the value of b.

b. How can you tell the initial value of a linear function from a table?

 A. It is the value of y when $x = 0$.

 B. It is the value of y when $x = 1$.

 C. It is the first value of y in the table.

 D. It is the first value of x in the table.

c. Compare the initial values of $y = 2x + 5$ and the function described by the table.

 A. The initial values are the same.

 B. The initial value of $y = 2x + 5$ is greater.

 C. The initial value of the function described by the table is greater.

7. a. Challenge Which two functions have the same rate of change?

> A. $y = 0.5x − 1$
>
> B. $y = 4x − 7$
>
> C. The function $N = 0.6r + 1$, where N is Nancy's pay in dollars, and r is the number of boxes she delivers
>
> D. The function $T = 0.5n + 1$, where T is Tony's pay in dollars, and n is the number of envelopes he fills

b. The rate of change is greatest for which function(s)?

c. What is the greatest rate of change?

See your complete lesson at MyMathUniverse.com

Topic 8 297 **Lesson 8-4**

Constructing a Function to Model a Linear Relationship

CCSS: 8.F.B.4

Part 1

Example Writing Linear Function Rules Using Initial Values

At time $t = 0$, a bicyclist begins riding at a constant speed. Ten minutes later, the bicyclist has traveled 2.5 miles.

Write the linear function rule that models the distance d the bicyclist has traveled after any number of minutes t.

Solution ·

Find the slope of the line:

$$m = \frac{rise}{sun}$$

$$= \frac{2.5}{10}$$

$$= 0.25$$

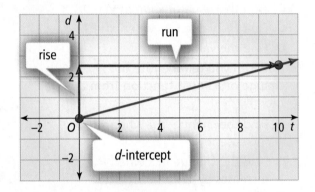

Find the d-intercept, where the bicycle started: $b = 0$

Finally, use the slope and d-intercept to find the rule:

$$d = mt + b$$

$$d = 0.25t + 0$$

So the linear function rule that models the distance the bicycle has traveled is $d = 0.25t$.

Key Concept

Points Two points determine a linear function.

Example: $(-4, -2)$ and $(3, 12)$

Graph

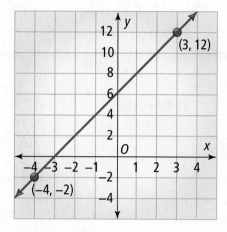

Linear Function Rule Use the values you know for m and one of the points to determine b in $y = mx + b$.

Find the rate of change.

$$m = \frac{12 - (-2)}{3 - (-4)}$$

$$m = 2$$

Use $m = 2$ and the point $(3, 12)$ to solve for b.

$$y = mx + b$$

$$12 = 2(3) + b$$

$$12 = 6 + b$$

$$b = 6$$

Use the values of m and b to write the function rule.

$$y = mx + b$$

$$y = 2x + 6$$

Part 2

Example Writing Linear Function Rules Without Initial Values

A jewelry store sells charm bracelets and charms. A bracelet with two charms costs $7.50. A bracelet with four charms costs $9.50.

Write a linear function rule to model the cost of a bracelet with any number of charms.

Solution

Know

- A bracelet with 2 charms costs $7.50.
- A bracelet with 4 charms costs $9.50.
- Two points: (2, 7.5) and (4, 9.5)

Need

- A function rule

Plan

- Let c be the number of charms.
- Let d be the cost, in dollars, of a bracelet with c charms.
- First, find the rate of change.
- Then, use the rate of change and one point to find the initial value.
- Last, write the function.

Two points: (2, 7.5) and (4, 9.5)

$$m = \frac{9.5 - 7.5}{4 - 2}$$

$$= \frac{2}{2}$$

$$= 1$$

Use $m = 1$ and the point (2, 7.5) to find the initial value.

$$d = m(c) + b$$

$$7.5 = 1(2) + b$$

$$5.5 = b$$

The equation should look like:

$$d = 1c + 5.5$$

$$d = c + 5.5$$

where c is the number of charms and d is the cost of a bracelet having c charms.

Part 3

Example Writing Linear Function Rules With Negative Rates of Change

A gardener collected 40 gallons of rainwater in a tank. Later, the bottom of the tank cracks, and the water starts to leak out. The water leaks at a constant rate of 2 cups per minute.

Write a function rule to model the amount of water in the tank at any given time.

Solution ·

Let t be the number of minutes the tank has been leaking.

Let w be the amount of water in the tank, in gallons, after t minutes.

To write a linear function rule, you need to know the initial value and the rate of change.

$b = 40$ — The tank starts with 40 gallons of water in it, so the initial value is 40.

1 gallon = 4 quarts, and 1 quart = 4 cups

1 gallon = 4 × 4 cups, or 16 cups — The water is leaking out of the tank at 2 cups per minute. Convert 2 cups per minute to gallons per minute.

$2 \text{ cups} = 2 \times \frac{1}{16} \text{ gal} = \frac{2}{16} \text{ gal} = \frac{1}{8} \text{ gal}$

$m = -\frac{1}{8}$

For every minute that passes, $\frac{1}{8}$ gallon leaks out. So the rate of change is $-\frac{1}{8}$.

The function rule is $w = 40 - \frac{1}{8}t$.

1. At time $t = 0$, water begins to drip out of a pipe into an empty bucket. After 26 minutes, there are 13 inches of water in the bucket. Write a linear function rule to model how many inches of water, w, are in the bucket after any number of minutes, t.

2. A car moving at a constant speed passed a timing device at $t = 0$. After 8 seconds, the car has traveled 840 ft. Write a linear function rule to model the distance in feet, d, the car has traveled any number of seconds, t, after passing the timing device.

3. An international food festival charges for admission and for each sample of food. Admission and 3 samples cost $5.75. Admission and 6 samples cost $8.75. Write a linear function rule to model the cost, y, for any number of samples, x.

4. A line passes through the points (4,19) and (9,24). Write a linear function rule in terms of x and y for this line.

5. At time $x = 0$, water begins to drip steadily out of a water tank. After 3 hours, there are 7.7 gallons of water in the tank. After 8 hours, 7.2 gallons remain. Write a linear function rule that models the number of gallons of water, y, left in the tank for any number of hours, x.

6. Each month, your phone company charges you a fee of 15 cents per minute as well as a service fee of $3.95. Write a linear function rule that models the number of dollars, y, you pay each month for any number of minutes, x.

7. **Writing** At time $x = 0$, water begins to drain steadily out of a bathtub. After 100 seconds, the water in the tub is 10 cm deep. After 200 seconds, the tub is empty.

   a. Write a linear function rule that models the depth of water in the tub, y, after any number of seconds, x.

   b. Suppose the drain rate of another bathtub is 0.2 cm/second. Describe a "draining race" between these two tubs. Be sure to include the initial depths of water in the tubs and which tub wins.

8. A meteorologist monitors the steady snowfall for a report on the news. After 4 hours, there are 12 inches of snow on the ground. There are 16 inches of snow 4 hours later.

   a. Write a linear function rule for y, the depth of the snow on the ground, after any number of hours x.

   b. If the meteorologist started measuring the snow at noon, how deep will the snow be when the news airs at 10 P.M.?

9. **Reasoning** A store sells packages of comic books with a poster. A poster and 6 comics cost $12.75. A poster and 13 comics cost $19.75.

   a. Write a linear function rule that models the cost, y, of a package containing any number of comic books, x.

   b. Suppose another store sells a similar package, modeled by a linear function rule with initial value $7.99. Explain which store has the better deal.

10. **Estimation** You and a group of 7 friends go out for pizza. One large pizza and 4 small drinks cost $21.95. One large pizza and 6 small drinks cost $25.93.

   a. Write a linear function rule that models the total cost, y, (in dollars) for one large pizza and any number of drinks, x.

   b. Use linear function rule to estimate the cost of one large pizza and 8 small drinks for you and your friends.

11. Think About the Process The line represents a linear function.

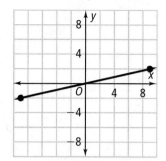

a. Which expression represents the rate of change of the function?

A. $\dfrac{2-(-2)}{-9-9}$ **B.** $\dfrac{2-9}{-2-(-9)}$

C. $\dfrac{2-(-2)}{9-(-9)}$ **D.** $\dfrac{-2-(-9)}{2-9}$

b. What is the function rule for the line?

12. Error Analysis Your friend incorrectly says that the linear function rule for the line through the points (0,0) and (7, 4) is $y = \frac{7}{4}x$.

a. What is the correct linear function rule?

A. $y = -\frac{4}{7}x$ **B.** $y = x + \frac{7}{4}$

C. $y = \frac{4}{7}x$ **D.** $y = -\frac{7}{4}x$

b. What was your friend's mistake?

  A. Your friend calculated the change in x incorrectly.

  B. Your friend reversed the numerator and denominator for the rate of change.

  C. Your friend did not simplify the fraction.

  D. Your friend calculated the change in y incorrectly.

13. Clothing Online An online clothing company sells custom sweatshirts. The company charges $3.99 for shipping plus $6.50 for each sweatshirt.

a. Write a linear function rule that models the total cost, y, (in dollars) for any number of sweatshirts, x.

b. Describe how the linear function rule would change if the shipping charge applied to each sweatshirt.

14. Find the function rule for the line that passes through the origin (0,0) and the point (−6, −14).

  A. $y = -14x - 6$

  B. $y = -6x - 14$

  C. $y = \frac{7}{3}x$

  D. $y = \frac{3}{7}x$

15. Think About the Process A line through the point (−0.24, 0) with slope 1 models a linear function.

a. Which equation below could you use to find b, the initial value of the linear function?

  A. $0 + (-0.24) = b + 1$

  B. $0 = (1)(-0.24) + b$

  C. $-0.24 = (1 + 0) + b$

  D. $-0.24 = (1)(0) + b$

b. Write a linear function rule in terms of x and y for this line.

16. Write a function rule in terms of x and y for the line that contains the points (−8.3, −5.2) and (6.4, 9.5).

17. What is a linear function rule in terms of x and y for the line passing through (4.5, −4.25) with y-intercept 2.5?

18. Challenge Stephanie is 5 years and 9 months older than her brother Michael.

a. What is the linear function rule for Stephanie's age, y, (in months) in terms of Michael's age, x?

  A. $y = 69 - x$ **B.** $y = 69x$

  C. $y = x - 69$ **D.** $y = x + 69$

b. Stephanie and Michael have a little sister, who was born when Stephanie was 10 years old. How old was Michael when their little sister was born?

19. Challenge A line passes through the points (11, 19.75) and (19, 29.75).

a. Write a linear function rule in terms of x and y for this line.

b. Which has the greater x-value?

  A. the point with y-coordinate 42.25

  B. the point with x-coordinate 35

CCSS: 8.F.B.4

Part 1

Example Using Linear Function Rules to Find Points

At time $t = 0$, a bicyclist begins riding at a constant speed. Ten minutes later the bicyclist has traveled 2.5 miles.

A road worker spilled yellow paint 3.5 miles down the road. At what time will the bicyclist ride through the paint spill?

Solution ·

The bicyclist is traveling at a constant speed, so his progress can be represented by a linear function.

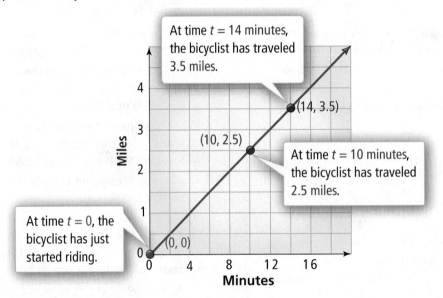

The bicyclist will ride through the paint spill after 14 minutes.

Part 2

Example Using Linear Function Rules to Describe Meanings of Points

A model train passes its model depot at time $t = 0$. After 3 minutes, the train has traveled a distance of 132 ft along the track.

Use a linear function to model the distance the train travels in t minutes. Find the value of the function for $t = -2$. Explain the meaning of the associated point on the graph of the function, in terms of the situation.

Solution ·

At time $t = 0$, the model train passes its model depot. Let this be the origin $(0, 0)$ of the graph. After 3 minutes, the train has traveled 132 feet along the track. This is represented by the point $(3, 132)$ on the graph.

You know two points on the graph. Remember that the origin of the graph represents the depot. Everything on the line to the right of the origin represents the train after it passes the depot. Everything on the line to the left of the origin represents the train before it passes the depot.

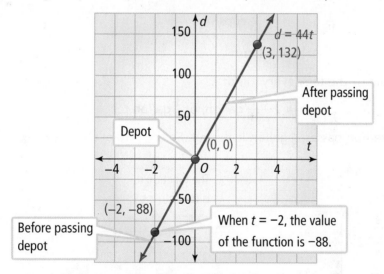

Two minutes before passing the model depot, the model train is 88 feet away.

Part 3

Example Writing Linear Function Rules to Solve Problems

A gardener collected 40 gallons of rainwater in a tank. Later the bottom of the tank cracks, and water starts to leak out. The water leaks at a constant rate of 2 cups per minute.

The gardener notices the leak after an hour. She needs 30 gallons of water to water the vegetable garden. Is there enough water in the tank?

Solution

The original volume of the tank is given in gallons and the rate at which the water leaks from the tank is given in cups. First, find the number of cups in one gallon.

Conversion Chart
1 gallon = 4 quarts
1 quart = 4 cups

1 gallon = 4 • 1 quart
1 gallon = 4 • 4 cups
1 gallon = 16 cups

Now find the number of gallons in one cup.

$$\frac{1}{16} \text{ gallon} = \frac{16}{16} \text{ cups}$$

$$\frac{1}{16} \text{ gallon} = 1 \text{ cup}$$

Two cups leak out of the tank every minute.

$$2 \text{ cups} = 2 \cdot \frac{1}{16} \text{ gallon, or } \frac{1}{8} \text{ gallon.}$$

For every minute that passes, $\frac{1}{8}$ gallon leaks out. So the rate of change is $-\frac{1}{8}$.

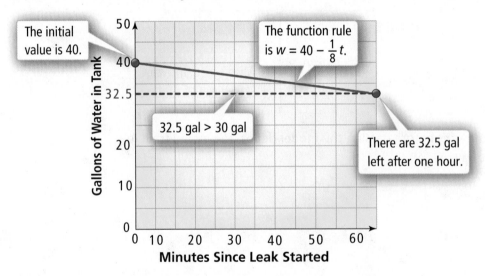

The initial value is 40.

The function rule is $w = 40 - \frac{1}{8}t$.

32.5 gal > 30 gal

There are 32.5 gal left after one hour.

Yes, after 1 hour there is still enough water in the tank to water the vegetable garden.

1. The after-school Activities Club charges $30 to join for the year. It charges a materials fee of $6 for each activity you choose.

   a. Write a linear function to model the cost, c, of joining the club and choosing t activities.

   b. Find the value of the function for $t = -4$.

   c. Which statement best explains the meaning of this value of the function in terms of the situation?

      A. If you choose 4 activities, you get a $6 discount.

      B. You cannot choose a negative number of activities, so this function makes sense for only nonnegative values of t.

      C. If you signed up 4 days ago, you would have saved $6.

      D. You may only choose fewer than 4 activities.

2. You go on a 7–day vacation and bring $188 for spending money. You spend $24 each of the first 6 days.

   a. Write a linear function that describes the amount of money, a, that you have after d days.

   b. On the last day, can you buy a sweatshirt that costs $45?

3. **Think About the Process** Most U.S. paper money weighs one gram per bill. To the nearest whole number, there are 454 grams in one pound.

   a. Which linear function models the value V of 3 pounds of U.S. bills of any given denomination d?

      A. $V = 454d$

      B. $V = 454d + 3$

      C. $V = 4,540d$

      D. $V = 1,362d$

   b. How would you find the value of 3 pounds of $10 bills?

      A. Use the linear function to find the value of V when $d = 3$.

   B. Use the linear function to find the value of d when $V = 10$.

   C. Use the linear function to find the value of d when $V = 1,362$.

   D. Use the linear function to find the value of V when $d = 10$.

   c. What is the value of 3 pounds of $10 bills?

4. **Think About the Process** At the beginning of the month, the price of 1 share of a certain stock was $10.00. Each day for a certain number of days, the price of the stock decreased by $1.25.

   a. Choose the linear function that models the price, p, of 1 share of this stock after d days.

      A. $p = -1.25d + 23.00$

      B. $p = 10.00 + 1.25d$

      C. $p = 1.25d + 10.00$

      D. $p = 1.25d + 23.00$

   b. How can you tell that the model does not make sense for some values of d?

      A. The model does not make sense if d is a negative number.

      B. The price of a share of stock cannot be negative, so this model does not make sense for the values of d that give negative values of p.

      C. The price of a share of stock cannot be a decimal, so this model does not make sense for values of d that give non-integer values of p.

      D. The price of a share of stock can be positive or negative, so this model does make sense for all values of d.

   c. Describe the values of d for which the model makes sense and those for which it does not.

5. You open a savings account with $75 and plan to save regularly each week. After 5 weeks you have $135.

   a. What is a linear function that models the amount, S, saved in w weeks?

   b. Find the value of the function for $w = -2$.

   c. Which statement best explains the meaning of this value of the function in terms of the situation?

     A. Since w is negative, you spent 51 dollars in the 2 weeks before opening the account.

     B. You had saved 51 dollars 2 weeks before opening the account. The value of S can be less than 75.

     C. The value has no meaning, since w represents time. The account did not exist at $w = -2$, so w can never be negative.

Change Over Time

6. a. Write a linear function for the graph in the form $y = mx$, where y is the total change and x is the number of years since 2000.

   b. What would the total change be by 2013?

   c. Describe a situation that can be modeled by the function.

7. A family has a supply of 60 logs to use in the fireplace during a vacation.

   a. Write a linear function to model this situation where G is the number of logs remaining after N nights.

   b. If the family uses exactly 7 logs each night, how many nights will the supply of logs last?

8. Your friend bought a plant that was 8 cm tall. He followed the care and watering instructions, and each week the plant grew at a constant rate. He recorded the plant's height each week in the table shown.

Plant Growth

Number of Weeks	Height (cm)
1	9.2
2	10.4
3	11.6
4	12.8

   a. Which linear function models the height of the plant after x weeks?

     A. $y = 1.2x - 2$ **B.** $y = 1.2x + 8$

     C. $y = -2x + 8$ **D.** $y = 8x + 1.2$

   b. Find the value of the function for $x = -2$.

   c. Can this value of y be used to represent the height of a plant?

9. You go shopping at a store where every item costs exactly $4. You have a $20 gift card to use in the store. When you pay, you will first use the gift card. Then you will pay for the remainder of your purchases with cash.

   a. Write a linear function that models the amount of your own cash C that you will spend when you purchase n items.

   b. How much cash will you spend if you purchase 7 items?

   c. Find the value of C when $n = 4$.

   d. Which statement best explains the meaning of this value of the function in terms of the situation?

     A. You must pay $4 in cash to cover your purchase.

     B. You may still purchase 4 items using the gift card.

     C. You do not have to spend any cash. You have a balance of $4 on the gift card.

     D. The value has no meaning, since C is in dollars.

English/Spanish Glossary

A

Absolute deviation from the mean Absolute deviation measures the distance that the data value is from the mean. You find the absolute deviation by taking the absolute value of the deviation of a data value. Absolute deviations are always nonnegative.

Desviación absoluta de la media La desviación absoluta mide la distancia a la que un valor se encuentra de la media. Para hallar la desviación absoluta, tomas el valor absoluto de la desviación de un valor. Las desviaciones absolutas siempre son no negativas.

Absolute value The absolute value of a number a is the distance between a and zero on a number line. The absolute value of a is written as $|a|$.

Valor absoluto El valor absoluto de un número a es la distancia entre a y cero en la recta numérica. El valor absoluto de a se escribe como $|a|$.

Accuracy The accuracy of an estimate or measurement is the degree to which it agrees with an accepted or actual value of that measurement.

Exactitud La exactitud de una estimación o medición es el grado de concordancia con un valor aceptado o real de esa medición.

Action In a probability situation, an action is a process with an uncertain result.

Acción En una situación de probabilidad, una acción es el proceso con un resultado incierto.

Acute angle An acute angle is an angle with a measure between 0° and 90°.

Ángulo agudo Un ángulo agudo es un ángulo que mide entre 0° y 90°.

Acute triangle An acute triangle is a triangle with three acute angles.

Triángulo acutángulo Un triángulo acutángulo es un triángulo que tiene tres ángulos agudos.

Addend Addends are the numbers that are added together to find a sum.

Sumando Los sumandos son los números que se suman para hallar un total.

English/Spanish Glossary

Additive inverses Two numbers that have a sum of 0.

Inversos de suma Dos números cuya suma es 0.

Adjacent angles Two angles are adjacent angles if they share a vertex and a side, but have no interior points in common.

Ángulos adyacentes Dos ángulos son adyacentes si tienen un vértice y un lado en común, pero no comparten puntos internos.

Algebraic expression An algebraic expression is a mathematical phrase that consists of variables, numbers, and operation symbols.

Expresión algebraica Una expresión algebraica es una frase matemática que consiste en variables, números y símbolos de operaciones.

Analyze To analyze is to think about and understand facts and details about a given set of information. Analyzing can involve providing a written summary supported by factual information, diagrams, charts, tables, or any combination of these.

Analizar Analizar es pensar en los datos y detalles de cierta información y comprenderlos. El análisis puede incluir la presentación de un resumen escrito sustentado por información objetiva, diagramas, tablas o una combinación de esos elementos.

Angle An angle is a figure formed by two rays with a common endpoint.

Ángulo Un ángulo es una figura formada por dos semirrectas que tienen un extremo en común.

Angle of rotation The angle of rotation is the number of degrees a figure is rotated.

Ángulo de rotación El ángulo de rotación es el número de grados que se rota una figura.

Annual salary The amount of money earned at a job in one year.

Salario annual La cantidad de dinero ganó en un trabajo en un año.

Area The area of a figure is the number of square units the figure encloses.

Área El área de una figura es el número de unidades cuadradas que ocupa.

English/Spanish Glossary

Area of a circle The formula for the area of a circle is $A = \pi r^2$, where A represents the area and r represents the radius of the circle.

Área de un círculo La fórmula del área de un círculo es $A = \pi r^2$, donde A representa el área y r representa el radio del círculo.

Area of a parallelogram The formula for the area of a parallelogram is $A = bh$, where A represents the area, b represents a base, and h is the corresponding height.

Área de un paralelogramo La fórmula del área de un paralelogramo es $A = bh$, donde A representa el área, b representa una base y h es la altura correspondiente.

Area of a rectangle The formula for the area of a rectangle is $A = bh$, where A represents the area, b represents the base, and h represents the height of the rectangle.

Área de un rectángulo La fórmula del área de un rectángulo es $A = bh$, donde A representa el área, b representa la base y h representa la altura del rectángulo.

Area of a square The formula for the area of a square is $A = s^2$, where A represents the area and s represents a side length.

Área de un cuadrado La fórmula del área de un cuadrado es $A = s^2$, donde A representa el área y l representa la longitud de un lado.

Area of a trapezoid The formula for the area of a trapezoid is $A = \frac{1}{2}h(b_1 + b_2)$, where A represents the area, b_1 and b_2 represent the bases, and h represents the height between the bases.

El área de un trapezoide La fórmula para el área de un trapezoide es $A = \frac{1}{2}h(b_1 + b_2)$, donde A representa el área, b_1 y b_2 representan las bases, y h representa la altura entre las bases.

Area of a triangle The formula for the area of a triangle is $A = \frac{1}{2}bh$, where A represents the area, b represents the length of a base, and h represents the corresponding height.

Área de un triángulo La fórmula del área de un triángulo es $A = \frac{1}{2}bh$, donde A representa el área, b representa la longitud de una base y h representa la altura correspondiente.

Asset An asset is money you have or property of value that you own.

Ventaja Una ventaja es dinero que tiene o la propiedad de valor que usted posee.

English/Spanish Glossary

Associative Property of Addition For any numbers a, b, and c:
$(a + b) + c = a + (b + c)$

Propiedad asociativa de la suma Para los números cualesquiera a, b y c:
$(a + b) + c = a + (b + c)$

Associative Property of Multiplication For any numbers a, b, and c:
$(a \cdot b) \cdot c = a \cdot (b \cdot c)$

Propiedad asociativa de la multiplicación Para los números cualesquiera a, b y c:
$(a \cdot b) \cdot c = a \cdot (b \cdot c)$

Average of two numbers The average of two numbers is the value that represents the middle of two numbers. It is found by adding the two numbers together and dividing by 2.

Promedio de dos números El promedio de dos números es el valor que está justo en el medio de esos dos números. Se halla sumando los dos números y dividiendo el resultado por 2.

B

Balance The balance in an account is the principal amount plus the interest earned.

Saldo El saldo de una cuenta es el capital más el interés ganado.

Balance of a checking account The balance of a checking account is the amount of money in the checking account.

El equilibrio de una Cuenta Corriente Bancaria El equilibrio de una cuenta corriente bancaria es la cantidad de dinero en la cuenta corriente bancaria.

Balance of a loan The balance of a loan is the remaining unpaid principal.

El equilibrio de un préstamo El equilibrio de un préstamo es el director impagado restante.

Bar diagram A bar diagram is a way to represent part to whole relationships.

Diagrama de barras Un diagrama de barras es una forma de representar una relación de parte a entero.

Base The base is the repeated factor of a number written in exponential form.

Base La base es el factor repetido de un número escrito en forma exponencial.

English/Spanish Glossary

Base area of a cone The base area of a cone is the area of a circle. Base Area $= \pi r^2$.

Área de la base de un cono El área de la base de un cono es el área de un círculo. El área de la base $= \pi r^2$.

Base of a cone The base of a cone is a circle with radius *r*.

Base de un cono La base de un cono es un círculo con radio *r*.

Base of a cylinder A base of a cylinder is one of a pair of parallel circular faces that are the same size.

Base de un cilindro Una base de un cilindro es una de dos caras circulares paralelas que tienen el mismo tamaño.

Base of a parallelogram A base of a parallelogram is any side of the parallelogram.

Base de un paralelogramo La base de un paralelogramo es cualquiera de los lados del paralelogramo.

Base of a prism A base of a prism is one of a pair of parallel polygonal faces that are the same size and shape. A prism is named for the shape of its bases.

Base de un prisma La base de un prisma es una de las dos caras poligonales paralelas que tienen el mismo tamaño y la misma forma. El nombre de un prisma depende de la forma de sus bases.

Base of a pyramid A base of a pyramid is a polygonal face that does not connect to the vertex.

Base de una pirámide La base de una pirámide es una cara poligonal que no se conecta con el vértice.

Base of a triangle The base of a triangle is any side of the triangle.

Base de un triángulo La base de un triángulo es cualquiera de los lados del triángulo.

Benchmark A benchmark is a number you can use as a reference point for other numbers.

Referencia Una referencia es un número que usted puede utilizar como un punto de referencia para otros números.

English/Spanish Glossary

Bias A bias is a tendency toward a particular perspective that is different from the overall perspective of the population.

Sesgo Un sesgo es una tendencia hacia una perspectiva particular que es diferente de la perspectiva general de la población.

Biased sample In a biased sample, the number of subjects in the sample with the trait that you are studying is not proportional to the number of members in the population with that trait. A biased sample does not accurately represent the population.

Muestra sesgada En una muestra sesgada, el número de sujetos de la muestra que tiene la característica que se está estudiando no es proporcional al número de miembros de la población que tienen esa característica. Una muestra sesgada no representa con exactitud la población.

Bivariate categorical data Bivariate categorical data pairs categorical data collected about two variables of the same population.

Datos bivariados por categorías Los datos bivariados por categorías agrupan pares de datos obtenidos acerca de dos variables de la misma población.

Bivariate data Bivariate data is comprised of pairs of linked observations about a population.

Datos bivariados Los datos bivariados se forman a partir de pares de observaciones relacionadas sobre una población.

Box plot A box plot is a statistical graph that shows the distribution of a data set by marking five boundary points where data occur along a number line. Unlike a dot plot or a histogram, a box plot does not show frequency.

Diagrama de cajas Un diagrama de cajas es un diagrama de estadísticas que muestra la distribución de un conjunto de datos al marcar cinco puntos de frontera donde se hallan los datos sobre una recta numérica. A diferencia del diagrama de puntos o el histograma, el diagrama de cajas no muestra la frecuencia.

Budget A budget is a plan for how you will spend your money.

Presupuesto Un presupuesto es un plan para cómo gastará su dinero.

English/Spanish Glossary

C

Categorical data Categorical data consist of data that fall into categories.

Datos por categorías Los datos por categorías son datos que se pueden clasificar en categorías.

Center of a circle The center of a circle is the point inside the circle that is the same distance from all points on the circle. Name a circle by its center.

Centro de un círculo El centro de un círculo es el punto dentro del círculo que está a la misma distancia de todos los puntos del círculo. Un círculo se identifica por su centro.

Center of a regular polygon The center of a regular polygon is the point that is equidistant from its vertices.

Centro de un polígono regular El centro de un polígono regular es el punto equidistante de todos sus vértices.

Center of rotation The center of rotation is a fixed point about which a figure is rotated.

Centro de rotación El centro de rotación es el punto fijo alrededor del cual se rota una figura.

Check register A record that shows all of the transactions for a bank account, including withdrawals, deposits, and transfers. It also shows the balance of the account after each transaction.

Verifique registro Un registro que muestra todas las transacciones para una cuenta bancaria, inclusive retiradas, los depósitos, y las transferencias. También muestra el equilibrio de la cuenta después de cada transacción.

Circle A circle is the set of all points in a plane that are the same distance from a given point, called the center.

Círculo Un círculo es el conjunto de todos los puntos de un plano que están a la misma distancia de un punto dado, llamado centro.

Circle graph A circle graph is a graph that represents a whole divided into parts.

Gráfica circular Una gráfica circular es una gráfica que representa un todo dividido en partes.

English/Spanish Glossary

Circumference of a circle The circumference of a circle is the distance around the circle. The formula for the circumference of a circle is $C = \pi d$, where C represents the circumference and d represents the diameter of the circle.

Circunferencia de un círculo La circunferencia de un círculo es la distancia alrededor del círculo. La fórmula de la circunferencia de un círculo es $C = \pi d$, donde C representa la circunferencia y d representa el diámetro del círculo.

Cluster A cluster is a group of points that lie close together on a scatter plot.

Grupo Un grupo es un conjunto de puntos que están agrupados en un diagrama de dispersión.

Coefficient A coefficient is the number part of a term that contains a variable.

Coeficiente Un coeficiente es la parte numérica de un término que contiene una variable.

Common denominator A common denominator is a number that is the denominator of two or more fractions.

Común denominador Un común denominador es un número que es el denominador de dos o más fracciones.

Common multiple A common multiple is a multiple that two or more numbers share.

Múltiplo común Un múltiplo común es un múltiplo que comparten dos o más números.

Commutative Property of Addition For any numbers a and b: $a + b = b + a$

Propiedad conmutativa de la suma Para los números cualesquiera a y b: $a + b = b + a$

Commutative Property of Multiplication For any numbers a and b: $a \cdot b = b \cdot a$

Propiedad conmutativa de la multiplicación Para los números cualesquiera a y b: $a \cdot b = b \cdot a$

Comparative inference A comparative inference is an inference made by interpreting and comparing two sets of data.

Inferencia comparativa Una inferencia comparativa es una inferencia que se hace al interpretar y comparar dos conjuntos de datos.

English/Spanish Glossary

Compare To compare is to tell or show how two things are alike or different.

Comparar Comparar es describir o mostrar en qué se parecen o en qué se diferencian dos cosas.

Compatible numbers Compatible numbers are numbers that are easy to compute mentally.

Números compatibles Los números compatibles son números fáciles de calcular mentalmente.

Complementary angles Two angles are complementary angles if the sum of their measures is 90°. Complementary angles that are adjacent form a right angle.

Ángulos complementarios Dos ángulos son complementarios si la suma de sus medidas es 90°. Los ángulos complementarios que son adyacentes forman un ángulo recto.

Complex fraction A complex fraction is a fraction $\frac{A}{B}$ where A and/or B are fractions and B is not zero.

Fracción compleja Una fracción compleja es una fracción $\frac{A}{B}$ donde A y/o B son fracciones y B es distinto de cero.

Compose a shape To compose a shape, join two (or more) shapes so that there is no gap or overlap.

Componer una figura Para componer una figura, debes unir dos (o más) figuras de modo que entre ellas no queden espacios ni superposiciones.

Composite figure A composite figure is the combination of two or more figures into one object.

Figura compuesta Una figura compuesta es la combinación de dos o más figuras en un objeto.

Composite number A composite number is a whole number greater than 1 with more than two factors.

Número compuesto Un número compuesto es un número entero mayor que 1 con más de dos factores.

Compound event A compound event is an event associated with a multi-step action. A compound event is composed of events that are the outcomes of the steps of the action.

Evento compuesto Un evento compuesto es un evento que se relaciona con una acción de varios pasos. Un evento compuesto se compone de eventos que son los resultados de los pasos de una acción.

English/Spanish Glossary

Compound interest Compound interest is interest paid on both the principal and the interest earned in previous interest periods. To calculate compound interest, use the formula $B = p(1 + r)^n$, where B is the balance in the account, p is the principal, r is the annual interest rate, and n is the time in years that the account earns interest.

Interés compuesto El interés compuesto es el interés que se paga sobre el capital y el interés obtenido en períodos de interés anteriores. Para calcular el interés compuesto, usa la fórmula $B = c(1 + r)^n$ donde B es el saldo de la cuenta, c es el capital, r es la tasa de interés anual y n es el tiempo en años en que la cuenta obtiene un interés.

Cone A cone is a three-dimensional figure with one circular base and one vertex.

Cono Un cono es una figura tridimensional con una base circular y un vértice.

Congruent figures Two two-dimensional figures are congruent ≅ if the second can be obtained from the first by a sequence of rotations, reflections, and translations.

Figuras congruentes Dos figuras bidimensionales son congruentes ≅ si la segunda puede obtenerse a partir de la primera mediante una secuencia de rotaciones, reflexiones y traslaciones.

Conjecture A conjecture is a statement that you believe to be true but have not yet proved to be true.

Conjetura Una conjetura es un enunciado que crees que es verdadero, pero que todavía no has comprobado que sea verdadero.

Constant A constant is a term that only contains a number.

Constante Una constante es un término que solamente contiene un número.

Constant of proportionality In a proportional relationship, one quantity y is a constant multiple of the other quantity x. The constant multiple is called the constant of proportionality. The constant of proportionality is equal to the ratio $\frac{y}{x}$.

Constante de proporcionalidad En una relación proporcional, una cantidad y es un múltiplo constante de la otra cantidad x. El múltiplo constante se llama constante de proporcionalidad. La constante de proporcionalidad es igual a la razón $\frac{y}{x}$.

English/Spanish Glossary

Construct To construct is to make something, such as an argument, by organizing ideas. Constructing an argument can involve a written response, equations, diagrams, charts, tables, or a combination of these.

Construir Construir es hacer o crear algo, como se construye un argumento al organizar ideas. Para construir un argumento puede usarse una respuesta escrita, ecuaciones, diagramas, tablas o una combinación de esos elementos.

Convenience sampling Convenience sampling is a sampling method in which a researcher chooses members of the population that are convenient and available. Many researchers use this sampling technique because it is fast and inexpensive. It does not require the researcher to keep track of everyone in the population.

Muestra de conveniencia Una muestra de conveniencia es un método de muestreo en el que un investigador escoge miembros de la población que están convenientemente disponibles. Muchos investigadores usan esta técnica de muestreo porque es rápida y no es costosa. No requiere que el investigador lleve un registro de cada miembro de la población.

Cost of attendance The cost of attendance of one year of college is the sum of all of your expenses during the year.

El costo de asistencia El costo de asistencia de un año del colegio es la suma de todos sus gastos durante el año.

Cost of credit The cost of credit for a loan is the difference between the total cost and the principal.

El costo de crédito El costo de crédito para un préstamo es la diferencia entre el coste total y el director.

Converse of the Pythagorean Theorem If the sum of the squares of the lengths of two sides of a triangle equals the square of the length of the third side, then the triangle is a right triangle. If $a^2 + b^2 = c^2$, then the triangle is a right triangle.

Expresión recíproca del Teorema de Pitágoras Si la suma del cuadrado de la longitud de dos lados de un triángulo es igual al cuadrado de la longitud del tercer lado, entonces el triángulo es un triángulo rectángulo. $a^2 + b^2 = c^2$, entonces el triángulo es un triángulo rectángulo.

Conversion factor A conversion factor is a rate that equals 1.

Factor de conversión Un factor de conversión es una tasa que es igual a 1.

English/Spanish Glossary

Coordinate plane A coordinate plane is formed by a horizontal number line called the *x*-axis and a vertical number line called the *y*-axis.

Plano de coordenadas Un plano de coordenadas está formado por una recta numérica horizontal llamada eje de las *x* y una recta numérica vertical llamada eje de las *y*.

Corresponding angles Corresponding angles lie on the same side of a transversal and in corresponding positions.

Ángulos correspondientes Los ángulos correspondientes se ubican al mismo lado de una secante y en posiciones correspondientes.

Counterexample A counterexample is a specific example that shows that a conjecture is false.

Contraejemplo Un contraejemplo es un ejemplo específico que muestra que una conjetura es falsa.

Counting Principle If there are *m* possible outcomes of one action and *n* possible outcomes of a second action, then there are *m* · *n* outcomes of the first action followed by the second action.

Principio de conteo Si hay *m* resultados posibles de una acción y *n* resultados posibles de una segunda acción, entonces hay *m* · *n* resultados de la primera acción seguida de la segunda acción.

Coupon A coupon is part of a printed or online advertisement entitling the holder to a discount at checkout.

Cupón Un cupón forma parte de un anuncio impreso o en línea que permite al poseedor a un descuento en comprueba.

Credit card A credit card is a card issued by a lender that can be used to borrow money or make purchases on credit.

Tarjeta de crédito Una tarjeta de crédito es una tarjeta publicada por un prestamista que puede ser utilizado para pedir dinero prestado o compras de marca a cuenta.

Credit history A credit history shows how a consumer has managed credit in the past.

Acredite la historia Una historia del crédito muestra cómo un consumidor ha manejado crédito en el pasado.

English/Spanish Glossary

Credit report A report that shows personal information about a consumer and details about the consumer's credit history.

Acredite reporte Un reporte que muestra información personal sobre un consumidor y detalles acerca de la historia del crédito del consumidor.

Critique A critique is a careful judgment in which you give your opinion about the good and bad parts of something, such as how a problem was solved.

Crítica Una crítica es una evaluación cuidadosa en la que das tu opinión acerca de las partes positivas y negativas de algo, como la manera en la que se resolvió un problema.

Cross section A cross section is the intersection of a three-dimensional figure and a plane.

Corte transversal Un corte transversal es la intersección de una figura tridimensional y un plano.

Cube A cube is a rectangular prism whose faces are all squares.

Cubo Un cubo es un prisma rectangular cuyas caras son todas cuadrados.

Cube root The cube root of a number, *n*, is a number whose cube equals *n*.

Raíz cúbica La raíz cúbica de un número, *n*, es un número que elevado al cubo es igual a *n*.

Cubic unit A cubic unit is the volume of a cube that measures 1 unit on each edge.

Unidad cúbica Una unidad cúbica es el volumen de un cubo en el que cada arista mide 1 unidad.

Cylinder A cylinder is a three-dimensional figure with two parallel circular bases that are the same size.

Cilindro Un cilindro es una figura tridimensional con dos bases circulares paralelas que tienen el mismo tamaño.

D

Data Data are pieces of information collected by asking questions, measuring, or making observations about the real world.

Datos Los datos son información reunida mediante preguntas, mediciones u observaciones sobre la vida diaria.

English/Spanish Glossary

Debit card A debit card is a card issued by a bank that is linked to a customer's bank account, normally a checking account. A debit card can normally be used to withdraw money from an ATM or to make a purchase.

Tarjeta de débito Una tarjeta de débito es una tarjeta publicada por un banco que es ligado la cuenta bancaria de un cliente, normalmente una cuenta corriente bancaria. Una tarjeta de débito puede ser utilizada normalmente retirar dinero de una ATM o para hacer una compra.

Decimal A decimal is a number with one or more places to the right of a decimal point.

Decimal Un decimal es un número que tiene uno o más lugares a la derecha del punto decimal.

Decimal places The digits after the decimal point are called decimal places.

Lugares decimales Los dígitos que están después del punto decimal se llaman lugares decimales.

Decompose a shape To decompose a shape, break it up to form other shapes.

Descomponer una figura Para descomponer una figura, debes separarla para formar otras figuras.

Deductive reasoning Deductive reasoning is a process of reasoning logically from given facts to a conclusion.

Razonamiento deductivo El razonamiento deductivo es un proceso de razonamiento lógico que parte de hechos dados hasta llegar a una conclusión.

Denominator The denominator is the number below the fraction bar in a fraction.

Denominador El denominador es el número que está debajo de la barra de fracción en una fracción.

Dependent events Two events are dependent events if the occurrence of the first event affects the probability of the second event.

Eventos dependientes Dos eventos son dependientes si el resultado del primer evento afecta la probabilidad del segundo evento.

Deposit A transaction that adds money to a bank account is a deposit.

Depósito Una transacción que agrega dinero a una cuenta bancaria es un depósito.

English/Spanish Glossary

Dependent variable A dependent variable is a variable whose value changes in response to another (independent) variable.

Variable dependiente Una variable dependiente es una variable cuyo valor cambia en respuesta a otra variable (independiente).

Describe To describe is to explain or tell in detail. A written description can contain facts and other information needed to communicate your answer. A diagram or a graph may also be included.

Describir Describir es explicar o indicar algo en detalle. Una descripción escrita puede incluir hechos y otra información necesaria para comunicar tu respuesta. También puede incluir un diagrama o una gráfica.

Design To design is to make using specific criteria.

Diseñar Diseñar es crear algo a partir de criterios específicos.

Determine To determine is to use the given information and any related facts to find a value or make a decision.

Determinar Determinar es usar la información dada y cualquier otro dato relacionado para hallar un valor o tomar una decisión.

Deviation from the mean Deviation indicates how far away and in which direction a data value is from the mean. Data values that are less than the mean have a negative deviation. Data values that are greater than the mean have a positive deviation.

Desviación de la media La desviación indica a qué distancia y en qué dirección un valor se aleja de la media. Los valores menores que la media tienen una desviación negativa. Los valores mayores que la media tienen una desviación positiva.

Diagonal A diagonal of a figure is a segment that connects two nonconsecutive vertices of the figure.

Diagonal La diagonal de una figura es un segmento que conecta dos vértices no consecutivos de la figura.

Diameter A diameter is a segment that passes through the center of a circle and has both endpoints on the circle. The term diameter can also mean the length of this segment.

Diámetro Un diámetro es un segmento que atraviesa el centro de un círculo y tiene sus dos extremos en el círculo. El término diámetro también puede referirse a la longitud de este segmento.

English/Spanish Glossary

Difference The difference is the answer you get when subtracting two numbers.

Diferencia La diferencia es la respuesta que obtienes cuando restas dos números.

Dilation A dilation is a transformation that moves each point along the ray through the point, starting from a fixed center, and multiplies distances from the center by a common scale factor. If a vertex of a figure is the center of dilation, then the vertex and its image after the dilation are the same point.

Dilatación Una dilatación es una transformación que mueve cada punto a lo largo de la semirrecta a través del punto, a partir de un centro fijo, y multiplica las distancias desde el centro por un factor de escala común. Si un vértice de una figura es el centro de dilatación, entonces el vértice y su imagen después de la dilatación son el mismo punto.

Direct variation A linear relationship that can be represented by an equation in the form $y = kx$, where $x \neq 0$.

Dirija variación Una relación lineal que puede ser representada por una ecuación en la forma $y = kx$, donde x no iguale 0.

Distribution (of a data set) The distribution of a data set describes the way that its data values are spread out over all possible values. This includes describing the frequencies of each data value. The shape of a data display shows the distribution of a data set.

Distribución (de un conjunto de datos) La distribución de un conjunto de datos describe la manera en que sus valores se esparcen sobre todos los valores posibles. Eso incluye la descripción de las frecuencias de cada valor. La forma de una exhibición de datos muestra la distribución de un conjunto de datos.

Distributive Property Multiplying a number by a sum or difference gives the same result as multiplying that number by each term in the sum or difference and then adding or subtracting the corresponding products.
$a \cdot (b + c) = a \cdot b + a \cdot c$ and
$a \cdot (b - c) = a \cdot b - a \cdot c$

Propiedad distributiva Multiplicar un número por una suma o una diferencia da el mismo resultado que multiplicar ese mismo número por cada uno de los términos de la suma o la diferencia y después sumar o restar los productos obtenidos.
$a \cdot (b + c) = a \cdot b + a \cdot c$ and
$a \cdot (b - c) = a \cdot b - a \cdot c$

Dividend The dividend is the number to be divided.

Dividendo El dividendo es el número que se divide.

English/Spanish Glossary

Divisible A number is divisible by another number if there is no remainder after dividing.

Divisible Un número es divisible por otro número si no hay residuo después de dividir.

Divisor The divisor is the number used to divide another number.

Divisor El divisor es el número por el cual se divide otro número.

Dot plot A dot plot is a statistical graph that shows the shape of a data set with stacked dots above each data value on a number line. Each dot represents one data value.

Diagrama de puntos Un diagrama de puntos es una gráfica estadística que muestra la forma de un conjunto de datos con puntos marcados sobre cada valor de una recta numérica. Cada punto representa un valor.

E

Earned wages Earned wages are the income you receive from an employer for doing a job. Earned wages are also called gross pay.

Sueldos ganados Los sueldos ganados son los ingresos que usted recibe de un empleador para hacer un trabajo. Los sueldos ganados también son llamados la paga bruta.

Easy-access loan The term easy-access loan refers to a wide variety of loans with a streamlined application process. Many easy-access loans are short-term loans of relatively small amounts of money. They often have high interest rates.

Préstamo de fácil-acceso El préstamo del fácil-acceso del término se refiere a una gran variedad de préstamos con un proceso simplificado de aplicación. Muchos préstamos del fácil-acceso son préstamos a corto plazo de cantidades relativamente pequeñas de dinero. Ellos a menudo tienen los tipos de interés altos.

Edge of a three-dimensional figure An edge of a three-dimensional figure is a segment formed by the intersection of two faces.

Arista de una figura tridimensional Una arista de una figura tridimensional es un segmento formado por la intersección de dos caras.

English/Spanish Glossary

Enlargement An enlargement is a dilation with a scale factor greater than 1. After an enlargement, the image is bigger than the original figure.

Aumento Un aumento es una dilatación con un factor de escala mayor que 1. Después de un aumento, la imagen es más grande que la figura original.

Equation An equation is a mathematical sentence that includes an equals sign to compare two expressions.

Ecuación Una ecuación es una oración matemática que incluye un signo igual para comparar dos expresiones.

Equilateral triangle An equilateral triangle is a triangle whose sides are all the same length.

Triángulo equilátero Un triángulo equilátero es un triángulo que tiene todos sus lados de la misma longitud.

Equivalent equations Equivalent equations are equations that have exactly the same solutions.

Ecuaciones equivalentes Las ecuaciones equivalentes son ecuaciones que tienen exactamente la misma solución.

Equivalent expressions Equivalent expressions are expressions that always have the same value.

Expresiones equivalentes Las expresiones equivalentes son expresiones que siempre tienen el mismo valor.

Equivalent fractions Equivalent fractions are fractions that name the same number.

Fracciones equivalentes Las fracciones equivalentes son fracciones que representan el mismo número.

Equivalent inequalities Equivalent inequalities are inequalities that have the same solution.

Desigualdades equivalentes Las desigualdades equivalentes son desigualdades que tienen la misma solución.

Equivalent ratios Equivalent ratios are ratios that express the same relationship.

Razones equivalentes Las razones equivalentes son razones que expresan la misma relación.

Estimate To estimate is to find a number that is close to an exact answer.

Estimar Estimar es hallar un número cercano a una respuesta exacta.

English/Spanish Glossary

Evaluate a numerical expression To evaluate a numerical expression is to follow the order of operations.

Evaluar una expresión numérica Evaluar una expresión numérica es seguir el orden de las operaciones.

Evaluate an algebraic expression To evaluate an algebraic expression, replace each variable with a number, and then follow the order of operations.

Evaluar una expresión algebraica Para evaluar una expresión algebraica, reemplaza cada variable con un número y luego sigue el orden de las operaciones.

Event An event is a single outcome or group of outcomes from a sample space.

Evento Un evento es un resultado simple o un grupo de resultados de un espacio muestral.

Expand an algebraic expression To expand an algebraic expression, use the Distributive Property to rewrite a product as a sum or difference of terms.

Desarrollar una expresión algebraica Para desarrollar una expresión algebraica, usa la propiedad distributiva para reescribir el producto como una suma o diferencia de términos.

Expected family contribution The amount of money a student's family is expected to contribute towards the student's cost of attendance for school.

Contribución familiar esperado La cantidad de dinero que la familia de un estudiante es esperada contribuir hacia el estudiante es costado de asistencia para la escuela.

Expense Money that a business or a person needs to spend to pay for or buy something.

Gasto El dinero que un negocio o una persona debe gastar para pagar por o comprar algo.

Experiment To experiment is to try to gather information in several ways.

Experimentar Experimentar es intentar reunir información de varias maneras.

English/Spanish Glossary

Experimental probability You find the experimental probability of an event by repeating an experiment many times and using this ratio: $P(\text{event}) = \dfrac{\text{number of times event occurs}}{\text{total number of trials}}$

Probabilidad experimental Para hallar la probabilidad experimental de un evento, debes repetir un experimento muchas veces y usar esta razón: $P(\text{evento}) = \dfrac{\text{número de veces que sucede el evento}}{\text{número total de pruebas}}$

Explain To explain is to give facts and details that make an idea easier to understand. Explaining can involve a written summary supported by a diagram, chart, table, or a combination of these.

Explicar Explicar es brindar datos y detalles para que una idea sea más fácil de comprender. Para explicar algo se puede usar un resumen escrito sustentado por un diagrama, una tabla o una combinación de esos elementos.

Exponent An exponent is a number that shows how many times a base is used as a factor.

Exponente Un exponente es un número que muestra cuántas veces se usa una base como factor.

Expression An expression is a mathematical phrase that can involve variables, numbers, and operations. See algebraic expression or numerical expression.

Expresión Una expresión es una frase matemática que puede tener variables, números y operaciones. Ver expresión algebraica o expresión numérica.

Exterior angle of a triangle An exterior angle of a triangle is an angle formed by a side and an extension of an adjacent side.

Ángulo externo de un triángulo Un ángulo externo de un triángulo es un ángulo formado por un lado y una extensión de un lado adyacente.

F

Face of a three-dimensional figure A face of a three-dimensional figure is a flat surface shaped like a polygon.

Cara de una figura tridimensional La cara de una figura tridimensional es una superficie plana con forma de polígono.

English/Spanish Glossary

Factor an algebraic expression To factor an algebraic expression, write the expression as a product.

Descomponer una expresión algebraica en factores Para descomponer una expresión algebraica en factores, escribe la expresión como un producto.

Factors Factors are numbers that are multiplied to give a product.

Factores Los factores son los números que se multiplican para obtener un producto.

False equation A false equation has values that do not equal each other on each side of the equals sign.

Ecuación falsa Una ecuación falsa tiene valores a cada lado del signo igual que no son iguales entre sí.

Financial aid Financial aid is any money offered to a student to assist with the cost of attendance.

Ayuda financiera La ayuda financiera es cualquier dinero ofreció a un estudiante para ayudar con el costo de asistencia.

Financial need A student's financial need is the difference between the student's cost of attendance and the student's expected family contribution.

Necesidad financiera Una necesidad financiera del estudiante es la diferencia entre el estudiante es costada de asistencia y la contribución esperado de familia de estudiante.

Find To find is to calculate or determine.

Hallar Hallar es calcular o determinar.

First quartile For an ordered set of data, the first quartile is the median of the lower half of the data set.

Primer cuartil Para un conjunto ordenado de datos, el primer cuartil es la mediana de la mitad inferior del conjunto de datos.

Fixed expenses Fixed expenses are expenses that do not change from one budget period to the next.

Gastos fijos Los gastos fijos son los gastos que no cambian de un período económico al próximo.

English/Spanish Glossary

Fraction A fraction is a number that can be written in the form $\frac{a}{b}$, where a is a whole number and b is a positive whole number. A fraction is formed by a parts of size $\frac{1}{b}$.

Fracción Una fracción es un número que puede expresarse de forma $\frac{a}{b}$, donde a es un entero y b es un número entero positivo. La fracción está formada por a partes de tamaño $\frac{1}{b}$.

Frequency Frequency describes the number of times a specific value occurs in a data set.

Frecuencia La frecuencia describe el número de veces que aparece un valor específico en un conjunto de datos.

Function A function is a rule for taking each input value and producing exactly one output value.

Función Una función es una regla por la cual se toma cada valor de entrada y se produce exactamente un valor de salida.

G

Gap A gap is an area of a graph that contains no data points.

Espacio vacío o brecha Un espacio vacío o brecha es un área de una gráfica que no contiene ningún valor.

Grant A type of monetary award a student can use to pay for his or her education. The student does not need to repay this money.

Grant Un tipo de premio monetario que un estudiante puede utilizar para pagar por su educación. El estudiante no debe devolver este dinero.

Greater than $>$ The greater-than symbol shows a comparison of two numbers with the number of greater value shown first, or on the left.

Mayor que $>$ El símbolo de mayor que muestra una comparación de dos números con el número de mayor valor que aparece primero, o a la izquierda.

Greatest common factor The greatest common factor (GCF) of two or more whole numbers is the greatest number that is a factor of all of the numbers.

Máximo común divisor El máximo común divisor (M.C.D.) de dos o más números enteros no negativos es el número mayor que es un factor de todos los números.

English/Spanish Glossary

H

Height of a cone The height of a cone, *h*, is the length of a segment perpendicular to the base that joins the vertex and the base.

Altura de un cono La altura de un cono, *h*, es la longitud de un segmento perpendicular a la base que une el vértice y la base.

Height of a cylinder The height of a cylinder is the length of a perpendicular segment that joins the planes of the bases.

Altura de un cilindro La altura de un cilindro es la longitud de un segmento perpendicular que une los planos de las bases.

Height of a parallelogram A height of a parallelogram is the perpendicular distance between opposite bases.

Altura de un paralelogramo La altura de un paralelogramo es la distancia perpendicular que existe entre las bases opuestas.

Height of a prism The height of a prism is the length of a perpendicular segment that joins the bases.

Altura de un prisma La altura de un prisma es la longitud de un segmento perpendicular que une a las bases.

Height of a pyramid The height of a pyramid is the length of a segment perpendicular to the base that joins the vertex and the base.

Altura de una pirámide La altura de una pirámide es la longitud de un segmento perpendicular a la base que une al vértice con la base.

Height of a triangle The height of a triangle is the length of the perpendicular segment from a vertex to the base opposite that vertex.

Altura de un triángulo La altura de un triángulo es la longitud del segmento perpendicular desde un vértice hasta la base opuesta a ese vértice.

Hexagon A hexagon is a polygon with six sides.

Hexágono Un hexágono es un polígono de seis lados.

English/Spanish Glossary

Histogram A histogram is a statistical graph that shows the shape of a data set with vertical bars above intervals of values on a number line. The intervals are equal in size and do not overlap. The height of each bar shows the frequency of data within that interval.

Histograma Un histograma es una gráfica de estadísticas que muestra la forma de un conjunto de datos con barras verticales encima de intervalos de valores en una recta numérica. Los intervalos tienen el mismo tamaño y no se superponen. La altura de cada barra muestra la frecuencia de los datos dentro de ese intervalo.

Hundredths One hundredth is one part of 100 equal parts of a whole.

Centésima Una centésima es 1 de las 100 partes iguales de un todo.

Hypotenuse In a right triangle, the longest side, which is opposite the right angle, is the hypotenuse.

Hipotenusa En un triángulo rectángulo, el lado más largo, que es opuesto al ángulo recto, es la hipotenusa.

I

Identify To identify is to match a definition or description to an object or to recognize something and be able to name it.

Identificar Identificar es unir una definición o una descripción con un objeto, o reconocer algo y poder nombrarlo.

Identity Property of Addition The sum of 0 and any number is that number. For any number n, $n + 0 = n$ and $0 + n = n$.

Propiedad de identidad de la suma La suma de 0 y cualquier número es ese número. Para cualquier número n, $n + 0 = n$ and $0 + n = n$.

Identity Property of Multiplication The product of 1 and any number is that number. For any number n, $n \cdot 1 = n$ and $1 \cdot n = n$.

Propiedad de identidad de la multiplicación El producto de 1 y cualquier número es ese número. Para cualquier número n, $n \cdot 1 = n$ and $1 \cdot n = n$.

Illustrate To illustrate is to show or present information, usually as a drawing or a diagram. You can also illustrate a point using a written explanation.

Ilustrar Ilustrar es mostrar o presentar información, generalmente en forma de dibujo o diagrama. También puedes usar una explicación escrita para ilustrar un punto.

English/Spanish Glossary

Image An image is the result of a transformation of a point, line, or figure.

Imagen Una imagen es el resultado de una transformación de un punto, una recta o una figura.

Improper fraction An improper fraction is a fraction in which the numerator is greater than or equal to its denominator.

Fracción impropia Una fracción impropia es una fracción en la cual el numerador es mayor que o igual a su denominador.

Included angle An included angle is an angle that is between two sides.

Ángulo incluido Un ángulo incluido es un ángulo que está entre dos lados.

Included side An included side is a side that is between two angles.

Lado incluido Un lado incluido es un lado que está entre dos ángulos.

Income Money that a business receives. The money that a person earns from working is also called income.

Ingresos El dinero que un negocio recibe. El dinero que una persona gana de trabajar también es llamado los ingresos.

Income tax Income tax is money collected by the government based on how much you earn.

Impuesto de renta El impuesto de renta es dinero completo por el gobierno basado en cuánto gana.

Independent events Two events are independent events if the occurrence of one event does not affect the probability of the other event.

Eventos independientes Dos eventos son eventos independientes cuando el resultado de un evento no altera la probabilidad del otro.

Independent variable An independent variable is a variable whose value determines the value of another (dependent) variable.

Variable independiente Una variable independiente es una variable cuyo valor determina el valor de otra variable (dependiente).

Indicate To indicate is to point out or show.

Indicar Indicar es señalar o mostrar.

English/Spanish Glossary

Indirect measurement Indirect measurement uses proportions and similar triangles to measure distances that would be difficult to measure directly.

Medición indirecta La medición indirecta usa proporciones y triángulos semejantes para medir distancias que serían difíciles de medir de forma directa.

Inequality An inequality is a mathematical sentence that uses $<$, $\leq$, $>$, $\geq$, or $\neq$ to compare two quantities.

Desigualdad Una desigualdad es una oración matemática que usa $<$, $\leq$, $>$, $\geq$, o $\neq$ para comparar dos cantidades.

Inference An inference is a judgment made by interpreting data.

Inferencia Una inferencia es una opinión que se forma al interpretar datos.

Infinitely many solutions A linear equation in one variable has infinitely many solutions if any value of the variable makes the two sides of the equation equal.

Número infinito de soluciones Una ecuación lineal en una variable tiene un número infinito de soluciones si cualquier valor de la variable hace que los dos lados de la ecuación sean iguales.

Initial value The initial value of a linear function is the value of the output when the input is 0.

Valor inicial El valor inicial de una función lineal es el valor de salida cuando el valor de entrada es 0.

Integers Integers are the set of positive whole numbers, their opposites, and 0.

Enteros Los enteros son el conjunto de los números enteros positivos, sus opuestos y 0.

Interest When you deposit money in a bank account, the bank pays you interest for the right to use your money for a period of time.

Interés Cuando depositas dinero en una cuenta bancaria, el banco te paga un interés por el derecho a usar tu dinero por un período de tiempo.

Interest period The length of time on which compound interest is based. The total number of interest periods that you keep the money in the account is represented by the variable *n*.

Período de interés La cantidad de tiempo sobre la que se calcula el interés compuesto. El número total de períodos de interés que mantienes el dinero en la cuenta se representa con la variable *n*.

English/Spanish Glossary

Interest rate Interest is calculated based on a percent of the principal. That percent is called the interest rate (r).

Tasa de interés El interés se calcula con base en un porcentaje del capital. Ese porcentaje se llama tasa de interés, (r).

Interest rate for an interest period The interest rate for an interest period is the annual interest rate divided by the number of interest periods per year.

El tipo de interés por un período de interés El tipo de interés por un período de interés es el tipo de interés anual dividido por el número de períodos de interés por año.

Interquartile range The interquartile range (IQR) is the distance between the first and third quartiles of the data set. It represents the spread of the middle 50% of the data values.

Rango intercuartil El rango intercuartil es la distancia entre el primer y el tercer cuartil del conjunto de datos. Representa la ubicación del 50% del medio de los valores.

Interval An interval is a period of time between two points of time or events.

Intervalo Un intervalo es un período de tiempo entre dos puntos en el tiempo o entre dos sucesos.

Invalid inference An invalid inference is false about the population, or does not follow from the available data. A biased sample can lead to invalid inferences.

Inferencia inválida Una inferencia inválida es una inferencia falsa acerca de una población, o no se deduce a partir de los datos disponibles. Una muestra sesgada puede llevar a inferencias inválidas.

Inverse operations Inverse operations are operations that undo each other.

Operaciones inversas Las operaciones inversas son operaciones que se cancelan entre sí.

Inverse Property of Addition Every number has an additive inverse. The sum of a number and its additive inverse is zero.

Propiedad inversa de la suma Todos los números tienen un inverso de suma. La suma de un número y su inverso de suma es cero.

English/Spanish Glossary

Irrational numbers An irrational number is a number that cannot be written in the form $\frac{a}{b}$, where a and b are integers and $b \neq 0$. In decimal form, an irrational number cannot be written as a terminating or repeating decimal.

Números irracionales Un número irracional es un número que no se puede escribir en la forma $\frac{a}{b}$ donde a y b, son enteros y $b \neq 0$. Los números racionales en forma decimal no son finitos y no son periódicos.

Isolate a variable When solving equations, to isolate a variable means to get a variable with a coefficient of 1 alone on one side of an equation. Use the properties of equality and inverse operations to isolate a variable.

Aislar una variable Cuando resuelves ecuaciones, aislar una variable significa poner una variable con un coeficiente de 1 sola a un lado de la ecuación. Usa las propiedades de igualdad y las operaciones inversas para aislar una variable.

Isosceles triangle An isosceles triangle is a triangle with at least two sides that are the same length.

Triángulo isósceles Un triángulo isósceles es un triángulo que tiene al menos dos lados de la misma longitud.

J

Justify To justify is to support your answer with reasons or examples. A justification may include a written response, diagrams, charts, tables, or a combination of these.

Justificar Justificar es apoyar tu respuesta con razones o ejemplos. Una justificación puede incluir una respuesta escrita, diagramas, tablas o una combinación de esos elementos.

L

Lateral area of a cone The lateral area of a cone is the area of its lateral surface. The formula for the lateral area of a cone is L.A. $= \pi r \ell$, where r represents the radius of the base and ℓ represents the slant height of the cone.

Área lateral de un cono El área lateral de un cono es el área de su superficie lateral. La fórmula del área lateral de un cono es A.L. $= \pi r \ell$, donde r representa el radio de la base y ℓ representa la altura inclinada del cono.

English/Spanish Glossary

Lateral area of a cylinder The lateral area of a cylinder is the area of its lateral surface. The formula for the lateral area of a cylinder is L.A. = $2\pi rh$, where r represents the radius of a base and h represents the height of the cylinder.

Área lateral de un cilindro El área lateral de un cilindro es el área de su superficie lateral. La fórmula del área lateral de un cilindro es A.L. = $2\pi rh$, donde r representa el radio de una base y h representa la altura del cilindro.

Lateral area of a prism The lateral area of a prism is the sum of the areas of the lateral faces of the prism. The formula for the lateral area, L.A., of a prism is L.A. = ph, where p represents the perimeter of the base and h represents the height of the prism.

Área lateral de un prisma El área lateral de un prisma es la suma de las áreas de las caras laterales del prisma. La fórmula del área lateral, A.L., de un prisma es A.L. = ph, donde p representa el perímetro de la base y h representa la altura del prisma.

Lateral area of a pyramid The lateral area of a pyramid is the sum of the areas of the lateral faces of the pyramid. The formula for the lateral area, L.A., of a pyramid is L.A. = $\frac{1}{2}p\ell$ where p represents the perimeter of the base and ℓ represents the slant height of the pyramid.

Área lateral de una pirámide El área lateral de una pirámide es la suma de las áreas de las caras laterales de la pirámide. La fórmula del área lateral, A.L., de una pirámide es A.L. = $\frac{1}{2}p\ell$ donde p representa el perímetro de la base y ℓ representa la altura inclinada de la pirámide.

Lateral face of a prism A lateral face of a prism is a face that joins the bases of the prism.

Cara lateral de un prisma La cara lateral de un prisma es la cara que une a las bases del prisma.

Lateral face of a pyramid A lateral face of a pyramid is a triangular face that joins the base and the vertex.

Cara lateral de una pirámide La cara lateral de una pirámide es una cara lateral que une a la base con el vértice.

Lateral surface of a cone The lateral surface of a cone is the curved surface that is not included in the base.

Superficie lateral de un cono La superficie lateral de un cono es la superficie curva que no está incluida en la base.

English/Spanish Glossary

Lateral surface of a cylinder The lateral surface of a cylinder is the curved surface that is not included in the bases.

Superficie lateral de un cilindro La superficie lateral de un cilindro es la superficie curva que no está incluida en las bases.

Least common multiple The least common multiple (LCM) of two or more numbers is the least multiple shared by all of the numbers.

Mínimo común múltiplo El mínimo común múltiplo (MCM) de dos o más números es el múltiplo menor compartido por todos los números.

Leg of a right triangle In a right triangle, the two shortest sides are legs.

Cateto de un triángulo rectángulo En un triángulo rectángulo, los dos lados más cortos son los catetos.

Less than < The less-than symbol shows a comparison of two numbers with the number of lesser value shown first, or on the left.

Menor que < El símbolo de menor que muestra una comparación de dos números con el número de menor valor que aparece primero, o a la izquierda.

Liability A liability is money that you owe.

Obligación Una obligación es dinero que usted debe.

Lifetime income The amount of money earned over a lifetime of working.

Ingresos para toda la vida La cantidad de dinero ganó sobre una vida de trabajar.

Like terms Terms that have identical variable parts are like terms.

Términos semejantes Los términos que tienen partes variables idénticas son términos semejantes.

Line of reflection A line of reflection is a line across which a figure is reflected.

Eje de reflexión Un eje de reflexión es una línea a través de la cual se refleja una figura.

Linear equation An equation is a linear equation if the graph of all of its solutions is a line.

Ecuación lineal Una ecuación es lineal si la gráfica de todas sus soluciones es una línea recta.

English/Spanish Glossary

Linear function A linear function is a function whose graph is a straight line. The rate of change for a linear function is constant.

Función lineal Una función lineal es una función cuya gráfica es una línea recta. La tasa de cambio en una función lineal es constante.

Linear function rule A linear function rule is an equation that describes a linear function.

Regla de la función lineal La ecuación que describe una función lineal es la regla de la función lineal.

Loan A loan is an amount of money borrowed for a period of time with the promise of paying it back.

Préstamo Un préstamo es una cantidad de dinero pedido prestaddo por un espacio de tiempo con la promesa de pagarlo apoya.

Loan length Loan length is the period of time set to repay a loan.

Preste longitud La longitud del préstamo es el conjunto de espacio de tiempo de devolver un préstamo.

Loan term The term of a loan is the period of time set to repay the loan.

Preste término El término de un préstamo es el conjunto de espacio de tiempo de devolver el préstamo.

Locate To locate is to find or identify a value, usually on a number line or coordinate graph.

Ubicar Ubicar es hallar o identificar un valor, generalmente en una recta numérica o en una gráfica de coordenadas.

Loss When a business's expenses are greater than the business's income, there is a loss.

Pérdida Cuando los gastos de un negocio son más que los ingresos del negocio, hay una pérdida.

English/Spanish Glossary

M

Mapping diagram A mapping diagram describes a relation by linking the input values to the corresponding output values using arrows.

Diagrama de correspondencia Un diagrama de correspondencia describe una relación uniendo con flechas los valores de entrada con sus correspondientes valores de salida.

Markdown Markdown is the amount of decrease from the selling price to the sale price. The markdown as a percent decrease of the original selling price is called the percent markdown.

Rebaja La rebaja es la cantidad de disminución de un precio de venta a un precio rebajado. La rebaja como una disminución porcentual del precio de venta original se llama porcentaje de rebaja.

Markup Markup is the amount of increase from the cost to the selling price. The markup as a percent increase of the original cost is called the percent markup.

Margen de ganancia El margen de ganancia es la cantidad de aumento del costo al precio de venta. El margen de ganancia como un aumento porcentual del costo original se llama porcentaje del margen de ganancia.

Mean The mean represents the center of a numerical data set. To find the mean, sum the data values and then divide by the number of values in the data set.

Media La media representa el centro de un conjunto de datos numéricos. Para hallar la media, suma los valores y luego divide por el número de valores del conjunto de datos.

Mean absolute deviation The mean absolute deviation is a measure of variability that describes how much the data values are spread out from the mean of a data set. The mean absolute deviation is the average distance that the data values are spread around the mean.

mean absolute deviation =
$$\frac{\text{sum of the absolute deviations of the data values}}{\text{total number of data values}}$$

Desviación absoluta media La desviación absoluta media es una medida de variabilidad que describe cuánto se alejan los valores de la media de un conjunto de datos. La desviación absoluta media es la distancia promedio que los valores se alejan de la media.

desviación absoluta media =
$$\frac{\text{suma de las desviaciones absolutas de los valores}}{\text{número total de valores}}$$

English/Spanish Glossary

Measure of variability A measure of variability describes the spread of values in a data set. There may be more than one measure of variability for a data set.

Medida de variabilidad Una medida de variabilidad describe la distribución de los valores de un conjunto de datos. Puede haber más de una medida de variabilidad para un conjunto de datos.

Measurement data Measurement data consist of data that are measures.

Datos de mediciones Los datos de mediciones son datos que son medidas.

Measures of center A measure of center is a value that represents the middle of a data set. There may be more than one measure of center for a data set.

Medida de tendencia central Una medida de tendencia central es un valor que representa el centro de un conjunto de datos. Puede haber más de una medida de tendencia central para un conjunto de datos.

Median The median represents the center of a numerical data set. For an odd number of data values, the median is the middle value when the data values are arranged in numerical order. For an even number of data values, the median is the average of the two middle values when the data values are arranged in numerical order.

Mediana La mediana representa el centro de un conjunto de datos numéricos. Para un número impar de valores, la mediana es el valor del medio cuando los valores están organizados en orden numérico. Para un número par de valores, la mediana es el promedio de los dos valores del medio cuando los valores están organizados en orden numérico.

Median-median line The median-median line, or median trend line, is a method of finding a fit line for a scatter plot that suggests a linear association. This method involves dividing the data into three subgroups and using medians to find a summary point for each subgroup. The summary points are used to find the equation of the fit line.

Recta mediana-mediana La recta mediana-mediana es un método que se usa para hallar una línea de ajuste para un diagrama de dispersión que sugiere una asociación lineal. Este método implica dividir los datos en tres subgrupos y usar medianas para hallar un punto medio para cada subgrupo. Los puntos medios se usan para hallar la ecuación de la línea de ajuste.

Million Whole numbers in the millions have 7, 8, or 9 digits.

Millón Los números enteros no negativos que están en los millones tienen 7, 8 ó 9 dígitos.

English/Spanish Glossary

Mixed number A mixed number combines a whole number and a fraction.

Número mixto Un número mixto combina un número entero no negativo con una fracción.

Mode The item, or items, in a data set that occurs most frequently.

Modo El artículo, o los artículos, en un conjunto de datos que ocurre normalmente.

Model To model is to represent a situation using pictures, diagrams, or number sentences.

Demostrar Demostrar es usar ilustraciones, diagramas o enunciados numéricos para representar una situación.

Monetary incentive A monetary incentive is an offer that might encourage customers to buy a product.

Estímulo monetario Un estímulo monetario es una oferta que quizás favorezca a clientes para comprar un producto.

Multiple A multiple of a number is the product of the number and a whole number.

Múltiplo El múltiplo de un número es el producto del número y un número entero no negativo.

N

Natural numbers The natural numbers are the counting numbers.

Números naturales Los números naturales son los números que se usan para contar.

Negative exponent property For every nonzero number a and integer n, $a^{-n} = \frac{1}{a^n}$.

Propiedad del exponente negativo Para todo número distinto de cero a y entero n, $a^{-n} = \frac{1}{a^n}$.

Negative numbers Negative numbers are numbers less than zero.

Números negativos Los números negativos son números menores que cero.

English/Spanish Glossary

Net A net is a two-dimensional pattern that you can fold to form a three-dimensional figure. A net of a figure shows all of the surfaces of that figure in one view.

Modelo plano Un modelo plano es un diseño bidimensional que puedes doblar para formar una figura tridimensional. Un modelo plano de una figura muestra todas las superficies de la figura en una vista.

Net worth Net worth is the total value of all assets minus the total value of all liabilities.

Patrimonio neto El patrimonio neto es el valor total de todas las ventajas menos el valor total de todas las obligaciones.

Net worth statement Net worth is the total value of all assets minus the total value of all liabilities.

Declaración de patrimonio neto El patrimonio neto es el valor total de todas las ventajas menos el valor total de todas las obligaciones.

No solution A linear equation in one variable has no solution if no value of the variable makes the two sides of the equation equal.

Sin solución Una ecuación lineal en una variable no tiene solución si ningún valor de la variable hace que los dos lados de la ecuación sean iguales.

Nonlinear function A nonlinear function is a function that does not have a constant rate of change.

Función no lineal Una función no lineal es una función que no tiene una tasa de cambio constante.

Numerator The numerator is the number above the fraction bar in a fraction.

Numerador El numerador es el número que está arriba de la barra de fracción en una fracción.

Numerical expression A numerical expression is a mathematical phrase that consists of numbers and operation symbols.

Expresión numérica Una expresión numérica es una frase matemática que contiene números y símbolos de operaciones.

English/Spanish Glossary

O

Obtuse angle An obtuse angle is an angle with a measure greater than 90° and less than 180°.

Ángulo obtuso Un ángulo obtuso es un ángulo con una medida mayor que 90° y menor que 180°.

Obtuse triangle An obtuse triangle is a triangle with one obtuse angle.

Triángulo obtusángulo Un triángulo obtusángulo es un triángulo que tiene un ángulo obtuso.

Octagon An octagon is a polygon with eight sides.

Octágono Un octágono es un polígono de ocho lados.

Online payment system An online payment system allows money to be exchanged electronically between buyer and seller, usually using credit card or bank account information.

Sistema en línea de pago Un sistema en línea del pago permite dinero para ser cambiado electrónicamente entre comprador y vendedor, utilizando generalmente información de tarjeta de crédito o cuenta bancaria.

Open sentence An open sentence is an equation with one or more variables.

Enunciado abierto Un enunciado abierto es una ecuación con una o más variables.

Opposites Opposites are two numbers that are the same distance from 0 on a number line, but in opposite directions.

Opuestos Los opuestos son dos números que están a la misma distancia de 0 en la recta numérica, pero en direcciones opuestas.

Order of operations The order of operations is the order in which operations should be performed in an expression. Operations inside parentheses are done first, followed by exponents. Then, multiplication and division are done in order from left to right, and finally addition and subtraction are done in order from left to right.

Orden de las operaciones El orden de las operaciones es el orden en el que se deben resolver las operaciones de una expresión. Las operaciones que están entre paréntesis se resuelven primero, seguidas de los exponentes. Luego, se multiplica y se divide en orden de izquierda a derecha, y finalmente se suma y se resta en orden de izquierda a derecha.

English/Spanish Glossary

Ordered pair An ordered pair identifies the location of a point in the coordinate plane. The *x*-coordinate shows a point's position left or right of the *y*-axis. The *y*-coordinate shows a point's position up or down from the *x*-axis.

Par ordenado Un par ordenado identifica la ubicación de un punto en el plano de coordenadas. La coordenada *x* muestra la posición de un punto a la izquierda o a la derecha del eje de las *y*. La coordenada *y* muestra la posición de un punto arriba o abajo del eje de las *x*.

Origin The origin is the point of intersection of the *x*- and *y*-axes on a coordinate plane.

Origen El origen es el punto de intersección del eje de las *x* y el eje de las *y* en un plano de coordenadas.

Outcome An outcome is a possible result of an action.

Resultado Un resultado es un desenlace posible de una acción.

Outlier An outlier is a piece of data that doesn't seem to fit with the rest of a data set.

Valor extremo Un valor extremo es un valor que parece no ajustarse al resto de los datos de un conjunto.

P

Parallel lines Parallel lines are lines in the same plane that never intersect.

Rectas paralelas Las rectas paralelas son rectas que están en el mismo plano y nunca se intersecan.

Parallelogram A parallelogram is a quadrilateral with both pairs of opposite sides parallel.

Paralelogramo Un paralelogramo es un cuadrilátero en el cual los dos pares de lados opuestos son paralelos.

Partial product A partial product is part of the total product. A product is the sum of the partial products.

Producto parcial Un producto parcial es una parte del producto total. Un producto es la suma de los productos parciales.

English/Spanish Glossary

Pay period Wages for many jobs are paid at regular intervals, such a weekly, biweekly, semimonthly, or monthly. The interval of time is called a pay period.

Pague el período Los sueldos para muchos trabajos son pagados con regularidad, tal semanal, quincenal, quincenal, o mensual. El intervalo de tiempo es llamado un período de la paga.

Payroll deductions Your employer can deduct your income taxes from your wages before you receive your paycheck. The amounts deducted are called payroll deductions.

Deducciones de nómina Su empleador puede descontar sus impuestos de renta de sus sueldos antes que reciba su cheque de pago. Las cantidades descontadas son llamadas nómina deducciones.

Percent A percent is a ratio that compares a number to 100.

Porcentaje Un porcentaje es una razón que compara un número con 100.

Percent bar graph A percent bar graph is a bar graph that shows each category as a percent of the total number of data items.

Gráfico de barras de por ciento Un gráfico de barras del por ciento es un gráfico de barras que muestra cada categoría como un por ciento del número total de artículos de datos.

Percent decrease When a quantity decreases, the percent of change is called a percent decrease. percent decrease = $\frac{\text{amount of decrease}}{\text{original quantity}}$

Disminución porcentual Cuando una cantidad disminuye, el porcentaje de cambio se llama disminución porcentual. disminución porcentual = $\frac{\text{cantidad de disminución}}{\text{cantidad original}}$

Percent equation The percent equation describes the relationship between a part and a whole. You can use the percent equation to solve percent problems. part = percent · whole

Ecuación de porcentaje La ecuación de porcentaje describe la relación entre una parte y un todo. Puedes usar la ecuación de porcentaje para resolver problemas de porcentaje. parte = por ciento · todo

Percent error Percent error describes the accuracy of a measured or estimated value compared to an actual or accepted value.

Error porcentual El error porcentual describe la exactitud de un valor medido o estimado en comparación con un valor real o aceptado.

English/Spanish Glossary

Percent increase When a quantity increases, the percent of change is called a percent increase.

Aumento porcentual Cuando una cantidad aumenta, el porcentaje de cambio se llama aumento porcentual.

Percent of change Percent of change is the percent something increases or decreases from its original measure or amount. You can find the percent of change by using the equation: percent of change $= \dfrac{\text{amount of change}}{\text{original quantity}}$

Porcentaje de cambio El porcentaje de cambio es el porcentaje en que algo aumenta o disminuye en relación a la medida o cantidad original. Puedes hallar el porcentaje de cambio con la siguiente ecuación: porcentaje de cambio $= \dfrac{\text{cantidad de cambio}}{\text{cantidad original}}$

Perfect cube A perfect cube is the cube of an integer.

Cubo perfecto Un cubo perfecto es el cubo de un entero.

Perfect square A perfect square is a number that is the square of an integer.

Cuadrado perfecto Un cuadrado perfecto es un número que es el cuadrado de un entero.

Perimeter Perimeter is the distance around a figure.

Perímetro El perímetro es la distancia alrededor de una figura.

Period A period is a group of 3 digits in a number. Periods are separated by a comma and start from the right of a number.

Período Un período es un grupo de 3 dígitos en un número. Los períodos están separados por una coma y empiezan a la derecha del número.

Periodic savings plan A periodic savings plan is a method of saving that involves making deposits on a regular basis.

Plan de ahorros periódico Un plan de ahorros periódico es un método de guardar que implica depósitos que hace con regularidad.

Perpendicular lines Perpendicular lines intersect to form right angles.

Rectas perpendiculares Las rectas perpendiculares se intersecan para formar ángulos rectos.

English/Spanish Glossary

Pi Pi (π) is the ratio of a circle's circumference, C, to its diameter, d.

Pi Pi (π) es la razón de la circunferencia de un círculo, C, a su diámetro, d.

Place value Place value is the value given to an individual digit based on its position within a number.

Valor posicional El valor posicional es el valor asignado a determinado dígito según su posición en un número.

Plane A plane is a flat surface that extends indefinitely in all directions.

Plano Un plano es una superficie plana que se extiende indefinidamente en todas direcciones.

Polygon A polygon is a closed figure formed by three or more line segments that do not cross.

Polígono Un polígono es una figura cerrada compuesta por tres o más segmentos que no se cruzan.

Population A population is the complete set of items being studied.

Población Una población es todo el conjunto de elementos que se estudian.

Positive numbers Positive numbers are numbers greater than zero.

Números positivos Los números positivos son números mayores que cero.

Power A power is a number expressed using an exponent.

Potencia Una potencia es un número expresado con un exponente.

Predict To predict is to make an educated guess based on the analysis of real data.

Predecir Predecir es hacer una estimación informada según el análisis de datos reales.

Prime factorization The prime factorization of a composite number is the expression of the number as a product of its prime factors.

Descomposición en factores primos La descomposición en factores primos de un número compuesto es la expresión del número como un producto de sus factores primos.

English/Spanish Glossary

Prime number A prime number is a whole number greater than 1 with exactly two factors, 1 and the number itself.

Número primo Un número primo es un número entero mayor que 1 con exactamente dos factores, 1 y el número mismo.

Principal The original amount of money deposited or borrowed in an account.

Capital La cantidad original de dinero que se deposita o se pide prestada en una cuenta.

Prism A prism is a three-dimensional figure with two parallel polygonal faces that are the same size and shape.

Prisma Un prisma es una figura tridimensional con dos caras poligonales paralelas que tienen el mismo tamaño y la misma forma.

Probability model A probability model consists of an action, its sample space, and a list of events with their probabilities. The events and probabilities in the list have these characteristics: each outcome in the sample space is in exactly one event, and the sum of all of the probabilities must be 1.

Modelo de probabilidad Un modelo de probabilidad consiste en una acción, su espacio muestral y una lista de eventos con sus probabilidades. Los eventos y las probabilidades de la lista tienen estas características: cada resultado del espacio muestral está exactamente en un evento, y la suma de todas las probabilidades debe ser 1.

Probability of an event The probability of an event is a number from 0 to 1 that measures the likelihood that the event will occur. The closer the probability is to 0, the less likely it is that the event will happen. The closer the probability is to 1, the more likely it is that the event will happen. You can express probability as a fraction, decimal, or percent.

Probabilidad de un evento La probabilidad de un evento es un número de 0 a 1 que mide la probabilidad de que suceda el evento. Cuanto más se acerca la probabilidad a 0, menos probable es que suceda el evento. Cuanto más se acerca la probabilidad a 1, más probable es que suceda el evento. Puedes expresar la probabilidad como una fracción, un decimal o un porcentaje.

Product A product is the value of a multiplication or an expression showing multiplication.

Producto Un producto es el valor de una multiplicación o una expresión que representa la multiplicación.

English/Spanish Glossary

Profit When a business's expenses are less than the business's income, there is a profit.

Ganancia Cuando los gastos de un negocio son menos que los ingresos del negocio, hay una ganancia.

Proof A proof is a logical, deductive argument in which every statement of fact is supported by a reason.

Comprobación Una comprobación es un argumento lógico y deductivo en el que cada enunciado de un hecho está apoyado por una razón.

Proper fraction A proper fraction has a numerator that is less than its denominator.

Fracción propia Una fracción propia tiene un numerador que es menor que su denominador.

Proportion A proportion is an equation stating that two ratios are equal.

Proporción Una proporción es una ecuación que establece que dos razones son iguales.

Proportional relationship Two quantities x and y have a proportional relationship if y is always a constant multiple of x. A relationship is proportional if it can be described by equivalent ratios.

Relación de proporción Dos cantidades x y y tienen una relación de proporción si y es siempre un múltiplo constante de x. Una relación es de proporción si se puede describir con razones equivalentes.

Pyramid A pyramid is a three-dimensional figure with a base that is a polygon and triangular faces that meet at a vertex. A pyramid is named for the shape of its base.

Pirámide Una pirámide es una figura tridimensional con una base que es un polígono y caras triangulares que se unen en un vértice. El nombre de la pirámide depende de la forma de su base.

English/Spanish Glossary

Pythagorean Theorem In any right triangle, the sum of the squares of the lengths of the legs equals the square of the length of the hypotenuse. If a triangle is a right triangle, then $a^2 + b^2 = c^2$, where a and b represent the lengths of the legs, and c represents the length of the hypotenuse.

Teorema de Pitágoras En cualquier triángulo rectángulo, la suma del cuadrado de la longitud de los catetos es igual al cuadrado de la longitud de la hipotenusa. Si un triángulo es un triángulo rectángulo, entonces $a^2 + b^2 = c^2$, donde a y b representan la longitud de los catetos, y c representa la longitud de la hipotenusa.

Q

Quadrant The x- and y-axes divide the coordinate plane into four regions called quadrants.

Cuadrante Los ejes de las x y de las y dividen el plano de coordenadas en cuatro regiones llamadas cuadrantes.

Quadrilateral A quadrilateral is a polygon with four sides.

Cuadrilátero Un cuadrilátero es un polígono de cuatro lados.

Quarter circle A quarter circle is one fourth of a circle.

Círculo cuarto Un círculo cuarto es la cuarta parte de un círculo.

Quartile The quartiles of a data set divide the data set into four parts with the same number of data values in each part.

Cuartil Los cuartiles de un conjunto de datos dividen el conjunto de datos en cuatro partes que tienen el mismo número de valores cada una.

Quotient The quotient is the answer to a division problem. When there is a remainder, "quotient" sometimes refers to the whole-number portion of the answer.

Cociente El cociente es el resultado de una división. Cuando queda un residuo, "cociente" a veces se refiere a la parte de la solución que es un número entero.

English/Spanish Glossary

R

Radius A radius of a circle is a segment that has one endpoint at the center and the other endpoint on the circle. The term radius can also mean the length of this segment.

Radio Un radio de un círculo es un segmento que tiene un extremo en el centro y el otro extremo en el círculo. El término radio también puede referirse a la longitud de este segmento.

Radius of a sphere The radius of a sphere, r, is a segment that has one endpoint at the center and the other endpoint on the sphere.

Radio de una esfera El radio de una esfera, r, es un segmento que tiene un extremo en el centro y el otro extremo en la esfera.

Random sample In a random sample, each member in the population has an equal chance of being selected.

Muestra aleatoria En una muestra aleatoria, cada miembro en la población tiene una oportunidad igual de ser seleccionado.

Range The range is a measure of variability of a numerical data set. The range of a data set is the difference between the greatest and least values in a data set.

Rango El rango es una medida de la variabilidad de un conjunto de datos numéricos. El rango de un conjunto de datos es la diferencia que existe entre el mayor y el menor valor del conjunto.

Rate A rate is a ratio involving two quantities measured in different units.

Tasa Una tasa es una razón que relaciona dos cantidades medidas con unidades diferentes.

Rate of change The rate of change of a linear function is the ratio $\frac{\text{vertical change}}{\text{horizontal change}}$ between any two points on the graph of the function.

Tasa de cambio La tasa de cambio de una función lineal es la razón del $\frac{\text{cambio vertical}}{\text{cambio horizontal}}$ que existe entre dos puntos cualesquiera de la gráfica de la función.

Ratio A ratio is a relationship in which for every x units of one quantity there are y units of another quantity.

Razón Una razón es una relación en la cual por cada x unidades de una cantidad hay y unidades de otra cantidad.

English/Spanish Glossary

Rational numbers A rational number is a number that can be written in the form $\frac{a}{b}$ or $-\frac{a}{b}$, where a is a whole number and b is a positive whole number. The rational numbers include the integers.

Números racionales Un número racional es un número que se puede escribir como $\frac{a}{b}$ o $-\frac{a}{b}$, donde a es un número entero no negativo y b es un número entero positivo. Los números racionales incluyen los enteros.

Real numbers The real numbers are the set of rational and irrational numbers.

Números reales Los números reales son el conjunto de los números racionales e irracionales.

Reason To reason is to think through a problem using facts and information.

Razonar Razonar es usar hechos e información para estudiar detenidamente un problema.

Rebate A rebate returns part of the purchase price of an item after the buyer provides proof of purchase through a mail-in or online form.

Reembolso Un reembolso regresa la parte del precio de compra de un artículo después de que el comprador proporcione comprobante de compra por un correo-en o forma en línea.

Recall To recall is to remember a fact quickly.

Recordar Recordar es traer a la memoria un hecho rápidamente.

Reciprocals Two numbers are reciprocals if their product is 1. If a nonzero number is named as a fraction, , then its reciprocal is .

Recíprocos Dos números son recíprocos si su producto es 1. Si un número distinto de cero se expresa como una fracción, , entonces su recíproco es .

Rectangle A rectangle is a quadrilateral with four right angles.

Rectángulo Un rectángulo es un cuadrilátero que tiene cuatro ángulos rectos.

Rectangular prism A rectangular prism is a prism with bases in the shape of a rectangle.

Prisma rectangular Un prisma rectangular es un prisma cuyas bases tienen la forma de un rectángulo.

English/Spanish Glossary

Reduction A reduction is a dilation with a scale factor less than 1. After a reduction, the image is smaller than the original figure.

Reducción Una reducción es una dilatación con un factor de escala menor que 1. Después de una reducción, la imagen es más pequeña que la figura original.

Reflection A reflection, or flip, is a transformation that flips a figure across a line of reflection.

Reflexión Una reflexión, o inversión, es una transformación que invierte una figura a través de un eje de reflexión.

Regular polygon A regular polygon is a polygon with all sides of equal length and all angles of equal measure.

Polígono regular Un polígono regular es un polígono que tiene todos los lados de la misma longitud y todos los ángulos de la misma medida.

Relate To relate two different things, find a connection between them.

Relacionar Para relacionar dos cosas diferentes, halla una conexión entre ellas.

Relation Any set of ordered pairs is called a relation.

Relación Todo conjunto de pares ordenados se llama relación.

Relative frequency relative frequency

of an event $= \dfrac{\text{number of times event occurs}}{\text{total number of trials}}$

Frecuencia relativa frecuencia relativa de un evento $=$

$\dfrac{\text{número de veces que sucede el evento}}{\text{número total de pruebas}}$

Relative frequency table A relative frequency table shows the ratio of the number of data in each category to the total number of data items. The ratio can be expressed as a fraction, decimal, or percent.

Mesa relativa de frecuencia Una mesa relativa de la frecuencia muestra la proporción del número de datos en cada categoría al número total de artículos de datos. La proporción puede ser expresada como una fracción, el decimal, o el por ciento.

Remainder In division, the remainder is the number that is left after the division is complete.

Residuo En una división, el residuo es el número que queda después de terminar la operación.

English/Spanish Glossary

Remote interior angles Remote interior angles are the two nonadjacent interior angles corresponding to each exterior angle of a triangle.

Ángulos internos no adyacentes Los ángulos internos no adyacentes son los dos ángulos internos de un triángulo que se corresponden con el ángulo externo que está más alejado de ellos.

Repeating decimal A repeating decimal has a decimal expansion that repeats the same digit, or block of digits, without end.

Decimal periódico Un decimal periódico tiene una expansión decimal que repite el mismo dígito, o grupo de dígitos, sin fin.

Represent To represent is to stand for or take the place of something else. Symbols, equations, charts, and tables are often used to represent particular situations.

Representar Representar es sustituir u ocupar el lugar de otra cosa. A menudo se usan símbolos, ecuaciones y tablas para representar determinadas situaciones.

Representative sample A representative sample is a sample of a population in which the number of subjects in the sample with the trait that you are studying is proportional to the number of members in the population with that trait. A representative sample accurately represents the population and does not have bias.

Muestra representativa Una muestra representativa es una muestra de una población en la que el número de sujetos de la muestra que tiene la característica que se estudia es proporcional al número de miembros de la población que tienen esa característica. Una muestra representativa representa la población con exactitud y no está sesgada.

Rhombus A rhombus is a parallelogram whose sides are all the same length.

Rombo Un rombo es un paralelogramo que tiene todos sus lados de la misma longitud.

Right angle A right angle is an angle with a measure of 90°.

Ángulo recto Un ángulo recto es un ángulo que mide 90°.

Right cone A right cone is a cone in which the segment representing the height connects the vertex and the center of the base.

Cono recto Un cono recto es un cono en el que el segmento que representa la altura une el vértice y el centro de la base.

English/Spanish Glossary

Right cylinder A right cylinder is a cylinder in which the height joins the centers of the bases.

Cilindro recto Un cilindro recto es un cilindro en el que la altura une los centros de las bases.

Right prism In a right prism, all lateral faces are rectangles.

Prisma recto En un prisma recto, todas las caras laterales son rectángulos.

Right pyramid In a right pyramid, the segment that represents the height intersects the base at its center.

Pirámide recta En una pirámide recta, el segmento que representa la altura interseca la base en el centro.

Right triangle A right triangle is a triangle with one right angle.

Triángulo rectángulo Un triángulo rectángulo es un triángulo que tiene un ángulo recto.

Rigid motion A rigid motion is a transformation that changes only the position of a figure.

Movimiento rígido Un movimiento rígido es una transformación que sólo cambia la posición de una figura.

Rotation A rotation is a rigid motion that turns a figure around a fixed point, called the center of rotation.

Rotación Una rotación es un movimiento rígido que hace girar una figura alrededor de un punto fijo, llamado centro de rotación.

Rounding Rounding a number means replacing the number with a number that tells about how much or how many.

Redondear Redondear un número significa reemplazar ese número por un número que indica más o menos cuánto o cuántos.

S

Sale A sale is a discount offered by a store. A sale does not require the customer to have a coupon.

Venta Una venta es un descuento ofreció por una tienda. Una venta no requiere al cliente a tener un cupón.

English/Spanish Glossary

Sales tax A tax added to the price of goods and services.

Las ventas tasan Un impuesto añadió al precio de bienes y servicios.

Sample of a population A sample of a population is part of the population. A sample is useful when you want to find out about a population but you do not have the resources to study every member of the population.

Muestra de una población Una muestra de una población es una parte de la población. Una muestra es útil cuando quieres saber algo acerca de una población, pero no tienes los recursos para estudiar a cada miembro de esa población.

Sample space The sample space for an action is the set of all possible outcomes of that action.

Espacio muestral El espacio muestral de una acción es el conjunto de todos los resultados posibles de esa acción.

Sampling method A sampling method is the method by which you choose members of a population to sample.

Método de muestreo Un método de muestreo es el método por el cual escoges miembros de una población para muestrear.

Savings Savings is money that a person puts away for use at a later date.

Ahorros Los ahorros son dinero que una persona guarda para el uso en una fecha posterior.

Scale A scale is a ratio that compares a length in a scale drawing to the corresponding length in the actual object.

Escala Una escala es una razón que compara una longitud en un dibujo a escala con la longitud correspondiente en el objeto real.

Scale drawing A scale drawing is an enlarged or reduced drawing of an object that is proportional to the actual object.

Dibujo a escala Un dibujo a escala es un dibujo ampliado o reducido de un objeto que es proporcional al objeto real.

English/Spanish Glossary

Scale factor The scale factor is the ratio of a length in the image to the corresponding length in the original figure.

Factor de escala El factor de escala es la razón de una longitud de la imagen a la longitud correspondiente en la figura original.

Scalene triangle A scalene triangle is a triangle in which no sides have the same length.

Triángulo escaleno Un triángulo escaleno es un triángulo que no tiene lados de la misma longitud.

Scatter plot A scatter plot is a graph that uses points to display the relationship between two different sets of data. Each point can be represented by an ordered pair.

Diagrama de dispersión Un diagrama de dispersión es una gráfica que usa puntos para mostrar la relación entre dos conjuntos de datos diferentes. Cada punto se puede representar con un par ordenado.

Scholarship A type of monetary award a student can use to pay for his or her education. The student does not need to repay this money.

Beca Un tipo de premio monetario que un estudiante puede utilizar para pagar por su educación. El estudiante no debe devolver este dinero.

Scientific notation A number in scientific notation is written as the product of two factors, one greater than or equal to 1 and less than 10, and the other a power of 10.

Notación científica Un número en notación científica está escrito como el producto de dos factores, uno mayor que o igual a 1 y menor que 10, y el otro una potencia de 10.

Segment A segment is part of a line. It consists of two endpoints and all of the points on the line between the endpoints.

Segmento Un segmento es una parte de una recta. Está formado por dos extremos y todos los puntos de la recta que están entre los extremos.

Semicircle A semicircle is one half of a circle.

Semicírculo Un semicírculo es la mitad de un círculo.

English/Spanish Glossary

Similar figures A two-dimensional figure is similar to another two-dimensional figure if you can map one figure to the other by a sequence of rotations, reflections, translations, and dilations.

Figuras semejantes Una figura bidimensional es semejante a otra figura bidimensional si puedes hacer corresponder una figura con otra mediante una secuencia de rotaciones, reflexiones, traslaciones y dilataciones.

Simple interest Simple interest is interest paid only on an original deposit. To calculate simple interest, use the formula where I is the simple interest, p is the principal, r is the annual interest rate, and t is the number of years that the account earns interest.

Interés simple El interés simple es el interés que se paga sobre un depósito original solamente. Para calcular el interés simple, usa la fórmula donde I es el interés simple, c es el capital, r es la tasa de interés anual y t es el número de años en que la cuenta obtiene un interés.

Simple random sampling Simple random sampling is a sampling method in which every member of the population has an equal chance of being chosen for the sample.

Muestreo aleatorio simple El muestreo aleatorio simple es un método de muestreo en el que cada miembro de la población tiene la misma probabilidad de ser seleccionado para la muestra.

Simpler form A fraction is in simpler form when it is equivalent to a given fraction and has smaller numbers in the numerator and denominator.

Forma simplificada Una fracción está en su forma simplificada cuando es equivalente a otra fracción dada, pero tiene números más pequeños en el numerador y el denominador.

Simplest form A fraction is in simplest form when the only common factor of the numerator and denominator is one.

Mínima expresión Una fracción está en su mínima expresión cuando el único factor común del numerador y el denominador es 1.

Simplify an algebraic expression To simplify an algebraic expression, combine the like terms of the expression.

Simplificar una expresión algebraica Para simplificar una expresión algebraica, combina los términos semejantes de la expresión.

English/Spanish Glossary

Simulation A simulation is a model of a real-world situation that is used to find probabilities.

Simulación Una simulación es un modelo de una situación de la vida diaria que se usa para hallar probabilidades.

Sketch To sketch a figure, draw a rough outline. When a sketch is asked for, it means that a drawing needs to be included in your response.

Bosquejo Para hacer un bosquejo, dibuja un esquema simple. Si se pide un bosquejo, tu respuesta debe incluir un dibujo.

Slant height of a cone The slant height of a cone, ℓ, is the length of its lateral surface from base to vertex.

Altura inclinada de un cono La altura inclinada de un cono, ℓ, es la longitud de su superficie lateral desde la base hasta el vértice.

Slant height of a pyramid The slant height of a pyramid is the height of a lateral face.

Altura inclinada de una pirámide La altura inclinada de una pirámide es la altura de una cara lateral.

Slope Slope is a ratio that describes steepness.

$$\text{slope} = \frac{\text{vertical change}}{\text{horizontal change}} = \frac{\text{rise}}{\text{run}}$$

Pendiente La pendiente es una razón que describe la inclinación.

$$\text{pendiente} = \frac{\text{cambio vertical}}{\text{cambio horizontal}}$$
$$= \frac{\text{distancia vertical}}{\text{distancia horizontal}}$$

Slope of a line slope =

$$\frac{\text{change in } y\text{-coordinates}}{\text{change in } x\text{-coordinates}} = \frac{\text{rise}}{\text{run}}$$

Pendiente de una recta pendiente =

$$\frac{\text{cambio en las coordenadas } y}{\text{cambio en las coordenadas } x}$$
$$= \frac{\text{distancia vertical}}{\text{distancia horizontal}}$$

Slope-intercept form An equation written in the form $y = mx + b$ is in slope-intercept form. The graph is a line with slope m and y-intercept b.

Forma pendiente-intercepto Una ecuación escrita en la forma $y = mx + b$ está en forma de pendiente-intercepto. La gráfica es una línea recta con pendiente m e intercepto en y b.

English/Spanish Glossary

Solution of a system of linear equations A solution of a system of linear equations is any ordered pair that makes all the equations of that system true.

Solución de un sistema de ecuaciones lineales Una solución de un sistema de ecuaciones lineales es cualquier par ordenado que hace que todas las ecuaciones de ese sistema sean verdaderas.

Solution of an equation A solution of an equation is a value of the variable that makes the equation true.

Solución de una ecuación Una solución de una ecuación es un valor de la variable que hace que la ecuación sea verdadera.

Solution of an inequality The solutions of an inequality are the values of the variable that make the inequality true.

Solución de una desigualdad Las soluciones de una desigualdad son los valores de la variable que hacen que la desigualdad sea verdadera.

Solution set A solution set contains all of the numbers that satisfy an equation or inequality.

Conjunto solución Un conjunto solución contiene todos los números que satisfacen una ecuación o desigualdad.

Solve To solve a given statement, determine the value or values that make the statement true. Several methods and strategies can be used to solve a problem, including estimating, isolating the variable, drawing a graph, or using a table of values.

Resolver Para resolver un enunciado dado, determina el valor o los valores que hacen que ese enunciado sea verdadero. Para resolver un problema se pueden usar varios métodos y estrategias, como estimar, aislar la variable, dibujar una gráfica o usar una tabla de valores.

Sphere A sphere is the set of all points in space that are the same distance from a center point.

Esfera Una esfera es el conjunto de todos los puntos en el espacio que están a la misma distancia de un punto central.

Square A square is a quadrilateral with four right angles and all sides the same length.

Cuadrado Un cuadrado es un cuadrilátero que tiene cuatro ángulos rectos y todos los lados de la misma longitud.

English/Spanish Glossary

Square root A square root of a number is a number that, when multiplied by itself, equals the original number.

Raíz cuadrada La raíz cuadrada de un número es un número que, cuando se multiplica por sí mismo, es igual al número original.

Square unit A square unit is the area of a square that has sides that are 1 unit long.

Unidad cuadrada Una unidad cuadrada es el área de un cuadrado en el que cada lado mide 1 unidad de longitud.

Standard form A number written using digits and place value is in standard form.

Forma estándar Un número escrito con dígitos y valor posicional está escrito en forma estándar.

Statistical question A statistical question is a question that investigates an aspect of the real world and can have variety in the responses.

Pregunta estadística Una pregunta estadística es una pregunta que investiga un aspecto de la vida diaria y puede tener varias respuestas.

Statistics Statistics is the study of collecting, organizing, graphing, and analyzing data to draw conclusions about the real world.

Estadística La estadística es el estudio de la recolección, organización, representación gráfica y análisis de datos para sacar conclusiones sobre la vida diaria.

Stem-and-leaf plot A stem-and-leaf plot is a graph that uses the digits of each number to show the data distribution. Each data item is broken into a stem and into a leaf. The leaf is the last digit of the data value. The stem is the other digit or digits of the data value.

Complot de tallo y hoja Un complot del tallo y la hoja es un gráfico que utiliza los dígitos de cada número para mostrar la distribución de datos. Cada artículo de datos es roto en un tallo y en una hoja. La hoja es el último dígito de los datos valora. El tallo es el otro dígito o los dígitos de los datos valoran.

Stored-value card A stored-value card is a prepaid card electronically coded to be worth a specified amount of money.

Tarjeta de almacenado-valor Una tarjeta del almacenado-valor es una tarjeta pagada por adelantado codificó electrónicamente valer una cantidad especificado de dinero.

English/Spanish Glossary

Straight angle A straight angle is an angle with a measure of 180°.

Ángulo llano Un ángulo llano es un ángulo que mide 180°.

Student loan A student loan provides money to a student to pay for college. The student needs to repay the loan after leaving college. Often the student will need to pay interest on the amount of the loan.

Crédito personal para estudiantes Un crédito personal para estudiantes le proporciona dinero a un estudiante para pagar por el colegio. El estudiante debe devolver el préstamo después de dejar el colegio. A menudo el estudiante deberá pagar interés en la cantidad del préstamo.

Subject Each member in a sample is a subject.

Sujeto Cada miembro de una muestra es un sujeto.

Sum The sum is the answer to an addition problem.

Suma o total La suma o total es el resultado de una operación de suma.

Summarize To summarize an explanation or solution, go over or review the most important points.

Resumir Para resumir una explicación o solución, revisa o repasa los puntos más importantes.

Supplementary angles Two angles are supplementary angles if the sum of their measures is 180°. Supplementary angles that are adjacent form a straight angle.

Ángulos suplementarios Dos ángulos son suplementarios si la suma de sus medidas es 180°. Los ángulos suplementarios que son adyacentes forman un ángulo llano.

Surface area of a cone The surface area of a cone is the sum of the lateral area and the area of the base. The formula for the surface area of a cone is S.A. = L.A. + B.

Área total de un cono El área total de un cono es la suma del área lateral y el área de la base. La fórmula del área total de un cono es A.T. = A.L. + B.

English/Spanish Glossary

Surface area of a cube The surface area of a cube is the sum of the areas of the faces of the cube. The formula for the surface area, S.A., of a cube is S.A. , where s represents the length of an edge of the cube.

Área total de un cubo El área total de un cubo es la suma de las áreas de las caras del cubo. La fórmula del área total, A.T., de un cubo es A.T. , donde s representa la longitud de una arista del cubo.

Surface area of a cylinder The surface area of a cylinder is the sum of the lateral area and the areas of the two circular bases. The formula for the surface area of a cylinder is S.A. L.A. $2B$, where L.A. represents the lateral area of the cylinder and B represents the area of a base of the cylinder.

Área total de un cilindro El área total de un cilindro es la suma del área lateral y las áreas de las dos bases circulares. La fórmula del área total de un cilindro es A.T. A.L. $2B$, donde A.L. representa el área lateral del cilindro y B representa el área de una base del cilindro.

Surface area of a pyramid The surface area of a pyramid is the sum of the areas of the faces of the pyramid. The formula for the surface area, S.A., of a pyramid is S.A. = L.A. + B, where L.A. represents the lateral area of the pyramid and B represents the area of the base of the pyramid.

Área total de una pirámide El área total de una pirámide es la suma de las áreas de las caras de la pirámide. La fórmula del área total, A.T., de una pirámide es A.T. = A.L. + B, donde A.L. representa el área lateral de la pirámide y B representa el área de la base de la pirámide.

Surface area of a sphere The surface area of a sphere is equal to the lateral area of a cylinder that has the same radius, r, and height $2r$. The formula for the surface area of a sphere is S.A. = $4\pi r^2$, where r represents the radius of the sphere.

Área total de una esfera El área total de una esfera es igual al área lateral de un cilindro que tiene el mismo radio, r, y una altura de $2r$. La fórmula del área total de una esfera es A.T. = $4\pi r^2$, donde r representa el radio de la esfera.

Surface area of a three-dimensional figure The surface area of a three-dimensional figure is the sum of the areas of its faces. You can find the surface area by finding the area of the net of the three-dimensional figure.

Área total de una figura tridimensional El área total de una figura tridimensional es la suma de las áreas de sus caras. Puedes hallar el área total si hallas el área del modelo plano de la figura tridimensional.

English/Spanish Glossary

System of linear equations A system of linear equations is formed by two or more linear equations that use the same variables.

Sistema de ecuaciones lineales Un sistema de ecuaciones lineales está formado por dos o más ecuaciones lineales que usan las mismas variables.

Systematic sampling Systematic sampling is a sampling method in which you choose every nth member of the population, where *n* is a predetermined number. A systematic sample is useful when the researcher is able to approach the population in a systematic, or methodical, way.

Muestreo sistemático El muestreo sistemático es un método de muestreo en el que se escoge cada enésimo miembro de la población, donde *n* es un número predeterminado. Una muestra sistemática es útil cuando el investigador puede enfocarse en la población de manera sistemática o metódica.

T

Taxable wages For federal income tax purposes, your taxable wages are the difference between your earned wages and your withholding allowance. Your employer divides your withholding allowance equally among the pay periods of one year.

Sueldos imponibles Para propósitos federales de impuesto de renta, sus sueldos imponibles son la diferencia entre sus sueldos ganados y su concesión que retienen. Su empleador divide su concesión que retiene igualmente entre los períodos de paga de un año.

Tenths One tenth is one out of ten equal parts of a whole.

Décimas Una décima es 1 de 10 partes iguales de un todo.

Term A term is a number, a variable, or the product of a number and one or more variables.

Término Un término es un número, una variable o el producto de un número y una o más variables.

Terminating decimal A terminating decimal has a decimal expansion that terminates in 0.

Decimal finito Un decimal finito tiene una expansión decimal que termina en 0.

English/Spanish Glossary

Terms of a ratio The terms of a ratio are the quantities *x* and *y* in the ratio.

Términos de una razón Los términos de una razón son la cantidad *x* y la cantidad *y* de la razón.

Theorem A theorem is a conjecture that is proven.

Teorema Un teorema es una conjetura que se ha comprobado.

Theoretical probability When all outcomes of an action are equally likely,
$$P(\text{event}) = \frac{\text{number of favourable outcomes}}{\text{number of possible outcomes}}.$$

Probabilidad teórica Cuando todos los resultados de una acción son igualmente probables, $P(\text{evento}) =$
$$\frac{\text{número de resultados favorables}}{\text{número de resultados posibles}}.$$

Third quartile For an ordered set of data, the third quartile is the median of the upper half of the data set.

Tercer cuartil Para un conjunto de datos ordenados, el tercer cuartil es la mediana de la mitad superior del conjunto de datos.

Thousandths One thousandth is one part of 1,000 equal parts of a whole.

Milésimas Una milésima es 1 de 1,000 partes iguales de un todo.

Three-dimensional figure A three-dimensional (3-D) figure is a figure that does not lie in a plane.

Figura tridimensional Una figura tridimensional es una figura que no está en un plano.

Total cost of a loan The total cost of a loan is the total amount spent to repay the loan. Total cost includes the principal and all interest paid over the length of the loan. Total cost also includes any fees charged.

El coste total de un préstamo El coste total de un préstamo es el cantidad total que es gastado para devolver el préstamo. El coste total incluye al director y todo el interés pagó sobre la longitud del préstamo. El coste total también incluye cualquier honorario cargado.

Transaction A banking transaction moves money into or out of a bank account.

Transacción Una transacción bancaria mueve dinero en o fuera de una cuenta bancaria.

English/Spanish Glossary

Transfer A transaction that moves money from one bank account to another is a transfer. The balance of one account increases by the same amount the other account decreases.

Transferencia Una transacción que mueve dinero de una cuenta bancaria a otro es una transferencia. El equilibrio de un aumentos de cuenta por la misma cantidad que la otra cuenta disminuye.

Transformation A transformation is a change in position, shape, or size of a figure. Three types of transformations that change position only are translations, reflections, and rotations.

Transformación Una transformación es un cambio en la posición, la forma o el tamaño de una figura. Tres tipos de transformaciones que cambian sólo la posición son las traslaciones, las reflexiones y las rotaciones.

Translation A translation, or slide, is a rigid motion that moves every point of a figure the same distance and in the same direction.

Traslación Una traslación, o deslizamiento, es un movimiento rígido que mueve cada punto de una figura a la misma distancia y en la misma dirección.

Transversal A transversal is a line that intersects two or more lines at different points.

Transversal o secante Una transversal o secante es una línea que interseca dos o más líneas en distintos puntos.

Trapezoid A trapezoid is a quadrilateral with exactly one pair of parallel sides.

Trapecio Un trapecio es un cuadrilátero que tiene exactamente un par de lados paralelos.

Trend line A trend line is a line on a scatter plot, drawn near the points, that approximates the association between the data sets.

Línea de tendencia Una línea de tendencia es una línea en un diagrama de dispersión, trazada cerca de los puntos, que se aproxima a la relación entre los conjuntos de datos.

Trial In a probability experiment, you carry out or observe an action repeatedly. Each observation of the action is a trial.

Prueba En un experimento de probabilidad, realizas u observas una acción varias veces. Cada observación de la acción es una prueba.

Triangle A triangle is a polygon with three sides.

Triángulo Un triángulo es un polígono de tres lados.

English/Spanish Glossary

Triangular prism A triangular prism is a prism with bases in the shape of a triangle.

Prisma triangular Un prisma triangular es un prisma cuyas bases tienen la forma de un triángulo.

True equation A true equation has equal values on each side of the equals sign.

Ecuación verdadera En una ecuación verdadera, los valores a ambos lados del signo igual son iguales.

Two-way frequency table A two-way frequency table displays the counts of the data in each group.

Tabla de frecuencia con dos variables Una tabla de frecuencia con dos variables muestra el conteo de los datos de cada grupo.

Two-way relative frequency table A two-way relative frequency table shows the ratio of the number of data in each group to the size of the population. The relative frequencies can be calculated with respect to the entire population, the row populations, or the column populations. The relative frequencies can be expressed as fractions, decimals, or percents.

Tabla de frecuencias relativas con dos variables Una tabla de frecuencias relativas con dos variables muestra la razón del número de datos de cada grupo al tamaño de la población. Las frecuencias relativas se pueden calcular respecto de la población entera, las poblaciones de las filas o las poblaciones de las columnas. Las frecuencias relativas se pueden expresar como fracciones, decimales o porcentajes.

Two-way table A two-way table shows bivariate categorical data for a population.

Tabla con dos variables Una tabla con dos variables muestra datos bivariados por categorías de una población.

U

Uniform probability model A uniform probability model is a probability model based on using the theoretical probability of equally likely outcomes.

Modelo de probabilidad uniforme Un modelo de probabilidad uniforme es un modelo de probabilidad que se basa en el uso de la probabilidad teórica de resultados igualmente probables.

English/Spanish Glossary

Unit fraction A unit fraction is a fraction with a numerator of 1 and a denominator that is a whole number greater than 1.

Fracción unitaria Una fracción unitaria es una fracción con un numerador 1 y un denominador que es un número entero mayor que 1.

Unit price A unit price is a unit rate that gives the price of one item.

Precio por unidad El precio por unidad es una tasa por unidad que muestra el precio de un artículo.

Unit rate The rate for one unit of a given quantity is called the unit rate.

Tasa por unidad Se llama tasa por unidad a la tasa que corresponde a 1 unidad de una cantidad dada.

Use To use given information, draw on it to help you determine something else.

Usar Para usar una información dada, apóyate en ella para determinar otra cosa.

V

Valid inference A valid inference is an inference that is true about the population. Valid inferences can be made when they are based on data from a representative sample.

Inferencia válida Una inferencia válida es una inferencia verdadera acerca de una población. Se pueden hacer inferencias válidas si están basadas en los datos de una muestra representativa.

Variability Variability describes how much the items in a data set differ (or vary) from each other. On a data display, variability is shown by how much the data on the horizontal scale are spread out.

Variabilidad La variabilidad describe qué diferencia (o variación) existe entre los elementos de un conjunto de datos. Al exhibir datos, la variabilidad queda representada por la distancia que separa los datos en la escala horizontal.

Variable A variable is a letter that represents an unknown value.

Variable Una variable es una letra que representa un valor desconocido.

Variable expenses Variable expenses are expenses that change from one budget period to the next.

Gastos variables Los gastos variables son los gastos que cambian de un período económico al próximo.

English/Spanish Glossary

Vertex of a cone The vertex of a cone is the point farthest from the base.

Vértice de un cono El vértice de un cono es el punto más alejado de la base.

Vertex of a polygon The vertex of a polygon is any point where two sides of a polygon meet.

Vértice de un polígono El vértice de un polígono es cualquier punto donde se encuentran dos lados de un polígono.

Vertex of a three-dimensional figure A vertex of a three-dimensional figure is a point where three or more edges meet.

Vértice de una figura tridimensional El vértice de una figura tridimensional es un punto donde se unen tres o más aristas.

Vertex of an angle The vertex of an angle is the point of intersection of the rays that make up the sides of the angle.

Vértice de un ángulo El vértice de un ángulo es el punto de intersección de las semirrectas que forman los lados del ángulo.

Vertical angles Vertical angles are formed by two intersecting lines and are opposite each other. Vertical angles have equal measures.

Ángulos opuestos por el vértice Los ángulos opuestos por el vértice están formados por dos rectas secantes y están uno frente a otro. Los ángulos opuestos por el vértice tienen la misma medida.

Vertical-line test The vertical-line test is a method used to determine if a relation is a function or not. If a vertical line passes through a graph more than once, the graph is not the graph of a function.

Prueba de recta vertical La prueba de recta vertical es un método que se usa para determinar si una relación es una función o no. Si una recta vertical atraviesa la gráfica más de una vez, la gráfica no es la gráfica de una función.

Volume Volume is the number of cubic units needed to fill a solid figure.

Volumen El volumen es el número de unidades cúbicas que se necesitan para llenar un cuerpo geométrico.

English/Spanish Glossary

Volume of a cone The volume of a cone is the number of unit cubes, or cubic units, needed to fill the cone. The formula for the volume of a cone is $V = \frac{1}{3}Bh$, where B represents the area of the base and h represents the height of the cone.

Volumen de un cono El volumen de un cono es el número de bloques de unidades, o unidades cúbicas, que se necesitan para llenar el cono. La fórmula del volumen de un cono $V = \frac{1}{3}Bh$, donde B representa el área de la base y h representa la altura del cono.

Volume of a cube The volume of a cube is the number of unit cubes, or cubic units, needed to fill the cube. The formula for the volume V of a cube is $V = s^3$, where s represents the length of an edge of the cube.

Volumen de un cubo El volumen de un cubo es el número de bloques de unidades, o unidades cúbicas, que se necesitan para llenar el cubo. La fórmula del volumen, V, de un cubo es $V = s^3$, donde s representa la longitud de una arista del cubo.

Volume of a cylinder The volume of a cylinder is the number of unit cubes, or cubic units, needed to fill the cylinder. The formula for the volume of a cylinder is $V = \pi r^2 h$, where r represents the radius of a base and h represents the height of the cylinder.

Volumen de un cilindro El volumen de un cilindro es el número de bloques de unidades, o unidades cúbicas, que se necesitan para llenar el cilindro. La fórmula del volumen de un cilindro es $V = \pi r^2 h$, donde r representa el radio de una base y h representa la altura del cilindro.

Volume of a prism The volume of a prism is the number of unit cubes, or cubic units, needed to fill the prism. The formula for the volume V of a prism is $V = Bh$, where B represents the area of a base and h represents the height of the prism.

Volumen de un prisma El volumen de un prisma es el número de bloques de unidades, o unidades cúbicas, que se necesitan para llenar el prisma. La fórmula del volumen, V, de un prisma $V = Bh$, donde B representa el área de una base y h representa la altura del prisma.

Volume of a pyramid The volume of a pyramid is the number of unit cubes needed to fill the pyramid. The formula for the volume V of a pyramid is $V = \frac{1}{3}Bh$, where B represents the area of the base and h represents the height of the pyramid.

Volumen de una pirámide El volumen de una pirámide es el número de bloques de unidades, o unidades cúbicas, que se necesitan para llenar la pirámide. La fórmula del volumen, V, de una pirámide es $V = \frac{1}{3}Bh$, donde B representa el área de la base y h representa la altura de la pirámide.

English/Spanish Glossary

Volume of a sphere The volume of a sphere is the number of unit cubes, or cubic units, needed to fill the sphere. The formula for the volume of a sphere is $V = \frac{4}{3}\pi r^3$.

Volumen de una esfera El volumen de una esfera es el número de bloques de unidades, o unidades cúbicas, que se necesitan para llenar la esfera. La fórmula del volumen de una esfera es $V = \frac{4}{3}\pi r^3$.

W

Whole numbers The whole numbers consist of the number 0 and all of the natural numbers.

Números enteros no negativos Los números enteros no negativos son el número 0 y todos los números naturales.

Withdrawal A transaction that takes money out of a bank account is a withdrawal.

Retirada Una transacción que toma dinero fuera de una cuenta bancaria es una retirada.

Withholding allowance You can exclude a portion of your earned wages, called a withholding allowance, from federal income tax. You can claim one withholding allowance for yourself and one for each person dependent upon your income.

Retener concesión Puede excluir una porción de sus sueldos ganados, llamó una concesión que retiene, del impuesto de renta federal. Puede reclamar una concesión que retiene para usted mismo y para uno para cada dependiente de persona sobre sus ingresos.

Word form of a number The word form of a number is the number written in words.

Número en palabras Un número en palabras es un número escrito con palabras en lugar de dígitos.

Work-Study Work-study is a type of need-based aid that schools might offer to a student. A student must earn work-study money by working certain jobs.

Práctica estudiantil La práctica estudiantil es un tipo de ayuda necesidad-basado que escuelas quizás ofrezcan a un estudiante. Un estudiante debe ganar dinero de práctica estudiantil por ciertos trabajos de trabajo.

English/Spanish Glossary

X

x-axis The x-axis is the horizontal number line that, together with the y-axis, forms the coordinate plane.

Eje de las x El eje de las x es la recta numérica horizontal que, junto con el eje de las y, forma el plano de coordenadas.

x-coordinate The x-coordinate is the first number in an ordered pair. It tells the number of horizontal units a point is from 0.

Coordenada x La coordenada x (abscisa) es el primer número de un par ordenado. Indica cuántas unidades horizontales hay entre un punto y 0.

Y

y-axis The y-axis is the vertical number line that, together with the x-axis, forms the coordinate plane.

Eje de las y El eje de las y es la recta numérica vertical que, junto con el eje de las x, forma el plano de coordenadas.

y-coordinate The y-coordinate is the second number in an ordered pair. It tells the number of vertical units a point is from 0.

Coordenada y La coordenada y (ordenada) es el segundo número de un par ordenado. Indica cuántas unidades verticales hay entre un punto y 0.

y-intercept The y-intercept of a line is the y-coordinate of the point where the line crosses the y-axis.

Intercepto en y El intercepto en y de una recta es la coordenada y del punto por donde la recta cruza el eje de las y.

Z

Zero exponent property For any nonzero number a, $a^0 = 1$.

Propiedad del exponente cero Para cualquier número distinto de cero a, $a^0 = 1$.

Zero Property of Multiplication The product of 0 and any number is 0. For any number n, $n \cdot 0 = 0$ and $0 \cdot n = 0$.

Propiedad del cero en la multiplicación El producto de 0 y cualquier número es 0. Para cualquier número n, $n \cdot 0 = 0$ and $0 \cdot n = 0$.

Formulas

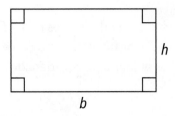

$$P = 2b + 2h$$
$$A = bh$$
Rectangle

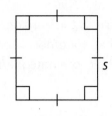

$$P = 4s$$
$$A = s^2$$
Square

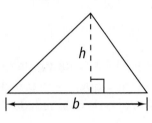

$$A = \tfrac{1}{2}bh$$
Triangle

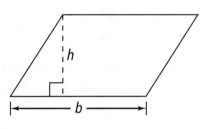

$$A = bh$$
Parallelogram

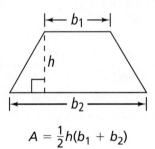

$$A = \tfrac{1}{2}h(b_1 + b_2)$$
Trapezoid

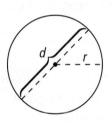

$$C = 2\pi r \text{ or } C = \pi d$$
$$A = \pi r^2$$
Circle

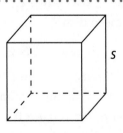

$$\text{S.A.} = 6s^2$$
$$V = s^3$$
Cube

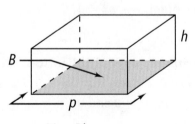

$$V = Bh$$
$$\text{L.A.} = ph$$
$$\text{S.A.} = \text{L.A.} + 2B$$
Rectangular Prism

Formulas

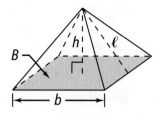

$V = \frac{1}{3}Bh$

L.A. $= 2b\ell$

S.A. = L.A. + B

Square Pyramid

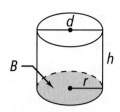

$V = Bh$

L.A. $= 2\pi rh$

S.A. = L.A. + $2B$

Cylinder

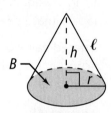

$V = \frac{1}{3}Bh$

L.A. $= \pi r\ell$

S.A. = L.A. + B

Cone

$V = \frac{4}{3}\pi r^3$

S.A. $= 4\pi r^2$

Sphere

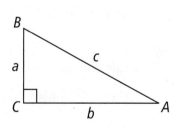

$a^2 + b^2 = c^2$

Pythagorean Theorem

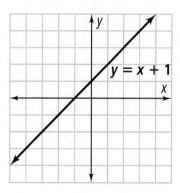

$y = mx + b$, where
m = slope and
b = y-intercept

Equation of Line

Math Symbols

Symbol	Meaning		Symbol	Meaning
+	plus (addition)		r	radius
−	minus (subtraction)		S.A.	surface area
×, ·	times (multiplication)		B	area of base
$\div, \sqrt{}, \frac{a}{b}$	divide (division)		L.A.	lateral area
=	is equal to		ℓ	slant height
<	is less than		V	volume
>	is greater than		a^n	nth power of a
≤	is less than or equal to		$\sqrt{x}$	nonnegative square root of x
≥	is greater than or equal to		π	pi, an irrational number approximately equal to 3.14
≠	is not equal to			
( )	parentheses for grouping		(a, b)	ordered pair with x-coordinate a and y-coordinate b
[ ]	brackets for grouping			
$-a$	opposite of a		$\overline{AB}$	segment AB
. . .	and so on		A'	image of A, A prime
°	degrees		$\triangle ABC$	triangle with vertices A, B, and C
$\lvert a \rvert$	absolute value of a			
$\overset{?}{=}, \overset{?}{<}, \overset{?}{>}$	Is the statement true?		$\rightarrow$	arrow notation
≈	is approximately equal to		$a : b, \frac{a}{b}$	ratio of a to b
$\frac{b}{a}$	reciprocal of $\frac{a}{b}$		≅	is congruent to
A	area		~	is similar to
ℓ	length		$\angle A$	angle with vertex A
w	width		AB	length of segment $\overline{AB}$
h	height		$\overrightarrow{AB}$	ray AB
d	distance		$\angle ABC$	angle formed by $\overrightarrow{BA}$ and $\overrightarrow{BC}$
r	rate		$m\angle ABC$	measure of angle ABC
t	time		⊥	is perpendicular to
P	perimeter		$\overleftrightarrow{AB}$	line AB
b	base length		∥	is parallel to
C	circumference		%	percent
d	diameter		P (event)	probability of an event

Measures

Customary	Metric
Length	**Length**
1 foot (ft) = 12 inches (in.) 1 yard (yd) = 36 in. 1 yd = 3 ft 1 mile (mi) = 5,280 ft 1 mi = 1,760 yd	1 centimeter (cm) = 10 millimeters (mm) 1 meter (m) = 100 cm 1 kilometer (km) = 1,000 m 1 mm = 0.001 m
Area	**Area**
1 square foot (ft^2) = 144 square inches ($in.^2$) 1 square yard (yd^2) = 9 ft^2 1 square mile (mi^2) = 640 acres	1 square centimeter (cm^2) = 100 square millimeters (mm^2) 1 square meter (m^2) = 10,000 cm^2
Volume	**Volume**
1 cubic foot (ft^3) = 1,728 cubic inches ($in.^3$) 1 cubic yard (yd^3) = 27 ft^3	1 cubic centimeter (cm^3) = 1,000 cubic millimeters (mm^3) 1 cubic meter (m^3) = 1,000,000 cm^3
Mass	**Mass**
1 pound (lb) = 16 ounces (oz) 1 ton (t) = 2,000 lb	1 gram (g) = 1,000 milligrams (mg) 1 kilogram (kg) = 1,000 g
Capacity	**Capacity**
1 cup (c) = 8 fluid ounces (fl oz) 1 pint (pt) = 2 c 1 quart (qt) = 2 pt 1 gallon (gal) = 4 qt	1 liter (L) = 1,000 milliliters (mL) 1000 liters = 1 kiloliter (kL)

Customary Units and Metric Units	
Length	1 in. = 2.54 cm 1 mi ≈ 1.61 km 1 ft ≈ 0.3 m
Capacity	1 qt ≈ 0.94 L
Weight and Mass	1 oz ≈ 28.3 g 1 lb ≈ 0.45 kg

Properties

Unless otherwise stated, the variables a, b, c, m, and n used in these properties can be replaced with any number represented on a number line.

Identity Properties
Addition $\quad\quad\ n + 0 = n$ and $0 + n = n$
Multiplication $n \cdot 1 = n$ and $1 \cdot n = n$

Commutative Properties
Addition $\quad\quad\ a + b = b + a$
Multiplication $a \cdot b = b \cdot a$

Associative Properties
Addition $\quad\quad (a + b) + c = a + (b + c)$
Multiplication $(a \cdot b) \cdot c = a \cdot (b \cdot c)$

Inverse Properties
Addition
$a + (-a) = 0$ and $-a + a = 0$
Multiplication
$a \cdot \frac{1}{a} = 1$ and $\frac{1}{a} \cdot a = 1,\ (a \neq 0)$

Distributive Properties
$a(b + c) = ab + ac \quad (b + c)a = ba + ca$
$a(b - c) = ab - ac \quad (b - c)a = ba - ca$

Properties of Equality
Addition $\quad\quad$ If $a = b$,
$\quad\quad\quad\quad\quad\quad$ then $a + c = b + c$.
Subtraction $\quad$ If $a = b$,
$\quad\quad\quad\quad\quad\quad$ then $a - c = b - c$.
Multiplication If $a = b$,
$\quad\quad\quad\quad\quad\quad$ then $a \cdot c = b \cdot c$.
Division $\quad\quad\ $ If $a = b$, and $c \neq 0$,
$\quad\quad\quad\quad\quad\quad$ then $\frac{a}{c} = \frac{b}{c}$.
Substitution $\quad$ If $a = b$, then b can
$\quad\quad\quad\quad\quad\quad$ replace a in any
$\quad\quad\quad\quad\quad\quad$ expression.

Zero Property
$a \cdot 0 = 0$ and $0 \cdot a = 0$.

Properties of Inequality
Addition $\quad\quad$ If $a > b$,
$\quad\quad\quad\quad\quad\quad$ then $a + c > b + c$.
$\quad\quad\quad\quad\quad\quad$ If $a < b$,
$\quad\quad\quad\quad\quad\quad$ then $a + c < b + c$.
Subtraction $\quad$ If $a > b$,
$\quad\quad\quad\quad\quad\quad$ then $a - c > b - c$.
$\quad\quad\quad\quad\quad\quad$ If $a < b$,
$\quad\quad\quad\quad\quad\quad$ then $a - c < b - c$.

Multiplication
If $a > b$ and $c > 0$, then $ac > bc$.
If $a < b$ and $c > 0$, then $ac < bc$.
If $a > b$ and $c < 0$, then $ac < bc$.
If $a < b$ and $c < 0$, then $ac > bc$.

Division
If $a > b$ and $c > 0$, then $\frac{a}{c} > \frac{b}{c}$.
If $a < b$ and $c > 0$, then $\frac{a}{c} < \frac{b}{c}$.
If $a > b$ and $c < 0$, then $\frac{a}{c} < \frac{b}{c}$.
If $a < b$ and $c < 0$, then $\frac{a}{c} > \frac{b}{c}$.

Properties of Exponents
For any nonzero number n and any integers m and n:

Zero Exponent $\quad\quad\quad a^0 = 1$
Negative Exponent $\quad\ a^{-n} = \frac{1}{a^n}$
Product of Powers $\quad\ a^m \cdot a^n = a^{m+n}$
Power of a Product $\quad (ab)^n = a^n b^n$
Quotient of Powers $\quad \frac{a^m}{a^n} = a^{m-n}$
Power of a Quotient $\left(\frac{a}{b}\right)^n = \frac{a^n}{b^n}$
Power of a Power $\quad\ (a^m)^n = a^{mn}$